W9-BMZ-404

Postmodernist Culture
SECOND EDITION

Postmodernist Culture

*An Introduction to Theories of the
Contemporary*

SECOND EDITION

Steven Connor
Birkbeck College, London University

First published 1989
Reprinted 1990, 1991, 1992 (twice), 1994, 1995, 1996
Second edition 1997
2 4 6 8 10 9 7 5 3 1

Blackwell Publishers Ltd
108 Cowley Road
Oxford OX4 1JF
UK

Blackwell Publishers Inc.
238 Main Street
Cambridge, Massachusetts 02142, USA

British Library Cataloguing in Publication Data

A CIP catalogue record for this book is available from the British Library.

Library of Congress Cataloging-in-Publication Data

Connor, Steven, 1955–
    Postmodernist culture: an introduction to theories of the contemporary /
Steven Connor. — 2nd ed.
        p.   cm.
    Includes bibliographical references and index.
    ISBN 0–631–20052–5 (pbk. : alk. paper)
    1. Postmodernism.   2. Literature, Modern—20th century—History
and criticism. I.   Title.
PN98.P67C66   1997   96–16125
306′.0904—dc20   CIP
ISBN 0–631–20052–5 (pbk.)

Commissioning Editor: Andrew McNeillie
Desk Editor: Tony Grahame
Production Controller: Lisa Eaton

Typeset in 10 1/2 on 12 1/2 pt Ehrhardt
by Pure Tech India Ltd, Pondicherry
Printed in Great Britain by T. J. Press Ltd, Padstow, Cornwall

This book is printed on acid-free paper

Contents

Part III Consequences

Preface to the Second Edition

When I began writing *Postmodernist Culture* in 1987, postmodernism seemed to be understood best as a complex simultaneity, a coincidence of different lines of development, in architecture, art, literature, film, popular culture and so on. I saw myself as trying to produce a sort of guidebook to the different kinds of postmodernism that had been identified in the different arts and different areas of cultural practice. At the time, it seemed to make sense to divide the book up in terms of the disciplines which had undergone or were undergoing their own particular forms of movement beyond modernism, which is to say, usually, their *own* modernisms.

At the same time, it was already obvious that there was another kind of postmodernism abroad, which required a different sort of explanation. As I remark at the beginning of the chapter on 'Postmodern Performance', the postmodern diagnosis has travelled to cultural spheres which may not have experienced any clearly defined modernist phase, such as TV, rock music and digital culture. Since the publication of the first edition of this book in 1989, the most noticeable change has been the steady overtaking of the first, shall we call it, genealogical kind of postmodernism by varieties of what may be termed the analogical postmodernism of the second kind. The global culture that it has occurred to me elsewhere to characterize as a 'culture of interruptions',[1] in which different artistic and cultural forms cross and combine promiscuously, operates to suggest and multiply affinities of this kind, as well as to consolidate the theoretical languages of postmodernism and to accelerate their circulation and turnover. Increasingly, disciplinary areas have sought to define their own postmodernist regimes in relation to those prevailing elsewhere, rather than by reference to their own histories. It would be possible to represent this generalization of 'pomo-envy' as one more symptom of the contemporary flattening of historical awareness were it not that looking over their were it not that; disciplinary shoulder at other kinds of postmodernism, seems to have driven many particular disciplines into a renewed investigation of their own genealogies. I think that this is the case, for example, with the development of theories of postmodernism in law and dance, as they are treated in new sections of this current edition.

This movement from genealogical to analogical postmodernism is signalled rather neatly in the orthographic standardization of the 'post-' word. Sally Banes's 1980 book, *Terpsichore in Sneakers*, refers in its subtitle to '*Post-Modern Dance*', the hyphen and the capitalization of the 'modern' element drawing attention to a particular defining narrative of a hiatus and transition between different phases in the history of dance.[2] The postmodernism of Sally Banes's more recent collection of essays on dance, *Writing Dancing in the Age of Postmodernism*,[3] is a more general cultural context, of which the pervasiveness and separation from particular histories is signalled by the removal of the hyphen that hiccups in the middle of 'Post-Modern', as well as of its awkwardly portentous capitalization. 'Post-Modern', 'Post-Modernism' and 'Post-Modernity' involve syncopation and interrupted passage; 'postmodern', 'postmodernism' and 'postmodernity' point to synthesis, simultaneity and coherence. In Sally Banes's second book, the rereading of dance, both within writing about it, and within dance itself, is no longer endogenous to dance, is no longer a question it asks about itself. Rather, it is derived from and driven by more generalized questions regarding the relations between all the arts and their histories, characterized not only by a more rapid interchange between the performance of different arts and interpretative reflections upon that performance, but also by an ever more finely tuned synchronization of the contretemps and failures of chronological fit between those different arts and their histories.

Another effect of this move from the genealogical to the analogical has been to multiply and accelerate those loops of what, at the end of my first chapter, I describe as 'perclusion', in the relations between theory and its objects. In fact, the last decade has seen a remarkable shift in the terms 'postmodern' and 'postmodernist' themselves, which now indicate, not so much the kinds of artistic and cultural object which a particular theory may have, as the kind of theory it is. As Hans Bertens has shown in his excellent *The Idea of the Postmodern* (1995), the dimensionless, travelling 'moment' of postmodernism's rupture and question has lengthened out into a substantial history.[4] Postmodernism is not so much an hypothesis about the world as a discipline, almost in some quarters, a career-choice, in its own right. It has become the name of our intense and undiminishable reflexivity, as well as the way in which we reflect upon that reflexivity (and so, exhilaratingly, on).

When I wrote *Postmodernist Culture* it was in order to offer a partial remedy for confusion and proliferation; to attempt to ascertain and describe the principal forms of postmodernism. What I now realize is that the book itself could not but assist the synchronic drawing-tight of postmodern commensurability. Perhaps the most ironic evidence of the cooperation between uniformity and difference, the postmodern movements of disaffiliation, disruption and dispersal and the postmodern urge to synoptic capture, is the proliferation in recent years of postmodern readers, anthologies, overviews, gazetteers and *vade mecums* of all kinds, of which, of course, this book is an example. My revisiting, rethinking and enlargement of *Postmodernist Culture* has been undertaken in the context of the bulging *overcoherence* of the concept of the postmodern. The substantial new discussions that are included in this edition are intended not only to bring the book up to date – by analysing more recent practical and theoretical developments, especially in law, dance, music, cultural studies, cyberculture, geography and ecological thought, as well as the more recent reflections of thinkers such as Jean-François Lyotard and Fredric Jameson – but also, I now begin to see, to provide some materials and occasions for accosting this overcoherence.

Notes

1 Steven Connor, 'Reading: The *Contretemps*', in *Strategies of Reading: Dickens and After*, *Yearbook of English Studies*, 26 (1996), pp. 246–8.
2 Sally Banes, *Terpsichore in Sneakers: Post-Modern Dance* (Boston: Houghton Mifflin, 1980).
3 Sally Banes, *Writing Dancing in the Age of Postmodernism* (Hanover, NH: Wesleyan University Press/University Press of New England, 1994).
4 Hans Bertens, *The Idea of the Postmodern: A History* (London: Routledge, 1995).

Acknowledgements

Part of chapter 5 appeared in a slightly different form in *New Formations* 3 (1987), and section of chapter 3 and the final section of chapter 9 appeared as a chapter in *Ethics and Aesthetics: The Moral Turn of Postmodernism*, ed. Gerhard Hoffmann and Alfred Hornung (Heidelberg: Univeritätsverlag C. Winter, 1986). I am grateful for permission to reproduce this material here.

One of the reasons that I have been easily persuaded to revise and expand this book for a second edition is that I seem to have learned so much more about its subject after writing it than I ever did before. This is due in large part to the generosity and vigour of those who have discussed with me the hindrances and exhilarations of the postmodern over the last decade or so. These include Andrew Benjamin, Hans Bertens, Christopher Butler, Jim Collins, Barry Curtis, Theo D'Haen, Thomas Docherty, Costas Douzinas, Andrew Gibson, Peter Goodrich, Ihab Hassan, Charles Jencks, Christopher Norris and Lisa Tickner, and my colleagues Isobel Armstrong, John Kraniauskas, Roger Luckhurst, Laura Marcus, Mpalive Msiska and Carol Watts.

Part I
Context

1
Postmodernism and the Academy

The difficulties of knowing the contemporary are well known. Knowledge, it is often claimed, can only be gained and enjoyed about what is in some sense over and done with. The claim to know the contemporary is therefore often seen as a kind of conceptual violence, a fixing of the fluid and formless energies of the urgently (but tenuously) present *now* into a knowable and speakable form, by fundamental and irrevocable acts of critical choosing. This formulation rests upon a sense of the inherent division between experience and knowledge, a belief that, when we experience life, we can only partially understand it, and when we try to understand life, we are no longer really experiencing it. According to this model, knowledge is always doomed to arrive too late on the scene of experience.

Much of the critical and theoretical work in philosophy and the social sciences over the last twenty or so years gives us reason to suspect this division, reason to wonder whether knowledge and experience may not be joined in a much more complex continuum. It may be that experience is always, if not actually determined, then at least interpreted in advance by the various structures of understanding and interpretation which hold at particular moments in particular societies, and different regions of those societies. Indeed, the very relationship in which experience and knowledge are taken to stand may also be a reflex of such structures of knowledge and understanding. From this it would follow that our present way of conceiving the opposition between experience and knowledge as (for example) one between transience and fixity, itself has its origin and history in particular knowledge structures.

This particular sense of the gap between experience and knowledge begins, or at least reaches a point of important focus, in some of the texts of the cultural and philosophical movement that is called modernism. When Baudelaire called for an art which would register the passing moment without doing violence to its fleeting transience, when Walter Pater urged us to snatch moments of intensity from flux, when Henri Bergson convinced a generation of a need for representations which would not falsely spatialize the purely temporal flow of consciousness, and when Virginia Woolf sought an art which would record the intensity of inner experience on its own terms, we can see stated and restated the principle of an apparently irrevocable tension between the way human beings felt they lived and the forms used to render that sensation.[1]

It is on these grounds that the modernist period is often credited with the discovery or rediscovery of those real intensities of experience which had for so long been concealed or distorted by false structures of understanding. But isn't it just as likely that this rediscovery of 'experience' was the result of a reorganization of categories and relationships, was, in other words, a product of a certain kind of knowledge? If this is the case, then it imposes a slightly greater responsibility upon the historian of such concepts. Modernism must be grasped henceforward, not just in terms of the way it experienced itself, but also in terms of its own modes of self-understanding – the ways it *thought* it was experiencing itself.

In fact, if one way of characterizing modernist culture and modernity in general is in terms of its discovery of experience, then another way is to see it as the moment when self-consciousness invaded experience. If a modern sensibility is characterized by a sense of the urgent, painful gap between experience and consciousness and the desire to replenish rational consciousness with the intensities of experience, then this itself marks an awareness of the necessary and inescapable dependence of experience upon consciousness and vice versa. Every kind of split between experience and self-understanding is itself produced from forms of knowledge, or self-understanding.

This line of reasoning might seem to take us well beyond any usable definition of the modern or of modernity. For Paul de Man at least, the struggle to understand and cope with the pressures of the absolutely unprecedented *now* is not at all the defining characteristic of modernity, or of 'our' modernity, since it is what the modern period shares with other periods, in which, similarly, the experience of the raw, unmediated present is set against the frozen structures of understanding inherited from the past.[2] But it isn't necessary to go quite this far. Though there may be structural resemblances between, say, the struggle of the Ancients and the Moderns in the eighteenth century and the struggle between tradition and modernity in the early twentieth century, this is not at all the same thing as saying that there is no difference between the two forms of modernity.

What these reflections amount to is the fact that we must be aware of the history and the constructed nature of our sense of what experience and knowledge are. One of the problems that will recur in this study is that, in seeking to understand modernity and its much-trumpeted sequel, postmodernity, we are forced to use modes of understanding that derive from the periods and concepts under consideration, forced to repeat histories of concepts that we might wish to stand clear of. But there is no way to avoid this, no way to duck the consequences of having to think about the relationship of experience and knowledge, present and past, with terms and structures that derive from these things. In trying to understand our contemporary selves in the moment of the present, there are no safely-detached observation-posts, not in 'science', 'religion', or even in 'history'. We are in and of the moment that we are attempting to analyse, in and of the structures we employ to analyse it. One might almost say that this terminal self-consciousness ('terminal' is glamorous, but imprecise, since the point is that such self-consciousness is never terminal) is what characterizes our contemporary or 'postmodern' moment. This reflexivity will necessarily be evident in what follows, for its argument is that, in trying to understand postmodernism and the postmodernism debate, we must look at the form as well as the content of that debate, must try to understand the priorities and questions which it produces as its own mode of self-understanding alongside the questions with which it seems to be dealing.

It will turn out that this involves considering another aspect of our immersion in inherited structures of knowledge. If what cultural theory has inherited from modernism is a particular set of conceptual relationships between experience and knowledge, then those relationships do not take a merely abstract form, within knowledge itself. That is to say, they do not have to do simply with academic or abstractedly philosophical issues or concepts, but are also related crucially to the social and institutional forms in which those abstract or conceptual relationships are embodied and from which they are operated. The development of structures and institutions of knowledge in the later twentieth century, universities and institutions of higher education, schools, publishing, and various sites of cultural production, has a crucial relationship to the forms of knowledge developed within those institutions, and their relationships with other forms of knowledge and representation.

Although the term 'postmodernism' had been used by a number of writers in the 1950s and 1960s, the concept of postmodernism cannot be said to have crystallized until about the mid-1970s, when claims for the existence of this diversely social and cultural phenomenon began to harden within and across a number of different cultural areas and academic disciplines, in philosophy, architecture, film studies and literary subjects. The legitimacy of this debate was established in two directions, effecting a conceptual stereoscopy. First of all, each discipline produced more and more conclusive evidence of the existence of postmodernism within its own area of cultural practice; secondly, and really more importantly, each discipline drew progressively upon the discoveries and definitions made in other disciplines. With the appearance of Jean-François Lyotard's *La Condition postmoderne* in 1979, and its translation into English in 1984, these different disciplinary diagnoses received an interdisciplinary confirmation, and there no longer seemed room for disagreement that postmodernism and postmodernity had come to stay.[3]

Naturally, with this critical success came controversy. What is remarkable about these controversies is the limited and predictable form which they took. Above all, they focused on the question of whether or not the term 'postmodernism' offers an adequate representation of the objects and practices of contemporary culture. The questions which were asked were: does postmodernism really exist, after all? Is there a 'unified sensibility' running across and between all the different areas of cultural life (Jürgen Peper)? Does postmodernism unjustly limit or prematurely curtail the 'unfinished project' of modernism (Jürgen Habermas)? Is there anything new or valuable in the alleged 'postmodernist breakthrough' (Gerald Graff)?[4] In other words, does postmodernist culture exist and if so (sometimes even if not) is it a 'good thing' or a 'bad thing'?

What had not yet become visible in this debate was the self-conscious density of the debate itself, which began to cast a progressively longer and longer shadow over its alleged object of analysis. It had become clear during the 1970s that there was a close and at times providential relationship between the various forms of *nouvelle critique*, or literary theory, which swept across America, Britain and Europe, and the contemporary writing and culture which often formed the object of analysis for these forms of theoretical criticism. A postmodernist fiction which had seemed to reject hierarchy, narrative closure, the desire to represent the world and the authority of the author, provided the perfect counterpart to a criticism which increasingly emphasized, in either positive or negative modes, the impossibility of representation or the unrestrainable freedom of the reader. Theory, therefore, slid neatly into its role as the mediator and validator of this new fiction (indeed, for some, began to outshine some of this primary material as evidence of the postmodern temper). If theory scratched the back of postmodernist culture, then that culture seemed to return the favour handsomely. Increasingly, postmodernist works were represented, and came to represent themselves, as self-conscious, quasi-critical activities – one needs to think only of the knowing metafictional musings of John Barth, John Fowles and Donald Barthelme, and the uncertain space between art and art-theory occupied by some forms of conceptual or performance art.

This is not to denounce an illicit fraternization between realms that should be distinct, or to imply that one can even keep such realms distinct. Rather, it is to draw attention to changing relationships of priority between cultural and critical activity, and the curious and significant self-designation that is involved in the critical discourses around postmodernism. My claim in this book will be, in fact, that this self-reflection is, if anything, more significant than the reflection upon, or description of contemporary culture which seemed to be offered in postmodernist critical theory. Postmodernism finds its object neither wholly in the cultural sphere, nor wholly in the critical-institutional sphere, but in some tensely renegotiated space between the two.

This leads to a difficulty. If I am right about the self-reflective structure of postmodernism, then it will not be easy simply to survey the field of postmodernist culture, as, for example, Brian McHale attempts to do, in his *Postmodernist Fiction*, a book which aims to be a 'poetics' of contemporary fiction, or to survey the field of critical writing, as Hans Bertens tries to do in his essay on 'the postmodernist *Weltanschauung*'.[5] The reason for this is that the two realms of the critical and the cultural have become so powerfully mingled and interrelated. This seems to imply that there is no space available for engaging with the postmodernist question from outside it, for to engage with postmodernism, even in the form of a detached survey, or a negative critique, however hostile, is to become part of it.

It is possible to become very cynical about this, and to see the whole postmodernism craze as being kept going Scheherezade-like by long-winded academics concerned simultaneously to perpetuate themselves and to distract attention from their growing irrelevance. Charles Newman has another, even less complimentary, metaphor. For him, postmodernism is only the representative system of an 'inflation of discourse', across all levels of society, but especially in the spheres of culture and communication. For Newman, critical and literary language have both deliberately abandoned any relationship with reliable use-value, and mount obscurity upon obscurity in endless spirals of self-validation.[6]

However, it is possible to take the idea of a self-validating discourse a little more soberly. It is clear that, if the postmodernism debate offers critical practice a means of self-advertisement and self-prolongation, it also reflects and embodies the real involvement of cultural criticism in what

Jürgen Habermas has called the 'legitimation crisis' which affects contemporary social life – the fact that there no longer seems to be access to principles which can act as criteria of value for anything else.[7] From now on, postmodern theorists will urge, there are no absolute grounds of value which can compel assent. But in such a situation, questions of value and legitimacy do not disappear, but gain a new intensity; and the struggle to generate and ground legitimacy in the contemporary academy is nowhere more intense than in the debates produced by and around postmodernism.

This is borne out by a striking paradox at the heart of the postmodernism debate. Jean-François Lyotard's formula for the emergence of postmodernism, the 'suspicion of metanarratives', those universal guiding principles and mythologies which once seemed to control, delimit and interpret all the diverse forms of discursive activity in the world, has compelled wide agreement.[8] The postmodern condition, we are told repeatedly, manifests itself in the multiplication of centres of power and activity and the dissolution of every kind of totalizing narrative which claims to govern the whole complex field of social activity and representation. The waning of the cultural authority of the West and its political and intellectual traditions, along with the opening up of the world political scene to cultural and ethnic differences, is another symptom of the modulation of hierarchy into heterarchy, or differences organized into a unified pattern of domination and subordination, as opposed to differences existing alongside each other but without any principle of commonality or order. The most famous image of such a situation of 'pure difference' is Michel Foucault's account of a passage in a story by Jorge Luis Borges, in which a certain Chinese encyclopaedia is quoted, which divides all animals into the following categories: '(a) belonging to the Emperor, (b) embalmed, (c) tame, (d) sucking pigs, (e) sirens, (f) fabulous, (g) stray dogs, (h) included in the present classification, (i) frenzied, (j) innumerable, (k) drawn with a very fine camelhair brush, (l) *et cetera*, (m) having just broken the water-pitcher, (n) that from a very long way off look like flies'.[9] Foucault argues that there is something disturbing and monstrous about this catalogue, because it does not allow one any recourse to an ordering principle outside itself. 'What is impossible', he writes, 'is not the propinquity of the things listed, but the very site on which their propinquity would be possible.'[10] Foucault calls this structure of radical incommensurability a 'heterotopia', and in doing so offers a name for the whole centreless universe of the postmodern.

But the obvious problem with this, which Foucault does not here confront, is that, once such a heterotopia has been named, and, more especially, once it has been cited and re-cited, it is no longer the conceptual monstrosity which it once was, for its incommensurability has been in some sense bound, controlled and predictively interpreted, given a centre and illustrative function. Something similar can be said to happen repeatedly in postmodernist theory, or theory of postmodernism, which names and correspondingly closes off the very world of cultural difference and plurality which it allegedly brings to visibility. What is striking is precisely the degree of consensus in postmodernist discourse that there is no longer any possibility of consensus, the authoritative announcements of the disappearance of final authority and the promotion and recirculation of a total and comprehensive narrative of a cultural condition in which totality is no longer thinkable. If postmodern theory insists on the irreducibility of the difference between different areas of cultural and critical practice, it is ironically the conceptual language of postmodern theory which flows into the trenches that it itself gouges between incommensurabilities and there becomes solid enough to bear the weight of an entirely new conceptual apparatus of comparative study.[11]

It would be easy to see this paradox as evidence of the essential fraudulence of the postmodernism debate, but such a response comes from a failure to attend closely to that debate's form and function rather than its content. True, given this kind of contradiction, it cannot be that postmodernist culture is quite the thing that postmodern theory contends that it is, but this is not to say that the whole debate is without meaning or function. If, for example, one sees postmodernism as inhering precisely in these forms of contradiction, then it becomes possible to read postmodernism as a *discursive* function, whose integrity derives from the regularity of its contexts and effects in different discursive operations, rather than from the consistency of the ideas within it.

We need, in other words, to ask different questions of the postmodernism debate. Instead of wondering how accurately postmodern criticism reflects real conditions obtaining in the cultural and social sphere, we need to consider the ways in which the debate comes out of a redefined relationship between the critical and the social-cultural spheres. Instead of asking, what is postmodernism?, we should ask, where, how and why does the discourse of postmodernism flourish?, what is at stake in its debates?, who do they address and how? This series of questions shifts attention from the meaning or content of the debate to its form and function, so that, to borrow Stanley Fish's formula, we ask, not, what does postmodernism mean?, but, what does it *do?*[12]

And this entails in large part a refusal to separate the themes of the postmodernism debate from its contexts in the real conditions of academic and critical writing and publishing and their relationships with cultural, political and other fields. It requires us above all to try to see the knowledge produced in and alongside critical and academic institutions in terms of the power-interests and relationships that sustain them. It is customary to think of these aspects as related but distinct. Necessarily a university teacher or writer of academic texts will spend most of his or her time, not engaged in producing texts of penetrating brilliance, but in much more mundane activities like applying for jobs, going to conferences, marking examinations, lecturing, ordering paper, putting in for promotion and trying to get on television. We are used to thinking of all these activities, as well as the more general functions of higher educational institutions, as being in most respects accessory to the main business of thinking and writing and significant only to the degree to which they facilitate or impede the real functions of the gathering or transmission of knowledge.

But what if one tried to think of the two dimensions simultaneously, seeing them as aspects one of the other, without subordinating one to the other as shadow to substance, or husk to kernel? Then we might approach something like the perspective offered in the work of Michel Foucault, which rests upon the determination to analyse knowledge in terms of all the material relationships within which it exists:

> No body of knowledge can be formed without a system of communications, records, accumulation and displacement which is in itself a form of power and which is linked, in its existence and functioning, to the other forms of power. Conversely, no power can be exercised without the extraction, appropriation, distribution or retention of knowledge. On this level, there is not knowledge on the one side and society on the other, or science and the state, but only the fundamental forms of knowledge/power.[13]

It is perhaps surprising, despite the notorious reflexivity of contemporary theoretical discourses in the humanities, and especially in postmodern theory, that not much interest has been shown in examining the knowledge-power formations embodied in academic institutions, practices and languages. This comes partly, I think, from a widespread resignation to the fact that academic institutions seem to have less and less social power and prestige, particularly in recent years in the traditionally 'soft' humanities subjects. If this produces a sense of resentment at being pushed from the centres of power and influence, it can also offer the customary consolations of life at the margins. In mourning their estrangement from the centres in which power is obviously formed, exercised and managed, those in the humanities can at least claim clean hands. Foucault's work suggests that we ought to try to think a little more carefully about this apparent impotence. This is especially the case if, as I believe, we can see the defining characteristic of the postmodern as lying not in a revolution in culture, but in an important readjustment of power relations within and across cultural and critical-academic institutions.

The story of the rise of the academy in mediating contemporary culture in the twentieth century usually lends itself to a sardonic narration. As far as its relationship with culture is concerned, the academy is usually represented as the means by which the subversive, experimental energies of the avant-garde culture of the early part of the century have been formulated, controlled, contained, marketed and cancelled. So, for instance, Charles Newman argues that the twentieth century has really seen two distinct revolutions in the field of culture, the first, 'real' revolution in which innovation and experiment swept across art and cultural activity throughout the countries of the West, destroying old certainties and urgently politicizing artistic activity, and the second revolution, apparently less dramatic, but really more fundamental and influential, in which the universities and other cultural institutions took over the various forms of modernism, canonized or popularized its works and artists, drained away its political charge, and set about the immense work of managing and administering it. As Newman shrewdly points out, the point of resistance for many forms of postmodernist culture is not modernist art *per se*, but this second revolution which has assimilated and institutionalized modernism.[14]

Alongside this account of the role of the academy in assimilating modernism goes a conventional account of the progressive withdrawal of the institutions of criticism from social, political and cultural engagement. For Terry Eagleton, the high point of criticism was the bourgeois 'public sphere' of the eighteenth century, when it was still possible for the activity of criticism to be seen as a form of conversation, its conflicts and disagreements set against a ground of consensus and free communicative exchange. The subsequent academicization of criticism during the nineteenth century and in accelerated form in the twentieth century provided it with an institutional basis and professional structure, but by the same token signalled the beginnings of its voluntary sequestration from the public realm.[15] If the upheavals of the 1960s and 1970s produced a body of theoretical discourses which, because of solid historical determinants (the diversification of the student population, for instance, and the growth of mass cultural forms), began to ask awkward questions of the academy and its marginalized practice, then these discourses may also be read as another writhe into introverted specialism. Eagleton is tempted to see deconstruction, for example, as a way of accommodating a crisis of legitimacy, rather than as the expression of that crisis; it is 'that crisis theorized, canonized, internalized, gathered up into the academy as a new set of textual techniques or fresh injection of intellectual capital to eke out its dwindling resources'.[16] Edward Said also sees the history of the twentieth century as a progressive withdrawal from general questions and responsibility and increasing collusion with a system that divides knowledge into specialisms to disallow in advance any radical or effective engagement with general issues.[17]

Both of these accounts are only partially true, for they assume in some sense that the academy has suffered simply from a failure of nerve, or intellectual confidence; if only these could be recovered, then the academy could claim once again its large and general effectiveness. For all the sensitivity of such accounts to the determining imprints of the institutional and the ideological, both Eagleton and Said risk falling into a purely internal intellectual history of the academy, a history of its ideas, debates, and theoretical conflicts separate from its particular material and social embodiments, in short, of knowledge separate from the conditions of power.

Perhaps the first point to be made about the academy in this sense is that, for all its apparent marginalization, the power and influence of literary and cultural institutions have increased enormously from the 1930s onwards. In Britain and the US, the numbers of higher education establishments grew enormously during this period, and, despite a temporary slowing-down during the 1980s, especially in Britain, the public visibility and prestige of such institutions remains enormous. The increasing professionalization of academic study, which Eagleton tends to take as a mark of its retreat from engagement with real issues, is in fact the mode in which it has consolidated and extended its influences over this period. Of course, during this period, the study of cultural forms, and especially, as the dominant discipline, the study of English literature, could represent itself as, and even perform the functions of, a 'counterpublic sphere', sustaining values of creativity, responsiveness, and intellectual and political critique against the purely instrumental function of the university as a mechanism of cultural accreditation.

But, in both Britain and the US, the sheer growth of English as a subject – imaged best of all in the vast annual conference of the Modern Languages Association of America, which has now grown so large that it requires a city to accommodate it – made the contradictions between its management and liberal-oppositional functions progressively more intense. If, during the 1960s and 1970s, the widening of the constituencies of the academic study of literature and culture broke open its fragile, class-based consensus, at this later stage, a quantum increase in size resulted in a massive introversion of the system, which now became concerned not so much with enlarging its space of cultural effectiveness, as with the internal regulation of its own activities. We can profitably stay with the example of English. If English had at one time moved confidently outwards, moving itself to the top of the hierarchy of disciplines and disseminating its standards throughout the cultural sphere and beyond, from the 1960s the subject began to expand from the inside. Its discursive principle became one of internal saturation. Every new approach in teaching and scholarship was required to extend itself over the whole field, in a confident encyclo-paedism, via the commissioning of complete works, concordances, bibliog-raphies, and so on, designed to map the whole field of literature. The system took to obsessively monitoring its scope and limits, in what seemed an attempt to produce and (oddly) to reproduce the repletion of the field. Elderly academics might smite their brows at the appearance of yet another newsletter devoted simply to listing every new article on sea-imagery in Shakespeare, but the fiction that such publications were only second-order phenomena, which had little to do with real critical judgement, could not last long in the face of the growing apprehension that the subject had come to consist in this self-referential activity of listing and mapping, generating gaps in order that they might be closed, but always leaving the possibility of more work, a different approach, another application. The bibliography, or its cross-disciplinary form, the computer-listing, like *Dissertation Abstracts International*, or the *Arts and Humanities Citations Index*, is a discursive image of the institution itself, for it is a structure which can always accommodate more detail, although these additions can never swell or burst the external limits of the system; rather, they are internal expansions, deepening the subject and making it denser without ever expanding it, or breaching its implicit, but always imperative boundaries. In such a vast and internally-expanding system, the principle of saturation is therefore accompanied by the principle of non-interfering plurality. Far from being the theoretical monolith that it has been represented as since the 1970s, the universe of English studies has actively fostered subuniverses of different approaches and practices, in frictionless rappro-chement.

Sheer size does not in itself disprove the charge of impotence levelled at the academic humanities, however, and it would be possible to point to this as the mode of the academy's withdrawal from real life, in a bureaucratic multiplication of devices for How Not To Do It, like Dickens's Circumlocution Office. The point is that, despite all this involution, the humanities in Britain and the US have maintained a clearly-visible and highly-successful function of accreditation for all the traditionally privileged professions and social functions – which includes banking, commerce and industrial management alongside 'humane' occupations like teaching and social work. Far from being merely 'irrelevant', or sacrificing their task of oppositionality, the humanities have come to act, as it were via their lack of direct effectuality, and in their claims to provide ideological completeness and adaptability, as an important kind of lubricant in the machine of higher education, in its reproduction of relations of power and privilege.

So we can see, alongside the narrowing and professionalization of the humanities, a certain broadening or consolidation, at least until the early 1980s, of their prestige and perceived value in the West. Most of this has to do with its function of imparting cultural competence in a unifying and filtering way to a widening constituency of consumers. But, partly as a consequence of this widening constituency, the sense of what constituted culture began to broaden and distort. It was not just that the sheer flood of contemporary writing and cultural production began to lap at the doors of literature and art-historical courses that tended not to recognize the significance of the contemporary, but also that a worrying fluidity began to affect the boundaries marking off the high culture which had traditionally become the preserve of universities and mass culture. Popular forms like television, film and rock music began to lay claim to some of the seriousness of high cultural forms and high culture responded with an equivalent adoption of pop forms and characteristics (Andy Warhol and pop art, or the semi-parodic annexation of forms like the Western or the detective story in contemporary literary fiction). The response to this explosion of culture, the increasing visibility as culture of forms that could previously be dismissed as simply not culture at all, was initially one of high-minded distaste, but increasingly took the form of appropriation as, with the (limited) growth of media studies, communications studies and women's studies, universities began to acknowledge that these forms might be studied with (nearly) as much profit and effectiveness as the high–cultural forms which had previously been the guarantee of the humanities in the academy. This is not to say that hierarchies of value did not survive – in Britain, for example, the field of study in the humanities is still institutionally distributed in such a way as to maintain the distinction between the polytechnics and, latterly, the 'new universities', in which popular culture is studied, and the high-prestige universities in which high culture is studied. But this should not distract us from the fact that the field of competence of the humanities has been extended and diversified.

In doing so, the academy has implicitly laid claim to a custodial or management function with regard to cultural experience which, at a time of threat, offered a way of enlarging its function and effectiveness. In this respect, the academy is not an anomaly in the field of contemporary culture, but its most representative form. For the expansion of the realm of culture which Fredric Jameson and others have spoken of as characteristic of the contemporary world of consumer capitalism, in which the earlier distinctions between cultural representations and economic activities have broken down, in an economy that thrives upon the manufacture and circulation of images and styles, also results in a vastly increased need for a management of this sphere. If the field of what counts as 'cultural' experience and competence has enlarged, then this also gives opportunities for the 'capitalization' of popular culture, its circulation as class-value, the manufacture and accreditation of forms of competence. 'Culture' has expanded, not because of any actual enlargement of opportunities for and varieties of cultural experience, but because of an expansion and diversification of the forms in which cultural experience is mediated. The academy may not be the only such mediating form, but it is a very important one.

This is not to say that there have not been developments within the academy which work against this enlarging of the field of the academic. For one thing, there has been the growth of theoretical approaches and languages which have broken or challenged the cultural histories inscribed within particular subjects. This has resulted in one sense in a deliberate disavowal of the previous link between cultural criticism and cultural practice, such that criticism is no longer patient with its role as intermediary or handmaiden of culture and tends instead to be concerned with the 'interrogation' of texts or artefacts, in this and other ways flaunting its distance from its object, and affecting a hard-boiled 'scientific' objectivity.

But this splitting of the terrain of culture at one level has been accompanied by a widening at another level, in the forms of affiliation between subjects that new theoretical discourses seem to make possible. If criticism has withdrawn in one direction from the close, enraptured study of patterns of alliteration in Spenser or the details of Manet's brushwork, then it has markedly expanded its competence to talk about pornography, pinball and the semiotics of the privy, in allegiances between subjects that share a body of legitimating theoretical material. There are, or have been, real gains and challenges in this 'deconstruction' of disciplinary boundaries, but, separated from a much more intense determination to interfere with and reconstruct the functions of the university, or of the academic system as a whole, these can become merely incidental mutations in a system that is becoming increasingly operationalized.

What is more, the new theoretical allegiances across disciplines are accompanied by a breakdown of the links between academic institutions and their national contexts. The language of the development of modern literary criticism began in England with a cultural analysis that sought to rescue and reformulate a myth of national identity to stand against the incursions of anonymous and international mass capitalism.[18] In other areas, especially philosophy and art-criticism, clear and continuous national 'traditions' were equally powerful constituents in the rise of academic disciplines. In the 1960s it was still possible to specify differences of emphasis and professional organization in different Western nations. With the arrival of the notorious structuralist 'revolution', along with the revival of Marxist and New Left theory in the 1960s and after, all that began to change. Just for a moment, the differences between French and Czech structuralism, Russian formalism, German hermeneutics, Swiss phenomenology, Anglo-Saxon empiricism and American New Criticism flared into visibility, before the serious work began of binding together those national differences into a unifying discursive frame, with a regularity of theme, concept and language. This is not in any way to mourn the loss of 'authentic' national traditions, but to highlight the process of simultaneous diversification and unification which took place across newly-cooperating academic disciplines. Where these different forms of study had previously constituted separate and noncoincident languages, the theoretical debates of the 1970s and the consolidation of these debates in the 1980s established these differences as a syntax of relations within a complete language. If this brought with it the obvious advantages of diversity and the possibility for enlightening and liberating exchange between different spheres, it also brought with it the disadvantage of containment and uniformity within a newly unified and now international academic field.

The most representative form of this paradoxical relationship between diversity and uniformity is the postmodernism debate itself, which advertises its commitment to indeterminacy, openness and multiplicity, but provides in itself the discursive means to limit the force and implications of such questions. The postmodern debate may be seen as an intellectual-discursive process which simultaneously multiplies critical options and binds them into recognizable and disseminable forms, or, as Dana Polan puts it, even more gloomily, 'intensely frames critical discourse as a kind of mechanistic *combinatoire* in which everything is given in advance, in which there can be no practice but the endless recombination of fixed pieces from the generative machine'.[19] A slightly different view, one that is closer to the emphasis proposed in this study, is apparent in John

Rajchman's description of the 'world market of ideas' which postmodern theory institutes and participates in; in its elasticity and theoretical centrelessness, postmodern theory 'is like the Toyota of thought: produced and assembled in several different places and then sold everywhere'.[20]

This may sound like a conventional protest against the life-denying abstractions of theory. But what is particular to postmodern theory (but perhaps by this very fact it has a sort of representative status, too) is the desire to project and to produce that which cannot be pinned down or mastered by representation or conceptual thought, the desire which has been identified by Jean-François Lyotard as the pull towards the sublime. Here, then, it is not simply a case of a theoretical-discursive practice which, like the second revolution spoken of by Charles Newman, arrives on the intellectual scene to mop up the challenges and distortions of a revolutionary art practice, but a theory which itself continually projects the categories of its own discomfiture, in a will-to-undoing which goes beyond (while also recapitulating) anything in Dadaism or surrealism. Here, will and surrender, mastery and renunciation spiral together in an indissoluble helix which is itself another version of the set towards the sublime. Such a theory asserts its legitimacy through the forms of its discrediting, unmakes and decentres itself only to produce suppler forms of authoritative discourse. Postmodern theory yields the vision of a cultural 'heterotopia' which has no edges, hierarchies or centre, but is nevertheless always framed by the theory that wills it into being, a theory that, in its authoritative disavowal of authority, prevents it everywhere, in a pervading inclusiveness, or 'perclusion' (in surrendering to the urge to neologism, I invoke a representative form of this critical discourse, in its simultaneous will to push language beyond itself and to objectify that movement in a repeatable formula).

If this account of the development of contemporary academic discourse diverges from those accounts which tell a simpler and more uniform story of the withdrawal of the academy from centres of power and influence, then it must agree with them in one particular – that contemporary conditions present the academy with a crisis of self-definition. But this must be read dialectically, as simultaneously the expression of crisis and the rhetorical means for managing and instrumentalizing that crisis. The advantage of this is that it allows us to see the academy as formulating, concentrating and redistributing powers at the same time as it is losing them. It is 'postmodern theory' – in that formulation that usefully allows us to speak simultaneously of theory about postmodernism in the cultural field and theory which mimics or evidences the qualities of postmodernism – which is the most complex form of this legitimation crisis.

One gain from this (if it is a gain) is that it may no longer be possible to deny that postmodernism exists, since the critical debate about post-modernism can be seen partly as the proof of its existence. Critical debates about postmodernism constitute postmodernism itself – such that even denials of the existence of postmodernism, by virtue of their implication in the debate, are thereby captured in its 'perclusive' pull. If this seems like another devious form of self-justification, a terminal squirm in the spiral of academic self-contemplation, then it may also offer a way of reading the postmodernism debate in terms of its strongest, most pressing conditions of cultural-theoretical power and self-legitimation, conditions that have, however, remained largely invisible within the debate itself. This may perhaps be due to the structural inattention implied by Paul Rabinow when he proposes that 'the postmodernist is blind to her own situation and situatedness because, qua postmodernist, she is committed to a doctrine of partiality and flux for which even such things as one's own situation are so unstable, so without identity, that they cannot serve as objects of sustained reflection'.[21] But such attention to the occasions and institutions of one's own critical discourse is important, not least because of their continuing power. As Paul Bové writes:

> For literary critics to join in this movement of forces opposed to tyrannical totalization and representation, they must begin by offering a thorough critique of the new ethics of professionalism that some leading figures and their followers now propel into the market of critical celebrity. Critical intellectuals will have to investigate the origins and contemporary functions of those ethics in order to negate them; then perhaps the work of building more positive institutions and progressive critical practices can go forward.[22]

In what follows, I will attempt to move through some of the most important areas of the debate about postmodernism and postmodernity, in the areas of architecture, art, literature, performance arts and popular culture studies. In noting the forms of thematic regularity and disconti-nuity between these different areas, I hope to give an explicit account of the terms of the debate for the reader who may not be expert in all (or any) of them, but at the same time to examine the more fundamental questions of meaning, judgement and disciplinary power that are embo-died in the different forms of the debate. Necessarily, this might be said to involve me in all of the problems that I am writing about, for, if the texts and arguments that I will be considering cannot be said to stand clear of postmodern issues, but are themselves cosubstantial with them, then my own account of these can pretend to no greater degree of detachment, especially given my stress on the need for postmodern theory to understand its own discursive functioning. Perhaps wilfully, I intend to resist the temptation to public agonies of rhetorical reflexivity; this is in the hope of being able to insinuate a certain knowledge about the political significance of processes of cultural self-reflection, even though, at a later stage of the argument, such knowledge may hardly appear immune from its own critical force.

Notes

1 Charles Baudelaire, 'The Painter of Modern Life' (1863), reprinted in *The Painter of Modern Life and Other Essays*, trans. J. Mayne (London: Phaidon, 1964), pp. 12–15; Walter Pater, 'Conclusion' to *The Renaissance: Studies in Art and Poetry* (1873), reprinted in *Walter Pater: Three Major Texts*, ed. William E. Buckler (New York and London: New York University Press 1986), pp. 217–20; Henri Bergson, *Time and Free Will*, trans. F. L. Pogson (1910), reprinted London: George Allen, 1950; Virginia Woolf, 'Modern Fiction' (1925), in *Collected Essays* Vol. 2 (London: Hogarth Press, 1966), pp. 106–7.

2 See Paul de Man, 'Literary History and Literary Modernity', in *Blindness and Insight: Essays in the Rhetoric of Contemporary Criticism*, first published 1971, 2nd edn (London: Methuen, 1983), pp. 142–65.

3 *The Postmodern Condition: A Report on Knowledge*, trans. Geoff Bennington and Brian Massumi (Manchester: Manchester University Press, 1984).

4 Jürgen Peper, 'Postmodernismus: Unitary Sensibility?', *Amerikastudien*, 22 (1977), pp. 65–89; Jürgen Habermas, 'Modernity: An Unfinished Project', in *Postmodern Culture*, ed. Hal Foster (London and Sydney: Pluto Press, 1985), pp. 3–15; Gerald Graff, 'The Myth of the Postmodern Breakthrough', in *Literature Against Itself: Literary Ideas in Modern Society* (Chicago and London: Chicago University Press, 1979), pp. 31–62.

5 Brian McHale, *Postmodernist Fiction* (New York and London: Methuen, 1987); Hans Bertens, 'The Postmodern *Weltanschauung* and its Relation With Modernism: An Introductory Survey', in *Approaching Postmodernism*, ed. Douwe Fokkema and Hans Bertens (Amsterdam and Philadelphia: John Benjamins, 1986), pp. 9–52.

6 *The PostModern Aura: The Act of Fiction in an Age of Inflation* (Evanston: Northwestern University Press, 1985).

7 Jürgen Habermas, *Legitimation Crisis*, first published 1973, trans. Thomas McCarthy (London: Heinemann, 1976).

8 *The Postmodern Condition*, pp. xxiv, 31–7.

9 Quoted in Michel Foucault, *The Order of Things: An Archaeology of the Human Sciences*, no translator named (London: Tavistock Press, 1970), p. xv.

10 Ibid., p. xvi.

11 Warren Montag has made similar observations about the totalizing force of postmodern theory in 'What is at Stake in the Postmodernism Debate?', in *Postmodernism and its Discontents: Theories, Practices*, ed. E. Ann Kaplan (London: Verso, 1988), pp. 91–2.

12 Stanley Fish, *Is There a Text in This Class? The Authority of Interpretive Communities* (Cambridge, Mass.: Harvard University Press, 1980), p. 3.

13 Théories et institutions pénales', *Annuaire du Collège de France, 1971–2*, quoted in Alan Sheridan, *Michel Foucault: The Will to Truth* (London and New York: Tavistock, 1980), p. 131.

14 *The Post-Modern Aura*, pp. 27–35.

15 Terry Eagleton, *The Function of Criticism: From 'The Spectator' to Post-Structuralism* (London: Verso, 1984), pp. 81–4.

16 Ibid., p. 102.

17 'Opponents, Audiences, Constituencies, and Community', in *The Politics of Interpretation*, ed. W. J. T. Mitchell (Chicago: University of Chicago Press, 1983), pp. 7–32.

18 Here I am clearly following the account given by Terry Eagleton in *Literary Theory: An Introduction* (Oxford: Basil Blackwell, 1983), pp. 17–53.

19 'Postmodernism and Cultural Analysis Today', in *Postmodernism and its Discontents*, p. 49.

20 'Postmodernism in a Nominalist Frame: The Emergence and Diffusion of a Cultural Category', *Flash Art*, 137 (1987), p. 51.

21 'Representations Are Social Facts: Modernity and Post-Modernity in Anthropology', in *Writing Culture: The Politics and Poetics of Ethnography*, ed. James Clifford and George E. Marcus (Berkeley: University of California Press, 1986), p. 252.

22 'The Ineluctability of Difference: Scientific Pluralism and the Critical Intelligence', in *Postmodernism and Politics*, ed. Jonathan Arac (Manchester: Manchester University Press, 1986), p. 22.

Part II
Posterities

2
Postmodernities: Postmodern Social and Legal Theory

It is necessary to distinguish between two separate areas of postmodern theory. On the one hand, there is the compendium of narratives about the emergence of postmodernism in world culture: the chapters that follow from this one will attempt to track through these narratives. But, associated with this side of the postmodern debate and in many ways serving as its structural support, is a different account, of the emergence of new forms of social, political and economic arrangement. These two accounts, one of the emergence of postmodernism out of modernism, the other of the emergence of postmodernity out of modernity, run on adjoining tracks, sometimes crossing, but also sometimes diverging from each other in significant ways. There are three writers whose work has orientated and continues to orientate discussion of social, economic and political postmodernity: Jean-François Lyotard, Fredric Jameson and Jean Baudrillard. The account that follows, of their work and of the concepts that their work has put into circulation, must necessarily be concentrated, but it is hoped that it will be enough to provide a working context for the more specific explorations of theories of postmodern culture in the later chapters.

Jean-François Lyotard

Lyotard's account of postmodernity is to be found in a book published originally in 1979, *La Condition postmoderne*. Although he has concerned himself with published work in a range of different areas, including linguistics, psychoanalysis and ethics, this short book is what has established Lyotard's reputation in the English-speaking world. Although the book calls itself an 'occasional' text, produced as it was at the request of the Conseil des Universités of the Quebec government as an interim 'report on knowledge', its influence on theorists of postmodernity has been immense. This is curious, since many of the arguments it sketches about the nature of knowledge and information in late twentieth-century scientific research seem very oblique to the concerns of such theorists. The immensity of its influence may be due to the fact that, as Fredric Jameson suggests in his introduction to the English translation, the book is a 'crossroads' in which debates in different areas such as politics, economics and aesthetics intersect.[1] It may also be due to the workings of a retroactive spiral of influence in which Lyotard's characterization of the postmodern condition, which originally drew much of its legitimating force from American ideas about the postmodern, such as those of Ihab Hassan, was itself seized upon as a legitimating source for those more properly cultural-aesthetic narratives. The skewing of the disciplinary audience for the book in English-speaking countries is indicated by the inclusion in the translated edition of a postscript in which Lyotard moves away from postmodernity towards the definition of cultural postmodernism.

Lyotard's argument in the book revolves around the function of narrative within scientific discourse and knowledge. His interest is not so much in scientific knowledge and procedures as such, as in the forms by which such knowledge and procedures gain or claim legitimacy. Firstly, Lyotard argues, modern science is characterized by its refusal or suppression of forms of legitimation which rely upon narrative. He defines narrative knowledge by drawing on anthropological accounts of primitive societies in which the function of narrative is embodied in clear sets of rules about who has the right and responsibility to speak and to listen in a given social group. The internalized rules, or 'pragmatics', of popular narrative among the Cashinahua Indians of South America, for instance, depend upon the fixed formulae whereby a storyteller begins his narrative by identifying himself with his Cashinahua name, thereby affirming his tribal authenticity and consequent right to speak (on the basis that he has heard the story from another Cashinahua), as well as his listener's responsibility to listen. This is an instance of self-legitimation. Telling the story in a certain way establishes the right of the storyteller to tell the story at all. Lyotard attaches great significance to this apparently rather feeble instance of self-legitimation, for he believes that 'what is transmitted through these narratives is the set of pragmatic rules that constitutes the social bond' (*PC*, 21). Another, surprising feature which Lyotard insists on is the rhythmic form of narrative which, by providing a regularizing metre or narrative 'beat', fixes and contains the irregularities of natural time. Lyotard's conclusion is that, far from calling attention to the passage of time in their own temporal unfolding, in what is conventionally assumed to be the distinguishing property of narrative, such narratives actually dissolve or suspend the sense of time. Lyotard here seems to be stretching the term 'narrative' to its limits – since what he says only really seems to apply to the particular case of a people like the Cashinahua, whose ritual narratives do indeed consist of 'interminably monotonous chants' (*PC*, 21).

For Lyotard, this form of narrative is the principal way in which a culture or collectivity legitimates itself, in a demanding tautology. These kinds of narrative only appear to refer to the past, he writes, for what they really refer to is the act of narrative itself in a continuing present, which requires no other authorization than itself; these narratives 'define what has the right to be said and done in the culture in question, and since they are themselves a part of that culture, they are legitimated by the simple fact that they do what they do' (*PC*, 23).

This kind of legitimation is what science from the eighteenth century onwards has been struggling against and trying to do away with, in Lyotard's view. The 'classical conception of the pragmatics of scientific knowledge' (*PC*, 23), as he puts it, requires a rather different structure of authorization. Depending as it does on assigned and agreed truth-value, scientific knowledge and language are set apart from the uses of language which form social bonds. Its dominating 'language-game' as Lyotard puts it, borrowing a term from the work of Wittgenstein, is denotative rather than narrative. Scientific language is actively opposed to the language-game of narrative, which it associates with ignorance, barbarity, prejudice, superstition and ideology (*PC*, 27). But there is another, more important, distinction between narrative and science. Where primitive narrative does not require any form of legitimation outside the fact of its own performance, certifying itself 'in the pragmatics of its own transmission without having recourse to argumentation and proof' (*PC*, 27), scientific knowledge can never validate itself simply by its own procedures (this is right because this is what we do). Since scientific knowledge, unlike narrative knowledge, is distinct from the forms of knowledge and communication which constitute social and collective bonds, the question of legitimation has another dimension: why should there be scientific activity at all and why should societies support scientific institutions of knowledge?

This is the point at which science inevitably returns to narrative, says Lyotard, since in the end it is by narratives alone that scientific work can be given authority and purpose. The two principal narratives to which science has recourse are political and philosophical. The one, associated with the Enlightenment and embodied in the ideals of the French

Revolution, is the narrative of the gradual emancipation of humanity from slavery and class oppression. Science is supposed to play a central part in this process as the representation of the knowledge which, once it has been made available to all, will assist in the attainment of this absolute freedom. This political 'narrative of emancipation' intersects with a philosophical narrative initiated and actualized in the work of Hegel, but massive in its general influence, in which knowledge is a prime part of the gradual evolution through history of self-conscious mind out of the ignorant unselfconsciousness of matter (*PC*, 31–7). Where earlier narratives had centred around the idea of rediscovering or being returned to original truth, both of these narratives, emancipatory and speculative, are teleological, that is, depend upon the idea of an itinerary towards some final goal. Both narratives are also 'metanarratives', which is to say, narratives which subordinate, organize and account for other narratives; so that every other local narrative, whether it be the narrative of a discovery in science, or the narrative of an individual's growth and education, is given meaning by the way it echoes and confirms the grand narratives of the emancipation of humanity or the achievement of pure self-conscious Spirit.

Lyotard is therefore proposing what he is happy to acknowledge as a paradox – that a scientific knowledge which depends at one level upon the suppression and denunciation of narrative, is thereby condemned to a dependence at a higher level on a narrative of legitimation, a 'metanarrative', or 'grand narrative'.

> Scientific knowledge cannot know and make known that it is the true knowledge without resorting to the other, narrative, kind of knowledge, which from its point of view is no knowledge at all. Without such recourse it would be in the position of presupposing its own validity and would be stooping to what it condemns: begging the question, proceeding on prejudice. But does it not fall into the same trap by using narrative as its authority? (*PC*, 29)

The attractive convolution of this paradox seems to me to be an illusion. It is clear that Lyotard is talking about two very different kinds of narrative here, one seeming to encompass lyric, chant, gossip and ritualized performance, the other having the features more usually associated with narrative – the extension through time of a causally-linked series of events and its direction towards resolution. In fact, if one declined to accept the designation 'narrative' for the kind of linguistic exchange practised by the Cashinahua, and similar non-scientific language-games, Lyotard's paradox would evaporate.

The most important part of Lyotard's analysis of scientific knowledge comes with his account of the contemporary condition. What has taken place since the Second World War, he argues, is a terminal wasting of the power of these grand narratives to provide a legitimating frame for scientific work. Lyotard is infuriatingly vague about what he takes the cause of this decline of metanarratives to be, suggesting only that it has something to do with the renewal of the spirit of capitalist free enterprise with the slow discrediting of its state communist alternative, along with the growth of techniques and technologies in science, with a consequent shift in emphasis from ends to means (*PC*, 37–8). The first of these is scarcely substantiated and the second is both unargued and tautological. Why is a shift from ends to means consequent upon the growth or multiplication of techniques and technologies? And if it is, then, as we shall see, this shift of emphasis might just as well be seen as a symptom of that decline rather than as its cause.

The effect on science of what Lyotard calls the 'incredulity towards metanarratives' is the loss of legitimacy with regard to those metanarratives. Science is therefore no longer held to be valuable and necessary because of the part it plays in the slow progress towards absolute freedom and absolute knowledge. With this loss of confidence in the metanarratives (and perhaps as a contribution towards such loss of confidence), comes the decline of general regulatory power in the paradigms of science itself, as science discovers the limits of its assumptions and procedures for verification, encountering paradoxes and throwing up questions (in mathematics, for example) that are undecidable, that is, not questions that have no answer, but questions that can be shown *in principle* to be unanswerable. Given this situation, the organizing power of science itself begins to weaken, as science develops into a cloud of specialisms, each with its own incompatible mode of proceeding, or language-game. None of these language-games has recourse any longer to external principles of justice or authority; in this situation, the goal is 'no longer truth but performativity' (*PC*, 46) – no longer what kind of research will lead to the discovery of verifiable facts, but what kind of research will work best, where 'working best' means producing more research along the same lines, and increasing the opportunities for more increases; that is to say, increasing the performance and operational output of the system of scientific knowledge.

We can detect here a clear correspondence between the resulting self-legitimations of science and the internal legitimation-through-narrative of the Cashinahua (who, as we can see, stand for Lyotard as a magical equivalent of the unspoilt linguistic innocence of all primitive peoples). Both science and Cashinahua narrative say 'We do what we do, because that's the way we do it.' The difference between them is that, where the Cashinahua's modes of communication and exchange form a comfortingly self-identical whole, such that their collective lives are dominated by one language-game, postmodern society encompasses a multitude of different, incompatible language-games, each with its own untransferable principles of self-legitimation. We have seen, therefore, a shift from the muffled majesty of grand narratives to the splintering autonomy of micronarratives.

This brings with it bad news and good news. The bad news is that there seems to be no way in this state of affairs to regulate science – or anything else, for that matter – in the name of justice or good. 'In the discourse of today's financial backers of research', Lyotard glumly admits, 'the only credible goal is power' (*PC*, 48). The university or institution of learning cannot in these circumstances be concerned with transmitting knowledge in itself, but must be tied ever more narrowly to the principle of performativity – so that the question asked by teacher, student and government must now no longer be 'Is it true?' but 'What use is it?' and 'How much is it worth?' (*PC*, 51). This side of Lyotard's analysis leads to the nightmare prospect envisaged by the Frankfurt school of Marxist social theorists, of a world subordinated not to a rational ideal, but to the absolute, and absolutely ungoverned, principle of rationalization, the search for higher output from lower input.

The good news about Lyotard's formulation is that the principle of performativity may not only bring with it the containment of innovative energies, but may also encourage unorthodox leaps out of existing para-digms, or governing structures of thought. Eventually, Lyotard predicts, science will have at its disposal a world of 'perfect information', in which all knowledge will have become in principle available to everybody, so that it will not be possible to base the claims of new knowledge on the discovery of new facts. (It has to be said here that Lyotard offers no explanation of how this situation of 'perfect information' is likely to come about on its own; certainly the expansion of technologies of information has shown little sign so far of increasing the general accessibility of information. Rather, it has tended to consolidate or even increase the disequilibrium in the possession of and access to information. But we had better leave this to one side.) Lyotard claims that, in this postulated condition of 'perfect information', the only way to make a new move in the game of science (he doesn't say why anyone would want to in this state of affairs) is to rearrange the information in a different and unpredictable way. It is these imaginative leaps which offer the prospect of destabilizing or renewing the paradigms of scientific knowledge.

The good news and the bad news are entwined together in complex ways in Lyotard's argument. If, on the one hand, the tendency of the dismantled grand narratives is to produce an inert saturation, in which a system of relations aims to keep reproducing itself, then, says Lyotard, it is this very saturation which may produce the surges of innovation required to jolt the system out of its inertia. We can imagine a model of how this might work with TV. Deregulated TV seems to promise absolute freedom of choice and variety of product. In fact, experience suggests that this freedom from economic or legislative control produces a deadening uniformity as TV companies struggle to guarantee the most revenue from the least input. The unlikely case that Lyotard would seem to be arguing is that at its absolute extreme of numb uniformity, this system would of itself produce the sudden daring innovation which would upset all its own protocols.

The example is a tendentious one, of course, and one that Lyotard, concerned as he is with science in particular, does not give – though many of those convinced by Lyotard's analysis have come much closer than this to the embrace of the ethos of the free market. Lyotard is more concerned to fit out science, so often accused of being the servant of tyranny, for the role of avant-garde liberator:

> Postmodern science – by concerning itself with such things as undecidables, the limits of precise control, conflicts characterized by incomplete information, '*fracta*', catastrophes and pragmatic paradoxes – is theorizing its own evolution as discontinuous, catastrophic, non-rectifiable, and paradoxical. It is changing the meaning of the word *knowledge*, while expressing how such a change can take place. It is producing not the known, but the unknown. (*PC*, 60)

Science of this kind depends not upon logic, but upon 'paralogy', faulty or deliberately contradictory reasoning, designed to shift and transform the structures of reason itself (*PC*, 61). What is representative about postmodern science is its abandonment of centralizing narratives. Lyotard embraces fondly a vision of a world in which multiple, incompatible language-games flourish alongside each other, believing that it is not worth attempting to create a conversation or consensus between them, since 'such consensus does violence to the heterogeneity of language games' (*PC*, xxv). Instead, we are enjoined to 'gaze in wonderment' (*PC*, 26) at this linguistic diversity and to cheer the language-games on in their cellular splitting and reduplication. Romantically sure that 'invention is always born of dissension', Lyotard is confident that 'postmodern knowledge is not simply a tool of the authorities; it refines our sensitivity to differences and reinforces our ability to tolerate the incommensurable' (*PC*, xxv).

Lyotard's formulation is one of the most powerful instances of the will to the sublime in contemporary thought and joins with the work of Deleuze and Foucault in suggesting the possibility of deliverance from the epochal delusions of metaphysical thinking into the 'nomadic', unregulated freedom of pure difference. It is in this immodest way that Lyotard's proposal has been read, largely by literary critics and cultural analysts (there has been little sign of any interest or response from among scientists themselves). This lack of engagement with the specific detail of Lyotard's claims about science, and the willingness of his readers to slide his analysis from one realm, the realm of scientific knowledge, to a host of other realms, is rather worrying.

It is made more so by the fact that, on the face of it, Lyotard's analysis of the condition of scientific knowledge is implausible on so many fronts. Although it is true that the conduct of scientific research in the universities and outside them is increasingly subject to the considerations of immediate use and profitability rather than pure considerations of the advancement of knowledge, it is hard to see how exactly this connects with the arguments about the breakdown of objectivist consensus within science itself. The kinds of scientific activity in which the questions which interest Lyotard so much are undeniably powerful – mathematics and theoretical physics – are, by and large, the forms which are suffering most from the economic instrumentalization of science. Lyotard paints a picture of the dissolution of science into a frenzy of relativism in which the only aim is to bound gleefully out of the confinement of musty old paradigms and to trample operational procedures underfoot in the quest for exotic forms of illogic. But this is simply not the case. If some forms of the pure sciences, mathematics and theoretical physics again being the obvious examples, are concerned with the exploration of different structures of thought for understanding reality, then this still remains bound, by and large, to models of rationality, consensus and correspondence to demonstrable truths. Otherwise, why would anyone postulating the existence of a new particle or force, go to so much trouble raising the money to burrow deep underground, or set up elaborate experiments under the polar ice, or build huge particle accelerators, to verify their existence?

Of course, not all science is as rawly dependent upon this empirical model. It is true that science today is much more aware of the ways in which a chosen paradigm of thought and investigation will always to some degree determine in advance the kind of results that are likely to be produced, and a science informed by such considerations is much less likely to claim universal validity for its discoveries. Lyotard draws here on the work of philosophers of science like Thomas Kuhn and Paul Feyerabend, both of whom have demonstrated that the achievements of science must always be a function of the paradigms governing scientific thought at any one time. But, as Richard Rorty and Axel Honneth have pointed out, Lyotard takes what Thomas Kuhn has specified as the general condition of all science at all times and turns it into the much more particular claim that this is the distinguishing characteristic of postmodern science.[2] Lyotard's analysis of the abandonment of the universal perspective in science hardly seems to accord, either, with one particular contemporary development in the sciences of matter. In theoretical physics, the drive is not towards outlandish forms of paralogy, for the sake of diversifying knowledges, nor are most scientists as benignly tolerant of incommensurability as Lyotard would have us believe, for the efforts of at least one important strain of theoretical research in physics have been towards the construction of unifying theories to account for the operations of all the forces known in nature – a grand narrative if ever there was one.[3]

What is most difficult to accept in Lyotard's account is the movement from the usefully specific, the account of the conduct and dissemination of scientific knowledge in universities and other institutions, to the globally generalized. Geoff Bennington has suggested that Lyotard might be accused of projecting his account of the inevitable 'diaspora' of knowledges away from centralizing metanarratives, as a metanarrative of his own.[4] In fact, Lyotard's model is doubly totalizing, for it depends not only upon a vision of the total collapse of metanarrative, everywhere and for always, but also upon an unshakeable belief in the absolute dominion of metanarrative before the arrival of the postmodern condition. It is this which leads Lyotard in his more recent thumbnail sketches of postmodernity, *Le Postmoderne expliqué aux enfants*, to accuse all such generalizing narratives as Marxism, Hegelian philosophy and liberal economic theory as totalitarian and conducing inevitably to 'crimes against humanity'.[5]

More recently, following those who have taken up his generalized account and generalized it still further, Lyotard has turned his eye to issues of cultural politics. Here the question of the decline of metanarrative has less to do with the possibilities or not of scientists agreeing with each other, or knowing why they do, and more to do with questions about the relationships within and between cultures. In an essay entitled 'Missive on Universal History', Lyotard has mounted an attack on the cultural imperialism of metanarrative by means of a linguistic argument. He argues that if we ask, or attempt to ask a question such as 'Should we continue to understand the multiplicity of social and nonsocial phenomena in the light of the Idea of a universal history of mankind?' the central problem lies in the very use of the word 'we'. This 'we', he writes, is a form of grammatical violence, which aims to deny and obliterate the specificity of the 'you' and the 'she' of other cultures through the false promise of incorporation within a universal humanity. We must therefore wean ourselves away from the 'we', that grammatico-political category that can never exist except as legitimating myth operating in the service of appropriative and oppressive cultures. Instead we must embrace and promote every form of cultural diversity, without recourse to universal principles.[6]

There are two different objections available to this argument against cultural universalism. The first objection is raized by Richard Rorty in a reply to Lyotard's 'Missive on Universal History'. Rorty argues that Lyotard is unable to conceive of anything in between absolute and dogmatic adherence to universals on the one hand and absolute delegitimation on the other – between totalitarianism and anarchy. This, he says, is to ignore a whole tradition of pragmatic thought represented by the American philosophers, William James, William Dewey and, latterly, Rorty himself, which, while professing absolutely no desire for metaphysical absolutes or ideals, nevertheless does not abandon the prospect of achieving human consensus. Lyotard insists on the absolute incompatibility of different cultural languages or 'name-worlds' as he calls them.[7] But Rorty, while prepared to accept that there are cultural differences, denies that these amount to principled incompatibility. Devastatingly, he points out that if Lyotard's claims about the absolute diversity of cultures and language-games were true, then it would not only be impossible for anyone ever to learn another language, but it would be impossible for anyone, a Frenchman, say, to be able to distinguish the ways in which another language – say, Cashinahua – was incompatible with his own. Indeed, one might go further and say that he might not be able to recognize that Cashinahua was a language at all. Rorty's recipe for consensus does not rely on abstract or universally accepted principles of human nature, but on a process of gradual mutual adjustment between opposed parties:

> what the pragmatist seeks are powerfully cosmopolitan narratives which are not narratives of emancipation. He believes that there has never been anything to emancipate and that human nature has never been in chains. On the contrary, humanity has created its own nature, little by little, through ever larger and richer 'compounds of opposed values'. In recent times, it looks as though it has managed to produce a particularly good form of this, the one that has resulted in the liberal institutions of the West.[8]

For Lyotard, the only way of avoiding the violent subordination of one language (and therefore cultural experience and identity) to another is by the abandonment of the expectation of ever being able to unify incompatible languages. For Rorty, such disagreements are a matter for tolerant understanding:

> Cultural differences are like the differences between old and new (or 'revolutionary') theories within the same culture. The respect which one pays to the Cashinahua point of view does not differ at all from the polite attention which one accords to a radically new idea in science, politics or philosophy, emanating from one of our Western Colleagues.

This vision of polite tolerance and persuasion is grounded for Rorty in an acknowledgement of the need to make sure that persuasion is not actually grounded in force, that cultures are not 'persuaded' to give up their identities by implied or actual threats, or other inducements which may interfere with the free, mutually-tolerant exchange of ideas and experiences. But Rorty offers little hint of how such tolerance may be guaranteed, other than by the assumption that cultures will naturally come to realize that such tolerance is desirable and productive.

It is possible to conceive a second objection to Lyotard's argument which is different from Rorty's and perhaps more powerful. In order to do this it will be necessary to consider the work of the writer who is Lyotard's implicit antagonist through *The Postmodern Condition* and much of his other work, the German social theorist, Jürgen Habermas. Habermas has been concerned, throughout a large and challenging body of work over the last 30 years, to develop a model of 'communicative action', an ethical scheme based upon the principles of reason, justice and democracy, but without running the risk of alienating or silencing seemingly aberrant minority voices within false or oppressive forms of consensus. Hence the focus of Habermas's philosophy upon free, undistorted communication as the ground of justice. Habermas differs from Rorty in seeking to discover grounds or guarantees for the multiplicity of competing interests in any one situation, rather than simply trusting in goodwill, or enlightened self-interest. In seeking such forms of legitimation, Habermas is continuing the modern search for a social ethics based upon reason, the 'Enlightenment project' which Lyotard believes has run itself into the ground. For Habermas, on the other hand, Lyotard's assault on the principle of reason is, ultimately, irrationalist and, in its willingness to sacrifice the principles of justice to the 'just gaming' of a moral-cultural free market, is also 'neo-conservative'.[10]

Lyotard's reply to Habermas's critique has been consistently to restate his scepticism about the grounds of universal reason and the necessity for a 'war on totality' (*PC*, 82), the absolute refusal of any kind of universalism. Ironically, in this absolute intolerance of absolutes, Lyotard removes the possibility of guaranteeing the diversity of cultural interests that he wishes to promote. To believe that conflict is a necessary guarantee of diversity and that dissension necessarily breeds innovation is to ignore the evidence of recent history. If the contemporary world is witnessing a continuation of the wholesale 'culturecide' that Lyotard abhors, then this may be the fault, not so much of tyrannous totality as of the failure to construct systems of relations which guarantee the freedom of minority groups and cultures – the product not of universalism, but of decentred greed and hostility. As Axel Honneth argues, Lyotard's distaste for any kind of universal or generalizable principle fatally deprives his theory of precisely the conditions which might sustain the free, productive agonistics of language-games:

> If recourse to universal norms is on principle blocked in the interests of a critique of ideology, then a meaningful argument in support of the equal right to coexistence of all everyday cultures cannot be constructed; this excludes the possibility of formulating a rule, let alone of institutionalising a form of law, which, beyond the internal moral perspectives of language-games, could take responsibility for the universal recognition of the equal rights of cultures.[11]

In fact, this point reveals the fundamental identity between Lyotard's and Rorty's positions; both are suspicious of the violent effects of totalizing thinking, both wish to promote diversity, but neither is willing to elaborate the grounds which might guarantee such diversity on anything but an *ad hoc* basis.

Another, perhaps equally serious, objection to Lyotard's characterization of the postmodern condition concerns his separation of the two opposite results of delegitimation in the contemporary world. As I argued earlier, one of these results is the empty functionalism of a system of production and exchange of information that has as its goal, not truth, but rationalized and accelerated production. The other, more benign, possibility is the encouragement of paralogical innovation. Lyotard makes it clear that, although the two currents in contemporary life derive from the same context of delegitimation, he is firmly on the side of paralogy. This is the point at which Lyotard's political theory merges most clearly with his earlier post-structuralist work in psychoanalysis and aesthetics, work which stresses the need to free the formless, fugitive intensities of desire and psychic drives from the binding, filtering effects of language and social forms.[12]

But Lyotard seems unwilling to follow through the implications of this structural equivalence between the two effects of delegitimation, performativity and paralogy, consolidation and subversion of systems of operation. Here is how Lyotard characterizes the interinvolvement of the two alternatives in world economics after the Second World War:

> the reconstitution of the world market after the Second World War and the intense financial and economic battles being fought out today between multinational banks and corporations, underwritten by national States, for domination of this market, lack any kind of cosmopolitan perspective. It would be hard to credit a participant in this game who claimed still to be aiming at the goals set by economic liberalism or the Keynesianism of the modern period; for it is quite clear that the game is not diminishing in the least but, on the contrary, is actually aggravating the inequalities of wealth in the world, and that, far from breaking down national frontiers, it takes advantage of them for financial and commercial speculation. The world market does not constitute a universal history in the modern sense. Cultural differences are in fact encouraged even more, by virtue of the whole range of tourist and culture industries.[13]

Lyotard's own analysis here suggests that diversity, far from being a desirable resistance to the global economic system, is its constitutive condition. Given this, it would seem a dangerous policy to embrace the delegitimated universe of postmodernity without an analytic framework which would tell you how to distinguish between a 'subversive' innovation and the constant diversity actually required to fuel and stimulate the global markets of advanced capitalism. Terry Eagleton puts the point more saltily:

> It is not difficult . . . to see a relation between the philosophy of J. L. Austin and IBM, or between the various neo–Nietzscheanisms of a post–structuralist epoch and Standard Oil. It is not surprising that classical models of truth and cognition are increasingly out of favour in a society where what matters is whether you deliver the commercial or rhetorical goods. Whether among discourse theorists or the Institute of Directors, the goal is no longer truth but performativity, not reason but power. The CBI are in this sense spontaneous post-structuralists to a man, utterly disenchanted (did they but know it) with epistemological realism and the correspondence theory of truth.[14]

If Eagleton is right, we must doubt the efficacy or wisdom of a trust in paralogy, which may be nothing more than an anarchist version of the emptily pragmatic ideology of capitalist performativity.

These questions may have a relation to the standing which Lyotard's work has achieved within postmodern literary theory as a whole, for *The Postmodern Condition*, like many other texts in the postmodernism debate, may also be seen as a disguised allegory of the condition of *academic* knowledge and institutions in the contemporary world. Lyotard exudes pessimism about the role of the intellectual in a modern world which has dispensed with the justifying horizon of universal history or absolute knowledge. The diagnosis of the postmodern condition is, in one sense, the diagnosis of the final futility of the intellectual:

> We, who try to think all this, are we condemned only to a kind of negative heroism? It is clear that one sort of intellectual figure (Voltaire, Zola, Sartre) has vanished with the decline of modernity . . . the violence of the critique mounted against the academy during the sixties, followed by the inexorable decline of educational institutions in all modern countries shows plainly enough that knowledge and its transmission have ceased to exercise the kind of authority required for intellectuals to get a hearing when they mount the rostrum. In a world in which success is identified with saving time, thinking has one, irremediable fault: it wastes time.[15]

But, despite this grim outlook, Lyotard does seem to offer an analytic panacea for the intellectual. *The Postmodern Condition* makes the scientist the real avant-garde 'negative hero', by virtue of his or her capacity to carry out intellectual guerrilla war on the inside of the system, inducing esoterically destabilizing moves in the language-games of authority. Although Lyotard directs his 'report on knowledge' towards the sciences, the book steadily detaches science from its disreputable associations with capitalism and imperialism and recreates it as a kind of art or philosophy on its own terms. In the end, as Axel Honneth and Kenneth Lea have observed, Lyotard sees the whole realm of the social under postmodernity as intrinsically aesthetic – organized in terms of narrative, linguistic and libidinal structure, rather than in terms of power.[16] This strategy enables Lyotard to enlist himself and those who would follow him in the glorious paralogical assault on stability. So the analysis which mourns the ghostly ineffectuality of the academy ends up not only giving the intellectual a central place in the struggle to bring about micropolitical multiplicity, but also, by transforming the field of postmodern society into an *aesthetic* field, giving the illusion of analytic dominion over it.

Lyotard's work is not itself responsible for these conditions, but it has an added potency in a situation characterized by the wholesale aestheticization of philosophy and the social sciences, in which terms like narrative, metaphor, text and discourse now have the advantage over an older, creaking vocabulary of function, determination, mechanism, and so on. (It is often felt in the humanities that the reverse has taken place, but the apparent invasion of critical language by sociological and philosophical technicality has gone along with a reciprocal migration of criticism into philosophy and the social sciences.)[17] The forms of interdisciplinarity which result from this exchange of languages and concepts are often claimed as postmodern destabilizations of the structures of knowledge. But this argument could be put the other way round. The form of interdisciplinarity which has been fostered across the social sciences and humanities by the vehicle of the postmodernism debate can also be seen as attempts to master the field, coercing it into intellectual performativity. This form of generalizing can restore a form (perhaps an illusory form) of that total dominion which, as Lyotard makes melancholically plain, the academy does not have. At the same time, in Lyotard's formulation it allows for a glamorously self-promoting vision of oppositional avant-garde practice, in which the institutions themselves are the places of difference, plurality and instability.

In other words, the postmodernism debate itself exhibits signs of the same functional equivalence between the consolidation of a system, and the fostering of plurality within it. Academic debates *about* postmodernity and postmodernism reproduce the conditions of the postmodern, and Lyotard's analysis of the operations of the performativity principle provide a model for the reception and circulation of his own texts and their concepts. The result of all this can be seen as an inertia, in which the real political questions and opportunities opened up by theories of postmodernism remain atomized and inconsequent. What follows is a curious amalgam of political oversell in the conjuring of glamorous images of total conceptual revolution and a sort of institutionalized paralysis. In the absence of a determined attempt to build any kind of effective oppositional or democratizing consensus, paralogy and subversion can be discharged harmlessly into strategies of professional and institutional consolidation.

In his work since *The Postmodern Condition*, Lyotard attempts to loosen the complex and unstable alliance between the deepening of systematic performativity and the liberation of paralogy and unpredictability. Perhaps provoked by Habermasian arguments for communicative ethics, or the utopian orientation to consensus buried within the conditions of speech as such, Lyotard himself turned to the analysis of discourse in *The Differend* (1984). This book is his attempt to make out, not so much an ethical system, as a set of ethical possibilities, in terms of the structures of address and communication within language itself. The book extends and deepens the claims for the multiplicity and incommensurability of language games launched in general terms in *The Postmodern Condition*. It proposes that all statements, utterances, communications and instances of address whatsoever, including a host of actions that one might previously not have suspected of being analysable in terms of a speech event (such as the Nazi extermination of the Jews) can be seen, not merely as reflecting a particular world or set of beliefs, but also as instituting a set of pragmatic relations between its participants – typically the addressor and the addressee. At the instant of their utterance, phrases such as 'How do you plead?', 'We have no choice but to operate', or 'I must ask you to accompany me to the station' bring into being certain relationships and expectations between addressors and those addressed by their phrases. Doubtless, the efficacy of such phrases, their capacity to make the social relations they posit stick and persist, is related to the existence of reinforcing nonlinguistic background conditions – where you are, how you got there, whether the person addressing you is wearing a wig, or a white coat. But Lyotard's interest is much more in the pragmatics of such linguistic events – the conditions and relationships conjured by the linguistic events as such – than in their defining and confirming contexts.

Phrases, and phrase-regimens, such as prescription, persuasion, prophecy and promising, and then, beyond these, the larger genres of discourse which aggregate, deploy and regulate such phrase-regimens – legal, philosophical, economic or aesthetic discourses, for example – are subject to a dual necessity. First of all there is the necessity of 'linkage'; phrases inevitably call forth other phrases, according with them, contradicting them, shifting their emphases. Even silence is a kind of phrase and a kind of linkage. Linkage implies the possibility of translatability or transition between the different pragmatic worlds posited by different genres of discourse. But the second necessity to which phrases are subject is the necessity of dispute and dissension between them. Every transition from one phrase to another implies a conflict of discursive worlds. We suppose that we have means for reconciling such conflicts of linguistic function, or for legislating over the clashes of interest and perspective they may imply. In fact, however for Lyotard, every apparent translation or mediation of two different phrases, phrase-regimens, or genres of discourse is subject to the conditions of incommensurability. Such conditions mean that any formalization of a conflict between name-worlds, or ways of being, or genres of discourse is in fact liable to constitute the unjust subjection of one genre of discourse to the imperatives of another.

When conflict between two parties, or their genres of discourse, is resolved by recourse to a third genre of discourse which is held to be applicable to both parties, Lyotard proposes that it be called a litigation. Where there is no such recourse, Lyotard asserts the existence of a 'differend', defined in the opening words of *The Differend* as 'a case of conflict, between (at least) two parties, that cannot be equitably resolved for lack of a rule of judgement applicable to both arguments'.[18] In the absence of such a discursive *tertium quid*, a wrong is committed; the wrong of subordinating one form of discourse, judgement, or culture to the norms of another. But for Lyotard, there is never a satisfactory *tertium quid*, and any and every instance of litigation must be seen as at best a deflection or dissimulation of the relations of the differend which are endemic in discourse. So the task of moral and philosophical argument is not to separate out the occasional hard cases of differend from the resolvable cases of litigation, or to chivvy differends into the tractable condition of litigations. Rather, it is to bear witness to the existence of such differends even, and especially, within what appear to be satisfactory relations of litigation. Blessed, so to speak, are the discursive trouble-makers.

Two related objections to this idea of generalized or absolute incommen-surability arise almost straight away. First of all, how can one speak of conflict under conditions of such absolute incommensurability? It is easy, of course, to come up with examples of limited incommensurability. One such example might be the failure of fit between the different forms of relationship to the land posited by occupying colonists and the peoples whose territories they appropriate; the treaty that gives an indigenous people rights of possession over a land with which they may previously have had a much more complex kind of relationship, of belonging, mutual responsibility, and so on, can be seen as forcing the colonized people into an acceptance of a way of thinking that is not their own, and is therefore a replication of the original wrong of colonial dispossession. But, insofar as the parties involved are in dispute, they must have something in common – there must be some form of commensurability which allows them to frame the dispute; this might, for example, be a normative assumption that human groups typically have and should retain some kind of defining relationship to particular places.

Secondly, how would you know that a wrong had been committed in subordinating the interests of one group to those of another, except according to some more or less explicit norm, applying not only to this case, but to all such cases whatsoever, that one genre of discourse should not be subordinated to another? For if the principle that one kind of discourse should not subordinate another wholly different kind of dis-course applies in all cases (and Lyotard does not allow that there could be any exceptions), then surely a universal rule of ethical – discursive functioning has been installed, a universal rule which is an instance of exactly the kind of thing that it itself countermands.

Far from being unaware of these issues, *The Differend* positively squirms with perplexity about them. In particular, Lyotard now appears very unsure as to what bearing his previous analysis of the postmodern condition might have on such moral–philosophical questions. In *The Postmodern Condition*, the analysis of the collapse and splintering of unified metanarratives in the contemporary world leads more or less directly to the ethical–political imperative to bear witness to difference articulated at the end of the book. *The Differend* may imply the existence of contemporary conditions which are propitious for the multiplication of differends, given the simultaneous diversification of forms of discourse and the increasing inevitability of interference or abrasion between them, but its ethical arguments no longer depend upon such an analysis of contemporary conditions. How could they, indeed, since this would be to derive an ethical or prescriptive way of talking from, or subordinate it to, a referential way of talking, which is a violence supposedly proscribed by prescriptive discourse? If the postmodern condition is supposed to be the condition of the differend, a notion which has had some philosophical success in some quarters, this claim about the way things are can have no bearing in principle upon what we ought to do about it. A cultural politics can be born from these conditions only on the strict principle (which can never be a principle, on pain of self-contradiction) that it retain an absolute distinction between itself and the conditions from which it might appear to arise.

These problems cast an interesting backward light on *The Postmodern Condition*. The English version of 1984 differed from the French version of 1979 in its inclusion of the appendix 'Answering the Question: What is Postmodernism?' As far as its readers have been concerned, this appendix brings together the social–political theories of postmodernity with theories of aesthetic postmodernism in culture and the arts. In its English version, the book appears to offer a passage from the analytic account of contemporary conditions to be found in the main body of the text to the recommendations and exhortations to be found in the appendix. Lyotard gives his appendix the title 'Answering the Question: What *is* Postmodernism', not, as he might well have done, 'Answering the Question: What Should Postmodernism Be?' And yet the difference of mood and purpose between the two segments is striking; where the main body of the text is conducted largely in the indicative mood, the appendix is thick with requirement and imperative. If the main part of the text is a 'report on knowledge', in the mode of knowledge itself, the appendix is a 'witnessing' of the incommensurable. The arguments elaborated in *The Differend* disclose the self-incriminating nature of the passage from cognitive *is* to ethical *ought* in *The Postmodern Condition*. If we try to read it as a unity, *The Postmodern Condition* falls apart; it seems to be saying that the postmodern *is* that set of conditions which determines that we *ought* to bear witness to the permanent estrangement of the *is* from the *ought*. The text can only be prevented from falling apart by carefully partitioning its two halves off from each other, in order to split its *is* from its *ought* and thereby insulate the text from the implications of its own argument.

In his more recent book, *The Inhuman*, Lyotard has attempted to resolve the dilemmas on which he had been spitted in *The Differend*. In effect, this has meant an ever more scrupulous segregation of report from witness, of the way things are from what we should do, of the postmodern condition from the postmodern imperative. In particular, Lyotard has sought to define with greater precision the nature of the human and that which exceeds it in contemporary life and thought. *The Postmodern Condition* had proposed that with the supersession of the prestige of metanarratives, would come a waning of the authority of the idea of the human – defined as Lyotard defines it as that inclusive, evolving 'we', or subject of history, which in practice involved the exclusion and extermination of those who did not accord with its own narrow and particular concerns. *The Postmodern Condition* proposes that it is the indifference to the concerns of the 'we' who constitute the collective hero of the metanarrative which makes the imperative of performativity liable to sudden anarchic jolts into paralogy; as though the deathly regime of the *is* might spontaneously generate the *ought* of newness and change.

In *The Inhuman*, Lyotard enlarges and particularizes his account of the performativity of knowledge and information systems in order to distinguish it from the principle of newness. *The Postmodern Condition* had suggested puzzlingly that knowledge and the avant-garde were linked by their refusal of the ideal of the human; *The Inhuman* proposes that they represent radically different orientations towards the inhuman. Lyotard sees the dominant culture of information as the sign of 'a cosmic process of complexification'.[19] This involves the move towards maximal retention – the ability to capture ideas and events in representation – and maximal synthesis – the ability to recombine such representations in more and more complex relationships. In that it appears to counter the universal slide into entropic noise, or disorganization, such a process can also be described as 'negentropic'. Lyotard sees this process as fundamentally aimed at cancelling the effects of temporal uncertainty. Knowledge, like money, aims to neutralize the effects of the unexpected, to take account of the future before it happens. The aim of maximal information is 'to subordinate the present to what is (still) called the "future", since in these conditions, the "future" will be completely predetermined and the present itself will cease opening onto an uncertain and contingent "afterward" ' (*Inhuman*, 65).

This process may have appeared for a while to be furthering and enlarging human self-knowledge and self-interest, but it now appears increasingly hard to reconcile with the human. Lyotard now defines modernity's metanarrative of human self-realization as only the temporary vehicle of this abstract principle of rational complexification, a vehicle which has come in its turn to seem like a clog or inertia to be overcome. The modern 'project' of human emancipation has given way to the postmodern programme, which is both an extension and a denial of the control of time proposed in modernity. Where the modern project attempted to realize the human through its very exposure to contingency, the postmodern programme attempts to neutralize all such contingency.

The modernist reassertion of the human against this process would be purposeless for Lyotard. Instead he proposes another mode of the inhuman, a mode associated with the modernist avant-gardes from which postmodernism draws its energies and force. Central to this activity is the notion of an attentive exposure to the actuality of the here and now of unsynthesized time. It is characterized by an attitude that Lyotard calls 'impassibility', by which he means a kind of resolute passivity, a determination to resist the transformation of events into explications. In psychoanalytic terms, this would resemble the attitude to free association counselled by Freud, in its determination to 'give itself as a passage to the events which come upon it from a "something" that it does not know' (*Inhuman*, 30). In philosophical terms, it is 'thought itself resolving to be irresolute, deciding to be patient, wanting not to want' (*Inhuman*, 19). In linguistic terms, this impassibility can be seen as a surrender to the 'other' in language, rather than the attempt to make language a more and more faithful instrument of the human mind.

> Sentences, in that case, far from being under the responsibility of the speakers, should rather be thought of as discontinuous and spasmodic concretions of a continuous 'speaking medium' . . . What these diverse or even heterogeneous forms have in common is the freedom and the lack of preparation with which language shows itself capable of receiving what can happen in the 'speaking medium', and of being accessible to the event. (*Inhuman*, 72–3)

Where the Lyotard of *The Postmodern Condition* had pinned his hopes upon the interwining of the two modes of the inhuman – the more-than-human process of negentropic complexification and the less-than-human openness to that which lies beneath the threshold of human self-consciousness and identity – he now regards it as imperative to keep them separate. 'What else remains as "politics" except resistance to this inhuman? And what else is left to resist with but . . . the other inhuman?' (*Inhuman*, 7). The problem with this other inhuman is that it can, in principle, yield no positive value, programme, or community of purpose, without instantly being betrayed into 'the great rule of controlled time' (*Inhuman*, 76). As though to dramatize this, *The Inhuman* itself resists its own centripetal tendency to gather together into a determinate argument. The book remains a series of brief reports on problems relating to technology, economics and aesthetics, which aims less to represent the conditions of postmodernism as they are, than to bear witness to the possibility of describing them otherwise. The 'report on knowledge' provided in *The Postmodern Condition* made the idea of the postmodern credible, comprehensible and describable. What belongs most 'authentically' to the postmodern moment for Lyotard is now its very indescribability; the faint and ever-more fugitive possibilities it appears to offer for resisting the transformation of 'report' into 'knowledge'.

Two other accounts compete with Lyotard's to form the dominant account of the social and economic conditions of postmodernity. I shall deal first with the work of Fredric Jameson, a Marxist whose early work attempted to graft the insights and challenges of post-structuralism on to a practice of Marxist literary criticism, and whose influential encounter with postmodern culture is perhaps another stage in this intellectual intersection.

Fredric Jameson

Jameson's principal contributions to the postmodernism debate are 'Postmodernism and Consumer Society', which reappeared in a much expanded and revised version as 'Postmodernism: or the Cultural Logic of Late Capitalism' in 1984, and an essay on experimental video, 'Reading Without Interpretation: Postmodernism and the Video-Text' first published in 1987.[20]

As we have seen, Lyotard conjoins the cultural/aesthetic realm of postmodernism with the socio-economic realm of postmodernity by aestheticizing the latter, reading the social as a species of the cultural (and we will see later how this same conjunction is achieved in the work of Jean Baudrillard). A similar merging takes place in the work of Jameson, but here it is not a spontaneous effect of Jameson's outlook or methodology so much as the analytic outcome of his determined attempt, as he puts it, 'to correlate the emergence of new formal features in culture with the emergence of a new type of social life and a new economic order' ('Postmodernism and Consumer Society', 113).

But in the first of these essays, Jameson's fulfilment of his promise to explore the relations between the cultural and the social is long deferred. Most of the essay is taken up with a discussion of the identifying formal and stylistic features of postmodernist culture, namely its fondness for pastiche, for the 'flat' multiplication and collage of styles, as opposed to the 'deep' expressive aesthetic of unique style characteristic of modernism, and its retreat from the idea of the unified personality to the 'schizoid' experience of the loss of self in undifferentiated time ('Postmodernism and Consumer Society', 114–23). On the way, Jameson hints at some of the causes of these cultural effects; postmodernism, he says, comes about in the wake of a modernism whose techniques and iconoclastic heroes have become safely institutionalized in museums and universities; the circulation or pastiche of multiple styles in postmodernist cultural forms mimics the actual tendency in contemporary social life towards the fragmentation of linguistic norms, with 'each group coming to speak a curious private language of its own, each profession developing its private code or dialect, and finally each individual coming to be a kind of linguistic island, separated from everyone else' ('Postmodernism and Consumer Society', 114). But nothing systematic is offered as evidence for these alleged tendencies and there is very little detail about how or why the causative link might work.

Indeed, the essay gropes for this solid relationship right until the end where, as it were in desperation, the following formula is offered. The key that connects the leading features of postmodern society – among others, the acceleration of cycles of style and fashion, the increased power of advertising and the electronic media, the advent of universal standardization, neocolonialism, the Green revolution – to the schizoid pastiche of postmodernist culture is the fading of a sense of history. Our contemporary social system has lost its capacity to know its own past, has begun to live in 'a perpetual present' without depth, definition, or secure identity ('Postmodernism and Consumer Society', 125). The essay leaves undeveloped the more central question of how to grasp or theorize what might turn out to be the oppositional aspects of postmodernist culture, the ways in which, as well as mutely giving expression to postmodernity, postmodernist culture might offer ways of resisting or surviving its most baleful tendencies.

That question is returned to in Jameson's longer version of the essay, 'The Cultural Logic of Late Capitalism'. It is here, as well, that Jameson offers his characterization of postmodernity in socioeconomic terms. As his title indicates, it is Jameson's purpose to demonstrate that there has been a fundamental shift in global economic organization. At the same time, he wishes to resist formulations (such as those of the conservative sociologist Daniel Bell), which suggest that we are living in postindustrial society, or that the world has gone beyond the epoch of class conflict, with all the disabling effects for a Marxist critique that such a diagnosis has.[21] Jameson will therefore wish to describe the contemporary global moment, not as a waning or surpassing of capitalism, but rather as an intensification of its forms and energies. Drawing heavily on Ernest Mandel's *Late Capitalism*, Jameson distinguishes three epochs of capitalist expansion: market capitalism, characterized by the growth of industrial capital in largely national markets (this running from about 1700 to 1850); monopoly capitalism, which is identical with the age of imperialism, during which markets grew into world markets, organized around nation-states, but depending on the fundamental exploitative asymmetry of the colonizing nations and the colonized who provide both raw materials and cheap labour; and, most recently, the postmodern phase of multinational capitalism, which is marked by the exponential growth of international corporations and the consequent transcending of national boundaries. Far from contradicting Marx's analysis of the operations of capitalism, multinational or consumer capitalism is 'the purest form of capital yet to have emerged, a prodigious expansion of capital into hitherto uncommodified areas' ('Cultural Logic of Late Capitalism', 78).

So far, this is an argument simply about size and intensification. But Jameson joins with other theorists of the postmodern condition in identifying the new area of commodification for multinational capitalism as pre-eminently *representation itself*. Where an older Marxist social theory saw cultural forms as part of the ideological veil or distorting mirror preventing the real economic relations in a society from being seen, this theory sees the production, exchange, marketing and consumption of cultural forms – considered in their widest sense and therefore including advertising, TV and the mass media generally – as a central focus and expression of economic activity. Here, images, styles and representations are not the promotional accessories to economic products, they are the products themselves. In a similar way, the explosion of information technology makes information not merely a lubricant of the cycles of exchange and profit, but itself the most important of commodities. If it is possible to imagine this nostalgically as a final greedy swallowing-up of culture by the forces of commodity capitalism, then this is in itself to reproduce a notion of the autonomy or separateness of culture which, Jameson wants us to believe, is itself out of date. A better way of modelling the situation is as 'an explosion: a prodigious expansion of culture throughout the social realm, to the point at which everything in our social life – from economic value and state power to practices and to the very structure of the psyche itself – can be said to have become "cultural" ' ('Cultural Logic of Late Capitalism', 87).

A later formulation, from Jameson's essay on postmodernist video, itself seems to transform the economic into the linguistic or representational, by recasting Mandel's three-stage history into a history of the sign. At the beginnings of bourgeois capitalist society is to be found division, the separation of different kinds of function and activity into unnaturally disjunct areas, all this resulting, for Jameson, in the phenomenon of 'reification', the conversion of social relationships into inert and frozen objects ('Postmodernism and the Video-Text', 222). In the early, 'heroic' phase of capitalist expansion, the force that separates capital from labour, exchange-value in the market from immediate social use-value, owner from worker, reaches into the linguistic realm to separate the sign from its referent. This is seen in the accompanying hegemony of scientific and other referential language, which is able to control at a distance the alien and rebarbative forces of nature just as the absentee landlord controls his unruly tenants, or the capitalist his workforce. But this process of separation and reification intensifies, so that language moves further and further away from what it was supposed to be referring to, though without ever quite losing sight of the referent. This is the moment of modernism, for Jameson, resulting from a separation of the realm of culture from social and economic life of a kind that allows for critique and utopian aspiration – even though this may also be shrouded by 'a certain otherworldly futility' ('Postmodernism and the Video-Text', 222). But the process of reification continues inexorably. In the next, postmodern stage, signs are entirely relieved of their function of referring to the world and this brings about the expansion of the power of capital into the realm of the sign, of culture and representation, along with the collapse of modernism's prized space of autonomy. We are left 'with that pure and random play of signifiers which we call postmodernism, and which no longer produces monumental works of the modernist type, but ceaselessly reshuffles the fragments of preexistent texts, the building blocks of older cultural and social production, in some new and heightened bricolage: metabooks which cannibalize other books, metatexts which collate bits of other texts' ('Postmodernism and the Video-Text', 222).

This self-acknowledged myth of Jameson's makes no distinction between dominant and oppositional. That is to say, even when dealing with modernist culture under the conditions of modernity, it attributes the same formative conditions both to social and economic life and to the cultural forms which, though standing in one sense separate from all this, also mirror its most fundamental conditions. In the case of postmodernist culture, no means seem to be available to separate culture from everything else, and there is greatly reduced scope for claiming that within culture there may be ways of thwarting the inexorable rhythms of appropriation and alienation of consumer capitalism. There is an unexpressed contradiction at the heart of the model: on the one hand, postmodern consumer capitalism represents the final term in a logic of reification (alienation, differentiation, splitting of the signifier and the signified), while on the other, there seems to be an absolute collapse of differentiation, as the cultural realm becomes identical with the socio-economic.

The problem for Jameson under these circumstances is how to remain true to the analysis of postmodernity which he has produced, while yet preventing the enormity of the analysis from overwhelming the possibility of critique. Far from simply bemoaning the loss of the long perspective of history, considered as inexorable progress, or, on the other hand, simply accepting the demise of this perspective (Jameson is routinely accused of both these things) he is concerned above all with the problem of how to go about analysing a situation which resists analysis so slyly. Although the cultural evidence of postmodernism seems palpable and ubiquitous, in the loss of history, the dissolution of the centred self, the fading of individual style and the predominance of pastiche, it proves immensely difficult for Jameson to specify the nature and direction of the postmodernity that he wishes to account for, pressing as it does so insistently into view, while resisting capture in any easy formulation or mapping. Seizing on the computer and information networks of the contemporary world as an instance of the centreless, but all-pervading labyrinth of the postmodern, Jameson immediately rejects it as inadequate, arguing that

> our faulty representations of some immense communicational and computer network are themselves but a distorted figuration of something even deeper, namely the whole world system of present-day multinational capitalism . . . a network of power and control even more difficult for our minds and imaginations to grasp – namely the whole new decentred global network of the third stage of capital itself. ('Cultural Logic of Late Capitalism', 79–80)

Like a postmodernist text, global capitalism flaunts its centreless ubiquity, its refusal to stand still and be itself for the analyst. In these circumstances, it proves more than ever difficult to offer a description of postmodernity which does not mutate into a meditation on the difficulties of offering such a description.

The dissolution of the privileged viewpoint, of science or of history, goes along with a seeming loss of sensitivity to the general tendency or evaluative polarities within postmodern culture. Jameson condemns the 'complacent (yet delirious) camp-following celebration of this aesthetic new world' ('Cultural Logic of Late Capitalism', 85) and yet, despite what many of these proponents of the postmodern liberation have had to say about him, and almost uniquely on the Left, he refuses to condemn the productions of postmodernist culture altogether. Rather, Jameson attempts to grasp postmodernist culture dialectically, in both its positive and negative aspects, just as Marx could perceive the progressive aspects in the bourgeois capitalism he condemned.

But the evidence of this dialectical reading that Jameson is able to offer is very thin. Postmodernist culture – the novels of Thomas Pynchon or the architecture of Paolo Portoghese, for instance – can be seen as attempts to 'explore', or 'express' the new decentred world of postmodernity. Such works are therefore to be read simultaneously as new forms of realism – in that they represent, perhaps critically, the central features of postmodern social existence – and as 'so many attempts to distract and to divert us from that reality or to disguise its contradictions and resolve them in the guise of various formal mystifications' ('Cultural Logic of Late Capitalism', 88). But Jameson gives us no clue as to how we would go about making the evaluative distinctions necessary for the dialectical grasping of postmodernist culture, nor indeed what we would use for evidence of one or the other tendency. His more recent essay on postmodernist experimental video ends on just such a note of irresolution. Having characterized the 'pure and random play of signifiers' in the third, postmodern stage of capitalism, he concludes that this logic can be seen in video 'in its strongest and most original and authentic form' ('Postmodernism and the Video-Text', 223). The terms used here encapsulate the paradoxes nicely. How can a culture which is allegedly defined by the decisive abandonment of originality and authenticity possibly be exemplified in any 'original' or 'authentic' way?

However, despite its final incapacity to deliver a resolution of the problems emanating from a sociology of the postmodern, Jameson's work provides the most suggestive account to date of the difficult and uneven relationship between postmodernist culture and socioeconomic postmodernity. That his account fails to achieve the high ground of critical detachment is not surprising, given the sensitivity which it shows to the continual imbrication of postmodern theory with what it aims to theorize. Rather than attempting to boost himself clear of the theoretical predicament to which postmodernity has brought him, Jameson acknowledges his necessary entanglement within that predicament. In a synoptic essay on other theories of postmodernism, he speaks powerfully of the folly of simply taking sides on postmodernism:

> The point is that we are *within* the culture of postmodernism to the point where its facile repudiation is as impossible as any equally facile celebration of it is complacent and corrupt. Ideological judgement on postmodernism today necessarily implies, one would think, a judgement on ourselves as well as on the artifacts in question.[22]

In more recent work, such as *The Seeds of Time* (1994), Jameson has continued to toil with the problem of how to generate a description of the complete dominion of multinational global capitalism, and the accelerated plurality of its cultural styles, which will help to propel one conceptually and politically beyond it. Though it works with very different intellectual and political resources, Jameson's more recent work resembles Lyotard's in its concern with the question of time in postmodernism. Specifically, this involves the attempt to read the end of history historically, and to confront the current unimaginability of any future substantially different from our own, in which 'the very experience of the future as such has come to seem enfeebled, if not deficient'[23], in such a way as to detect the tiny shifts and foreshocks that may yet trigger a futurity. Jameson struggles to grasp and represent the limits of a postmodern condition which presents itself as a dissolution of every limit, its relentless, polymorphous flux loosening every analytic fixative. By imagining the limits of postmodern plurality, Jameson aims, not to transcend the postmodern, but, more cautiously, 'to suggest an outside and an unrepresentable exterior to many of the issues that seem most crucial in contemporary (that is to say, postmodern) debate'. The possibility of a future that might be other than the present condition is dependent upon the identification of this exterior, or sense of an exterior: 'the future lies entangled in that unrepresentable outside like so many linked genetic messages'.[24]

In the first, formidably abstract chapter of *The Seeds of Time*, Jameson proposes to manipulate four apparently irresolvable and characteristically postmodern antinomies into the more tractable form of contradictions –

which is to say resolvable dilemmas, or dilemmas with a dialectical future. These four antinomies concern the relationships, in turn, between post-modern change and permanence, as crystallized in Jameson's insight into the 'equivalence between an unparalleled rate of change on all the levels of social life and an unparalleled standardization of everything';[25] between homogeneity and heterogeneity, in a postmodern world in which every principle of heterogeneous excess seems to have been programmed to meet the needs of the very system it seems to exceed; between the widespread suspicion, in postmodern theory and post-Fordist economic practices alike, of any kind of philosophical foundation, and the ecological revival of foundational thinking in the idea of nature; and between the universal bar on utopian thought and that irrepressible impulse to the utopian which Jameson himself, at least since his *The Political Unconscious* (1983),[26] has been able to find in every form of collectivity, however apparently repressive, and which is here to be discerned, by a small dialectical miracle, concealed in the folds of anti-utopianism itself.

It is hard not to be awed by Jameson's majestic command over the multiple lines of his argument here, which he maintains like a chess master playing four games simultaneously; hard, too, at times, not to wish for a slower, more stumbling and substantiated progress, or to suspect that the encrusted majesty of Jameson's writing is a substitute for the perspectival command the absence of which he laments in the postmodern condition. As the prestige of Marxist cultural theory has waned, so the political purpose and content of Jameson's work seem to have been driven into this kind of stylistic hiding, in the great unfolding, enfolding trance of his prose, here more magisterially mythic than ever. The fact that Jameson has himself been such an authoritative analyst of precisely this displacement of politics into aesthetics redoubles the irony. As Jameson well knows, the aesthetic can be anaesthetic; as with certain sentences of James, Proust or Joyce, the sheer effort of sifting the clauses and pinning down the subject can sometimes leave his reader too dazed to argue with what has actually been said. But Jameson's work also teaches us that form is never merely formal. Perhaps the most telling and characteristic device – or symptom – of his own writing is the hovering uncertainty of his tenses in this book. The proliferation of conditionals and varieties of the future perfect leave us permanently unclear whether what we are reading about is past, or passing, or to come. But this can hardly be an accident, since it so amply attests not only to the puzzling virtuality of time in our time, but also to Jameson's continuing commitment to the theme of utopia which might yet lie on its further side.

Jean Baudrillard

This question of distance and involvement is one that is central to the work of the French social theorist Jean Baudrillard. Baudrillard's work begins with an attempt to modify Marx in order to take account of the emergence of mass culture and the technologies of mass reproduction. In his *The Mirror of Production*, Baudrillard refers to Marx's three-stage genealogy of the growth of the market and its identifying feature, exchange value. In *The Poverty of Philosophy*, Marx suggests that in a first stage (in feudal society, for instance), only a small proportion of what is produced in handicrafts, agriculture, etc. is surplus and therefore available to be sold or exchanged in the market-place. As a result, in this situation, use-value predominates over exchange-value. In a second phase, the phase of industrial production, everything that is produced by the new industrial forms of production becomes a commodity to be sold and exchanged on the market. A third phase supervenes when abstract qualities, like love, goodness and knowledge, which had previously been thought to be immune from the operations of buying and selling, themselves enter into the realm of exchange-value. This model parallels fairly clearly the three stages of development spoken of by Mandel and Jameson, with the third stage, Marx's era of 'general corruption', brought about by the penetration of the market much further into the realm of culture and signification, seeming to equate neatly with Mandel's and Jameson's 'late' or 'consumer' capitalism.

Baudrillard assents to this genealogy, but claims that Marx misunderstood the enormity of the qualitative transformation wrought between stages two and three.[27] For in this situation, he argues, it is no longer possible to separate the economic or productive realm from the realms of ideology or culture, since cultural artefacts, images, representations, even feelings and psychic structures have become part of the world of the economic. This analysis should remind us immediately of Jameson's evocation of the 'explosion' of culture into the economic sphere and indeed Baudrillard and Jameson acknowledge a debt to a shared source in the work of the Situationists, a group of radical social critics writing in France during the 1960s, who were the first to diagnose in contemporary life a 'society of the spectacle', in which the most developed form of the commodity was the image rather than the concrete material product. Guy Debord, the spokesman of the group, wrote in 1967 that an estimated 29 per cent of the yearly national product of the US was already – this before the information revolution – expended on the distribution and consump-

tion of knowledge, and forecast that the image would replace the railway
and the automobile as the driving force of the economy in the second half
of the twentieth century.[28]

This situation, in a sense an extension of a Marxist model, requires for
Baudrillard a fundamental rethinking. Traditional Marxism subordinates
the operations of culture and signification to economic activity, says
Baudrillard, by grounding everything upon the notion of *production*; what
underlies every social and economic system, what forms its secret identity-
principle, is its 'mode of production', what products get produced, by
whom and how. Baudrillard argues that the explosion and acceleration of
cultural commodities, or, more generally, of social images or 'signs'
functioning as commodities, produces a 'political economy of the sign', in
a passage from 'the abstraction of the exchange of material products under
the law of general equivalence to the operationalization of all exchanges
under the law of the code' (*Mirror of Production*, 121).

It is not altogether clear what Baudrillard means here by the 'code'. He
seems to have in mind a new predominance of technologies and practices
concerned with the exchange, promotion, distribution and manipulation of
signs in general, from raw information, to cars, to fashion, to the 'images'
of pop stars, actors and governments, as well as, more generally, the
fabrication of public opinion and what Hans Magnus Enzensberger calls
the 'consciousness industry'.[29] All these are processes that Baudrillard calls
the 'general operationalization of the signifier' (*Mirror of Production*, 122).
It might be thought that such things function only as the superficial
markers of social and/or class relationships which are themselves ultimately grounded in economic relationships, but Baudrillard believes that we
have moved irrevocably beyond this mode of signification. Once, indeed,
the cut of your clothes, the lines of your car, or the style of the façade in
front of your mansion signified or referred to your social position, but
now, Baudrillard says, these signs have no referential function: 'the
signified and the referent are now abolished to the sole profit of the play
of signifiers, of a generalized formalization in which the code no longer
refers back to any subjective or objective "reality", but to its own logic'
(*Mirror of Production*, 127).

This is not to say that the code is not repressive in its effects.
Baudrillard instances the exclusion of ethnic and linguistic minorities from
signification, the rigorous focusing of sexuality around genital sexuality
and the family, the remorseless domination of women and the constructed
and sustained invisibility of youth, age and the unemployed, saying that,
in all of these, 'capitalism crosses the entire network of natural, social,
sexual and cultural forces, all languages and codes' (*Mirror of Production*,

138). All of this complex machinery of regulation works through the control of signs, signs which cannot be seen as the disguised emanation of some more real and fundamental system of exploitation at the economic level. In fact, says Baudrillard, it is the economic realm which is used by the capitalist system as a diversion from and displacement of the remorseless domination at the level of the symbolic. Orthodox Marxist criticism, in its unswerving devotion to the principle of the economic, is an accomplice rather than an adversary of this fact. So, in a reversal of the usual direction of the insult, economistic Marxism can be called 'idealist', since it is only the social critic who pays attention to the workings of semiotic or significatory oppression who can justly call his or her work 'materialist' (*Mirror of Production*, 139).

If Baudrillard is at one with Lyotard and Jameson in his view of the autonomy of the cultural sphere from the economic, he differs from them markedly in his early work in his vision of a monolithically single code, operating, admittedly with varying effects, uniformly through mass culture. Certainly, nothing could be further from Lyotard's conception of the agonistics of language-games in a decentred social space. In Baudrillard's earlier work, *For a Critique of the Political Economy of the Sign* (1972), *The Mirror of Production* (1973) and *L'Échange symbolique et la mort* (1975), this notion produces as its reactive opposite the dream of a 'symbolic exchange', a spontaneous exchange or communication which is based, neither upon the dominating logic of the 'code', nor upon the logic of general equivalence, in which everything has its price in terms of something else, via the intermediary abstraction of the market, but upon open and spontaneous communication.[30] Baudrillard is nowhere very clear about what would count as this kind of 'symbolic exchange', but gives some indication in an essay entitled 'Requiem for the Media'.[31] Here Baudrillard attacks the notion that the mass media possess intrinsic liberating or democratic potential which is blocked or suppressed by the ruling groups and power interests in whose hands they lie – and the consequent belief that it is the role of the Left to wrest control of these media from such narrow or oppressive interests. Baudrillard argues that it is not possible simply to take over the form of the mass media and change their content to any good purpose, since what is oppressive about the media is precisely the 'code' which in their very form they embody. This code functions by the denial of response or exchange in mass communication. A mass medium talks to its audience, says Baudrillard, while never allowing that audience to respond to it and, indeed, confirms its audience's muteness by simulating audience response, via phone-ins, studio audiences, viewers' polls and other forms of bogus 'interaction'. The mass media, Baudrillard declares roundly, 'fabricate non-communication' ('Requiem', 169). The experience of the events of May 1968 in France, in which radio and TV stations were taken over by revolutionary groups, was that every form of subversive message can be made harmless by this means, since 'transgression and subversion never get "on the air" without being subtly negated as they are: transformed into models, neutralized into signs, they are eviscerated of their meaning' ('Requiem', 173).

Against this synthesized communication, Baudrillard posits his ideal of free, immediate exchange, in which the hierarchical split between the transmitter and the receiver is transmuted into a mutual responsiveness and discursive responsibility in spontaneous dialogue. Perhaps a little romantically, Baudrillard finds this form of exchange in the discursive activities of the street:

> The real revolutionary media during May were the walls and their speech, the silk-screen posters and the hand-painted notices, the street where speech began and was exchanged – everything that was an *immediate* inscription, given and returned, spoken and answered, mobile in the same space and time, reciprocal and antagonistic. The street is, in this sense, the alternative and subversive form of the mass media, since it isn't, like the latter, an objectified support for answerless messages, a transmission system at a distance. It is the frayed space of the symbolic exchange of speech – ephemeral, mortal: a speech that is not reflected on the Platonic screen of the media. ('Requiem', 176–7)

Baudrillard's conception of symbolic exchange derives from the anthropological theories of Marcel Mauss and the radical economics of Georges Bataille.[32] The primitivism of Baudrillard's view is clearly apparent in his attack on the tendency of Marxist economics to subsume everything in primitive societies to the principle of economic production; on the contrary, he argues, everything in primitive society is based upon the principle of continuous symbolic exchange, which maintains social stability and reciprocal relations between man and nature by never allowing the process of exchange to be blocked, cornered or constrained to produce profit (*Mirror of Production*, 82–3). Indeed, what identifies 'symbolic exchange' for Baudrillard is the necessary principle of pure loss in it, the arbitrary and spontaneous expenditure or discharge of goods or utterances without expectation of equivalence or profit. This is opposed to conditions under capitalism in which every apparent disposal or giving away of value is really only a detour on the way to a greater accumulation of value or profit. It is for this reason that symbolic exchange can sometimes appear to Baudrillard in the light of an unconditional discharge or waste, on the model of the 'potlatch', the practice among primitive tribes of sacrificing large amounts of amassed goods, to no obvious economic end.

This kind of symbolic exchange can only take place among the disenfranchised groups in modern society, among those who do not form part of the code of general exchangeability: blacks, ethnic minorities, women, youth, the old. Symbolic exchange also has subversive potential, in setting at nought the code of the mass media – the hastily-scrawled graffito over an advertising poster transgressing the code because it gives an immediate response to what is designed to disallow response ('Requiem', 183).

All through these early works, Baudrillard's hold on the ideal of symbolic exchange is a tenuous one, and his analysis is consequently liable to slip into wishful fantasies of free spontaneous speech which are inattentive to the functioning of power and exclusion in the most intimate forms of social contact and communication. In *L'Échange symbolique et la mort*, Baudrillard is already gloomily suggesting that the only thing that can really resist the incursions of the repressive code is death itself, a view which does not suggest much in the way of affirmative political applications. Since that book, Baudrillard's confidence in the possibility of resisting the domination of signs has dramatically leaked away.

It is this later Baudrillard, the theorist of the regime of the 'simulacrum', who has been most influential in the postmodern debate, and perhaps the most influential of all his work has been his short essay 'The Precession of Simulacra' (1981).[33] Baudrillard here extends the point made in 'Requiem for the Media' about the capacity of the mass media to neutralize dissent simply by representing it, to the claim that nothing can resist the conversion of reality into empty signs. We live in an age, says Baudrillard, in which signs are no longer required to have any verifiable contact with the world they allegedly represent, and he provides a handy and much-quoted synopsis of the four stages through which representation has historically passed on its way to the condition of pure simulation. Initially, the sign 'is the reflection of a basic reality' (this might be the stage of scientific or referential language which Jameson dates from the reifying emergence of bourgeois knowledge). In the second stage, the sign 'masks and perverts a basic reality' (this might be the stage or theory of ideology as the false consciousness which prevents people from seeing their true alienation or exploitation). In the third stage, the sign 'masks the *absence* of a basic reality' (harder to think of examples for this one, though Baudrillard instances the ideas of the iconoclasts, who feared and despised images of the deity because they believed that the images were testimony to the absence of any deity). In the fourth, terminal stage, the sign 'bears no relation to any reality whatsoever: it is its own pure simulacrum' (*Simulations*, 10). In the regime of simulation which is contemporary culture, Baudrillard diagnoses the incessant production of images with no attempt to ground them in reality. Alongside this, as though in response to the awareness of the fading out of the real, is a compensatory attempt to manufacture it, in 'an escalation of the true, of the lived experience' (*Simulations*, 12); in other words, the cult of immediate experience, of raw, intense reality, is not the contradiction of the regime of the simulacrum, but its simulated effect. Baudrillard gives a number of examples to support this oddly powerful hypothesis, of which the most striking is this one. Evidently, in 1971, the Philippine government decided to return a small tribe of Tasaday Indians to the jungle where they had been discovered, far away from the corrupting influence of civilization. Baudrillard's point is that here science, in seeming to protect the Tasaday people from its own destructive hunger for knowledge, is actually extending its power by seeming to give it away. By turning the Tasaday into a scale-model, or simulation of a primitive, pre-scientific civilization – the universal Other of science – science both turns its gaze away from the Tasaday and remorselessly recaptures them as representation. Baudrillard's exposition of this is typical of his later intellectual style, in its playful, but chilling camp:

> The Indian thereby driven back into the ghetto, into the glass coffin of virgin forest, becomes the simulation model for all conceivable Indians *before ethnology*. The latter thus allows itself the luxury of being incarnate beyond itself, in the 'brute' reality of these Indians it has entirely reinvented – Savages who are indebted to ethnology for still being Savages: what a turn of events, what a triumph for the science which seemed dedicated to their destruction!
>   Of course, these particular Savages are posthumous: frozen, cryogenised, sterilised, protected to *death*, they have become referential simulacra, and the science itself a pure simulation. (*Simulations*, 15)

Baudrillard generalizes from this sort of example to the claim that all of contemporary life has been dismantled and reproduced in scrupulous facsimile. But the mood of all this is far from that of quiet satisfaction or indifference; rather, it produces 'a panic-stricken production of the real and the referential' (*Simulations*, 13), such that simulation takes the form, not of unreality, as many of Baudrillard's followers wish to believe, but of manufactured objects and experiences which attempt to be more real than reality itself – or, in Baudrillard's term, 'hyperreal'.

Hyperreality also brings with it the collapse of all real antagonisms or dichotomies of value, especially in the political sphere. Baudrillard claims that, with the whole of the political spectrum being dominated by the logic of the simulacrum, even the most inveterate antagonisms, like that of capitalism and socialism, are annulled by the dependence of one upon the other; authority depends upon subversion, just as subversion draws its energies from authority. Seemingly, no events can shatter or destabilize the models of political relationship which precede and hermeneutically intercept these events; Baudrillard gives as an example a bombing outrage which could equally well be interpreted as the work of leftist extremists, or of extreme right-wing provocateurs, or of centrists concerned to discredit political extremism. The responses are all preprogrammed, all equally available and can all be activated at once. The upshot of this is that power and effectiveness are no longer asymmetrical (one group has power, while another group lacks it; one group benefits from a certain situation, another group suffers) but are distributed evenly across the political spectrum by the model of simulation. Everybody benefits from an infraction of the code, because the code is thereby consolidated. In this situation, opposites collapse into each other; as Baudrillard says, they 'implode', producing 'a floating causality where positivity and negativity engender and overlap with one another, where there is no longer any active or passive', in which 'every act terminates at the end of the cycle having benefited everyone and been scattered in all directions' (*Simulations*, 30–1).

This might seem to produce a situation of inoperable inertia, in which nothing can challenge or upset the system of interchangeable simulacra. The obvious objection to this might seem to be that political life shows no sign of settling into this smooth complacency. Baudrillard's analysis here has surely contributed something to Jameson's more particularized worry about the imperviousness of late capitalism to political challenges which 'are all somehow secretly disarmed and reabsorbed by a system of which they themselves might be considered a part, since they can achieve no distance from it' ('Cultural Logic of Late Capitalism', 87), but is in direct opposition in its generalized inertia to Lyotard's vision of competing language-games in social and political life, or Michel Foucault's influential analysis of the way in which power works, not in terms of centrality and possessive concentration, but in terms of dispersed and localized networks of 'micro-power'. In a typical move, Baudrillard replies by going one step further to suggest that power has been so evenly diffused as to be totally neutralized. If power, like everything else, has modulated into signs and appearances, then in a strangely distorted vision of egalitarianism, it has disappeared: 'it is useless . . . to run after power or to discourse about it *ad infinitum*, since from now on it also partakes of the sacred horizon of appearances and is also there only to hide the fact that it no longer exists'.[34]

The resulting system does indeed involve conflict and anxiety, except that the goal of conflict is not so much power, but the signs of power, and what haunts the players in this game is not the fear of losing power, but the fear that power itself is about to disappear. This produces a yearning for tonic encounters with reality, in the form of danger, or crisis, even though these very encounters work to stabilize the control of simulation even further. Where Kennedy was murdered because there was still the possibility that he might possess real power, Johnson, Nixon, Ford and Reagan, who inhabit the realm of the simulacrum, require 'puppet attempts' at murder, need the threat of death to conceal the fact that they are themselves only simulated puppets. The principle of proving the simulational real by allowing it to come into contact with its potentially disastrous negative occurs everywhere in the system. 'It is always a question', Baudrillard writes, 'of proving the real by the imaginary, proving truth by scandal, proving the law by transgression, proving work by the strike, proving the system by crisis and capital by revolution' (*Simulations*, 36). So Baudrillard describes a system that is simultaneously energized by the consciousness of decay and disaster, and emptied of energy by the relentless dominion of the code of simulation. The central metaphor for this is nuclear deterrence, which encompasses anxiety and compulsive activity on the one hand and a goal of absolute inertia on the other. The system of nuclear deterrence is a metaphor for a situation in which avowed antagonists are locked together in systematic complicity, which 'conveys the impossibility of a determinate point of power' (*Simulations*, 34). It is a world simultaneously of absolute risk and absolute forethought, a system producing 'a generalised deterrence of every chance, of every accident, of every transversality, of every finality, of every contradiction, rupture, or complexity' (*Simulations*, 64).

In later works, Baudrillard has extended this account to the idea of the social itself, which can no longer be said to exist, since it is entirely the simulated effect of the frantic desire to produce representations of the masses, to give them an identity, opinions and desires. The masses 'reply' to this only with inertia, with a refusal to come together except as simulation. This may mean that 'our "society" is perhaps in the process of putting an end to the social, of burying the social beneath a simulation of the social'.[35] But this produces a second effect, because the more the actuality of 'the social' vanishes from view, the greater is the distance between these simulacra and the dumb indifference of 'the masses' who were traditionally held to embody the social. In other words, this looks like a regression from the final stage of Baudrillard's four-stage genealogy to an earlier stage, in which signs – the representations of the social – strive to mask the fact of an emptiness, the masses' refusal to *be* the social in the ways required of them by opinion polls, referenda and revolutionary movements. It is not that the masses are a storehouse of subversive potential, rather that they form a sort of brute resistance, an unselfconscious, but nevertheless clumsily authentic, negativity:

> the masses function as a gigantic black hole which inexorably inflects, bends and distorts all energy and light radiation approaching it: an implosive sphere, in which the curvature of spaces accelerates, in which all dimensions curve back on themselves and 'involve' to the point of annihilation, leaving in their stead only a sphere of potential engulfment. (*Silent Majorities*, 9)

Baudrillard accuses the social sciences of complicity in the process by which the fantasy of the social is simulated and manipulated – for a sociology which, like the State, requires the existence of the entity called the social confronts the fact of its own death in the hypothesis of the death of the social. It is a mark of the increasingly complex irony of Baudrillard's more recent writing, that it seems perfectly aware of the self-accusation that this brings with it, for his work, if not exactly the kind of sociology that he denounces here, itself attempts and depends upon a characterization of the social, and one which, despite all its best attempts, ends up by hypostatizing an ideal notion of the masses as intransigently resistant to the play of simulation. In other words, it makes a claim about the *real* spaces and functions of the social, even if this definition is entirely negative, as against the falsely positive images of the social which are routinely manufactured in sociology and politics. There is obviously a kind of logical contradiction, though it is hard to make such a charge stick on a writer like Baudrillard for whom the protocols of logic are increasingly subordinated to the play of irony and rhetoric. More important, perhaps, is the fact that he fundamentally mistakes the nature of theories of the social in postmodern society. He claims that the idea or image of the social is only ever produced in positive terms, to enable the ever greater administration of an abstract social totality – and if it is not surprising that he identifies socialism as the arch-proponent of such simulations of the social, it is because he shares the hatred of post-1968 French intellectuals for any social movement that even suggests centralized or unified effort. But in recoiling from this model of the social into its opposite, Baudrillard uncritically reproduces the dominant form in which sociality is actually represented in the advanced West. When Baudrillard breezily dismisses concepts like state, class and power as empty mystifications, it is in the service of that well-nigh official mystification of our time, the nullification of collective life in any form, and its ruthless processing into fiction. Baudrillard ends up a conspirator in something like the double-process he describes, in which the idea of the social is fabricated at the same time as the experience of the social is discredited.

It might even be that Baudrillard would not dispute this, given the way that his later work takes so literally the idea of the collapse or 'implosion' of social theory and the situation that it theorizes:

> The space of simulation confuses the real with the model. There is no longer any critical and speculative distance between the real and the rational. There is no longer really even any projection of models in the real . . . but an in-the-field, here-and-now transfiguration of the real into model. A fantastic short-circuit: the real is hyperrealised. Neither realised, nor idealised: but hyperrealised. The hyperreal is the abolition of the real not by violent destruction, but by its assumption, elevation to the strength of the model. Anticipation, deterrence, preventive transfiguration, etc.: the model acts as a sphere of absorption of the real. (*Silent Majorities*, 83–4)

Given this situation, there seems no reason why theory should struggle against its complicity in the process of hyperrealizing the social, and not acknowledge itself frankly as the symptom of what it describes: as Dick Hebdige writes, 'the critic-as-surgeon cutting out and analysing diseased or damaged tissue is replaced by the critic-as-homeopath "shadowing" and paralleling the signs of sickness by prescribing natural poisons which produce in the patient's body a simulation of the original symptoms.'[36] In this contraction of the distance between reality and theory, Baudrillard's work comes close to Lyotard's and Jameson's. In Lyotard's aestheticization of knowledge via the agonistics of language-games, in Jameson's anxious awareness of the loss of critical distance between culture and theory and, at its most extreme, in Baudrillard's adaptive transformation of theory itself into the condition of simulation that it theorizes, what began as an attempt to specify the relationship between the fixed and distinct poles of postmodernity in social and economic life and postmodernism in cultural life ends by dissolving the boundaries between the two realms. For all these writers, postmodernity may be defined as those plural conditions in which the social and the cultural become indistinguishable. Although Baudrillard goes further than the others in collapsing the distinction between theory and its object, all three of the theorists of the postmodern discussed in this section arrive at the difficult question of the hermeneutic entanglement of theory with the social reality that it describes. This is to say that postmodernity must be considered partially in terms of the difficulty of describing 'it'; or rather, in terms of the difficulty of specifying the 'it' which is postmodernity after the drawing of knowledge and theory into the sphere of culture, even as culture itself alters its scope and coordination.

Not all accounts of the postmodern condition exhibit this degree of reflexivity so openly; nor is it true that every form of reflexivity is the same, with the same values and effects. Indeed, in moving on to consider the particular narratives of the emergence of postmodernism which have compelled conviction in the disciplines concerned with different cultural practices like architecture, art, literature, the performing arts and the electronic media, what may strike us is rather the inhibition of awareness of the ways in which diagnoses of postmodernism partake of the field they describe. But we will need to hold on to this troubled perspective in order to understand the role of theory itself in the production of the postmodern.

Postmodern Law

Much of the suspicion and uncertainty attaching to the imaging or representation of social life in social theory has come about because of a heightened sense of the role of representation in maintaining relations of power. In certain areas, the equation has proved apt to be run the other way, in order to disclose the ways in which the mechanisms by means of which societies are ordered and regulated are also governed by broadly textual or representational imperatives. Over the last ten or fifteen years, this work has been carried through with particular vigour in the areas of law and legal theory.

Postmodern conditions and postmodernist critique have come to have a particularly strong purchase and vocation in law and legal theory because of the close relation between the formation of societies in the modern sense and the institution of law in the form which it has taken in the West. Modernity meant the dissolution of the norms shared by communities, or imposed absolutely upon them, to be replaced on the one hand by the sovereign individual, conceived as the ground of knowledge and rational truth, and on the other the State, conceived abstractly as the mechanism for governing the relations between sovereign individuals and poetically as the sovereign individual write large, the very embodiment of the rational, self-knowing will of the nation or people. Modern law, as a complex, autonomous, internally consistent set of norms and rules, comes into being as a simultaneous expression of and defence against a world deprived of external or transcendent guarantees, of moral and ethical absolutes traceable in the end back to the revealed truth of a supernatural force. No longer guaranteed as the will of the king, or of the Lord God, the law seemingly must either reinvent those principles – perhaps by its cooperation in a metanarrative which substitutes the story of the unfolding to some necessary end for the myth of an absolute and infallible origin – or by generating its own legitimacy from the inside.

Law was subjected to a process of autonomization, whereby it was detached from the values and beliefs of particular groups and communities and reconstrued as a self-sufficient and ethically neutral mechanism, supposedly driven by the abstract imperatives of logic and reason rather than particular political interests and purposes. Judgement – the implementation and interpretation of laws, the processes of assessing evidence, balancing competing claims and arriving at judicial decisions – became separated from justice, truth and value. On the one hand, law is the most detailed and concrete expression of a society's collective moral values. But on the other, it has become imperative in the administration of law to protect it from mere considerations of morality, associated as these are with the shifting relativities of individual prejudice.

The morality of law thus becomes identified with the maintenance of its self-consistency. This principle was embodied most clearly in what may be thought of as the modernist moment of twentieth-century jurisprudence, in the varieties of 'legal formalism' proposed by H. Kelsen, in *The Pure Theory of Law* (1934) and H.L.A Hart in *The Concept of Law* (1961). Both of these accounts emphasize the closed and self-referring unity of the law, as a system of interconnected and logically consistent norms (Kelsen), or rules (Hart), rather than a repository of moral truths or machinery of moral deliberation. There are obvious relations between the passing of particular laws and a society's vision of what is morally good or bad (the proscription of murder, the promotion of equal rights), but those relations belong to the sphere of politics and are not supposed to be operative within law itself, which aims to operate neutrally. The purpose of the law is not to promote goodness, but to protect and extend the self-consistency of the law itself. If this makes the law sound like it has a merely executive function, then there are also times when the law can assert its supremacy over the moral and political realms. Thus a law passed by an elected assembly and with the full consent of the people can nevertheless be shown to be illegal by the courts, insofar as it is not consistent with other existing laws, the operation of which it would render arbitrary and oppressive.

The self-consistency of the law is perpetually under threat, however, since law is not only an inert system of rules, but a set of procedures for dealing with infractions of those rules. Law dreams of a purely legal world, in which rules, their formulation, interpretation and application would be transparent and entirely regular in their operation; but it lives in a chronically contingent or alegal world. The very retreat from or denial of contingency which is necessary to ensure the self-consistency of law is what will always thwart its dream of self-consistency. Legal theory must therefore confront the fact that law exists not just as a body of precedents and doctrine, but as a system of judgement and interpretation. The work of Ronald Dworkin has attempted to extend the legal formalism of such accounts of Kelsen and Hart to take in these acts of judgement, and to meet the challenge of those more sceptical accounts which have flourished in philosophy and literary criticism during the 1970s and 1980s which emphasize the indeterminacy of judgements and interpretations. Nowhere has the gap between law and its application become so perplexingly large as in the USA, in which so much law depends upon the meanings and values held to be embodied by *fiat* in the Constitution. Everybody agrees to take the Constitution for their guide, but there is no agreement as to the particular guidance offered in the Constitution. Ronald Dworkin provides the most energetic and influential argument for a legal hermeneutics, or theory of interpretation, which would ensure that, when lawyers argue about the meanings of the Constitution, they are at least in agreement as to the kind of argument they are having. Thus Dworkin accepts that legal application and interpretation belong to the essence of law just as much as its preexisting system of norms and rules. But he argues that the act of legal interpretation must be guided and constrained, not by the search for the original truth of statute or Constitutional documents, nor by the assumed good of any prospective moral or political purpose, but by the need both to confirm and extend the integrity of law. Coming to a judicial decision requires a judge 'to test his interpretation of any part of the great network of political structures and decisions of his community by asking whether it could form part of a coherent theory justifying the network as a whole'.[37] His theory is designed to ensure that the dynamic and evolutionary nature of law-in-application will only ever extend and consolidate rather than fracture and dissolve 'law's empire'. For all its pragmatic tolerance of the variable conditions of interpretation, Dworkin's legal theory remains modern, or even modernist, in its commitment to the unity of the law, even if this is founded, not upon the authority given in texts, but upon the shared purposes embodied in communities. Modernist jurisprudence, according to Costas Douzinas and

Ronnie Warrington, is founded on and driven by the desire to establish legal propriety:

> Jurisprudence sets itself the task of determining what is proper to law and of keeping outside law's empire the non-legal, the extraneous, law's other. It has spent unlimited effort and energy demarcating the boundaries that enclose law within its sovereign terrain, giving it its internal purity, and its external power and right to hold court over the other realms. For jurisprudence the corpus of law is literally a body: it must either digest and transform the non-legal into legality, or it must reject it, keep it out as excess and contamination. Jurisprudence's task is to impose upon law the law of purity and order, of clear boundaries and well-policed checkpoints.[38]

In concert with Lyotard's assault upon the idea of metanarrative and the allegedly oppressive unity of the human assumed in modernity, legal postmodernism comes into being with challenges to the unity and coherence of law assumed in previous jurisprudential accounts. As Costas Douzinas and Ronnie Warrington see it:

> Legal language games have proliferated endlessly and cannot be presented as the embodiment of the public good, the general will, the wishes of the sovereign electorate or of some coherent system of principle. The condition of postmodernity has irredeemably removed the possibility of the unity of the law and of reconciliation of differences, an always impossible and slightly comical hope on which modernist jurisprudence based itself.[39]

Three versions of legal postmodernism would appear to have defined themselves; the critical, as embodied principally in Critical Legal Studies and feminist legal theory; the pragmatic, as embodied chiefly in the work of Stanley Fish; and the ethical, as instanced in the work of Costas Douzinas, Peter Goodrich and Ronnie Warrington.

Critical Legal Studies submits the operations of the law to forms of scrutiny which aim to expose its blindness, inconsistency or concealed interests. It has its roots in a series of broadly Marxist critiques of law, which suggest that law is the expression and enactment of the dominative class and economic relations at work in any particular historical period. Marxist and *marxisant* critique of this kind denies law its claimed autonomy by revealing the systematic complicity of its forms and procedures with the interests of a ruling class or dominant ideology. Critical Legal Studies, which arose and spread rapidly from the late 1970s in North America, broadens the base of this kind of critique, and diversifies the ways and levels in which critique of the law may be elaborated. Critical

Legal Studies offers critique of the law openly in the service of the goal of emancipation, but does not believe that such emancipation must take only one form; it thus begins with, and does not attempt prematurely to unify, the interests of marginal or disenfranchized social groups of all kinds, including women, ethnic minorities, homosexuals and workers. Working in highly specific ways on a range of different legal topics and problems, Critical Legal scholars nevertheless have in common the aim of revealing the historicity, the constructedness and sometimes the sheer arbitrariness of rules and structures which legal theory assumes to be, or legal procedures persuade us to view as natural, permanent and essential. Central to the work of Critical Legal Studies is a refusal of law's 'modernist' tendency to universalize itself and its operations, and an eschewal of those forms of social critique which tended to mimic that universalization. Thus Critical Legal scholars attempted to show, against functionalist arguments, that law has no natural role as the supplier of particular evolving social needs. Other forms of Critical Legal theory employ linguistic analysis to show the indeterminacy of all interpretation of documents, statutes and constitutions, and to challenge the grounds of judgements that speak in terms of knowable intention or specifiable meaning. In more general terms, the purpose of such analysis is to resist the processes of reification and abstraction that define the operations of the law, and conceal its messy, contingent relations with social life and process; it is to substitute a vision of legal operations for the paralysing transhistorical idealization of Law. Thus Gary Peller uses an analysis of the metaphorical effects at work within the language of contract law to reveal the unacknowledged and unjustifiable assumptions on which it rests, in particular the positing of a transcendental subject, able to exercise choice and embody intentions free from any constraints imposed by their interpretative context. The transcendental freedom assumed in such liberal accounts of law is in fact a reified freedom, one that is abstract and metaphysical in its suppression of the contingency of social relations, in which actors are always placed within determinate contexts which limit and predetermine the nature of the choices open to them. For Peller, such metaphysical assertions of freedom in fact add up to a form of unfreedom, for, in refusing to recognize the contingency both of subjective choices and legal interpretations, they also 'suppress the extent to which we create the social language that mediates our social relations . . . [so that] accordingly we subordinate ourselves to our own creations, which we mistake for objective things existing in the world'.[40]

Critical Legal Studies therefore draws heavily from what might be termed a postmodern version of critical theory derived largely from the work of Michel Foucault, which sees power not as homogeneous and split symmetrically between rulers and ruled, but as unevenly distributed in different ways, in different sites, and among different social groupings. Along with other strains of critical thought which flourished during the 1970s and 1980s, such as feminism and new historicism, Critical Legal Studies attempts to criticize the claims of universal reason without exercising them itself. Central to Critical Legal Studies is a conception, derived largely from the work of Roberto Unger, of the contextual and situated nature of all thought and practice; a belief that ideas and judgements are always formed within historically limited and therefore limiting fields of possibility.[41] But if Critical Legal studies is sustained by a broadly postmodern acceptance of the localized or contingent nature of all judgement and interpretation, its critical and emancipatory ambitions are also fuelled by the belief that it may be possible to build outwards from particular contexts to more benign, more self-aware and provisional models of social association and generality, which would not be subject to the false overtotalizations produced within modern social and legal theory in response to earlier eruptions of anxiety at the loss of external or metaphysical moorings. James Boyle concludes his magisterial survey of the field of Critical Legal Studies with a refusal of 'the grandiose picture of a totalizing rational theory that will both describe and prescribe social life and that rests on "neutral" features of biology, or human nature, or historical progress', recommending instead the spirit of 'the *bricoleur*, the artisan who uses the materials that come to hand to create an artifact that is shaped both by intention and the constraints of circumstance'.[42] Duncan Kennedy, one of the most determined of emancipatory legal theorists, has a qualified but still emphatic sense of the epistemological and political advantage that the bringing to light of contradiction and contingency can bring: 'The task of criticism is to demystify our thinking by confronting us with the fact that the contradiction is a historical artifact. It is no more immortal than is the society that created and sustains it. Understanding this is not salvation, but it is a help.'[43]

In a series of affably brawling polemics, directed not only at Critical Legal Studies, but also at other versions of the emancipatory hermeneutics of suspicion in literary and cultural studies, Stanley Fish has insisted on the implausibility of this position. Fish is in agreement with what he calls the pragmatic and antifoundationalist thrust of Critical Legal Studies and other cognate forms of contemporary legal and interpretative theory, or in other words with the argument that there are no objective, transhistorical truths or bottom lines which might serve to stabilize the interpretation of the particular historical purposes of groups and individuals. For Fish, as for many other postmodern critics of law and literature (the two disciplines in which Fish is simultaneously active), there are no essences, no final or founding truths, no absolute and unchanging values; all is contingency, rhetoric and historicity.

> In a heterogeneous world, a world in which persons are situated – occupying particular places with particular purposes pursued in relation to particular goals, visions, and hopes as they follow from holding (or being held by) particular beliefs – no one will be in a situation that is universal or general (that is, no situation at all), and therefore no one's perspective (a word that gives the game away) can lay claim to privilege.[44]

Where Fish disagrees with postmodern anti-foundationalism, whether of the deconstructive type practised for example by analysts of law like Clare Dalton or Peter Goodrich, or the more genially open-ended pragmatist variety evidenced in the recent work of the legal theorist Richard Posner, or the philosopher Richard Rorty, is in its assumption that the awareness of this condition confers any kind of advantage, epistemological or otherwise, over those still mired in relativity or self- contradiction.[45] There are no grounds for what Fish has called 'anti-foundationalist theory hope'; neither the condition of indeterminacy nor the awareness of that condition can supply a principle of reform or transformation.[46] Fish has not shown much direct interest in debates about the nature or consequences of the postmodern condition, though the word 'postmodern' might without distortion be substituted for the word 'pragmatic' in the following summary of his views on the blurring of descriptions of our foundationless condition into prescriptions as to what we should do with it. Such accounts

> confuse a pragmatist account with a pragmatist program and thereby fail to distinguish between pragmatism as a truth we are all living *out* and pragmatism as a truth we might be able to live *by*. We are all living *out* pragmatism because we live in a world bereft of transcendent truths and leak proof logics . . . and therefore must make do with the ragtag bag of metaphors, analogies, rules of thumb, inspirational phrases, incantations, and jerry-built 'reasons' that keep the conversation going and bring it to temporary, and always revisable, conclusions; but we could only live by pragmatism if we could grasp the pragmatist insight – that there are no universals or self-executing methods or self-declaring texts in sight – and make it into something positive, use an awareness of contingency as a way either of mastering it or perfecting it (in which case it would no longer be contingency) turn ourselves (by design rather than as the creatures of history) into something new.[47]

One might say that the very success of Critical Legal Studies is the confirmation of Fish's argument here. Critical Legal Studies proposes that the law should not and will not be able to be practised as it has been practised hitherto in the face of its revelations of contradiction and inconsistency. But, like the law itself, Critical Legal Studies itself operates and even flourishes in its argumentative purposes in spite of the seemingly toxic contradiction at its own heart between its strategies of suspicion and its emancipatory principles. The very success of Critical Legal Studies as a mode of legal–theoretical discourse might be the most potent proof for Fish of the insufficiency of its claims to be a mode of transformative critique.

In a sense, Fish pushes to an extreme the paradoxical principle of discursive justice proclaimed by Jean-François Lyotard in *Just Gaming* and *The Differend*, namely that it is illegitimate to derive from one genre of discourse – the description of how things are – a set of recommendations for how we should act. Describing and analysing are one thing, doing is another. The difference between Fish and Lyotard is that Fish refuses to allow this conception of the heterogeneity of human actions, beliefs and purposes to become a foundational principle, and thus fends off the paradox that Lyotard perplexedly embraces. In a world accustomed to the idea of the increasing indistinguishability of theoretical models and real actualities, Fish goes against the grain in insisting on the inconsequence of theory, by which he means, not that theory has no meaning or purpose, only that it does not and cannot have the kind of real world consequences it thinks it has, or thinks it should have. Just as there are no necessary consequences of any theory, so there are no politics in particular that follow automatically from the recognition, itself strongly urged by Fish, that everything is political. In refusing to allow a 'postmodern' condition to be wrenched into a 'postmodern' programme, Fish is in one sense arguing against the desire for coherence, the desire to make everything connect and add up. 'Give me a break', he represents himself as saying. I am not in the business of organizing my successive actions so that they all conform to or are available to a coherent philosophical account'.[48] Crucial to his argument is the demand that we do not seek or pretend to impose long-range and once-and-for-all rules and explanations on changing circumstances and contingencies. But the unsleeping zeal with which Fish roots out the self-contradictoriness of anti-foundationalist theory betrays a coherentist streak in his own work that is far stronger than that of any of the opponents he submits to such cordially pitiless pummelling. If Fish declines to acknowledge any principle or theory underlying or emerging from his attacks on principles and theories, it is above all because this would be flagrantly self-contradictory: 'the point is that there *is* no point, no yield of a positive programmatic kind to be carried away from these analyses . . . it would be contradictory for me to have a point beyond *that* point'.[49] There is a strong, strange contradiction between Fish's eschewing of strong coherence and his unbending demand that he and others should be consistent in this eschewal, or (what is a version of the same thing) should come clean about their inconsistency.

During the trial at the end of *Alice in Wonderland*, Alice anticipates Critical Legal theory in her refusal to recognize the force of Rule 42, '*All persons more than a mile high to leave the court*', on the grounds that, as she explains to the Red King, 'That's not a regular rule. You made it up just now.' When the King insists that it's 'the oldest rule in the book', Alice responds icily, 'Then it ought to be Number One.'[50] Fish's work insists on the necessity of a certain forgetting of critical self-consciousness, a relinquishing of the modernist or Enlightenment privilege of knowing one's mind as one makes it up, or knowing all the contingencies that have always made up the way one goes about making up one's mind. Fish is on the King's side and not Alice's, because for Fish all acts of judgement, not least in the operations of the law, must operate under the auspices of Rule 42, in their endless fabrication of the ground upon which they need to take their stand. The problem seems to be that Fish regards law's forgetting of its own incoherence as so urgent a necessity, seeing his own work as a reminder to law and legal theory to remember to forget, to stay below the threshold of self-consciousness. I cannot imagine how Fish is ever going to be able to make up his mind about whether to be consistently inconsistent or inconsistently consistent on these questions. (In the meantime, though, the unflagging energy of his assault on legal and literary theory and their claims to coherence seems to be an indication of how much, for him, the question of whether theory matters, *matters*.)

The jurisprudence associated with the work of Costas Douzinas, Ronnie Warrington and Peter Goodrich similarly emphasizes the incommensurability of judgement and justice, or law and ethics. This work nevertheless insists that law needs to confront and, if not to overcome, then at least to negotiate the divide between itself and the sphere of the ethical, which latter is defined, following the work of the philosopher Emmanuel Levinas, not as a body of precepts and prescriptions, but as a primary condition of liability to and responsibility for others. For this reason, ethical relations are always contingent relations – actual, unpredictable and irreducible to rule. The postmodern legality called for by Douzinas and his collaborators is founded upon a vision of ethics as a disruptive force, which shakes the complacency and formality of legal-political relations:

A postmodern ethics of law thus starts from the (Kantian) recognition that we are called to ethics before we begin its and our questioning. Before, prior to and in front of the law of the institution comes the law of ethics.[51]

A postmodern ethics of law shares with Critical Legal Studies the aim of exposing the gaps in law's empire, and with the work of Stanley Fish a sense of the contingency of truth and interpretation in law. But it also refuses the reassuring neutrality of the 'view from nowhere' assumed by Critical Legal Studies, and the numbing of critique in the extreme contextualism of Fish's position. It urges that law expose itself to, and find ways of inhabiting, the plural and uncertain condition of a world without metaphysical guarantees. Postmodern jurisprudence can then be defined as 'the attempt to open a clearing for reason(s), ethics and law(s) once all strategic moves of modern philosophy and jurisprudence to ground them on some single principle, form or meaning lie shattered'.[52] Crucial to such a reassociation of law and ethics is the rethinking of the relations between the ethical and the aesthetic. An ethics conceived in terms of exposure, liability, uncertainty and implicated responsibility has more in common with the modes of aesthetic experience and judgement as defined by Kant in his *Critique of Judgement* than the formal or analytic language of ethics. For this reason, the postmodern ethics of law also insists that law acknowledge the operations within it of the aesthetic – of the constitutive powers of language, rhetoric, imagery and the senses. The ethical relations of law are, on this view, acknowledgements of its embodiment, in the material forms and sites of its practices (the architecture of law courts, the iconography of legal power and privilege, the abstraction and regulation of sound, image and the material body), and in the irreducibly concrete nature of its encounters and effects.

> The postmodern judge is implicated, he stands in proximity to the litigant who comes before the law and hears his speech or request. Justice returns to ethics when it recognizes the embedded voice of the litigant, when it gives the other in her concrete materiality a *locus standi* or place of enunciation. The law is necessarily committed to the form of universality and abstract equality; but a just decision must also respect the requests of the contingent, incarnate and concrete other, it must pass through the ethics of alterity in order to respond to its own embeddedness in justice.[53]

A postmodern ethics of law must therefore also be a postmodern aesthetics of law, in confirmation of Aristotle's anti-Platonic proposition that *en aisthesis hé krisis* (in feeling lies judgement):

Notes

1 *The Postmodern Condition: A Report on Knowledge*, trans. Geoff Bennington and Brian Massumi (Manchester: Manchester University Press, 1984), p. vii. References hereafter to *PC* in text.

2 See Thomas Kuhn, *The Structure of Scientific Revolutions*, 2nd edn (Chicago: University of Chicago Press, 1970); Richard Rorty, 'Habermas and Lyotard on Post-Modernity' in *Habermas on Modernity*, ed. Richard Bernstein (Cambridge, Mass. MIT Press, 1985), pp. 161–76; Axel Honneth, 'An Aversion Against the Universal: A Commentary on Lyotard's *Postmodern Condition*', *Theory, Culture and Society*, 2:3 (1985), p. 151. See, too, Stephen Toulmin's 'The Construal of Reality: Criticism in Modern and Postmodern Science', in *The Politics of Interpretation*, ed. W. J. T. Mitchell (Chicago: University of Chicago Press, 1983), pp. 99–117, which is in more general agreement with Lyotard's characterization of postmodern science.

3 See Paul Davies, *Superforce: The Search for a Grand Unified Theory of Nature* (London: William Heinemann, 1984).

4 Geoff Bennington, *Lyotard: Writing the Event* (Manchester: Manchester University Press, 1988), pp. 114–17.

5 Jean-François Lyotard, *Le Postmoderne expliqué aux enfants: Correspondance, 1982–1985* (Paris: Galilée, 1986), pp. 121–2. All translations from this text are my own.

6 'Missive sur l'Histoire', first pub. *Critique* 41:456 (1985), repr. in *Le Postmoderne expliqué aux enfants*, pp. 43–64.

7 Ibid., p. 57.

8 Richard Rorty, reply to Jean-François Lyotard, in *Critique*, 41:456 (1985) pp. 570–1 (my translation).

9 Ibid., p. 573.

10 Habermas's position with regard to Lyotard's postmodernity is sketched out in his 'Modernity – an Incomplete Project', in *Postmodern Culture*, ed. Hal Foster (London and Sydney: Pluto Press, 1985), pp. 3–15. His reaction to postmodern tendencies in philosophy more generally is set out in his *The Philosophical Discourse of Modernity*, trans. Frederick Lawrence (London: Polity Press, 1987).

11 Honneth, 'An Aversion Against the Universal', p. 155.

12 See, for example, *Libidinal Economy*, trans. Iain Hamilton Grant (London: Athlone, 1993).

13 *Le Postmoderne expliqué aux enfants*, pp. 62–3.

14 Terry Eagleton, 'Capitalism, Modernism and Postmodernism', in *Against the Grain: Essays 1975–1985* (London: Verso, 1986), p. 134.

15 *Le Postmoderne expliqué aux enfants*, p. 63.

16 See Honneth, 'An Aversion Against the Universal', p. 149, and Kenneth Lea, ' "In the Most Highly Developed Societies": Lyotard and Postmodernism', *Oxford Literary Review*, 9:1–2 (1987), pp. 101–2.

17 Christopher Norris discusses one form of this, Richard Rorty's claim that philosophy must learn to see its activity not as the search for truth but as the

strategic construction of fictions, in 'Philosophy as a Kind of Narrative: Rorty on Post-Modern Liberal Culture', in *Contest of Faculties: Philosophy and Theory After Deconstruction* (London: Methuen, 1985), pp. 139–66. See, too Richard Rorty, *Philosophy and the Mirror of Nature* (Princeton: Princeton University Press, 1980).

18   Jean-François Lyotard, *The Differend: Phrases in Dispute*, trans. Georges Van Den Abbeele (Manchester: Manchester University Press, 1988), p. xi.

19   Jean-François Lyotard, *The Inhuman: Reflections on Time*, trans. Geoffrey Bennington and Rachel Bowlby (Cambridge: Polity Press, 1991), p. 67. References hereafter to *Inhuman* in the text.

20   Fredric Jameson, 'Postmodernism and Consumer Society', in Foster, *Postmodern Culture*, pp. 111–25; 'Postmodernism: or the Cultural Logic of Late Capitalism', *New Left Review*, 146 (July/August, 1984)), pp. 53–92; 'Reading Without Interpretation: Postmodernism and the Video-Text', in *The Linguistics of Writing: Arguments Between Language and Literature*, ed. Derek Attridge, Nigel Fabb, Alan Durant and Colin McCabe (Manchester: Manchester University Press, 1987), pp. 198–223. References to these texts hereafter in text.

21   Daniel Bell, *The Cultural Contradictions of Capitalism* (New York: Basic Books, 1976).

22   Fredric Jameson, 'The Politics of Theory: Ideological Positions in the Postmodernism Debate', *New German Critique*, 33 (Fall, 1984), p. 63.

23   Fredric Jameson *The Seeds of Time* (New York: Columbia University Press, 1994), p. 31.

24   Ibid., p. xiii.

25   Ibid., p. 15.

26   Fredric Jameson *The Political Unconscious: Narrative as a Socially Symbolic Act* (London and New York: Methuen, 1983).

27   Jean Baudrillard, *The Mirror of Production*, first published 1973, trans. Mark Poster (St. Louis: Telos Press, 1975), pp. 119–21. References hereafter in text.

28   Guy Debord, *Society of the Spectacle*, no translator named (Exeter?: Rebel Press, 1987), paragraph 193.

29   Hans Magnus Enzensberger, *The Consciousness Industry* (New York: Seabury Press, 1974).

30   *For a Critique of the Political Economy of the Sign*, first published 1972, trans. Charles Levin (St. Louis: Telos Press, 1981); *L'Echange symbolique et la mort* (Paris: Gallimard, 1975).

31   *For a Critique of the Political Economy of the Sign*, pp. 164–84. References hereafter to 'Requiem' in the text.

32   See Michele H. Richman, *Reading Georges Bataille: Beyond the Gift* (Baltimore: Johns Hopkins University Press, 1982).

33   First published in *Simulacres et simulation* (Paris: Galilée, 1981), trans. Paul Foss and Paul Patton in *Simulations* (New York: Semiotext(e), 1983), pp. 1–79. References hereafter to *Simulations* in the text.

34   *Forget Foucault*, trans. Nicola Dufresne (New York: Semiotext(e), 1987), p. 51.

35 *In the Shadow of the Silent Majorities . . . or, the End of the Social*, trans. Paul Foss, Paul Patton and John Johnston (New York: Semiotext(e), 1983), p. 67. References hereafter to *Silent Majorities* in the text.

36 *Hiding in the Light: On Images and Things* (London: Comedia, 1988), p. 209.

37 Ronald Dworkin, *Law's Empire* (London: Fontana 1994), p. 245.

38 Costas Douzinas and Ronnie Warrington with Shaun McVeigh, *Postmodern Jurisprudence: The Law of Text in the Text of Law* (London and New York: Routledge, 1991), p. 25.

39 Ibid., p. 27.

40 'The Metaphysics of American Law', in *Critical Legal Studies*, ed. James Boyle (New York: New York University Press, 1994), p. 502.

41 See Roberto Unger, *Knowledge and Politics* (New York: Free Press, 1975), and *The Critical Legal Studies Movement* (Cambridge, Mass. and London: Harvard University Press, 1986).

42 *Critical Legal Studies*, pp. 599, 600.

43 Duncan Kennedy, 'The Structure of Blackstone's Commentaries', in Boyle, ed., *Critical Legal Studies*, p. 15.

44 'Almost Pragmatism: The Jurisprudence of Richard Posner, Richard Rorty, and Ronald Dworkin', *There is No Such Thing As Free Speech And It's A Good Thing, Too* (Oxford and New York: Oxford University Press, 1994), p.218

45 Clare Dalton, 'An Essay in the Deconstruction of Contract Doctrine', *Yale Law Review*, 94 (1985), pp. 999–1114; Peter Goodrich, *Legal Discourse: Studies in Linguistics, Rhetoric and Legal Analysis* (Basingstoke and London: Macmillan, 1987); Richard Posner, *The Problems of Jurisprudence* (Cambridge, Mass.: Harvard University Press, 1990); Richard Rorty, *Contingency, Irony, and Solidarity* (Cambridge: Cambridge University Press, 1989).

46 'Anti-Foundationalism, Theory Hope, and the Teaching of Composition', in *Doing What Comes Naturally: Change, Rhetoric, and the Practice of Theory in Literary and Legal Studies* (Oxford: Clarendon Press, 1989), pp. 342–55.

47 Ibid., p. 67.

48 Gary A. Olson, 'Fish Tales: A Conversation With "The Contemporary Sophist" ', *There's No Such Thing As Free Speech And It's A Good Thing, Too*, p. 299.

49 Ibid., p. 307.

50 *The Annotated Alice: Alice's Adventures in Wonderland and Through the Looking-Glass*, ed. Martin Gardner (Harmondsworth: Penguin, 1976), p. 156.

51 Costas Douzinas, Peter Goodrich and Yifat Hachamovitch, 'Introduction', in *Politics, Postmodernity and Critical Legal Studies: The Legality of the Contingent*, ed. Costas Douzinas, Peter Goodrich and Yifat Hachamovitch (London and New York: Routledge, 1994), p. 22.

52 Douzinas, Warrington and McVeigh, *Postmodern Jurisprudence*, p. 18.

53 Douzinas, Goodrich and Hachamovitch (eds), *Politics, Postmodernity and Critical Legal Studies*, p. 24.

3

Postmodernism in Architecture and the Visual Arts

If we live in a 'post-culture', a culture wedded to all kinds of supersession – post-Holocaust, post-industrial, post-humanist, post-cultural, indeed – then there remain, residually, two sides or aspects to the 'post'-prefix and debates about the postmodern in the humanities and social sciences have tended to reproduce this duality. On the one hand, to designate oneself as 'post' anything, is to admit to a certain exhaustion, diminution or decay. Someone who inhabits a post-culture is a late-comer to the party, arriving only in time to see the bottles and cigarette-ends being swept up. Belatedness may also imply a certain dependence, for the post-culture cannot even define itself in any free-standing way, but is condemned to the parasitic prolongation of some vanished cultural achievement. Such a reading of the 'post' underlies, for example, Charles Newman's sardonic characterization of postmodernism as 'a band of vainglorious contemporary artists following the circus elephants of Modernism with snow shovels'.[1] Other evocations of the postmodern stress this sense of decline. Irving Howe sees postmodernism as a failure of nerve, intelligence and commitment, while Arnold Toynbee, in what is acknowledged to be the first use of the epithet, 'Post-Modern', uses it to characterize the decline of Western civilization into irrationality and relativism since the 1870s.[2]

More recently the claims of postmodernism have been advanced in a much more affirmative way. In the work of Leslie Fiedler, Ihab Hassan and Jean-François Lyotard, postmodernism is seen as a positive birth from the fallen giant of modernism. In the work of these writers, the 'post' of postmodernism signifies not the fatigue of the late-comer, but the freedom and self-assertion of those who have awoken from the past.

In fact, what is striking about the function of the 'post'-prefix is not so much the difference between the two kinds of connotation, the one submissive and dismissive, the other iconoclastic and promotional, as the way in which these connotative fields tend to intersect. We might say that the characteristic of postmodernism is this peculiarly complex relationship which it has to the modernism which in its very name is at once invoked, admired, suspected or rejected. This relationship is overlaid with further complexities in the different disciplinary discourses of postmodernism, in which the struggle with modernism often represents an internal struggle with the history and institutions of the discipline.

Architecture

The clearest place to start in examining the relationship between modernism and postmodernism is in architecture. This may be because architecture, though closely concerned with all the debates about modernism and modernity of this century, is an area of cultural practice in which movements and stylistic dominants are much more conspicuous and less arguable than elsewhere; even if this is not the case, architectural historians and theorists are much more willing to make these categorical judgements than others.

The reason that postmodernism is provided with such a relatively unarguable definition in architecture turns out, interestingly, to rest upon the visible dominance in twentieth-century experience of architectural modernism. This had its beginnings in the upsurge of utopian architectural theory and practice in the early years of the century. This revolution was centred primarily upon the Bauhaus school founded in Germany in 1919, and the ideas of the Bauhaus found expression in the work and writing of Walter Gropius, Henri Le Corbusier and Mies van der Rohe. Despite their differences, the work of these three theorists amounts to a unified programme of change for architecture.

From now on, architecture was to belong to and express the 'new'. It was to use new materials and embrace the techniques of construction which industrial development had made available. The newness of the modern movement would lie principally in forms of reduction, simplification and concentration. Line, space and form were to be pared to their essentials and the self-sufficient functionality of every building frankly proclaimed. Content for so long to be distracted from its mission by the falsities and vanities of decoration, symbolism, etc., twentieth-century architecture announced itself purely and simply as what it was. Its beauty was no longer to be incidental or supplementary to its function, for its beauty would now *be* its function. Le Corbusier, for example, argued that the engineer was the representative artist of the new spirit because his exclusive concern with function led him inevitably to the creation of beauty. 'The engineer', he wrote, ' . . . has his own aesthetic . . . In handling a mathematical problem, a man is regarding it from a purely abstract point of view, and in such a situation, his taste must follow a sure and certain path'.[3] The most vigorous proponent of pure functionalism was Henry van der Velde, who wrote that all forms determined by their function were 'of the same kind, marked by the generating operation of intelligence, all equally pure, yes, equally perfect'.[4]

The utopian language of the modern movement in architecture expresses a renewed faith in the rational, and this movement's break with the past is seen as a restoration of the essential identity of architecture. Stylistically, modern architecture was to be the expression, at different levels, of the principle of unity, and essential meaning. The American architect Frank Lloyd Wright wrote in 1910 that the modern building would be 'an organic-entity . . . as contrasted with that former insensate aggregation of parts . . . one great thing instead of a quarrelling collection of so many little things'.[5] In a similar way, Walter Gropius insisted that the modern building 'must be true to itself, logically transparent and virginal of lies or trivialities'.[6] The prophets of modern architecture insisted time and again on the unity of the building, as the organic expression of an inner principle, rather than the external imposition of form. Le Corbusier praised Michelangelo's Capitol in Rome for the way that 'it heaps itself together, in a unity, expresses the same law throughout', and wrote that a building was like a bubble which 'is perfect and harmonious if the breath has been evenly distributed and regulated from the inside. The exterior is the result of an interior.'[7]

This extraordinarily intense drive for unity of being in architecture does not prevent some interesting transferences of the idea of unity. For Ludwig Mies van der Rohe, architecture was to serve as the single most powerful expression of the *Zeitgeist*; in being thoroughly itself, architecture was to be the essence of the modern. 'Architecture depends on its time', he wrote. 'It is the crystallization of its inner structure, the slow unfolding of its form.'[8] At the same time, architecture was to be the visible expression of a new unity of art, science and industry. Walter Gropius fought throughout his life for the reunification of the separated realms of art and industry. The final words of his manifesto for the Bauhaus in 1919 express well the utopian and universalist aims of the modern movement in architecture: 'Together let us desire, conceive, and create the new structure of the future, which will embrace architecture and sculpture and painting in one unity and which will one day rise toward heaven from the hands of a million workers like the crystal symbol of a new faith.'[9]

So there is an odd contradiction in the midst of these epochal statements about the purification of architectural practice. Committed as they were to an aesthetic of purity and essence, modernist theorists of architecture are drawn to speak of architecture's relationships to the modern world, and to other arts, in ways that compromise the austerity of their essentialist formulae. Not the least of the latent contradictions in modernist architectural aesthetics is the fact that the unrelenting demand for architecture to discover its own immanent or essential laws is what links it to the aesthetics predominating elsewhere in painting, and in literature, in which, as we will see, the demand is equally for a determined exploration of the specific truth of each art form.

However, it is true to say that, in architecture, the forces of essentializing self-designation were much stronger than elsewhere. What is more, architecture succeeded in carrying through its aims in a more unified way than any other form of art. This is partly because architecture had a much less ambivalent relationship with the social and economic spheres than other art forms in the early years of the twentieth century. As many have noted, modernism in the arts arises in parallel with an extraordinary surge forward in industrial and technological development. If modernism is a part and reflection of the new age of iron, steel and telecommunications, taking its symbols and energies for its own, then it is also true that many painters, sculptors, writers and musicians also had very ambivalent relationships toward the material triumphs of modernity and took up adversary postures to the emerging machine culture. This is not so obviously the case with architecture, which is materially and ideologically wedded to the public, economic world; if painters and writers can make a living at the Bohemian edges of modern technological society, this is never quite possible for an architect, who is usually dependent upon his or her visionary forms being realized. For these and other reasons, architecture was forced early on to make its peace with the worlds of commerce and government. For all the Utopian drive of its prophets – and it may be that this very Utopianism is an expression of resentment at this situation – architecture is that area of cultural production in which the artistic and the technological, modernism and modernity, are forced into collaboration.

It is perhaps for something like these reasons that architectural modernism became through the later years of this century the dominant sign of the 'new'. By the 1950s, the world was familiar with the International Style, buildings expressing the simple, geometrical intensity imagined by

Posterities

Gropius and van der Rohe. It is this visible dominance which gave the 'postmodernist' reactions against the International Style, when they came, such clarity and definition. Charles Jencks, who is the single most influential proponent of architectural postmodernism, can therefore declare with smilingly absolute conviction that 'Modern Architecture died in St. Louis, Missouri on July 15, 1972 at 3.32 pm.'[10] This turns out to be the date on which the infamous Pruitt-Igoe housing scheme was dynamited, after the building had swallowed up millions of dollars in attempted renovation of the energetic vandalism it had suffered at the hands of its unimpressed inhabitants. For Jencks, this moment crystallizes the beginnings of a plural set of resistances to the hegemony of modernism. It will help us to specify some of the lines of this resistance, for they form a conceptual template which other accounts of postmodernism will employ in their respective narratives.

Jencks focuses first of all on what he calls the 'univalence' of modern architecture. By this he means the simple, essential forms typified by the near-universal glass and steel boxes of Mies van der Rohe and his followers. The univalent building is one which advertises its simplicity of form, insisting on the one theme which dominates its construction. Usually, this is achieved by the device of repetition, as, for example, in the Chicago Civic Centre, with its assemblage of horizontal spans, or Mies van der Rohe's 'curtain wall' construction, the Lake Shore housing units in Chicago. At one and the same time, such buildings assert and deny their form. If they proclaim their simplicity and integrity, saying, this square, this concrete box, is what I am and nothing else – then they also claim a kind of otherworldliness in their approximation to geometrical perfection. The univalence of the modernist building seems to establish its absolute self-sufficiency, as an ideal principle made solid and visible. Univalence also means exclusion. The modernist building is simultaneously pure materiality, and pure sign, which does not refer to anything outside itself by quotation or allusion. Like the ideal poem described by the American New Critics of the 1940s and 1950s, the modernist building should not 'mean' but 'be'.

Postmodernist architecture is characterized, says Jencks, by the various ways in which it refuses this principle of univalence. The first and most obvious of these is through a return to the sense of the meaningful or referential function of architecture. In the work especially of the architects Robert Venturi and Denise Scott-Brown, there is to be found a new tolerance for architecture that is prepared to gesture beyond itself, to acknowledge its meaning, purpose or environment. Robert Venturi's *Learning From Las Vegas* urges architects to try to recover a sense of the ways in which buildings are read and translated by their contexts, finding a demonstration of this in the streets of Las Vegas, with their multiplicity of roadside signs, painted, illuminated, literal and emblematic.[11]

Charles Jencks concurs in seeing postmodernism as arising out of a renewed sensitivity to 'the modes of architectural communication'. He praises, for example, the use of a sculpture of 'Portlandia', an athletic modern culture-goddess who seemed to embody appropriately the civic aspirations of Michael Graves's 'Portland' building in Portland, Oregon (*LPMA*, 6–7). In fact, for Jencks, this aspect of postmodernist architecture is an awakening to the fact that all architecture is inherently symbolic all the time. A failure to attend to the banal visual overtones of one's architectural abstraction can lead to embarrassing results, as with Herman Hertzberger's Old Age Home in Amsterdam, the intricate tessellations of which form an unintended but unignorable pattern of white crosses and black coffins, or Gordon Bunshaft's Hirschhorn Museum in Washington, a building which houses an art collection but resembles a defensive pillbox; Jencks 'translates' the message of this building as ' "keep modern art from the public in this fortified stronghold and shoot 'em down if they dare approach" ' (*LPMA*, 20).

In fact, as both Jencks and Venturi point out, modern buildings can never escape the play of connotation, even when they seem to have expunged all possible symbolism or reference. The very modernist language of power and sleek functionalism derives, not from a Platonic vocabulary of absolute forms, but from the industrial forms and materials of the early part of the century, from railway lines to grain elevators, which are taken as allegories of the 'new':

> Their buildings were explicitly adapted from these sources, and largely for their symbolic content, because industrial structures *represented*, for European architects, the brave new world of science and technology . . . the Moderns employed a design method based on typological models and developed an architectural iconography based on their interpretation of the progressive technology of the Industrial Revolution.[12]

So, in a surprising turn-around, what Venturi criticizes in modernist architecture is not its parched abstraction, but its failure to recognize its own modes of communication and its refusal to acknowledge the iconography of power which underpins it.

For both Jencks and Venturi, postmodernism has meant a renewed awareness of this suppressed linguistic or connotative dimension in architecture. Jencks is concerned in particular with emphasizing a semiotic view of the way that architecture functions, that derives from Saussurean theories of language. This means two things in particular for Jencks. Firstly, the language of architecture is not, as modernist architects would have it, a language of archetypal or absolute forms; rather, its structural elements derive their meanings from their relationships of contrast and similarity with other elements. So, for instance, the associations of the Doric order of columns – sobriety, impersonality, rationality, restraint, etc. – are not uniformly and transhistorically opposed to the so-called elegance, femininity and insubstantiality of the Corinthian Order; Jencks points out how John Nash makes the Corinthian play the part of the 'masculine', by setting it in various ways against other forms of column in his Brighton Pavilion of 1815–18 (*LPMA*, 72–3).

Secondly, the language of architecture, as well as depending upon internal relationships of difference, is itself part of a much larger field of intersecting language and communication structures. This clearly challenges the modernist conception of architectural integrity. Where, for Le Corbusier, an architectural construction was to be seen in the rigorously reduced terms of its own lines, surfaces and masses, for Jencks these abstractions are always placed in signifying contexts. What is more, the codes which are used to understand or interpret the abstract forms of architecture are not fixed or unchanging, since they always derive from and reflect the multiple contexts in which any work of architecture is experienced and 'read'.

The movement marked by postmodernist architecture and architectural theory is therefore from univalence to multivalence. In this climate, modernist assumptions about the simplicity of primary forms and the 'natural' responses they elicit from human observers begin to seem specious and voluntaristic. If architecture cannot guarantee the ways in which it will be read, then larger claims such as Le Corbusier's that 'harmony . . . is indeed the axis on which man is organized in perfect accord with nature and probably with the universe' also begin to dissolve.[13]

Postmodernist architecture therefore begins to mutate away from the geometric univalence of modernist architecture, as though allowing into its own form something of the multiplicity of ways of reading it, or, in a sense, reading itself in advance. Where modernist architects stressed the absolute unity of intention and execution in a building, postmodernist architecture signals its departure from this austere requirement by exploring and displaying incompatibilities of style, form and texture. In an early book, Robert Venturi argued for what he called in his title 'complexity and contradiction' in architecture and Charles Jencks, too, admires the display of architectural differences.[14]

A parallel move away from unified or essential form is to be seen in the embrace of ornamentation in postmodernist architecture, as opposed to the contempt shown by modernist architects for the inessential or superfluous – for Adolf Loos in 1908, ornament was 'crime'.[15] Ornament was the object of ontological dread by modernist artists because it encrusted the essential essence of a building with something alien to its nature. But, for many champions of postmodernism, architecture always consists precisely in its relationships to what is not itself. Robert Venturi has laid particular stress on these contingent relationships. In place of the unified city, planned according to one consistent principle, as Le Corbusier recommended, Venturi would have architects learn from the urban sprawl of Las Vegas about the way in which incompatible elements are laid side by side and work in collaboration. The unity of the Las Vegas Strip is not fixed and static, but emerges in process:

> The emerging order of the Strip is a complex order. It is not the easy, rigid order of the urban renewal project or the fashionable 'total design' of the megastructure . . . the order of the Strip *includes*; it includes at all levels . . . It is not an order dominated by the expert and made easy for the eye. The moving eye in the moving body must work to pick out and interpret a variety of changing, juxtaposed orders.[16]

Other architects, notably those associated with the movement known as Contextualism, emphasize the failure of modern architecture to understand and respond to the physical contexts of a building, the complex and various spaces and experiences that fill out the intervals that lie between the soaring and indifferent modernist monuments (*LPMA*, 110–11).

This movement from 'text' to 'context' has another dimension, too. One of the contradictions of modernist architectural theory is the disparity between its ambitions for an architecture which, in its spare functionality, can be seen as impersonal, and a desire to seize the opportunities for heroic individual vision and expression – architecture as the 'pure creation of the mind', as Le Corbusier put it.[17] In arguing for an architecture which is more responsive to its contexts, postmodernist architects like Robert Venturi have turned away from such heroic individualism. Charles Jencks similarly emphasizes the collaborative as opposed to the individualistic nature of postmodernist architecture, looking back with approval to the intimate, mutual comprehension between architect and client of earlier times, in which aims and intentions were pragmatically shared, as opposed to the distant and professionally impersonal relationships between client and architect in modern times. Jencks admires attempts to restore this intimacy of relationship in forms of participatory design, as, for instance, in Ralph Erskine's housing renewal project in Bkyer, in which local people were continuously involved in the processes of design and construction (*LPMA*, 104–5). One of the advantages of this is that it frees the postmodernist architect from the charge that, in adapting and combining different styles, he or she is indulging in mere professional display. When authorship is truly collaborative, Jencks claims, 'plural coding' is a natural embodiment of local and particular priorities.

The most obvious and frequently remarked-on form of pluralism in postmodernist architecture is its openness to the past. Where modernist architecture seemed to celebrate its absolute break with the past in its rigorous purging of all archaism, postmodernism shows a new willingness to retrieve and engage with historical styles and techniques. In Jencks's terms, this is a further consequence of the relativity of architecture's language; in the various forms of revivalism which have been brought to notice in postmodernist theory, we can see an attempt to fill out the temporal, or diachronic, context of architecture as well as its synchronic context.

There are two main forms which this historicism can take. One is what Jencks calls 'straight revivalism', in which architecture simply reinstates traditional forms, or produces wholesale historical simulations, like the Paul Getty Museum in Malibu, California, which is an exact recreation of the Villa of the Papyri at Herculaneum. But the use of the past can also take more critical and self-conscious forms, which are concerned to negotiate and even accentuate historical differences even when they are apparent in the same building. One famous example of this is Philip Johnson's A.T. & T. Building in New York City, which gives the traditional skyscraper's glass and steel box the more humane shape and scale of a grandfather clock, topping it off cutely with a Chippendale broken pediment. For Jencks, the unity created from this is an ironic one, which seems to depend both on the knowing disparity of the codes at work, the contemporary and the antique, the functional and the decorative, the domestic and the public, and their harmonization. Jencks looks forward confidently to a period of what he calls 'Radical Eclecticism', in which a multivalent architecture will pull together 'different kinds of meaning, which appeal to opposite faculties of the mind and the body, so that they interrelate and modify each other' (*LPMA*, 132).

In some formulations, the attention to context and the attention to history can intersect significantly. In an influential article Kenneth Frampton has argued for what he calls a 'Critical Regionalism'. What he means by this is an architecture that resists the tendency to flatten out cultural differences into the uniformity of a universal architectural grammar. This involves the assertion of local particularities within and against modern building forms. Frampton is careful to distinguish this form of regionalism from a simple nostalgic return to preindustrial models or building methods; this regionalism is 'critical' precisely because it investigates new combinations of the new and the traditional. In asserting the language of a particular locality, albeit in forms modified by the language of modernism, an architecture may be produced which expresses a 'dual coding', of the new and the old, remaining sensitive to the regional inflections of climate and geography, as well as local traditions.[18] Like Jencks, Frampton sees the abstraction of the modern movement as resulting in a brutal domination of the sense of sight, traditionally associated in the West with rationality and epistemological command, and argues for an 'architecture of resistance' which will enlarge the range of the senses which are brought into play to 'read' a building, to accommodate the awareness of 'the intensity of light, darkness, heat and cold; the feeling of humidity; the aroma of material; the almost palpable presence of masonry as the body senses its own confinement; the momentum of an induced gait and the relative inertia of the body as it traverses the floor; the echoing resonance of our own footfall'.[19]

We have seen, then, that postmodernist theory in architecture encompasses the following set of resistances to and reformulations of modernism: the principle of abstraction is countered by a renewed interest in the connotative or referential languages of architecture; the introverted and contemplative concentration on the building as 'text' gives way to an awareness of the various kinds of relational contexts for architecture; timelessness gives way to a critical engagement with history; univalence and identity are replaced by the principles of multivalence or plurality; and this brings about a corresponding shift from heroic individuality to collaborative authorship.

We will find that this sort of binary or oppositional logic is very characteristic of theories of postmodernism in general. No doubt this cognitive habit derives from an anxiety about definition and a need to fix clearly in their places the two terms of the opposition. It is undoubtedly true that, in this projection of modernism as a necessary and absolute Other, contemporary architectural theories of postmodernism are guilty of caricature, particularly in their occasional suppressions of the differences and variety within modernist architecture itself, and Andreas Huyssen has pointed out that 'in order to arrive at his postmodernism, Jencks ironically had to exacerbate the very view of modernist architecture which he persistently attacks'.[20]

There are reasons why the split between modern and postmodern should be produced so starkly in architecture, and we have touched on one of these already. The fact that architecture belongs so undeniably to the public world brought about a close affiliation between the avant-garde theory and experimentation of van der Rohe, Gropius and Le Corbusier and the requirements of the modernizing city. Ironically, the ideas and techniques of the architects who saw their work as part of a huge social transformation in the direction of rationality and egalitarianism, have been used to glorify the power of banks, airlines and multinational companies; Le Corbusier could not have suspected the part that architecture would play in the dehumanizing spread of global capital when he proclaimed that 'the morality of industry has been transformed: big business is to-day a healthy and moral organism'.[21]

If modernism has become so closely identified with modernity in its worst aspects, this may increase the demand among postmodernist theorists for an absolute break from it. This creates an odd paradox, since, in proclaiming such an absolute break, postmodernism actually seems to be repeating one of the founding gestures of modernism itself, the gesture of absolutely refusing the past; in other words, postmodernism is most like modernism in its stark refusal of it. The bad dream that haunts architectural postmodernism is that announcing the parricide may only be a way of keeping the family line going. This fear produces in its turn more attempts to decontaminate the concept of the postmodern. This can be seen, for example, in Charles Jencks's invention of the category 'Late Modern' to describe those buildings which take the stylistic ideas and values of modernism to an exaggerated extreme in order to squeeze out a terminal spurt of novelty from them. The most famous examples of Late Modern are Renzo Piano's and Richard Rogers's Pompidou Centre in Paris and Norman Foster's Hong Kong Shanghai Bank. These buildings display their modernity in a way that almost makes them seem archaic, each of them relentlessly pointing to its structural elements, pipes, ducts and girders. If these buildings are in one sense a condensed and intensified form of modernism, they are in another sense the revelation of the ornamentality at the heart of modernism, in their decorative display of the self-conscious signs of functionality. Jencks is understandably anxious to separate this hybrid area of cultural practice off from postmodernism. The following quotation shows that the question of definition is not a trivial one; for all of the alleged fluidity of boundaries and openness to influence of postmodernism, the need to secure the category is paramount:

It is a difference of values and philosophy. To call a Late Modernist a Post-Modernist is tantamount to calling a Protestant a Catholic because they both practise a Christian religion. Or it is to criticise a donkey for being a bad sort of horse. Such category mistakes lead to misreadings and this may be very fruitful and creative – the Russians read Don Quixote as tragedy – but it is ultimately violent and barren.[22]

The point about Late Modernism which Jencks uses to distinguish it is that it no longer has the clear commitment to modernist ideals of sheer functionality. In fact, however, it is hard to see quite why the knowing 'quotation' of the modernist iconography of power and function in the Pompidou Centre does not count as the critical or ironically 'dual-coded' relation to the past which Jencks specifies as uniquely postmodern.

Jencks has to negotiate a very tricky paradox here. In order to be genuinely 'new' (and not 'old' like Late Modernism), postmodernism must eschew modernism's commitment to the new, restoring or sustaining connections with the past. In order to be truly new, then, postmodernism must be old. And yet, as Jencks insists, it cannot be confused with straight revivalism, either. Postmodernism is defined, therefore, in that difficult space between the old new and the new old. This means that there is no longer any unarguable space which is purely 'new' into which architecture could simply and irrevocably leap. In this situation, in which every attempt at novelty stands condemned in advance as repetition, the only way to avoid repetition seems to be to repeat *knowingly* – to return to the past, in Victor Burgin's words, not 'to celebrate the timelessness and immutability of the values of the present status quo', but 'to demonstrate that it is never simply past; rather it is the locus of meanings which are lived by, and struggled over, in the present'.[23] The problem with this formulation is that it is never a simple matter to define the difference between the two modes. And if the 'past' that is returned to happens to be the 'tradition' of modernism – as it is in many postmodernist ventures – then how are we to know whether our 'critical relation' to that tradition is not just a hidden replication of it?

All this is not to deny the usefulness of the distinctions made by theorists of the postmodern in architecture. Rather, it is to suggest that the relationship between the old and the affirmation of the new can never be set out as simply and categorically as many theorists would wish. This is not just a question of a lack of information or of interpretative delicacy. It has to do rather with a certain complexity intrinsic to theories of the contemporary, in which theory and its object have been mingled with, or become aspects of each other.

This might seem at first scarcely credible. As the most palpable and public of cultural forms architecture is, in a sense, the least dependent of all forms upon theory (postmodernist theory, after all, derives much of its energy from the widespread antagonism to modernist architecture among those with no architectural training – one of the most influential intuitive postmodernists being Prince Charles). Furthermore, theories of postmodernism in architecture tend to exhibit much less of the convoluted reflexivity of ther postmodern theory, content as they often are simply to specify and catalogue the stylistic markers of postmodernism. It is the relative clarity and confidence of its definitions that gives architectural theory its key position in more general or applied descriptions of postmodernism (and is the reason for dealing with it first in this account). But, even here, questions of definition reveal at their heart fundamental uncertainties, which can no longer be resolved simply by appeal to the 'evidence'. This is partly because postmodernist architectural theory gives its object, the postmodernist building itself, the status of a kind of theory, or critical reflection on itself – if postmodernist architectural theory is about the problem of adequately defining the boundaries of postmodernism, then postmodernist architecture, read and given significance by that theory as an interrogation of the architectural past, is a version of the same enquiry. So it is not so much that theory has become detached from its object, as that the theory of postmodernist architecture has penetrated its object, to the point where there is no possibility of the object or the theory standing wholly distinct from each other. For example, it is common to argue that postmodernist architecture rejects univalent style in favour of an exploration of multiple styles, the incompatibility of which gives this architecture its ironic energy. But this exploitation of stylistic difference depends crucially upon a theoretical self-consciousness 'in' the building or assumed to be induced in its viewer which is sufficiently intense to allow awareness of the forms of incompatibility. But, as well as giving awareness of the forms of difference, such self-consciousness may also act to give unity and coherence to these forms of difference. As with Foucault's 'heterotopia', the announcement or theoretical recognition of heterogeneity always to some degree flattens or 'percludes' the possibility of such heterogeneity. So here, as elsewhere, problems of definition turn out to be intrinsic to the enquiry. The postmodern condition in architectural theory is precisely that condition of not being able consistently or precisely to formulate one's relationship to one's object. Postmodernism, in this 'master' discourse of postmodernism, is never purely the distanced *diagnosis* of the relationship between modernism and its successor, but is rather the narrative process which is articulated in order to produce the diagnosis.

Another form of this paradox concerns postmodernist architecture's alleged move away from the dehumanizing uniformity of a modernism whose technical language depended upon standardized mass-production, into new hybrid languages of difference and plurality. Surprisingly, the postmodernist multiplication of difference *also* depends upon mass-production, but this time mass-production at so heightened a scale that it produces, not uniformity, but difference:

> The new technologies stemming from the computer have made possible a new facility of production. This emergent type is much more geared to change and individuality than the relatively stereotyped productive processes of the First Industrial Revolution. And mass-production, mass-repetition, was of course one of the unshakeable foundations of Modern Architecture. This has cracked apart, if not crumbled. For computer modelling, automated-production, and the sophisticated techniques of market research and prediction now allow us to mass-produce a variety of styles and almost personalized products. (*LPMA*, 5)

Jencks seems unaware of the ironies implicit in this enthusiastic account of the brave new world of simulation. The new language of difference that Jencks proposes is not a splitting apart of the modernist dream of universality, but a morbid intensification of it. The 'hybrid', 'complex' and 'dual-coded' language of postmodernist architecture ought to testify to a new sense of rootedness or locality, but when hybridization itself becomes universal, regional specificity becomes simply a style which can be transmitted across the globe as rapidly as a photocopy of the latest glossy architectural manifesto. Paradoxically, the sign of the success of the anti-universalist language and style of architectural postmodernism is that one can find it *everywhere*, from London, to New York, to Tokyo and Delhi. The same relationship between plurality and universality is to be found in the critical discourses of postmodernism itself, in architecture and elsewhere. Postmodernist theory reproduces everywhere, and with everywhere increased allure and potency, the story of the dissolution of the universal perspective. The problem faced by postmodernist theory is how to speak of and bring plurality into being, in a way that does not itself limit and neutralize that plurality.

Art

As with architecture, there can be no doubt about the sheer visibility of modernism in painting. The two realms are so closely intermingled, both in terms of works and their practitioners (modernist artists and architects often worked closely together and certain artists worked in both realms) and in terms of the institutional deployments of the subject, that we would expect this to be the case. Accordingly, there is a considerable degree of overlap between the debates about the emergence of postmodernism in architecture and art.

Nevertheless, there are clear differences between the two realms. Where architectural modernism crystallized into the International Style which could be read and recognized by all, it would be theoretical suicide to try to deduce such a single stylistic norm from the extraordinary diversity of work produced in painting and sculpture over 50 years and across three continents, in order to be able to locate a single modernist point of departure for postmodernism. This means that it would scarcely be possible to determine the presence or not of postmodernism in art on purely stylistic grounds, in terms of the details of line, colour, or volume. What holds modernism together in art is a programme or ideology, rather than any particular, identifiable form of practice; correspondingly, what underlies debate about postmodernism is a shift in this programme. This is to say that, even more than in architecture, artistic modernism is defined at some point between practice and theory, between artistic objects and their definitions. The postmodernism debate makes this interrelationship even more complex.

The American art theorist Clement Greenberg is often credited with having provided artistic modernism with its most influential form of legitimation. Since theories of postmodernism usually derive their impetus from their reaction to his formulations, his work provides an obvious starting point. For Greenberg, the modernist revolution in the arts is to be understood primarily not as an expression of the turbulence of the newly-emerging technological world, nor as a movement of political renewal, nor again as a return to 'primitive' truths about the function of art, but as nothing less than art's discovery of itself, as form, subject and practice. In support of this, Greenberg can draw on the proclamations of many early modernist artists, especially the pioneers of abstraction, such as Kandinsky, Klee and Mondrian, as well as critics like Clive Bell, who wrote in 1914 of the radical separateness of the aesthetic from 'life': 'what quality is shared by all objects that provoke our aesthetic emotions? . . . significant form . . . lines and colours combined in a particular way, certain forms and relations of forms, stir our aesthetic emotions. To appreciate a work of art we need bring with us nothing from life.'[24]

What is distinctive about Greenberg's position is, first of all that he focuses upon the purity and the singleness of each particular art form's absorption in itself, and secondly that he sees this as the culmination of an historical process. The era of modernism therefore begins for Greenberg

not with the twentieth century nor even with the innovations of impress-
ionism, but with the intense activity of self-reflection associated with the
philosopher Kant. Greenberg believes that, because Kant was the first
philosopher thoroughly to scrutinize the nature and limitations of reason
itself, he is the first real modernist. Just as Kant subjected philosophy to
an internal auto-critique, so in the succeeding centuries, successive forms
of cultural activity have equally been anxious to explore and affirm their
own essential natures. Greenberg sees the development of the specificity
of the work of art as a kind of purging. Where painting in the nineteenth
century fell under the sway of the other arts, especially literature, the
painting of the twentieth century set itself to rediscover what was specific
and proper to painting alone:

> The task of self-criticism became to eliminate from the effects of each art
> any and every effect that might conceivably be borrowed from or by the
> medium of any other art. Thereby each art would be rendered 'pure', and
> in its 'purity' find the guarantee of its standards of quality as well as of its
> independence.[25]

Other writers had insisted upon the primacy of purely aesthetic categories, but Greenberg is alone in his emphasis on the separation of the
arts that must result from this. Painting can never be itself until it has
discovered what belongs to it and it alone, and expelled everything that it
shares with other arts. Writing in 1940, he is able to celebrate the fact that
the avant-garde arts have achieved a 'purity' and a radical delimitation of
their fields of activity for which there is no previous example in the history
of culture. 'The arts lie safe now, each within its "legitimate" boundaries,
and free trade has been replaced by autarchy.'[26]

For Greenberg, the undeniable dominance of painting in modernism is
due to the achievement of this absolute self-possession and self-govern-
ment, and to painting's absolute dependence upon its own medium. What
is the prime characteristic of this medium? Greenberg's reply is that
painting, unlike any of the other arts, is applied to a flat, two-dimensional
surface. Despite all its historical attempts to dissuade the viewer from
recognizing this flatness, painting is reducible in the end to this one
characteristic. For every other feature of painting is shared with some
other art form; the principle of the enclosing frame is shared with the
theatre, line, mass and colour are shared with sculpture and architecture.
Curiously, therefore, Greenberg's case does not depend upon the abandonment of representation, only on the remorseless exclusion from representation of objects from a three-dimensional world which contradict the

condition of the painting surface. In principle, then, there is nothing in this theory to prevent painting representing or referring to other objects that possess this quality of two-dimensional flatness: the problemis, that not many things do. Greenberg's demand for flatness was both echoed and intensified in the work of minimalist artists such as Morris Louis, whose flatness-insurance procedures are viciously, but deliciously derided by Tom Wolfe:

> So Louis used unprimed canvas and thinned out his paint until it *soaked right into* the canvas when he brushed it on. He could put a painting on the floor and lie on top of the canvas and cock his eye sideways like a robin and look along the surface of the canvas – and he had done it! Nothing existed above or below the picture plane, except for a few ultramicroscopic wisps of cotton fray, and what reasonable person could count that against him. . . . Did I hear the word *flat*? well, try to outflat this, you young Gotham rascals![27]

Greenberg's attempt, then, is to affirm the 'univalence' of painting, as Le Corbusier wanted to affirm the essential identity of architecture. More recently another art theorist, Michael Fried, has attempted an equivalent defence of the particularity of painting. Although his approach differs sharply from that of Greenberg, there are striking congruities between the two. Like Greenberg, Fried is concerned to trace the forms in which painting establishes and consolidates itself as representational activity – that is to say, the ways in which it defines itself against other representational forms. And like Greenberg, Fried develops an historical trajectory which has modernism as its triumphant conclusion.

If, for Greenberg, the dominating influence which painting had to shrug off was literature, for Fried it is much more often the theatre. Fried begins his analysis of burgeoning modernism a little earlier than Greenberg, with his study of French painting in the latter half of the eighteenth century, *Absorption and Theatricality: Painting and Beholder in the Age of Diderot* (1980).[28] Fried focuses in this book upon the growing demand among art-critics and theorists in the eighteenth century for an art which would escape from the coy falsity of the condition that Diderot called *le théatral*, the theatrical. For Diderot, theatricality takes the form of an exaggerated awareness of and implied address to the spectator (which Diderot objected to in painting and in the theatre itself). So, for instance, Diderot mistrusted the still-life painting which somehow, in the very exquisiteness of its hovering stillness, archly called attention to itself, seemed to be aware of being watched. He approved of history painting, however, in which the action could seem to be so intense as to be performing itself, without casting a flirtatious eye over its shoulder for the approval of the spectator.

Fried argues that, following Diderot, anti-rococo criticism and theory (and, to an extent, painting itself) through the eighteenth century grew to rest on the requirement that each individual painting should project an absolute self-absorption and obliviousness of its beholder. The paradox here is that this obliviousness is required precisely in order to stimulate that which 'theatrical' art denied or blocked – the complete absorption of the beholder in the painting. The painting must repress the fluttering eyelashes of the theatrical come-on, in order to allow access to some deeper central truth.

In later works, Fried developed his theory of the anti-theatrical mission of painting into the modern period and his work converged with that of Greenberg in identifying art's absorption in itself as the essential principle of modernism. Already, in his studies of French eighteenthcentury painting, he had insisted on the formal or compositional means employed to give hermetic unity to a picture, stressing the ways in which advanced taste settled on the principles of unity, instantaneity and artistic self-sufficiency. In his work on the modern period, Fried stresses modernism's withdrawal from the task of representing the world and consequent preoccupation with its own styles, forms and media. His most famous and influential essay is 'Art and Objecthood', in which he inveighs against minimalist art because of the ways in which it calls attention distractingly to its social and institutional placings, that is to say those elements of theatricality which threaten the simple integrity of the work of art as object.[29] Fried sees this in turn as a justification for a criticism such as Greenberg's which focuses exclusively upon the formal aspects of the work in question. It is not so much that history is removed from the criticism of painting, but rather that the detachment from social and political matters throws into prominence the *interior* history of art, in its struggle to arrive at a purely formal language. Fried is not inclined to go so far as Greenberg in representing this as a remorseless process of purification, and therefore does not agree that the interior history of art can have even a notional end-point of absolute self-identity; but the development of modern art is nevertheless argued in Fried's work in Hegelian terms which suggest the dialectical engagement of the new with the old and an intensified self-consciousness at each stage of renewal. This forms a sort of alternative history for painting, a history that gathers some of the solidity of human history itself:

while modernist painting has increasingly divorced itself from the concerns of the society in which it precariously flourishes, the actual dialectic by which it is made has taken on more and more of the denseness, structure and complexity of moral experience – that is, of life itself, but life lived as few are inclined to live it: in a state of continuous intellectual and moral alertness.[30]

Modernism seems to represent some kind of culmination of this process. For Fried, the split between the painterly-aesthetic and the social-economic is not an accident, but is irresistibly the means by which painting (and sculpture) become themselves, achieve the limit of self-absorption. An example which Fried gives of modernism at this peak of development is the work of the British sculptor Anthony Caro, and especially his work on a small scale. Fried wants to highlight the way in which Caro makes the size of his sculptures an intrinsic and not an accidental fact about them:

the problem of smallness that Caro found so challenging may be phrased quite simply. How was he to go about making pieces whose modest dimensions would strike the viewer not as a contingent, quantitative in that sense merely literal fact about them but rather as a crucial aspect of their identity as abstract works of art – as internal to their 'form', as part of their very essence as works of sculpture?[31]

The rather banal answer Fried gives is that Caro puts handles on his sculptures, to keep them in the manual scale – and then, progressively adds elements that run beneath the surface of the table on which they are to be set, thus precluding the actual or imaginative transfer of the sculpture to the ground. It is not in the least clear how this is supposed to result in the assertion of the intrinsic or essential qualities of smallness enjoyed by the sculpture; in that the handle or projection establishes the sculpture's size relative to some other surface and relative to the normal expectations of sculpture, it can hardly be said that it makes the size of the sculptures internal to their form or part of their very essence – quite the opposite, in fact.

Fried wants to assert in a contradictory way the work's autocritical awareness of its nature and history alongside its spontaneous 'thisness'. 'The convincingness of *Table Piece XXII* as art', he writes, 'depends on something that defies exhaustive analysis, namely, the sheer rightness of *all* the relevant relations at work in it . . . Intuition of that rightness is the critic's first responsibility as well as his immediate reward.'[32] The secret advantage of this double focus, on the unending historical conflict between works of art as they struggle to perfect their absorption, and on the mystical self-sufficiency of the work of art, is the warrant it gives to the discipline of art criticism and its associated discursive forms in the market place; for it simultaneously allows the flaunting of a specialized and particular knowledge to do with forms and techniques, and the defensive guarantee of the intuitive rightness, not of the work of art, but of the critic. In Fried, as in Greenberg, the insistence on the particularity of the work of art can become a territorial insistence on the part of the discipline of art history itself.

Fried's views on modernism are shared by the philosopher Stanley Cavell. 'Whatever painting may be about', he writes, 'modernist painting is about *painting*, about what it means to use a limited two-dimensional surface in ways establishing the coherence and interest we demand of art'.[33] Modernism is characterized for Cavell equally by an intense self-consciousness, in which each art confronts its own history: 'The new difficulty which comes to light in the modernist situation is that of maintaining one's belief in one's own enterprise, for the past and the present become problematic together.'[34] But where Fried is able to rely upon the self-absorption and intrinsic 'rightness' of an art which is moving inexorably closer to its true nature, Cavell argues that the willingness of modern art to question its own basis actually threatens the self-identity of art:

> The trouble is that the genuine article – the music of Schoenberg and Webern, the sculpture of Caro, the painting of Morris Louis, the theatre of Brecht and Beckett – really does challenge the art of which it is the inheritor and voice. Each is, in a word, not merely modern, but modernist . . . The task of the modernist artist, as of the contemporary critic, is to find what it is his art really depends upon; it doesn't matter that we haven't a priori criteria for defining a painting, what matters is that we realize that the criteria are something we must discover, discover in the continuity of painting itself.[35]

The paradox which Cavell opens out but does not deal with here, is that the genuine always risks being a fake, and as such his definition puts in question the a priori beliefs by which we hope to distinguish the real from the fake. Two essays in his book *Must We Mean What We Say?* (1976) are devoted to the question of genuineness and imposture in modernist art; but, surprisingly, although Cavell repeats that the condition of modernist art is precisely that it throws up such questions in extreme forms, he is unable to do more than assert the difference between the genuine and the fraudulent as it is revealed to intuition. His critique joins with Fried's in seeking to identify the authentic strains of modernism against the various

forms of modish imposture, minimalism, pop art, etc. which follow in its
wake, but is unable to do more than merely *assert* the distinction in terms
of intrinsic rightness. Pop art, he says, 'is not painting'. 'Why not?' we
want to ask, and the answer twangs back, 'it is not painting not because
paintings *couldn't* look like that, but because serious painting doesn't'. The
mixture of glibness and caution is extraordinary as Cavell then struggles
to parachute himself out of contradiction in a feverishly billowing mass of
qualifications. Serious painting does not look like this, he says

> not because serious painting is not forced to change, to explore its own
> foundations, even its own look; but because the *way* it changes – what will
> count as a relevant change – is determined by the commitment to painting
> as an *art*, in struggle with the history which makes it an art, continuing and
> countering the conventions and intentions and responses which comprise
> that history.[36]

It might be said that Cavell has run into a certain crucial switchpoint in
the division of modernism from postmodernism in the visual arts, a
point at which modernism's intensity of self-definition flips over into a
radical uncertainty about art's very means and identity. Cavell's struggle
is to maintain the belief that modernist art somehow forms and sustains
itself in the very act of dissolving its grounds. Nevertheless, in what is
actually a representative way, his account reveals all the time contradictions that it can barely suppress, as it attempts to delimit a region of the
purely aesthetic in the face of the awareness of the instability of that
region.

Most accounts of the postmodernist break in art turn precisely upon this
sense of the radical instability of the aesthetic, denying the drive towards
'presentness' as Fried calls it. Where Greenberg, Fried and others have
tried to argue for a modernism that becomes what it is by purging itself
of what it is not, theories of postmodernism in art stress the deep
connectedness between what it acknowledges as its own and what it
excludes. This argument takes many forms: sometimes, it will involve the
embrace of the 'theatricality' which is stigmatized by Fried, for example
in the promotion of pop art, conceptual and performance art, or in the
return to discredited modes such as figurative painting; and sometimes it
will take the form of an assault against the formalist-aestheticist beliefs that
constitute official or institutionalized doctrine about modernism – 'modernism', that is to say, as opposed to modernism. Sometimes, often,
indeed, the two will overlap or combine to form hybrid positions; but in
all cases there remains a crucial and irreducible overlayering of theory and

practice, to the extent that it is no longer possible to speak of the two realms in isolation one from the other.

Theories of postmodernism in art encompass two principal strands, though these strands twist together in intriguing ways. The first, exemplified by the work of Charles Jencks and those associated with him, can be called 'conservative-pluralist'; it embraces the enlarged conditions of possibility apparently released by the fading of modernism, and shows little sign of mourning its passing. The second, which might be called 'critical-pluralist', is evidenced notably by Rosalind Krauss, Douglas Crimp, Craig Owens, Hal Foster, and other writers for the journal *October*, and attempts to go beyond modernism by revealing the instabilities within it, and, more particularly within its official and institutionalized forms; but, in doing so, 'critical-pluralist' postmodernism aims to preserve some of the oppositional, exploratory ethic of suspicion which characterized many forms of modernism and avant-garde practice.

Charles Jencks has identified himself as the central figure in conservative-pluralist theories of artistic postmodernism. For him the supersession of modernism in painting takes forms equivalent to the emergence of postmodernism in architecture. His characterization of postmodernism lays its stress in two main areas – the multiplication of stylistic norms and the return of symbolism. Whereas modernism emphasized the integrity of style of the artist, along with the self-generated integrity of a building, postmodernism breaks down this norm, by encouraging multiplicity of style and method. This may involve the frank embrace of artificiality, though now this is no longer part of the pursuit of an ideal and complete self-absorption in the work of art. Instead, it involves the hesitantly ironic adaptation of other modes, historical and contemporary. Discussing *Figures With a Landscape*, a puzzling painting by the London artist William Wilkins, which depicts what seems to be a dormitory bedroom, with two clothed men playing flute and violin, a voluptuously posed nude woman on a bed, and a sumptuous landscape hanging on the wall behind them, Jencks emphasizes the way that the painting leaves us unsure whether we are looking at a realistic scene, or a parody of a number of painting styles. The central point is the way that the painting, for all its simplicity, defies reduction to essentials:

> If the subject of Modern art, according to one oversimplification of Clement Greenberg, is the perfection of its medium, then the subject of Post-Modern art is about [sic] past art which acknowledges its artificiality. This cliché lets us look at Wilkins' and so much other historicist work without regarding it as cynical: the presence of quotation marks, the self-conscious artificiality,

make it instead ironic. Thus we enter Wilkins' sparkling world of daubs, of *pointillisme* à la Seurat and *déjeuners* à la Manet, as we would a theatre with painted screens and stage. Each level of reality is a perfectly plausible representation of the present, but it also alludes to a previous world of painting or myth.[37]

The form of painting, which, like the postmodernist architecture admired and promoted by Jencks, can encompass forms of straight revivalism as well as the mixing of incompatible styles, roams hungrily, not only through history, but across national borders. In place of the universalizing internationalism of modernism, postmodernism offers the sensibility of the world village, of 'ironic cosmopolitanism'. This can permit a return to national styles and traditions, as in the 1980 painting *Constellazione del Leone (Scuola di Roma)* by the Italian artist Carlo Maria Mariani, which represents a range of contemporary artists and dealers in the mock-heroic style of eighteenth-century allegory painting; but the return is always partial, provisional, tongue-in-cheek. Mariani's 'Italianness', like that of other Italian painters such as Sandro Chia and Mimmo Paladino, is 'always in quotation marks, an ironic fabrication of their roots made as much for the New York they occasionally inhabit as from inner necessity'.[38]

This critical embrace of stylistic diversity is part of a larger mistrust of the modernist aesthetic of exclusion. For Howard Fox, 'modernist art was modern to the degree that it excluded the prevailing aesthetic, ethical, and moral codes of the larger culture'; postmodernist art is characterized, in contrast, by 'the willingness of artists and audiences to embrace subjects of mutual and perennial interest, to acknowledge all of the uses of art'. Fox sees the logical end-point of the modernist requirement of the purification of means in the Minimalism of the 1960s, which set itself the goal of producing objects which 'would refute all but a single experience and a single signification . . . would be acausal, complete, and perfect', and the thrust of postmodernism in the benign denial of this:

> At root Post-Modern art is neither exclusionary nor reductive but synthetic, freely enlisting the full range of conditions, experiences, and knowledge beyond the object. Far from seeking a single and complete experience, the Post-Modern object strives toward an encyclopedic condition, allowing a myriad of access points, an infinitude of interpretive responses.[39]

One of the signs of this openness to that which lies beyond the self-absorbed work, is the unabashed return to representation, symbolism, connotation, and all the other forms of referentiality. This may take the fuzzily indeterminate form evoked by Charles Jencks, when he speaks of a postmodern style of allegory; in contrast to more familiar forms of allegory, like *Pilgrim's Progress*, in which the manifest story and its latent meaning are distinct and clearly apprehensible, postmodernist allegory does not allow us to be sure of what the main story is, nor what the underlying myth may be that it alludes to.[40] Such enigmatic forms of allegory may be seen in the painting of Ron Kitaj, or the ironic Arcadianism of Lennart Anderson. Or it may take the much more obvious form of the return to traditional figurative painting, which is trumpeted at regular intervals by art critics.

The theory that underlies this conservative-pluralist form of postmodernism has been made dismayingly apparent in the recent writings of Charles Jencks. This shows a marked waning in the rhetoric of opposition and critique which he sometimes allowed himself in his earlier crusades on behalf of architectural postmodernism. After the definitive passing of the avant-garde, with its tedious compulsion to shock the bourgeoisie and assault the sensibilities of the art public, Jencks believes that art can now acknowledge itself as what it always was, thoroughly bourgeois, and return itself to the forms and subjects tabooed by modernism. Jencks finds nothing distasteful in this new realism. In place of the uncompromisingly universal horizons of modernism, he believes we must adopt an attitude of amused, agnostic pragmatism. Although this view takes its impetus from the critique of the institutionalization of the avant-garde energies of modernism, it sets itself in no way against the institutions of art or the structures of the international art market. Jencks, whose own promotional power and status within this field is not inconsiderable, is disingenuous when he paints his picture of the diffusion of the avant-garde into a collection of individuals of modest and unassertive liberal sensibilities, the 'post-avant-garde', who believe, in an affable sort of way, 'that humanity is going in several different directions at once, some of them more valid than others, and it is their duty to be guides and critics'.[41] There is little to distinguish this attitude, however much it represents itself as liberal and participatory, from a complacent tolerance of the falsity, exclusion and brazen centralization of the international art market, for whom the various forms of artistic postmodernism have all been moneyspinners, and whose central purpose, in recent years, seems to have been to reconstitute art in the way that Jencks so openly acknowledges, as 'the image of the bourgeoisie triumphant and enjoying itself'.[42]

For Rosalind Krauss and the other writers who embody the oppositional, or critical-pluralist strand of postmodernist theory, it is precisely the question of the power invested in institutions and canonical traditions which is to be challenged in postmodernist art and postmodernist theory.

This involves much of the same analytic repertoire as Jencks and his supporters employ, in the claim that postmodernist art aims to undermine the modernist imperatives of the formal and stylistic integrity of the individual work, the cult of the individual artist, and the radically subtractive mode of modernist aesthetics. Like Jencks, the *October* group refuse to credit the myth of the heroic avant-garde standing uncompromisingly outside the social and political world, and promote the exploration of the multiple relationships between art and its contexts. The structure of oppositions which frames the postmodernist analysis of the two groups therefore has much in common, in setting multivalence against univalence, impurity against purity, and intertextuality against the singleness of the 'work'. Both Jencks and the *October* group may be said to be trying positively to open up Michael Fried's proscribed, but usefully defined realm of the 'theatrical'; in this, as we shall see in later chapters, they are in tune with a recurrent movement in different areas of postmodernist theory, a movement towards what Scott Lash has called the 'de-differentiation' of the separate spheres of art, and the deliberate exploration of what lies – so scandalously for Fried – between, rather than securely within, different art forms.[43]

The principal tactical and theoretical difference between the conservative-pluralism of Jencks and the critical-pluralism of the *October* group, is that, where the former simply resign themselves to the vanishing of the avant-garde and its passage into the institutions and the market, the latter, in subjecting avant-garde and modernist aesthetics to critique, seek to reimagine forms and models of oppositional art practice. This requires a more complicated aesthetic-political map than that provided by Jencks. Where Jencks imagines a simple break between the restriction of modernist 'absorption' and the openness of postmodernist 'theatricality', the *October* group seek to understand the complex relationships between the terms of the binary opposition.

A representative voice in this debate is Stephen Melville, who has mounted an important critique of Michael Fried's absorption/theatricality model. Melville argues that Fried is right to draw attention to the growing fear among artists and art theorists since the time of Diderot that art is threatened by the forces of theatricality, entertainment, kitsch and mass-culture. Where Fried's analysis is limited, however, is in accepting on its own terms the neurotically self-defensive response of art to this threat. In attempting to deny or eschew reference to the beholder, Melville says, art simultaneously asserts its own purity and integrity, and denies a necessary condition of its own being as art. If the theatrical in some way invades the integrity of art, then the suppression of the necessary condition of art, that it be seen, or beheld, is equally a threat to the nature of art. In fact, Melville argues, art since the eighteenth century has always come into being on the risky borderline between absorption and theatricality. In asserting itself, it is always, in some curious way, acknowledging the force of that which is not–itself, including that which it seeks to exclude: 'the . . . attempt to (re)establish the autonomy of the aesthetic can be posed initially in terms of a problem of purification – but the attempt at purification has become necessary only because painting has already glimpsed (and would suppress) its openness to and implication in the "impurity" of the extra-aesthetic.'[44]

Melville's argument therefore seems to assert the simple priority of the theatrical over the absorptive mode, an aesthetic of 'impurity' over an aesthetic of purity – 'there is no way to absorption', he writes, 'because absorption is, in the last analysis, a lie'.[45] However, he is claiming something a little more complicated than this, namely, that the two extremes of absorption and theatricality are always mutually dependent on each other (it is not possible to assert what is proper to 'pure' painting except by reference to what is 'improper' to it). If modernism is a name that we can give to the movement of thought that attempts to expel the improper from the domain of art, postmodernism is the deconstructive intensification of that logic of modernism to the point where the two binary extremes are seen to include and imply each other. The place of art, at this point, is no longer securely inside itself, or outside in the no-man's-land of the theatrical, but always on a risky edge between what it is and what it is not: 'One is tempted to say that what has happened here is that painting has finally come into its truth, has appropriated for itself its proper field or problematic – except that this problematic is precisely that of painting's essential impropriety, its essential – if pro- foundly difficult – possibility of losing itself.'[46]

This play with the impropriety of painting is demonstrated in Jasper Johns's depiction of the stars and stripes, in *Flag*, painted in 1954 or 1955 and first exhibited in 1958. As Fred Orton observes in his rich analysis of the painting, *Flag* marks an inauguration for Johns; it was not only the painting by which he became known and established, but also marked his personal sense of his beginning as an artist, such that he set about systematically destroying as much of his previous art as he could lay his hands on. Orton shows how Johns keeps returning to this moment of autogenetic *fiat*, repainting the flag, or the *Flag*, to mark and monitor the progress of his painting by reference back to its beginnings. If the gesture of beginning appears to be thoroughly modernist in its fusion of the *ab initio* with the *ex nihilo*, then the repetition of that beginning in Johns's work is something distinctly other than modernist in its complex loops of precognition and *déjà vu*; the Stars and Stripes 'is not the assignable origin of "Jasper Johns" but the sign of the fiction and arbitrary character of any such origin'.[47] The viewer of *Flag* and its derivative images is kept off-balance, forced to decide, but forbidden to conclude, what kind of thing she is looking at:

> The peculiar character of *Flag*, where the Stars and Stripes and the art object, flag and factitiousness, are so thoroughly congruent, is such that wherever one looks there is both flag and painting (or something that is neither painting nor collage, but painting and collage) . . . . Neither the Stars and Stripes nor a painting (or something that is neither painting nor collage, but painting and collage) of the Stars and Stripes, it is simultaneously both the Stars and Stripes and a painting (or something that is neither painting nor collage, but painting and collage).[48]

In all of this, the legal and political implications hanging on the question of whether Johns is specifically representing a US flag, and, if so, with what purposes and effects, make this much more than a connoisseurial conundrum.

Another characteristic form of intimacy with the improper in postmodernist art is its embrace of textuality, for example in the collocation of images and captions in the work of Barbara Kruger, the elaborate interplay between image, substance, and inscribed and typographic markings in Mary Kelly's record of and reflection on her maternity, *Post-Partum Document* (1975–79), the provocative cooperation between images and discourse in the installation work of Hans Haacke, and the remarkable transmutations of books performed by Tom Phillips, both in physical form, and in electronic form, as the visual basis for his collaboration with Peter Greenaway in *A TV Dante*. Stephen Melville and Bill Readings suggest that such encounters between image and text are to be understood as an enactment of a 'postmodern sublime', which explores the consequences, not of the sense of thrilling and unencompassable largeness, as in the Romantic sublime, but of 'the shock of heterogeneity'. In such works,

> postmodernism seems oriented . . . to the presentation of modes of visual and textual co-presence that do not offer themselves to synthetic appreciation. That is to say, the incommensurability of visual and textual materials is not overcome in the act of understanding: apprehension of objects prolongs their heterogeneous co-presence . . . . The postmodern sublime can thus be understood as the *active consequence* of foregrounding the simultaneous incommensurability and intimacy of the visual and the textual.[49]

Rosalind Krauss provides two interesting examples of critical-pluralist critique. In her influential essay 'The Originality of the Avant-Garde', she sets out to examine and undermine the cult of absolute originality in modernist aesthetics. Referring to the famous passage in Marinetti's first *Futurist Manifesto* in which he describes being precipitated by his motor-car into a factory ditch filled with water and emerging, as though new-born, Krauss observes that 'more than a rejection or dissolution of the past, avant-garde originality is conceived as a literal origin, a beginning from ground-zero, a birth'.[50] This desire for absolute originality extends to the individual artistic products of modernism, which were to proclaim themselves independent of all reference; no longer having the role of repeating or reproducing the world, they are pure signs of nothing but themselves. But Krauss's argument, which weaves in a complex way from nineteenth-century conceptions of the picturesque to the figure of the grid in modernist painting, is that no sign can ever really function in this purely autonomous or self-originating way. Just as in the nineteenth century a landscape or natural prospect could strike the viewer as 'spontaneously' beautiful or sublime only because it accorded to the educated eye with the prior images of the picturesque (the very term indicating the ways in which the landscape must always already in some sense have been imaginatively 'pictured'), so the modernist aesthetic requirement of the picture-space as absolutely identical to itself is always penetrated by repetition:

> If modernism's domain of pleasure is the space of auto-referentiality, this pleasure-dome is erected on the semiological possibility of the pictorial sign as nonrepresentational and non transparent, so that the signified becomes the redundant condition of a reified signifier. But from *our* perspective, the one from which we see that the signifier cannot be reified; that its objecthood, its quiddity, is only a fiction; that every signifier is itself the transparent signified of an already-given decision to carve it out as the vehicle of a sign – from *this* perspective there is no opacity, but only a transparency that opens onto a dizzying fall into a bottomless system of reduplication.[51]

This complex passage argues that the nonrepresentational sign of the modernist painting always represents something, if only the desire to embody nonrepresentation. This is perhaps a twentieth-century version of the nineteenth-century picturesque; pure abstraction is always to some degree an image or copy of the ideal of non-referentiality. As such, it is a sign which is drawn into relationship with other signs, in relationships of reduplication and repetition.

So, like Melville, Krauss is asserting that what is conceived of as secondary and threatening in painting – the possibility of repetition – is in fact always primary. Her argument connects implicitly with Melville's, since what stand as the theatrical 'other' for twentieth-century painting, what threaten its integrity as a medium, are precisely those media of mechanical reproduction which allow for exact repetition. Her interest in this essay is in the promotion of a postmodernist art which explores the possibilities of reproduction alongside the production of pure, unique and original works, the work, for example, of the American artist Robert Rauschenberg, whose silk-screen canvases blend photographic reproductions of images such as Velázquez's *Rokeby Venus* and Rubens' *Venus at her Toilet* with painted and other images. This bringing together of heterogeneous images and technologies seems to throw into question the idea of pure origin or authorship (Rauschenberg has not attempted to imitate Velázquez or Rubens, he has simply incorporated them into his picture), as does the work of appropriation of artists like Sherrie Levine, who photographs other famous photographs and represents them as her own (see discussion below, p. 107).

The aesthetic that emerges from this is not quite one of anonymity, but rather of simulated authorship, in which ideas of originality and repetition, authenticity and theft are teased out to their problematic limits. A similar strategy is set forth in Krauss's discussion of postmodernist sculpture, 'Sculpture in the Expanded Field'. This essay presents the question of sculpture as primarily one of definition, and therefore, in a sense, of institutional power. The struggle in the 1960s and 1970s was between a sculptural practice that all the time pushed beyond the limits of what sculpture was, with the exhibition of piles of bricks, heaps of waste thread, tons of earth, records of walks through the country, and of curtains erected across miles of desert, and an art criticism that attempted to incorporate this practice into the history of modern art, seeing it as new variations of the same. Krauss argues that such experiments are in fact not easily to be assimilated to the (then reigning) modernist consensus as to what sculpture was – an abstract form, which was largely self-referential and unrelated to its setting. It is this last aspect that interests Krauss in particular, for, after a period of limit-modernism, in which sculpture reached the end-point of pure self-absorption and denial of its surroundings, sculpture began to explore seriously the boundaries between itself and what was not-itself. Examples of this are the 'site constructions' of Robert Smithson, structures of natural and other materials built on, or partially buried in, landscapes, and the manipulations and markings of landscape and buildings, such as Christo's projects to wrap up in fabric large well-known buildings, and to run curtains over miles of terrain.[52]

Although Krauss does not characterize the work she is interested in as ecological, for indeed she observes that what such work explores is a network of cultural possibilities rather than natural qualities, the work of certain more recent artists, especially the British artists Richard Long and Andy Goldsworthy would suggest that the movement beyond the permanence and self-absorption of the monument can also be seen as an ecological movement or aspiration to move beyond the cultural as such.

Richard Long's work consists principally of various forms of intervention or action performed upon the natural environment.[53] Although Long does produce and display objects in museums and galleries, they tend to have interest and importance not in themselves, but as the residuary evidence of these actions or performances. A great deal of Richard Long's displayed work takes the form of maps combined with short documentary accounts of walks across a variety of terrains in different parts of the world, during the course of which certain orderings or disorderings of the environment may be brought about – turning stones to face the wind, for example. Long's ritual, obsessive art aims to inhabit impermanence, to find a kind of nonappropriative belonging in the world. Often his work occupies a strange, ghostly borderline between the present and the absent – standing as a trace of a kind of passage through a landscape that is itself the leaving of the lightest possible trace, as in the photographs of lines that Long has walked through fields of grass. The maps which Long displays are not a capturing or objectification of a performance or process, but the very demonstration of the incapacity of the map to coincide with or take possession of what it represents. In some recent exhibitions, Long seems to want to unfold the interior space of the museum, atmospherically, stylistically and politically regulated as this space has traditionally been, to the outside of the natural environment, by, for instance, installing complex, swirling geometrical patterns of daubing with mud taken from a favourite river, or tessellating stones and slates. But the turning outwards of the museum is never a simple nor ever wholly achieved evacuation of the human space of the cultural. It is only ever, so to speak, an interval or aperture of exteriority hollowed out of the secure, bounded, indoor space of the museum.

Andy Goldsworthy works in a very similar manner. For Goldsworthy too, artistic practice is not orientated towards the production of self-bounded objects which are wrested out of the amorphousness of the natural. For Goldsworthy, the aesthetic is not the product, but the process – of making holes, rolling monumental snowballs, digging trenches, sewing leaves together with thorns.[54] The process is the process of coming to inhabit a particular space. Like other artists such as Alan Kaprow, Robert Smithson, Joseph Beuys and Damien Hirst, Goldsworthy is particularly interested in processes of decay, and the evolution of form into its collapse or absence. Goldsworthy's attitude towards the natural world is far from Romantic or primitivist. He resists that form of anthropocentric self-abasement which would deny the possibility of any contact between man and nature by seeking to restore nature wholly to 'itself'. His interest is in the inhabitation of nature, the quality of the reciprocal impingements of the human and the natural.

In the work both of Richard Long and of Andy Goldsworthy, there is a recognition of the always-already entanglement of the natural and the human. If their work appears to discover and present the natural in its self-evidence, then it is a self-evidence that is always and only disclosed through the mediation of consciousness, culture and history. Hence their willingness to tolerate the contamination of the event by the photographic record, or the decay of that event into photographic residue. The photograph is necessary not in order simply that the event be known and preserved, but also in order to preserve the acknowledgement of what inevitably slips out of the grasp of the archive.

Certainly, there remains in the work of both artists, perhaps as a sort of practical necessity, a certain blindness to the degree to which the opening to the self-evidence of the natural and the human involvement with it is always a potential violence. Nevertheless, the work of both artists is also characterized precisely by an appetite for cultural afterlife – afterlife in the sense of all the interviews, documents, images, evidences, residues and supplements to the 'primary' events that constitute the work of these artists, and that prove to be intrinsic to forming the events themselves. In the work of Long and Goldsworthy, the simplicity of the encounter with the natural is always a complex, construed simplicity; the quality of the way in which their art lets the natural into its own being is always also an incising of a cultural way of being on to it.

We might expect a postmodernist theory with such an interest in the disputed boundaries of art and non-art to engage with that cultural form which is so clearly representative of modern culture, and yet which also in itself straddles the border between high art and popular cultural practice. This form is photography, and, indeed, the *October* group have focused very closely upon it.

Photography

As the quintessentially modern art, photography has been one of the most threatening adversaries to the integrity of painting in the twentieth century. Indeed, one may say that it was partly in reaction to the widespread dissemination of photographic technology that modern painting was forced to turn from representation into the abstract interrogation of its own forms and conditions. But, if photography functions as that sphere of theatricality which most threatens the self-absorption of painting, it is interesting that photography itself, or that particular brand of it known as art photography, has sought self-definition in something of the same recoil from photography as a social practice. The problem for art photographers in the early part of the century was how to define and defend their own practice against the rapidly-widening ownership of cameras, as well as the spread of photographs in non-artistic media such as magazines and newspapers. The initial stage in this activity of self-definition was camouflage, an art photography that attempted to pass itself off as art by replicating the styles and subjects of painting. But this stage, associated with the work of Edward Steichen, Alfred Stieglitz and the Photo-Secession school in New York, as embodied in Stieglitz's publication *Camera Work* from 1903 to 1917, was soon superseded by a photography which sought dignity and autonomy on its own terms. Like the modernist painting defined by Clement Greenberg, modernist photography was to define itself '*only* through the most scrupulous attention to those effects which were irreducibly derived from, and specific to, the very functioning of the photographic apparatus itself'.[55] Allan Sekula relates this to the aestheticism of Clive Bell, Roger Fry and Benedetto Croce when he writes that 'the invention of the photograph as high art was only possible through its transformation into an abstract fetish, into "significant form".'[56] Rosalind Krauss adds to this with her description of the way that historians of photography have validated their subject as art by insisting on the modernist quality of flatness, for example in nineteenth-century landscape photography. For Krauss, the flatness of modernist painting its its acknowledgement and internalization of the flat exhibition wall which was its space of visibility; by drawing attention to its own flatness, the work of art mimics the wall-space that will be its place of exhibition and evaluation. (Krauss gives no explanation of the fact that it is particularly in the twentieth century that painting should have embraced this flatness – after all, it is hardly anything very new to exhibit paintings on flat walls.) Krauss sees the history of the incorporation of photography into the realms of art as requiring a rewriting of the representational three-dimensionality of photography to accord with the modernist promotion of the surface.[57]

Victor Burgin's view is rather different. He argues that the rise in status of the art photograph has to do with the enshrined belief in the metaphysical priority of images over words, the belief that an image directly shows us the reality which words can only communicate in a fragile and untrustworthy manner. But for Burgin, this pure and ineffable intelligibility of the image is an illusion, since all images, photographic or otherwise, operate in a dense network of relationship with other forms of representation, textual, visual and psychic. Against the attempts of critics such as Greenberg to expunge the alien presence of narrative from photography, Burgin asserts that any photograph 'inescapably implicates a world of activity responsible for, and to, the fragments circumscribed by the frame: a world of causes, of "before and after", of "if, then . . .", a *narrated* world'.[58]

In this, Burgin joins with the centrifugal movement of postmodernist photographic theory, a movement to implicate it in a more inclusive web of relationships and determinants. For Abigail Solomon Godeau, postmodernist photography comes into being in the reaction against the 'aesthetic self-referencing' of the modernist photograph; the most significant postmodernist photographers are therefore those who, like Barbara Kruger, Sylvia Kolbowski and Richard Prince, actively engage with photography-in-the-world, acknowledging the contingency of cultural codes and embracing the various mass-cultural uses of photography. Barbara Kruger produces posters that overlay media images with alienating political slogans, and sometimes hires hoarding space to display them publicly, while Richard Prince works with sophisticated advertising images, reproducing in intense, near-hallucinatory detail images of watches, cigarettes and whisky logos, in order to .make fascinatingly visible forms of the contemporary fetishism of the commodity.[59]

But there is another element which overlaps with the cult of the aestheticized autonomous image in modernist photographic theory. Many influential statements about the role and dignity of photography stress, not only the end-production of a hygienically detached object, but also the ways in which this object encapsulates the perceiving subjectivity of the photographer. According to this account, the aesthetically self-regarding image, in its exploration of line, form and shadow, is merely a metaphorical occasion for the representation of a state of feeling in the artist.[60] What is striking is the compacting in one apparently unified programme of two such contradictory notions: on the one hand an art which is absorbedly impersonal, in which the hand of the artist scarcely intervenes (in the nineteenth century, photography had been called 'heliography' – the writing of the sun) and, on the other, an art which is saturated with the personality of the artist.

In fact, this contradiction can be explained, if not exactly reconciled, at a structural level, by the fact that both the cult of the pure image and the

cult of the artist as pure maker were required as marks of the differentiation of high art photography from the threatening ubiquity of photography
as popular practice; if anyone can take a photograph, then only the
inspired or specially gifted individual can take a photograph with a claim
to be a work of art.

This emphasis on the heroic subjectivity of the photographer – artist has
been superseded in various ways by a postmodernist photography and
photographic theory. The American artist Sherrie Levine, for example,
specialized for some years in a form of art photography which aimed to
assault the cult of authorial personality. She rephotographed classic
photographs by such artists as Edward Weston and Walker Evans and then
exhibited them as her own. The point of this exercise inhered in the
obviousness of the plagiarism, in the fact that the photographs which
Levine 'confiscated' were so well known as to make it impossible for her
really to be trying to pass them off as her own. By making the act of
confiscation manifest, Levine attempted to throw into confusion the
conventional distinction by means of which the concept of the art
photograph can continue to function, the distinction between the high art
'original' work, on the one hand, and the public reproduction on the other.
But the reverberations may go even further than this, for Levine's work
may also be seen as a fundamental attack on capitalist conceptions of
ownership and property, along with the patriarchal identification of
authorship with the assertion of self-sufficient maleness.[61]

Photography, therefore, is a specially revealing instance of the struggle
between a modernist restricted field, with its stress on individuality, purity
and essence, and the postmodernist expanded field, with its embrace of the
contingent conditions which attend upon photography as a social practice.
It is not surprising to find that the struggle of definitions in photography
takes the form of a miniaturization of the struggle over definitions in the
field of art as a whole, since photography stands at the problematic edge
of art, marking the point where absorption has to be defended against
theatricality, the aesthetic against the non-aesthetic.

Characteristic of all the forms of 'critical-pluralist' postmodernist theory
that we have been looking at is its mistrust of the position of outsider, its
belief that the only space to operate is alongside and within the institutions
of art itself. If there is no simple outside, then there is no simple way of
setting aside modernist orthodoxies, as the more optimistic forms of
postmodernism such as Jencks's seem to suggest. These orthodoxies must
be problematized, displaced, unsettled, rather than simply forgotten.

What is striking about these formulations is the closing of the gap that
they require between art practice and criticism. In what is quite acknow-

ledgedly a transgression of one of the most sacred boundaries of modernist aesthetics, that between the self-sufficient 'work' and the 'commentary' upon that work, postmodernist art is characterized increasingly by means of the critical accounts that it can give of itself, or the forms of rapprochement that it can make with advanced art theory. What remains unclear is whether this will really prove to be a means of resisting or challenging the forms of cultural power that are concentrated in art and its institutions, or whether this merging of distinct realms, along with the abandonment of the avant-garde dream of the critical space 'outside' traditions and formations of power, might not serve in the end as a strategic alliance to consolidate rather than to threaten the paradigms of art and art criticism.

Notes

1 *The Post-Modern Aura: The Act of Fiction in an Age of Inflation* (Evanston: Northwestern University Press, 1985), p. 17.

2 Irving Howe, *The Decline of the New* (New York: Harcourt, Brace and World, 1970); Arnold Toynbee, *A Study of History* Vol. IX (London: Oxford University Press, 1954).

3 *Towards a New Architecture* (1920), trans. Frederick Etchells (London: John Rodker, 1927), p. 15.

4 *Programmes and Manifestoes on Twentieth-Century Architecture*, ed. Ulrich Conrads (London: Lund Humphries, 1970), p. 152.

5 Ibid., p. 25.

6 *The New Architecture and the Bauhaus*, trans. P. Morton Shand (London: Faber and Faber, 1965), p. 82.

7 *Towards a New Architecture*, pp. 79, 181.

8 'Technology and Architecture' (1950), in Conrads, *Programmes and Manifestoes*, p. 154.

9 Ibid., p. 49.

10 *The Language of Post-Modern Architecture*, 4th edn. (London: Academy Editions, 1984), p. 9. References hereafter to *LPMA* in text.

11 *Learning From Las Vegas* (Cambridge, Mass.: MIT Press, 1977).

12 Ibid., pp. 135–6.

13 *Towards a New Architecture*, p. 79.

14 Robert Venturi, *Complexity and Contradiction in Architecture* (New York: Museum of Modern Art and Graham Foundation, 1966).

15 Adolf Loos, 'Ornament and Crime' (1908), repr. in Ludwig Münz and Gustav Künstler, *Adolf Loos: Pioneer of Modern Architecture* (New York: Praeger, 1966).

16 *Learning From Las Vegas*, pp. 52–3.

17 *Towards a New Architecture*, p. 218.

18 'Towards a Critical Regionalism', in *Postmodern Culture*, ed. Hal Foster (London and Sydney: Pluto Press, 1985), pp. 16–30.

19 Ibid., p. 28.

20 *After the Great Divide: Modernism, Mass Culture, Postmodernism* (Bloomington: Indiana, University Press, 1987), p. 187.

21 *Towards a New Architecture*, p. 284.

22 *What Is Post-Modernism?* (London: Academy Editions, 1986), p. 38.

23 *The End of Art Theory: Criticism and Postmodernity* (London: Macmillan, 1986), p. 45.

24 'The Aesthetic Hypothesis' (1914), in *Modern Art and Modernism: A Critical Anthology*, ed. Francis Frascina and Charles Harrison (London: Harper and Row and Open University Press, 1982), p. 68.

25 'Modernist Painting' (1965), ibid., pp. 5–6.

26 'Towards a Newer Laocoon' (1940), repr. in *Pollock and After: The Critical Debate*, ed. Francis Frascina (London: Harper and Row, 1985), pp. 41–2.

27 Tom Wolfe, *The Painted Word* (New York: Bantam Books, 1976), p. 59.

28 *Absorption and Theatricality: Painting and Beholder in the Age of Diderot* (Berkeley and Los Angeles: University of California Press, 1980).

29 'Art and Objecthood' (1967), reprinted in *Minimalist Art*, ed. Geoffrey Battcock (New York: E. P. Dutton and Co., 1968), pp. 116–47.

30 *Three American Painters: Kenneth Noland, Jules Olitski, Frank Stella*, quoted in Frascina and Harrison, *Modern Art and Modernism*, p. 119.

31 'How Modernism Works: A Response to T. J. Clark', repr. in Frascina, *Pollock and After*, p. 73.

32 Ibid., p. 75.

33 *Must We Mean What We Say? A Book of Essays* (Cambridge: Cambridge University Press, 1976), p. 207.

34 Ibid., p. xxii.

35 Ibid., p. 219.

36 Ibid., p. 222.

37 'The Classical Sensibility', in *The Post-Avant-Garde: Painting in the Eighties*, ed. Charles Jencks (London: Academy Editions, 1987), p. 61.

38 Jencks, *What is Post-Modernism?*, p. 27.

39 Howard Fox, 'Avant-Garde in the Eighties', in *The Post-Avant-Garde*, pp. 29, 30.

40 'Interview With Charles Jencks', in *The Post-Avant-Garde*, p. 47.

41 Ibid., p. 20.

42 Ibid., p. 17.

43 See Scott Lash, 'Postmodernism as a "Regime of Signification" ', *Theory, Culture and Society*, 5: 2–3 (1988), p. 312.

44 *Philosophy Beside Itself: On Deconstruction and Modernism* (Manchester: Manchester University Press, 1986), p. 9.

45 Ibid., p. 11.

46 Ibid., p. 14.

47 Fred Orton, *Figuring Jasper Johns* (London: Reaktion Books, 1994), p. 97.

48 Ibid., p. 139.

49 'General Introduction', *Vision and Textuality*, ed. Stephen Melville and Bill Readings (Basingstoke and London: Macmillan, 1995), p. 20.

50 *The Originality of the Avant-Garde and Other Modernist Myths* (Cambridge, Mass.: MIT Press, 1986), p. 157.

51 Ibid., p. 161.

52 'Sculpture in the Expanded Field', in Foster, *Postmodern Culture*, pp. 31–42.

53 Richard Long's work is represented in the following exhibition catalogues: *Touchstones* (Bristol: Arnolfini, 1983); *Muddy Water Marks* (Noordwijk: MW Press, 1985); *Old World New World* (London: Anthony D'Offay, 1988); *Mountains and Waters* (London: Anthony D'Offay, 1992); *Walking in Circles* (London: South Bank Centre, 1991).

54 The range of Andy Goldsworthy's work is to be seen in his *Hand to Earth: Andy Goldsworthy Sculpture 1976–1990*, ed. Terry Friedman and Andy Goldsworthy (Leeds: Leeds City Art Gallery).

55 Burgin, *End of Art Theory*, p. 67.

56 'On the Invention of Photographic Meaning', in *Thinking Photography*, ed. Victor Burgin (London: Macmillan, 1982), p. 103.

57 'Photography's Discursive Spaces', in *The Originality of the Avant-Garde*, pp. 131–50.

58 Burgin, *End of Art Theory*, p. 69.

59 ' "Winning the Game When the Rules Have Been Changed": Art Photography and Postmodernism', *Screen*, 25:6 (1984), p. 99.

60 In an analysis of Alfred Stieglitz's account of how he came to take his famous 1907 photograph of immigrants on board ship, *The Steerage*, Allan Sekula has demonstrated how powerfully aestheticism and subjectivism are intertwined; 'On the Invention of Photographic Meaning', in Burgin, *Thinking Photography*, pp. 98–100.

61 See Abigail Solomon Godeau, ' "Winning the Game When the Rules Have Been Changed" ', pp. 89–92. See, too, the discussion of Levine's work in Douglas Crimp, 'The Photographic Activity of Postmodernism', *October*, 15 (Winter, 1980), pp. 91–100.

4
Postmodernism and Literature

The narrative of the decline or supersession of modernism is perhaps least clear, but no less pervasive, in literary studies. This is in inverse proportion to the influence which is wielded by literature and literary criticism in the academy, and there may be a connection here. For, if the years since the 1930s have seen a steady professionalization of the teaching and study of literature, with an ever more detailed organization and dissemination of its forms of knowledge and expression, then the result has been a much less monolithic discipline than academic architecture or art history. The sheer spread and diversity of the institutions of literature, comprehending publishing, journalism, electronic media and others, as well as the institutions of education and research, along with the deep penetration of literary studies into schools, entails a corresponding diversity of discursive means and practice. One symptom of this is that it is much harder to put together a history of the subject in terms of a conflict between clearly-defined schools or antagonistic groups – the academy and its norms on the one hand, the experimentalist, avant-garde or revolutionary on the other. In literary studies, the idea of an academy imposing or radiating aesthetic and critical norms has never been so well established as in architecture or art. At the same time, and perhaps more importantly, the relationship of literary studies to the market-place is much looser and takes more various forms than in other cultural disciplines; the norms of criticism have never exerted the same influence over publishing and literary reputation that the theories of modernism have elsewhere. This is not to deny any connection at all between the academy and the market-place, since undoubtedly universities and schools can determine to a very large degree which authors stay in print (especially in a larger market like the US) – but literary institutions exert much less direct influence on contemporary writing, simply because the economic means do not exist in the same way to restrict those who do not fit, and the channels of communication between departments of literature and publishing houses do not exist. (The situation is very different in art history, for example, in which the links between the academic world and the world of exhibitions and sale-rooms are much closer.)

None of this is to say that there are no powerful or unconscious paradigms at work in the institutions of literature; it is simply to establish that the field is more extensive and more various than elsewhere. If academic architecture theory and art history can be compared to large and successful businesses, marketing a range of variations on a single product in a world market, then literary studies are much more like a multinational conglomerate, selling and distributing a large number of diverse products in different ways and by different means.

It is for this reason that the contours of the postmodern paradigm are much less clear in literary studies than elsewhere. For one thing, the idea of modernism (though powerful) has never taken hold quite so strongly in literary studies as in, say, art history. Modernism in art and architecture represented itself and was represented as the avant-garde pitting itself remorselessly against the ingrained repressions of the past, and heroically transforming human destiny. Although literary studies depend upon this notion of the shock of the new – every student knows Ezra Pound's battle-cry of 'Make it new' – it is also strangely the case that the ugly duckling of the avant-garde in literature was always quickly transformed into a sleek canonical swan. If, on the one hand, literary modernists like Pound, Eliot and Woolf were opposed to and horrified by the automated mass culture of the twentieth century, then it is also true that these writers were quickly and aptly accommodated to the cultural and political mainstream; hence the peculiar contradiction, which is nowhere so sharp as in literary modernism, between radical disruption of form and traditionalism of content and ideology – in the work, for instance, of Pound, Eliot, Woolf and Yeats. These sorts of factor make it hard to construct a narrative of the slow betrayal of the avant-garde ideals of modernism, since literary modernism (at least in Britain and the US) never had such an openly iconoclastic phase.

A similar complexity attends the relationship between modernism in writing and the rise of professional literary criticism in the twentieth century. It must first of all be said clearly that there is a certain complicity between the formation and reproduction of the discipline of English (the dominant form of literary studies) and the notion of modernism itself. It is no coincidence that Eliot's *The Waste Land*, Joyce's *Ulysses*, Pound's first *Cantos* and I. A. Richards's *Principles of Literary Criticism* all appeared within a few years of each other in the early 1920s. Richards's theory of reading, with its emphasis upon the harmonization of conflicting affective impulses in the reader, worked wonderfully well as an account of the work of the new writers, and the work of Eliot in particular – indeed, *Principles of Literary Criticism* ends openly with a defence of Eliot.[1] It has been correctly observed that the New Criticism, the critical practice which was so influential in the US and Britain in the middle years of the century, with its fierce emphasis on the play of irony, tension and resolution within a text which is considered as an autonomous artefact, provides an ideal way of reading a body of modernist texts which seemed more and more to deny their readers the pleasures of immediate comprehension, and indeed to demand a highly self-conscious attention to verbal or poetic substance over and above meaning.

But it is also true that academic literary criticism, especially in Britain, turned away from the modernist writing which its theory seemed to foster. F. R. Leavis and the Scrutiny group were much less concerned to act as public relations agents for modernist writing than to assimilate, where it seemed appropriate, the forms and energies of modernism to the native (that is, 'English') traditions of literature.[2] So when Charles Newman speaks of the academic legitimating and containing of the dangerous energies of modernism as a 'second revolution', there is a double simplification: first of all, literary modernism was never exactly the 'revolution' which it might have been elsewhere, and secondly, the literary academy has accommodated and identified itself with modernism in a much less extensive way than Newman believes.[3]

Nevertheless, the idea of the *post*modern has taken root very firmly in literary studies. It even seems that the urge to identify and celebrate the category of the postmodern has been so strong as to produce by back-formation a collective agreement about what modernism was, in order to have something to react against. As Helmut Lethen puts it, 'the postmodern situation created the possibility to see Modernism as a closed and rather rigid entity. If one wants to deconstruct, one has to homogenize one's subject first so that it becomes deconstructible.'[4] The account of the emergence of literary postmodernism which follows will accord in many respects with this back-formation. I will not be attempting here to decide whether or not modernism corresponds to the account of it given in various theories of postmodernism, but it is at least necessary to recognize that such accounts always require there to have been something called modernism in the first place.

If theories of modernist art and architecture are founded on the desire to discover the essence or limit of each art practice, or, in other words, to affirm the aesthetic and material identity of that practice, then it is difficult at first to see how this might transfer to writing. If it is plausible to a degree to say that architecture is essentially 'lines and masses organized in space' and painting is essentially 'lines and forms organized on a flat surface', what essential formal principle might one discover for writing, or literature? If one works by strict analogy, then one should say, surely, that the essence of literature lies in the materiality of language, shapes on the page and sounds in the air. Indeed, modernist theorists and theorists of modern literature have stressed just this aspect of writing, for the Futurist leader, Marinetti, produced sound-poems which were nothing more than onomatopoeic boomings, while in Russia, artists like Khlebnikov also produced a language of pure sounds, along with books in which the physical arrangements of the words on the page were promoted above the semantic content of those words. But this hardly provides a very satisfying image of the essence of literature. Indeed, the irony is, that in reducing literature to its most basic material conditions, one risks actually turning it into something other than itself – into music in the case of Marinetti, or visual art in the case of Khlebnikov. Clearly, literature will need to look to other forms of pure definition.

The group of writers in the 1920s who are now known to us as the Russian Formalists might seem to have provided such a definition, for they saw the principle of literariness of a particular work as inhering not so much in its material nature as in its form – that is to say, the particular ways in which style and convention were deployed in that particular work of art. Literariness, they declared, lay in the intense capacity of the literary work to meditate upon and draw attention to the qualities of its form. Modern or progressive writing refused to allow the reader the illusion that he or she was reading about the real world, for literature remorselessly 'defamiliarized' that world. Many contemporary theoretical accounts of modernism extend and develop this formalist position. As Andreas Huyssen has observed, much of the French post-structuralist literary theory associated with the 1960s and 1970s, and centred particularly around the periodical *Tel Quel*, acts as a justification for the formalist account of modernism, and offers as exemplars of its aesthetic – the endless play of the signifier – the works of archmodernists like Mallarmé and Joyce.[5]

This, however, is not the only, or even the most influential definition of literary modernism. Alongside it we should place those accounts which stress, for example, the subjectivist relativism of modernism. According to this account, modernism begins with the move away from a belief in a world of ideas or substances which may be objectively known in themselves, to the apprehension of a world which can be truly known and experienced only through individual consciousness; the favoured locations for this view of modernism are Pater's 'Conclusion' to his *The Renaissance*, Conrad's Preface to *The Nigger of the Narcissus*, the later novels and prefaces of Henry James, and Virginia Woolf's essay 'Modern Fiction', in which she speaks famously of the 'semi-transparent envelope' of consciousness, and the necessity of finding a narrative language to render the shifting intensities of the subjective life.[6]

Ironically, this subjectivism has to be accommodated alongside a whole series of announcements of the end of individual subjectivity, from Eliot's famous defence of impersonality in 'Tradition and the Individual Talent', to Joyce's promotion (via his charactor Stephen Dedalus) of an aesthetic of authorial detachment, in which the author of a literary work removes himself, god-like, from the work. But, in fact one can also discern a principle which underlies and unites these two opposites. Whether conceived of as a cold, dry, impersonal jewel, or as a richly saturated tissue of subjectivity, the principle of the modernist artwork is that it be complete in itself. Both objectivity and subjectivity conduce to formal integrity of this kind, one giving the literary work the stony self-sufficiency of Cleanth Brooks's 'well-wrought urn,' the other, the 'intricately wrought composure', as I. A. Richards puts it, of a network of subjectivity. What this principle in turn seems to involve or guarantee, is an aesthetic of extreme artistry. The work of literary creation, under modernism, can now no longer be represented as the humble subjugation of the will to the task of representing the world, or conforming to a body of aesthetic precepts; the commitment to produce a work of art that will know no other rules but its own, and will transform the vulgar contingency of worldly relations into purified aesthetic terms, requires an extreme of vigilance, knowledge and mastery on the part of the artist, who is now divine artificer rather than humble workman.

As we might expect, theories of postmodernist writing postulate a regression from or progression beyond such notions of self-sufficient form. One early manifestation of this is the movement towards modest realism in British writing of the 1950s and 1960s, typified in the work of Alan Sillitoe, Kingsley Amis and Philip Larkin, writers who refused what seemed to them the high-minded and elitist obscurity of the modernist inheritance and fostered a return to a writing which was lodged in experience rather than form. In theory, at least, such writing would be less closed off and more permeable to 'life'. Although a case is occasionally made for calling such writers postmodernist, most accounts of literary postmodernism would want to insist on some form of critical engagement with modernism rather than a simple turning away from it.

A more positive challenge to the idea of the integrity of the literary artefact was provided by Leslie Fiedler in an essay of 1969, entitled 'Cross That Border – Close That Gap'.[7] The gap evoked in the title of this essay is that between high culture and mass culture. Fiedler argues that the writing of the present challenges and should continue to challenge the generic integrity of high culture, that integrity that had been hitherto guaranteed by its distance from the Western, the romance, the detective story. Where modernist novels either purged away all contamination by such writing or repudiated them by internal parody – examples might be Conrad's novels, with their partial recapitulation of the characters and incidents of the adventure story, or Joyce's parodies of girls' romance in the 'Nausicaa' section of *Ulysses* – Fiedler sees the signs of a new hospitality to the popular in the novels of Kurt Vonnegut and John Barth, with their embrace of the Western and science fiction. Fiedler's influential essay is an early definition of postmodernism as a movement of merging, a deliberate complication of the idea of generic integrity.[8]

An account such as this tends to see postmodernism in literature as a break or breakthrough; but for many, the postmodernist transformation, or advance, can be seen as a selective intensification of certain tendencies within modernism itself. Such accounts tend to view the rejection of formal integrity or essence as intrinsic to modernism, and the appearance of postmodernism as only another phase in that process. Probably the most influential exponent of this point of view in literary studies is Ihab Hassan.

Unmaking and Irony

Hassan's *The Dismemberment of Orpheus: Towards a Postmodern Literature* was first published in 1971, and centres around the story of the fate of Orpheus the poet, who was dismembered by Maenads, because they were jealous of the attention he gave to young men. The head of Orpheus, cast with the poet's lyre into the river Hebrus, continued singing after dismemberment. For Hassan, this narrative provides a way of understanding what he sees as the deliberate disarticulation of the traditions of literature by the generations of writers since 1914. The most significant literature of this century, says Hassan, has been a 'literature of silence', which consents to dismemberment, but yet continues somehow to sing 'on a lyre without strings'.[9]

'Silence' connotes more for Hassan than the simple absence of utterance. He writes that modernist literature enacts a 'complex' silence, which encompasses a number of meanings from refusal to subversion; so that the principle of silence is to be found in the alienation from reason, society, nature and history alike, the repudiation and subversion of language, convention and artistic form, the exploration of ecstasy, trance and other extreme states of feeling, the turning of consciousness in upon itself, and in the intense awareness of imminent apocalypse (*TPL*, 13–14). Hassan sees the beginning of the modernist 'will to unmaking' in the works of the Marquis de Sade, in which 'the dialectic of transgression moves toward infinity', for 'the true spirit of the Sadian self is priapic and continuous denial' (*TPL*, 46–7). This tradition of denial bubbles up again rumbustiously in the work of Alfred Jarry, and the Dadaists and Surrealists. But here as elsewhere, Hassan wants to insist on the dual nature of the modern Orpheus, who not only tolerates unmaking and dismemberment, but also, against all the odds, continues singing, in the affirmation of 'a new creative force, intact in destruction'.

The heroics of unmaking are a consistent quality in modernism and postmodernism alike for Hassan. When he arrives at the work of Beckett, which has seemed to many to inaugurate the era of postmodernist writing, he celebrates Beckett's 'heroic absurdity' in terms which are oddly similar to those which are earlier used of de Sade. Beckett's heroism is that of the ethical pioneer, the questing, lonely, self-scrutinizing male. About Beckett's exile from his country and language, Hassan has this to say: 'All exiles, Henry Miller reminds us in his book about Rimbaud, exile themselves from the world's body, the mother's flesh' (*TPL*, 213). Henry Miller is a quirky, but oddly appropriate authority, since what Hassan wants to assert is the heroic maleness of modernist/postmodernist denial against the disgusting 'female' acquiescence of matter, of the world, history, tradition. This is a history that incorporates de Sade alongside Beckett, and Hemingway alongside Kafka, in a remorseless sexualizing of aesthetics which is paradoxically obsessed with the need for literature to purify itself.

Modernist and postmodernist writers are equally characterized by the looping together of unmaking and heroic recreation. There is the familiar claim that in Beckett's work the excesses of disintegration are the guarantee of authentic speech – 'it is pain that presses silence into speech and speech back into silence' (*TPL*, 237) – and Hassan also makes out the 'two accents of silence', the one negative, 'auto-destructive, demonic, nihilist', the other positive, 'self-transcendent, sacramental and plenary' (*TPL*, 248) in contemporary American writers like John Barth and William Burroughs. But the most representative figure of all, presumably because of the way that he links modernism and postmodernism, is not a writer but the artist Marcel Duchamp, the Dadaist of the earlier years of the century, whose assault on the conventions of art led him for twenty years literally to silence and the actual renunciation of art, but who came back into view and began to influence artists again in the 1960s. The paradoxes of negativity and positivity in his work exemplify postmodernism for Hassan: 'A supreme intelligence of anti-art, he dedicates his existence to the artistic avant-garde. A total skeptic, Cartesian without a method, he emanates a sacramental irony toward creation, and says always to his friends: "yes" ' (*TPL*, 256).

So one of the more obvious problems for anyone trying to extract from Hassan's work a definition of what postmodernism might be, is his unsurrendering insistence that 'the postmodern spirit lies coiled within the great corpus of modernism' (*TPL*, 139). This is to see postmodernism partly as a kind of Dionysiac virus within modernism, tempting it to the extremes of madness and self-dissolution, and partly as the secret inner principle of modernism.

But *The Dismemberment of Orpheus* contains a 'Postface' added for the 1982 edition which makes a different move. Although Hassan continues to assert that there is no absolute break between modernism and postmodernism, since 'history is a palimpsest, and culture is permeable to time past, time present, and time future' (*TPL*, 264), he is now much more confident of setting out the terms in which postmodernism may be seen as opposed to modernism rather than a reformulation of it. He provides a representative table of such forms of opposition, as follows:

Modernism	Postmodernism
Romanticism/Symbolism	'Pataphysics/Dadaism
Form (conjunctive/closed)	Antiform (disjunctive, open)
Purpose	Play
Design	Chance
Hierarchy	Anarchy
Mastery/Logos	Exhaustion/Silence
Art Object/Finished Work	Process/Performance/Happening
Distance	Participation
Creation/Totalization	Decreation/Deconstruction
Synthesis	Antithesis
Presence	Absence
Centering	Dispersal
Genre/Boundary	Text/Intertext
Paradigm	Syntagm
Hypotaxis	Parataxis
Metaphor	Metonymy
Selection	Combination

Root/Depth	Rhizome/Surface
Interpretation/Reading	Against Interpretation/Misreading
Signified	Signifier
Lisible (Readerly)	*Scriptible* (Writerly)
Narrative/*Grand Histoire*	Antinarrative/Petit Histoire
Master Code	Idiolect
Symptom	Desire
Genital/Phallic	Polymorphous/Androgynous
Paranoia	Schizophrenia
Origin/Cause	Difference-Differance/Trace
Metaphysics	Irony
Determinacy	Indeterminacy
Transcendence	Immanence

(*TPL* 267–8)

Although some of the oppositions in this table (semantics and rhetoric, for example, or metaphor and metonymy) are literary–stylistic, many of the terms derive from other fields, from linguistics, philosophy, psycho-analysis and theology. Despite Hassan's attempts to protect himself from too rigid an application of his theoretical model, there is no doubt that it is a powerful and seductive one. What impresses most of all is the implicit evaluative hierarchy in the table. Invisibly but unmistakably, the mark of discredit hovers over the left hand column, while the right hand column reads like a litany of all that is obviously desirable (that it runs together alluring things like 'play', 'participation' and 'process' with less clearly desirable things like 'exhaustion' and 'schizophrenia' does not diminish the glamour of the package). The effect of associating modernism with such drearily authoritarian principles as 'form', 'hierarchy', 'totalization' and 'synthesis' is actually to deny the will-to-unmaking in modernism itself about which Hassan has had so much to say. Modernism now becomes the name for the purblind logocentric past, expressive as it is of a totalitarian will to absolute power.

Interestingly, one term that we might have expected to turn up in Hassan's sinister column of dishonour is 'binarism', the fixation upon strict and homogeneous contrasts. Hassan here has to rely upon this binary logic to promote the very things that appear to stand against binary logic, the ideas of dispersal, displacement and difference; he gives us difference *as opposed to* origin, irony *as opposed to* metaphysics, and so on, projecting the sense that these parallel lists of cultural symptoms could be extended infinitely without ever threatening the modernism/postmodernism oppo-sition that sustains and produces them.

This might be seen as a mere ironic kink in Hassan's argument, a symptom of the 'will and counter-will to power' which he acknowledges as dominating academic debates about postmodernism (*TPL*, 262). But more seriously damaging for the argument of his book as a whole are the consequences of this new, expanded conception of postmodernism for the concept of the literary itself. Hassan here acknowledges that the postmodernist era is marked by a radical decomposition of all the central principles of literature, the falling into deep questionability of critical ideas about authorship, audience, the processes of reading, and criticism itself. But this apprehension hardly seems to ruffle the surface of Hassan's work. Throughout *The Dismemberment of Orpheus*, Hassan fiercely defends the idea of literature, in the very terms which are so discredited in his table of contrasts, authenticity, depth, synthesis and transcendence.

Above all, Hassan seeks to differentiate the realm of the aesthetic from other realms. For him, the retreat of modern art and literature from the particularities of modern life is an act of pure and transcendent denial – and perhaps, like the act of repression according to Freud, a double denial, that also purges the fact of denial from memory, and so yields it a ghostly, self-sustaining positivity. The beginnings of this are to be found in Hassan's comments on de Sade: 'His works are almost wholly independent of time, place and person, and their autistic purpose is single. Without full comprehension of his role in Western thought, Sade may thus be the first to wrench the imagination free from history, to invert the will of art, and to set language against itself' (*TPL*, 45).

The only place where the negations evoked in *The Dismemberment of Orpheus* actually lock into or react in any particular way against social, economic or political conditions comes with a fleeting allusion to Lucien Goldmann's account of the French New Novel. Goldmann's argument is that the New Novel of Alain Robbe-Grillet and others is a representation of a response to the extreme of commodification of life under late twentieth-century capitalism, in which meaning and significance pass decisively from living beings to objects. But Hassan sees this entirely in the shrunken terms suggested by the novels themselves. Rather than attempting to restore the context of the negation, he simply celebrates the pure negativity of the fiction he calls 'aliterature', allowing alienation to somersault into transcendence: 'Such fictions can refer only to the internal time of consciousness, not of history or the stars; they refer to the phenomenological present, where discontinuous reality escapes from each word, even as it is read or uttered' (*TPL*, 161). Elsewhere, Hassan praises Beckett's characters in the same terms, as 'pure voices of subjectivity' (*TPL*, 233) and, going even further, discovers the supreme value of such literature in its enforced self-legitimations: 'There is the sufficiency of truth in the best work of Beckett; and also the sufficiency of poetry. Without faith in art or human consciousness, without benefit of ideology or dogma, Beckett still manages to regulate his "fundamental sounds" in the way poetry regulates itself from within' (*TPL*, 246).

In a sense, the gap between this belief in the self-creating unity of art and the sense of the constituting relations of art and its contexts is the gap between the modern and the postmodern, although in Hassan's work the gap is not satisfactorily negotiated. The growing apprehension of the determinate relations between the artistic and the non-artistic gives the lie to the fond, anxious hope voiced in the last words of the original edition of *The Dismemberment of Orpheus*, that, after all its modern and postmodern paroxysms of self-mutilation, 'art may move toward a redeemed imagination, commensurate with the full mystery of human consciousness' (*TPL*, 258). Although Hassan's work after this book has engaged in much more flexible ways with the uncertainties of definition thrown up by postmodernist literature and theories of it, his writing has clung to a vision of the transcendent separateness of art.

Another, more supple, reading of the movement from modernism to postmodernism in literature is offered by Alan Wilde in his *Horizons of Assent: Modernism, Postmodernism and the Ironic Imagination* (1981).[10] Wilde is concerned, like Hassan, with the literary response to the apprehension of disorder. But, where Hassan finds the spirit of modernism in its most delinquent practitioners of the aesthetics of silence and unmaking, Wilde focuses on 'high' modernism, with its more aristocratically unrevolutionary exponents, Eliot, Woolf and Forster. For Wilde, disorder is contained by that all-purpose New Critical device, the principle of irony, that term which, encompassing technique and cast of mind simultaneously, allows for the articulation of opposing attitudes and contradictory literary forms together.

Wilde identifies two forms of irony which are characteristic of modernism and postmodernism respectively: the 'disjunctive' and the 'suspensive'. Disjunctive irony is the response to a world perceived to be in fragments, and represents the desire simultaneously to be true to incoherence and to transcend it. Typically, in the works of Woolf and Joyce, who provide Wilde with his instances, radical incoherence is not 'resolved' or 'unified' in the manner imagined by I. A. Richards and Cleanth Brooks, but controlled by being projected in the form of binary conflicts (flesh and spirit, self and society). Paradox and disconnection are thus not redeemed, but delimited within a recognizable aesthetic shape. Joyce's *A Portrait of the Artist as a Young Man* provides an example of this aestheticizing. The text offers us no definitive way of reading it, hovering as it does between approval and ironic disapproval of its central character Stephen Dedalus. But, for Wilde, the novel derives its shape and integrity precisely from this formal projection of alternatives: 'Isn't the locus of the irony precisely the aesthetic and aestheticizing consciousness unable to solve or resolve the dilemma it posits, except by hovering over it in the sublimity of form?' (*HA*, 40).

In fact, this solution (not really a solution at all, more a neurotic containment of a problem) marks an imminent crisis. Disorder fixed in this way into the rictus of the aesthetic only internalizes pressures which are to erupt to the surface with postmodernism. In postmodernism, says Wilde, the disjunctive irony of modernism gives way to suspensive irony. Suspensive irony marks an intensification of the awareness of incoherence, to the point where it seems no longer capable of being accounted for and contained even in the ordering frames of the aesthetic, along with a decline in the need for order, and consequent lowering of organizational intensity. Postmodernist 'suspensive' irony is, therefore, the mark of an art grown out of modernist tantrums, which combines a tough-minded knowledge of the worst of incoherence and alienation with a benignly well-adjusted tolerance towards them; as Wilde puts it, 'an indecision about the meanings or relations of things is matched by a willingness to live with uncertainty, to tolerate, and, in some cases, to welcome a world seen as random and multiple, even, at times, absurd' (*HA*, 45). In postmodernism, 'a world in need of mending is superseded by one beyond repair' (*HA*, 131).

Wilde struggles against the transcendent idea of literature which dominates Hassan's account. Firstly, he finds in postmodernist literature a mistrust of the idea of depth, the idea that the inconstant spray of phenomena conceals secret and universal principles of truth. The need for depth brings with it the desire for origins, whether it be in the form of a return to the primitive, or of the desire for moments of intensity – the epiphany in Joyce, the moment of vision in Woolf. The metaphysics of depth is associated, Wilde says, with an aesthetic of detachment in modernism; the notion that the way to grasp the underlying principles of things is to retract oneself from them to a position of percipience. None of this is possible or desirable after the passing of modernism. Instead of the metaphysics of the hidden, postmodernism asserts 'that truth inheres in the visible' (*HA*, 108). Since there is nothing other than appearance, then, equally, there is no conceivable position of detachment from which one might hope to survey the field of appearances. Under postmodernism, one is always irretrievably *in* the world, which is organized, if at all, in local, temporary structures, which operate without reference to secret or final causes.

It is this involvement in the world which embodies Wilde's resistance to claims for the transcendence of art, and for this reason he gives short shrift to those writers like Ronald Sukenick, Raymond Federman and the school of American 'Surfictionists' who, in announcing that the novel 'invents its own reality', recirculate the rhetoric of the artist's supreme and unconditioned artistic freedom.[11] The postmodernist fiction that Wilde admires (the work of Donald Barthelme, Max Apple and Stanley Elkin) does not aim to abstract the world through structures of imaginative control, or absent itself from reality; it is modestly engaged in experiencing the world, overcoming or modifying the disorder of appearances through a generous absorption in them. This is the poetics of assent, writes Wilde, a vision which 'attempts to activate consciousness as a whole, making of its relationship with the world something dynamic, kinetic and reciprocal' (*HA*, 154).

There is undoubtedly something attractive in this friendly reaccommodation between text and world, but it has its own kind of abstractedness, too. For Wilde, the world is a cosy, welcoming place that, given the right positive attitude towards it, shapes itself into congruity with the self, hugging its contours like a comfortable quilt. This is to say that, in opposing himself to the abstractedness of modernism as well as some forms of postmodernist fiction, Wilde underestimates the determinate forms of negation which create real historical alienation. The alienation of modernist art and its anxious attempts to negotiate incoherence are not just the result of a failure of will, or elitist *hauteur*, they are the marks of actual struggles over meaning. The condition of this kind of alienation is not to be overcome simply by shrugging one's shoulders or pulling one's socks up. Wilde's position is therefore opposite to that of Hassan. Where Hassan seeks to protect literature from conflict and contamination by aesthetically distancing it from the world, Wilde's postmodernism bypasses conflict by simply submerging the literary in the nonaesthetic other of the world.

Beyond Spatialism

One of the most striking preoccupations of modernist and postmodernist aesthetics in literature is the question of time. Clearly, the obsession with time in all its senses is to be found throughout modernism, from the massive imaginative archaeology of time past to be found in Proust's *A la recherche du temps perdu* to the fragmentation of clock-time into mythic time in Eliot's *The Waste Land*, the melding of contemporary time and the times of history in Joyce's *Ulysses* and Pound's *Cantos*, and the visions of cyclical or universal time in Joyce's *Finnegans Wake* and Yeats's *A Vision*. Although things are as complex and various here as anywhere else in literary modernism, contemporary accounts have tended to assume that the modernist challenge to bourgeois clock-time can be reduced to a single principle – the flattening of time into space. To run together the time of epic with contemporary time, or to view history and human life as an endless series of cycles, is to attempt to defeat transience, by bending it into pattern. Even those writers (and there were many) who followed Henri Bergson's counsel that time should be rendered as pure and fluid process rather than artificially frozen into instants, found themselves condemned to spatialize or suspend time in attempting to be true to it. Virginia Woolf's 'moments of vision' and Joyce's 'epiphanies' are both instances of the distillation of time into spatial significance, time yielding its meaning by being suspended.[12] Clearly such a vision of spatialized time works easily alongside the modernist requirement of aesthetic autonomy; for, if the passage of time is what threatens every achievement of stasis, every moment of significance seized from the flux, then the denial of time is what might seem to guarantee the unyielding, unchanging permanence of the work of art.

One of the most powerfully and consistently articulated critiques of the spatialist norm of modernism is to be found in the work of W. V. Spanos, and the journal that he has edited since 1972, *Boundary* 2. Spanos offers as evidence of spatializing thought such things as the modernist cult of the timeless moment of being, or epiphany, the concentration of time into the sculpted essential instant in Imagism and what he sees as the thematic defeat of time in works such as Proust's *A la recherche du temps perdu* and Joyce's *Ulysses*, which, although they both seem to allow themselves to be saturated by the exigencies of personal and historical time, do so to the ultimate end of thwarting or subduing time, in order, in Joyce's words, to 'awaken from the nightmare of history'. The literary spatialization of time via the distilled instant or the flattened circle of recurrence is complemented by the methods of the New Criticism, which similarly arrest the open-ended existence of a text and its readings through time by seeing that text as an icon or 'well-wrought urn' that blends and binds tensions and contraries into a timeless unity. Along with this goes a belief in the power of criticism, which positions itself outside all the imprecisions and partialities of the reading process at the moment of ideal, total comprehension, as projected in the neutral gaze of metaphysics. (Spanos explains this last term by etymology, saying that metaphysics aims to see things as they are from the outside – *meta-ta-physica*, from above or beyond the physical.)[13]

Postmodern literature breaks from this by emphasizing the contingent flow of temporarily at the expense of the atemporal stasis of metaphysics. Spanos argues that in the work of contemporary American poets like Robert Creeley and Charles Olson, the process of reading and composition is highlighted against the still contemplation of meaning.[14] An apt metaphor for this kind of poetry is the *periplus*, a term that Ezra Pound used to describe the technique of his *Cantos*. A periplus is a map that projects the stages of a journey as they succeed each other for the traveller, as opposed to a map that gives an image from outside and above the terrain of every point on it simultaneously. Such a map forms a temporal narrative rather than a spatial image.

Spanos's critique of the metaphysical bases of modernist aesthetics derives from the work of Martin Heidegger, which is unstintingly devoted to understanding questions of 'being' and identity' not as essential and unhistorical principles, but as grounded in the particularity of historical circumstances – 'being-in-the-world' rather than abstract Being. This Heideggerian perspective promotes dynamic movement over the static presence of pure ideas or pure being, and similarly denies the possibility of any disinterested or objective act of interpretation, insisting that all such acts must be from a particular perspective and therefore 'interested', or involved in its material. Heidegger's aim, which Spanos shares, is the 'de-struction' of traditional forms of frozen hermeneutic disinterest, and the opening of texts and their readers to the play of opinions and partialities through time. For Spanos, this is the purpose of formal reflexivity in postmodern writing – not, as in modernism, to promote and assert the integrity of the artistic medium, closing it off against time, but to dislodge the reader from his or her position of spatializing command outside time:

> Postmodern literature not only thematizes time in the breakdown of metaphysics following the 'death of God' (or at any rate the death of God as Omega), but also makes the 'medium' itself the 'message' in the sense that its function is to perform a Heideggerian 'de-struction' of the traditional metaphysical frame of reference, that is, to accomplish the phenomenological reduction of the spatial perspective by formal violence, thus, like Kierkegaard, leaving the reader *inter esse* – a naked and unaccommodated being-in-the-world, a Dasein in the place of origins, where time is ontologically prior to being.[15]

Spanos argues the necessity, alongside this, of a postmodern literary criticism which will engage with the open temporary of a text, in the interests of breaking the interpretative will-to-power of criticism, which always construes a text from the standpoint of its ultimate or single timeless meaning. For a postmodern criticism 'what was conceived as an artifact to be read from a printed page, an image to be looked at from a distance, an It to be mastered, becomes "oral speech" to be heard immediately in time'.[16] Spanos is for this reason particularly interested in the explorations by poets such as David Antin of improvized or oral poetry. In contrast to Derrida, who regards the privileging of the idea of voice as a metaphysical desire for pure meaning, Spanos is fascinated by the exploration of 'the real, the occasional speech of temporally and historically situated human beings'.[17]

Other theorists of postmodern poetry have followed Spanos in his stress upon the poetry of the particular and the contingent, rather than of the abstract and the eternal. Charles Altieri finds a metaphor for this in the title of a volume by David Antin, *Tuning* (1984). Like Antin's previous work, *Talking* (1972) and *Talking at the Boundaries* (1976), the volume is a collection of the improvized anecdotal reflections which Antin has performed at various locations and in various contexts (Antin stresses, indeed, that the volumes are not the poems themselves, but only transcriptions of them). In some of his work, for example, the poem 'Talking at Pomona' from the collection *Talking*, Antin sets himself to consider precisely the question of whether there can be an art which is more fundamentally responsive to the experience of being in the world than the abstraction of modernism. In his talk-poems, Antin can be seen actually negotiating this problem, attempting, as Altieri says, 'to compose a space less exalted by its own differences from the real and more responsive to the possibility of continually testing the construct by its implications for our practices when we are not rapt before an art object'.[18] When talk poetry of this kind reflects on its own practice the effect is not to confirm the meaning-giving authority of the poet, but to draw author and audience into an interactive collusion:

> In this situation to accomplish anything together at all we have to find out what the other person's pace is we have to find what our pace is . . . we have to adjust our paces each to the other
> so that we can come more or less into step . . . it is this kind of negotiation which I would like to call 'tuning'[19]

For Marjorie Perloff, this relaxation of tension in postmodernist poetry distinguishes itself as a movement beyond the domination of the lyric in modernism, that poetic form 'in which the isolated speaker (whether or not the poet himself), located in a specific landscape, meditates or ruminates on some aspect of his or her relationship to the external world, coming finally to some sort of epiphany, a moment of insight with which the poem closes'.[20] This movement out of the 'impasse' of the lyric involves a new toleration of narrative. Although narrative exists in the modernist poetry of Yeats, Eliot and Stevens, it is often a closed and egocentric form of narrative, which rotates around single images or limited image-clusters, in the interests of the 'expression of a moment of absolute insight, of emotion crystallized into timeless patterns'.[21] Postmodernist poetry returns to narrative of a less exalted, less egocentric kind, a narrative which is hospitable to the loose, the contingent, the unformed and the incomplete in language and experience. Correspondingly, such poetry embraces casual and unpoetic forms of language like letters, journals, conversation, anecdotes, and news reports. For Perloff, the founding father of this form of poetry is Ezra Pound, and his *Cantos* testify to the emergence within modernism itself of a postmodernist poetry of historical openness; *The Cantos* blur the distinctions between poetic and everyday language, dissolve the centring principle of the Romantic author-self and, in their multiplication and intercalation of different historical time-frames, remain unfinished, temporary, and porous to historical process. Pound's legacy includes work like Louis Zukovsky's 800-page poem *A*, written between 1928 and 1974, whose freely-incorporative collage-mode enacts 'experience as always unfinished, indeed as always only potential – moving toward something that never quite happens', the improvised or performance poems of John Cage and David Antin, and the work of L=A=N=G=U=A=G=E group poets such as Ron Silliman and Charles Bernstein, who use puns and wordplay to reaffirm the historical materiality of words in a culture that consistently ignores or effaces this materiality.[22]

Others have characterized postmodernist poetry in similar terms. For Jerome Mazzaro, one of the most important marks of post-modernism (which he finds instanced not so much by Charles Olson, Robert Creeley, John Cage and David Antin, as by an earlier generation of American poets which includes the later Auden, Randall Jarrell, Theodore Roethke, John Berryman and Elizabeth Bishop) is its renewed hospitality to the long poem, and simultaneous suspicion of the cult of impersonality. Mazzaro diagnoses in postmodernism an acceptance of the fallen, contingent nature of language, which stands in marked contrast to the desire of the modernist poet to remake or purify language in the form of the lyric. The result is a greater spread and variability of poetic forms:

The formulation of the essential differences between 'modernism' and
'postmodernism' becomes: in conceiving of language as a fall from unity,
modernism seeks to restore the original state often by proposing silence or
the destruction of language; postmodernism accepts the division and uses
language and self-definition much as Descartes interpreted thinking – as the
basis of identity. Modernism tends, as a consequence, to be more mystical
in the traditional senses of that word, whereas postmodernism, for all its
seeming mysticism, is irrevocably worldly and social.[23]

If theorists of postmodernist poetry have tended increasingly to embrace
nonpoetic literary genres, then this may be part of a more general swing
away from the dominance of poetry, or a modernist definition of the
poetic. We might say that, in the modernist period, the values invested in
poetry, unity, autonomy of form, concentration and completeness, were
paramount and were actually transposed to the novel; correspondingly, the
project of writers like James, Joyce and Woolf was construed as the
organization of the messy open-endedness of fiction into closely-packed
'poetic' structures, via tight patterning, symbolic recurrence, and so on.
The modernist impulse to subvert or transform narrative conventions can
therefore be seen, as Matei Calinescu suggests, not as an attempt to
liberate narrative itself, but rather to harness its dangerous or distracting
energies; this view depends on the belief that 'standards of literary
composition are to be looked for in poetry, in its self-contained and
self-sufficient character, in its "epiphanic" nature, and ultimately in its
stubborn resistance to any kind of linguistic "displacement" – summary,
commentary, recounting, translation – were notoriously unable to capture
the "ineffable" essence of the poem'.[24]

In contrast to this, it certainly seems as though the values associated
with fiction or narrative, open-endedness, extension in time, generic
impurity, have come to hold sway in postmodernist literary theory.
Calinescu and others associate this with a move towards narrative modes
of thought in other areas, in anthropology, theology and philosophy.
Thomas Docherty's interesting call for a 'chrono-political' hermeneutic
similarly aims to move away from the notion of the timeless, static poetic
text. Where modern and modernist criticism constitutes its text simply as
a kind of 'noun' whose proper name is to be enunciated by the act of
criticism, Docherty proposes a Bergsonian vision of the text as a 'verb'
and therefore as 'a space characterized not by its spatial identity or
difference but rather by its *temporal* difference from itself; that is, a text
conditioned by its historicity or by the temporal dimension of its civil war
with itself'.[25]

But this stress on the temporal extensiveness of narrative has curiously not been so dominant within the most influential theorists of postmodernist fiction. If there is wide and public agreement that the postmodernist spirit in literature is best exemplified in the fictions of such writers as Samuel Beckett, John Barth, Donald Barthelme, Thomas Pynchon, Don DeLillo and William Burroughs in English, Peter Handke in German, Italo Calvino in Italian, and Jorge Luis Borges, Julio Cortázar and Carlos Fuentes in Spanish, then this is not on the grounds that these writers restore simply and unproblematically the rhythm of narrative unfolding through time. Instead, the most influential accounts of postmodernist fiction stress the prevalence of parodic 'metafiction', or the exploration by literary texts of their own nature and status as fiction.[26]

Ontology and Metafiction

Many accounts of postmodernist fiction lay emphasis on the capacity of fiction to create and sustain worlds. If modernist fiction – *Ulysses*, say, or *Pilgrimage*, or *The Sound and the Fury* – uses techniques such as interior monologue and the collaging of separate minds and points of view in the service of an enlarged and more subtly responsive realism, fiction like that of Alain Robbe-Grillet employs its innovative techniques to the end of creating pure and autonomous worlds (it is not so much that this kind of fiction creates worlds of pure fantasy, as that it no longer seeks to suppress its own part in the making of fiction). One of the earliest formulations of this principle is to be found in Robbe-Grillet's *Towards a New Novel*, in which he insists that the novel should own up to its own fictionalizing function. This can produce in Robbe-Grillet's own work a purely combinatorial mode of composition, as in his *In the Labyrinth*, which is a multiplicity of false starts, digressions, variations and repetitions on a number of narrative themes, arising from the wanderings of a soldier around a strange town; these variations come to constitute the novel itself. Samuel Beckett's novels from *Molloy* onwards similarly require us to remain aware all the time of the process by which the fiction we are reading is coming painfully into being on the page. Since the French 'new novel' of the 1950s and 1960s, a veritable epidemic of reflexivity has swept the fiction-writing world, from the work of American writers like William Gass (who declares that 'there are no descriptions in literature, there are only constructions'), to the ostentatious puzzle-making of Borges, the Scheherezade-like improvisations of John Barth, the fables of Italo Calvino and the nightmarish fairytales of Robert Coover.

One question that nags at theorists of postmodernist fiction is how all this differs from the obvious preoccupation with their own fictionality displayed by modernist texts like *Ulysses* and *To the Lighthouse*. One answer to this is given by Brian McHale, who suggests that there has been a shift in the dominant tendency of twentieth-century fiction. He argues that the modernist novel of the earlier twentieth century was concerned above all with epistemological questions – that is, with questions having to do with knowledge and interpretation – so that the plurality of techniques in the modernist novel is induced by anxieties about what can be truthfully known, understood and communicated about the world. The dominating concerns of the modernist novel are, therefore, with the limits and possibilities of individual consciousness, or the difficult relationships between separate subjectivities. In the end, stylistic multiplicity can always be explained or 'recuperated' by a theory of psychology; generations of students, for example, have become competent in reading the opening pages of Joyce's *Portrait of the Artist as a Young Man* as a rendering of the thoughts and feelings of a child in the language of infancy (and never mind the contradiction contained in those last two words, the fact that Joyce is writing as a child would if it had adult language).

McHale suggests that this kind of epistemological concern has given way in the postmodernist epoch to an ontological concern. Where epistemology is the study of knowledge and understanding, ontology is the study of the nature of being and existence; but McHale uses the term in a slightly more specific way. According to McHale, the ontological character of the postmodernist novel is shown in its concern with the making of autonomous worlds. So, instead of asking questions about how a world may be known, postmodernist fiction asks questions like 'What is a world?; What kinds of world are there, how are they constituted, and how do they differ?; What happens when different kinds of world are placed in confrontation, or when boundaries between worlds are violated?'[27]

McHale recognizes that epistemological and ontological concerns are by no means mutually exclusive, for to ask about how a world is constituted and how it differs from other possible worlds is always to ask implicitly about the conditions of that world's comprehensibility. We are involved here, not in an absolute transformation, but in rather a shift of emphasis or literary-philosophical 'dominant'. The ontological dominant means that the recuperation of distortion, deviation and other non-realistic effects as the effects of distorted or intensified consciousness is no longer possible. Instead, the worlds summoned up by literary texts are grounded simply in their own textual mechanisms; subjectivity gives way to textuality. McHale gives a number of examples of the movement from epistemological modernism to ontological postmodernism, but perhaps the most instructive is Alain Robbe-Grillet's novel *Jealousy*. The novel is constructed entirely according to the limited point of view of a jealous husband spying on his wife and her lover, except that the husband is never identified as the viewer. Point of view has therefore shrunk to the condition of a pure, unembodied textual function, a cinematic aperture which allows the action to be seen and reported. In Robbe-Grillet's later novels like *In the Labyrinth*, it is only with difficulty that we can read the puzzling involutions of the narrative as the ramblings of a shell-shocked soldier, and in other Robbe-Grillet novels it is no longer possible at all.

There is no shortage of examples of this building of textual worlds and McHale's book is an inventory of all the different forms of it to be found in the recent fiction produced in Europe, the US and Latin America. The book offers a hedge against being taken absolutely literally, since it emphasizes that its theory is a kind of construction rather than an exact tabulation of the facts. But it remains true that the book aspires to offer a detached 'poetics' of the postmodernist novel, a catalogue of the motifs and devices which would enable one to recognize and securely identify any example of the genre or movement. McHale's account is characterized by a serene belief in the givenness of the category of literature, or the 'literary system', and is unafraid of the charge of metaphysical illusion in announcing its search for the 'underlying systematicity' of postmodernist literature.[28] Curiously, this goes alongside a critical account which from time to time stresses the plurality of forms and languages in the postmodernist literary text. Mikhail Bakhtin's account of the plural, competing discourses to be found within the novel is enlisted to give a sheen to McHale's account of the postmodernist literary condition; where other genres are tight-fistedly 'monologic' in their stylistic regularity, McHale says, postmodernist fiction is a carnivalesque interweaving of styles, voices and registers which allegedly disrupts the decorous hierarchy of literary genres. But this kind of carnivalization is bent back into the smooth historical regularity of literary history, considered by McHale as a regularly developing organism or genealogy. If literary postmodernism can be defined as McHale wishes to define it, as a riotous cacophony of conflicting discourses or 'heterotopia' of incompatible geographies, then a strange kind of constraint is being exercised to leave the category of the literary an unanalysed or unanalysable blank, or as an elastic frame which expands obediently to contain every kind of subversion.

Other accounts of postmodernist poetics do not rely upon such an obviously stable model of the literary. Linda Hutcheon, for example, sees the most characteristic form of postmodernist literature as 'historiographic metafiction'.[29] By this she means works of fiction which reflect knowingly upon their own status as fiction, foregrounding the figure of the author and the act of writing, and even violently interrupting the conventions of the novel, but without relapsing into mere technical self-absorption. She focuses on works like Salman Rushdie's *Shame*, D. M. Thomas's *The White Hotel*, Ishmael Reed's *Mumbo Jumbo*, Robert Coover's *The Public Burning* and E. L. Doctorow's *The Book of Daniel*, all of which take as their ostensible subject characters and events from known history, but then subject them to distortion, falsification and fictionalization. The essential point, for Hutcheon, is that such texts expose the fictionality of history itself. These texts deny the possibility of a clearly sustainable distinction between history and fiction, by highlighting the fact that we can only ever know history through various forms of representation or narrative. In this sense, all history is a kind of literature.

For this reason, Hutcheon withholds the designation 'postmodernist' from the pure reflexivity promoted by other postmodern theorists, such as the French New Novel, or the surfiction of Raymond Federman and Ronald Sukenick. The literary work which is about nothing else but its own verbal textures is, in Hutcheon's terms, 'ultra-modernist' rather than truly postmodernist, for postmodernism involves the re-angling of literary self-reflectiveness back to the real, historical world. This is achieved through a neat paradox; for, while modernist literature had been contentedly grooming itself in self-reflective seclusion from what it took to be a solidly and mutely undiscursive real world, the real world had turned into literature – into a matter of texts, representations, discourses. The link between text and world is reforged in postmodernism, not by an effacement of the text in the interests of a return to the real, but by an intensification of textuality such that it becomes coextensive with the real. Once the real has been rendered into discourse, there is no longer any gap to be leapt between text and world.

Hutcheon's model of literary postmodernism, therefore, in one sense fundamentally contradicts Hassan's or McHale's, in that it seems to undermine the underlying essence of the literary. Literature is revealed in Hutcheon's account as no longer simply, transcendently itself, for 'historiographic metafiction' is always part of a larger set of discursive practices, that is to say, languages and linguistic rules conditioned by their relationship to specific social institutions or relationships and having a close and effective role in relationships of power. Along with other theorists of the postmodern in literature and elsewhere, Hutcheon welcomes the crossing of generic or disciplinary boundaries, the infiltration of history into literature and the blurring of the distinctions between literature and theory.

What is not clear, however, is the degree to which this alleged undermining of the literary acts in the service of any actual or effective form of subversion. Literature departments and such 'para-academic' institutions as publishing, journalism and arts broadcasting have undoubtedly been threatened to a certain degree by such loosening definitions of what 'literature', the cohering object of their activity, really is. But it is also true that what characterizes literary study, which is still the most institutionally rooted and secure of disciplines in the humanities, is its extraordinary capacity to assimilate such intellectual challenges and mobilize them in its own interests. And in fact, one of the clearest forms in which radical or unsettling theory is currently being operationalized is in the deployment of the category of the postmodernist literary text. Self-conscious, decentred, sceptical and playfully polymorphous, the postmodernist literary text from Borges to Beckett to Rushdie is an ideal object of analysis for a theory of reading which has grown suspicious of every form of identity or fixity, but still requires some object upon which to practise. Postmodernist literature obediently falls into step with the motifs and preoccupations of institutionalized post-structuralist theory (and naturally, it is hard to imagine what form a non-institutionalized or 'amateur' post-structuralist theory might possibly take), resonating in sympathy with all its hermeneutic requirements. More importantly, the postmodernist literary text – or prevailing critical conceptions of the postmodernist literary text – serves to concentrate radical or sceptical theory into an institutionally usable form, allowing the business of the literary academy – the interpretation of texts, the production and accreditation of readings and methodologies – to go on as usual.

It is precisely because of this extreme adaptability that the discipline of literary study, and, in particular, the discipline of English, have been able to survive and even to thrive on such apparently lethal doses of radical theory. Indeed, although literary departments were for a period the beneficiaries of this theory developed elsewhere, the institutional centrality and prestige of such departments is clearly evidenced in the way in which this flow is being reversed, with literary studies now looking for ways to diversify into the areas which had previously provided them with so much theoretical capital, like philosophy and cultural studies. Indeed, far from being a net importer of theoretical ideas, literary study may now often act as a kind of hothouse in which exotic forms of theory may be incubated before being transferred to other, less immediately hospitable intellectual climates. This is not to mention the new intellectual market in theoretical stars and personalities, in which literary study leads the field.

Let this not be mistaken for the crassness of mere antitheoreticism, or taken as a call for a return to some fantasized consensus of ideas about truth, beauty or traditional values. Theory is the name that we give to the process by which all such absolute claims are remorselessly put to the question, and should therefore be the name that we give to civilization and culture themselves. My suggestion is, however, that theory can – and perhaps to a degree always must – act simultaneously as a way of containing or regularizing the implications of intellectual self-scrutiny. Postmodern literary theory, in the dual sense of a dominant set of ideas and critical practices (characterized by post-structuralism and deconstruction), and a theory of a dominant mode of contemporary literature, may experience and project itself in a mode of euphoric crisis, but to interpret its operations entirely in these terms is to make the common mistake of only attending to the manifest *content* of that theory, rather than assessing its discursive effects: looking at what it says, rather than at what it does.

Possible Worlds: Science Fiction and Cyberpunk

One of the most remarkable developments in postmodernist writing and writing about postmodern writing during the 1980s has been the increased prominence and standing of science fiction, especially that brand of science fiction known as 'cyberpunk', identified especially with the work of such writers as William Gibson, Bruce Sterling, John Shirley and Greg Bear, which concerns itself with the postmodern technologies of media, information and bioengineering. Science fiction is a particularly intriguing case for postmodernist theory, precisely because the genre of science fiction belongs, chronologically at least, to the period of modernism's emergence. In fact, 'genre' or 'classic' science fiction may be seen as a kind of mass-cultural accompaniment or counterpoint to the distinctively modernist experiments of the first half of the century. Where modernist works such as *Ulysses*, *Pilgrimage* and *The Waves* often combined formal experimentation with a familiar and ultimately realistic content, science fiction employed more conventional or realistic fictional modes to render less familiar or impossible worlds. Modernism experimented with ways of seeing and saying the real; science fiction experimented realistically with forms of reality themselves. From the 1970s onwards, as a result perhaps of the shift of dominant spoken of by Brian McHale, the epistemological distinction between narrated world and narrative mode gradually closed, as 'literary' fiction took over from science fiction the 'ontological' interest in creating and exploring other and multiple worlds. The challenges to inherited notions of narrative form posed by Thomas Pynchon's *Gravity's Rainbow*, Angela Carter's *The Infernal Desire Machines of Dr. Hoffmann* or Christine Brooke-Rose's *Xorandor*, for instance, were inseparable from the nested proliferation of different worlds or orders of reality in those narratives. As literary fiction borrowed more and more deeply from science fiction, so science fiction itself drew upon the kinds of formal innovation being developed in literary fiction, as well as from the analyses being developed within postmodernist cultural theory. As Brian McHale suggests, cyberpunk, as a particular kind of science fiction 'which derives certain of its elements from postmodernist mainstream fiction which itself has, in its turn, already been "science-fictionized" to some greater or lesser degree' provides evidence, not of the collapse of cultural distinctions, but of the acceleration of their alternation.[30]

This came about particularly because of a new sense that reality had begun to catch up with science fiction, rendering its proliferation of possible worlds ever more plausible as a realistic representation of prevailing contemporary conditions, especially those brought about by the development of digitized experiences. Science fiction comes to correspond to the reality of technological society because that society has become in the meantime science-fictionized; as Jonathan Benison has suggested, 'it has become possible . . . to envisage our world as (merely) a "possible world" '.[31] This accounts perhaps for the curious blend of the familiar and the futural in much contemporary science fiction. This is especially true of cyberpunk, which blends the evocation of extravagant technological possibilities with the most hard-bitten and unillusioned of narrative styles, borrowed from the historical forms of the detective story and the *film noir*, which choke off the exhilaration of futurity. Classic or quasi-modernist science fiction extrapolated a future from the present, establishing both a logical continuity and a fictive distinction between the present and the future. Contemporary science fiction is characterized by a more complex mixture of temporal modes, in which the rich potentiality of the future appears somehow already used up and out of date. Hence the strange compounding, in works such as William Gibson's *Count Zero* and *Mona Lisa Overdrive* and Bruce Sterling's *Schismatrix*, of technological hyper-development and decrepitude, the sense of simultaneous expectation and exhaustion. The cinematic visualization of this temporal ambivalence is to be found in the darkened, oppressive urban environments of films like Terry Gilliam's *Brazil* and Ridley Scott's *Blade Runner*. Such fictions constitute a meditation upon the vocation of science fiction to posit and actualize futures, setting the space of fictional extrapolated alterity within a frame of weary retrospection, in a kind of futural version of the historiographic metafiction described by Linda Hutcheon. The variation upon cyberpunk known as 'steampunk', in which the evocation of futurity is grafted on to the rewriting of the history of classical or modern technologies, as in William Gibson's and Bruce Sterling's *The Difference Engine*, confirms this looping together of the historical and the speculative.

Some commentators have seen cyberpunk and related science fiction as a kind of anticipatory phenomenology, a means of imaginative orientation to the distinctive and disorientating experiences of digital culture. Scott Bukatman explores the development of what he calls, borrowing a phrase from William Burroughs, 'terminal identity' – to signify the simultaneous fading out of subjectivity in the diffused simulations of cyberspace and its regathering in that new 'scene' of postmodern experience, the interface with the video or the computer screen. Tracking the fascination with the shifting, indefinite, but strangely consoling 'consensual hallucination' of cyberspace, through the fiction of William Gibson, Bruce Sterling and Walter Jon Williams, and its cinematic correlates such as *TRON*, *Video-drome* and the *Terminator* films, Bukatman focuses upon the dissolution of the boundaries between humans and machines, and the reforming of the body, either in bio-digital simulation, or in sometimes monstrous bio-mechanical amalgams.

Particularly important to Bukatman's conception of what he calls the 'virtual subject' of such postmodern science fiction are the new relations between selves and the spaces they inhabit. Cyberpunk acquaints the self, accustomed to thinking of itself in visual-spatial terms, as a point or a visible volume moving determinately through an actual coherent space, with the shifting and fluid as if spaces of spectacle and data. Interestingly, narrative fiction, which traditionally requires the reader to build imaginary spaces from the prompts provided by language, has an advantage over more directly visual media such as film, in which the very presentness and immediacy of the visual spectacle may be a kind of distraction from the activity of construction essential to the experience of cyberspace. Film may just insist too much on the phenomenality of vision, when what counts in the evocation of cyberspace is the invisibility of the structures that contain and connect information, and the projection of imaginary spaces that lie behind or between what is given on the computer screen.

Bukatman convincingly isolates two contrasting modes in the evocation of cyberspace. On the one hand there is the surrender of the subject to the experience of the 'parallel spaces' of contemporary science fiction, within which 'the reader finds a polymorphous stage for the dissolution of ontological boundaries; for the collision of competing and transmutating worlds', and which 'stage the breakdown of language, rationality, and subjectivity'.[32] There is both fear and exhilaration in this loss of subjective definition and fixity. At the same time, the very notion of a 'staging' or visual scene implies something like a compensatory mechanism, in which the subject conjures the illusion of location and inhabitable space out of such radically derealizing experiences. As one character thinks to herself in Gibson's *Mona Lisa Overdrive*, '*There's no there, there*': the oxymoron expressing the sense of paradoxical persistence of place even within its denegation.[33] Cyberpunk is a way both of estranging the reader/viewer and of habituating him or her to this condition of estrangement. Such fictions create as it were temporary utopia out of atopia.

In one sense such fictions point to the final collapse of the autonomy of the word, in a world of ever more immediate sensory stimulations and simulations, and ever more complex sensory amalgams. At the same time, as we have seen, the very immateriality of the word gives it a kind of epistemological advantage, building into the short-circuit of media stimulation and response a time-lapse which allows for the possibility of reflection and differentiation. This is perhaps why cyberpunk fiction can prompt such judgements as that of Fredric Jameson, when he declares that it is 'the supreme *literary* expression if not of postmodernism, then of late capitalism itself'.[34] Cyberpunk not only helps to make the estranged conditions of contemporary technology familiar and livable, it also, like the theory which speaks on its behalf, reflects on the strangeness of the habituation it effects.

Notes

1 I. A. Richards, *Principles of Literary Criticism* (London: Routledge and Kegan Paul, 1924).

2 See Terry Eagleton, 'The End of English', *Textual Practice*, 1:1 (1987), pp. 1–9.

3 Charles Newman, *The Aura of Postmodernism: The Act of Fiction in an Age of Inflation* (Evanston: Northwestern, University Press, 1985), pp. 27–35.

4 Helmut Lethen, 'Modernism Cut in Half: The Exclusion of the Avant-Garde and the Debate on Postmodernism', in *Approaching Postmodernism*, ed. Hans Bertens and Douwe Fokkema (Philadelphia and Amsterdam: John Benjamins, 1986), p. 233.

5 Andreas Huyssen, *Beyond the Great Divide: Modernism, Mass Culture, Postmodernism* (Bloomington: Indiana University Press, 1986), pp. 206–16.

6 Virginia Woolf, 'Modern Fiction' (1925), in *Collected Essays*, vol. 2 (London: Hogarth Press, 1966), pp. 106–7. For this view of modernism, see Michael Levenson, *A Genealogy of Modernism* (Cambridge: Cambridge University Press, 1984), pp. 1–22.

7   Repr. in *The Collected Essays of Leslie Fiedler*, Vol. 2 (New York: Stein and Day, 1971), pp. 461–85.
8   For further consideration of the use of popular genres in postmodern fiction, see Stefano Tani, *The Doomed Detective: The Contribution of the Detective Novel to Postmodern American and Italian Fiction* (Carbondale and Edwardsville: Southern Illinois University Press, 1984) and Theo D'Haen, 'Popular Genre Conventions in Postmodern Fiction: The Case of the Western', in *Exploring Postmodernism*, ed. Matei Calinescu and Douwe Fokkema (Amsterdam and Philadelphia: John Benjamins, 1987), pp. 161–74.
9   *The Dismemberment of Orpheus: Towards a Postmodern Literature*, 2nd edn. (New York: Oxford University Press, 1982), p. xvii. References hereafter to *TPL* in the text.
10 *Horizons of Assent: Modernism, Postmodernism and the Ironic Imagination* (Baltimore: Johns Hopkins University Press, 1981). References hereafter to *HA* in the text.
11 See Raymond Federman, 'Fiction Today, or the Pursuit of Non-Knowledge', *Humanities in Society*, 1:2 (1978), p. 122, and the essays collected by Federman under the title *Surfiction: Fiction Now and Tomorrow*, first published 1975 (Chicago: Swallow Press, 1981).
12 See Joseph Frank, 'Spatial Form in Modern Literature', in *The Widening Gyre* (Bloomington: Indiana University Press, 1963), pp. 3–62.
13 Outi Pasanen, 'Postmodernism: An Interview With William V. Spanos', *Arbeiten aus Anglistik und Amerikanistik*, 11:2 (1986), p. 197.
14 William V. Spanos, 'Heidegger, Kierkegaard and the Hermeneutic Circle: Towards a Postmodern Theory of Interpretation as Disclosure', in *Martin Heidegger and the Question of Literature: Toward a Postmodern Literary Hermeneutics*, ed. William V. Spanos (Bloomington: Indiana University Press, 1979), p. 121.
15 Ibid., p. 135.
16 Ibid., p. 139.
17 Pasanen, 'Interview with W. V. Spanos', p. 206.
18 'The Postmodernism of David Antin's *Tuning*', *College English*, 48:1 (1986), p. 13.
19 David Antin, *Tuning* (New York: New Directions, 1984), p. 130.
20 'The Return of Story in Postmodern Poetry', in *The Dance of the Intellect: Studies in the Poetry of the Pound Tradition* (Cambridge: Cambridge University Press, 1985), pp. 156–7.
21 'Postmodernism and the Impasse of Lyric', ibid., p. 181.
22 'Postmodernism and the Impasse of Lyric', ibid., p. 185; 'The Word as Such: L=A=N=G=U=A=G=E Poetry in the Eighties', ibid., pp. 215–38; ' "No More Margins": John Cage, David Antin, and the Poetry of Performance', in *The Poetics of Indeterminacy: Rimbaud to Cage* (Evanston: Northwestern University Press, 1981), pp. 288–340.
23 *Postmodern American Poetry* (Chicago: University of Illinois Press, 1980), p. viii.

24 'Ways of Looking at Fiction', in *Romanticism, Modernism, Postmodernism*, ed. Harry R. Gavin (Lewisburg, PA: Bucknell University Press, 1980), p. 156.
25 *After Theory: Postmodernism/Postmarxism* (London: Routledge, 1990), p. 50.
26 See Linda Hutcheon, *Narcissistic Narrative: The Metafictional Paradox* (Waterloo, Ont.: Wilfred Laurier University Press, 1980).
27 *Postmodernist Fiction* (London: Methuen, 1987), p. 10.
28 Ibid., p. 7.
29 Linda Hutcheon, *A Poetics of Postmodernism: History, Theory, Fiction* (New York and London: Routledge, 1988).
30 Brian McHale, *Constructing Postmodernism*, (London and New York: Routledge, 1992), p. 229.
31 'Science Fiction and Postmodernity', in *Postmodernism and the Re-Reading of Modernity*, ed. Francis Barker, Peter Hulme and Margaret Iversen (Manchester: Manchester University Press, 1992), p. 149.
32 Scott Bukatman, *Terminal Identity: The Virtual Subject in Postmodern Science Fiction* (Durham, NC: Duke University Press, 1993), p. 18.
33 William Gibson, *Mona Lisa Overdrive* (London: HarperCollins, 1995), p. 55.
34 *Postmodernism, or, The Cultural Logic of Late Capitalism* (London: Verso, 1991), p. 419.

5
Postmodern Performance

Theatre

The accounts of postmodernism that we have been looking at so far have depended upon linear narratives of precedence and succession. However, the postmodern diagnosis has also migrated to areas of cultural life for which no satisfactory, pre-existing 'modernism' can be seen to exist, such as film, TV, opera and rock music. This transposability of the postmodern narrative is one of its most striking features, and takes two forms. The first is the production for cultural forms that have no obvious modernist moment – TV and rock music, for example – of an accelerated interior history, in which earlier periods in the history of the form come to constitute its modernism (the music of the Beatles and Rolling Stones, for example) in order to prodict the linear break of postmodernism. The second is the claim that forms such as rock music and TV belong so inescapably to the contemporary world of global electronic culture, that they are thereby *more* postmodern than those forms which have to drag their modernist shadows behind them.

An interestingly hybrid form, in that it lies somewhere in between these 'genealogical' and 'analogical' postmodernisms, as they may be called, is drama. Of course, drama has a long and involved history of its own in the twentieth century and played a significant part in the rise of modernism, especially in Europe, with the experiments of the German expressionists, Dadaist and Futurist performance, the work of Maeterlinck and Yeats and, in the later years of the century, of Artaud and Brecht. Nevertheless, historians of drama have been less anxious than others to claim a distinctively modernist movement in drama itself. It may be that drama is more resistant to radical formal innovation than other cultural forms, given its close dependence upon commercial conditions and professional structures;

but, for whatever reason, drama's modernism seems to have been muted, or at least long delayed, at least until Brecht and, in some accounts, until the emergence and successful critical promotion of the Theatre of the Absurd in the 1950s. None of this has inhibited the migration of the postmodern narrative to drama, but it has made that narrative more various in its manifestations. Most importantly, the lack of an agreed and coherent version of the modernist history of drama has meant that theories of postmodern drama have had to draw upon postmodern theory in other cultural fields.

All this is a little odd, since, on the face of it, the condition of theatricality connects with many of the most important preoccupations of the postmodern debate. Any theatrical work exemplifies the tension between product and process, for a dramatic work can never exist fully either in its script version, or in an individual performance of that script. Any script must advertise its incompleteness, its necessity of being embodied in more than mere printed words, while any performance must always refer back to some notional script (as we will see, this may apply even to improvised or scriptless performance). This split is actualized in socio-economic forms as well. More than any other cultural form, the theatre encompasses the extremes of high and low culture; the radiant glory of 'classic drama', which embodies, in Shakespeare, or classical tragedy, culture at its highest peak, is always in conflict with the grimy and necessary facts of what Yeats calls 'theatre business, management of men' – the inescapable physical and commercial pressures on the theatre as a social and economic institution.

In these senses the theatre, or theatrical form, encompasses many of the themes that we have already encountered in the postmodern debate, especially the refusal of notions of essential form, the dispersal of the identity of the work of art, and its immersion in social and political contexts. We have seen already how, as a radically impure form of art, theatricality threatens Michael Fried's ideal of absorbed presence. Theatricality stands for all those falsifying divisions which complicate, diffuse and displace the concentrated self-identity of a work of art, and so encompasses a number of different effects, including self-consciousness of the spectator, the awareness of context and the dependence upon extension in time. Theatricality is the name for the contamination of any artefact that is dependent upon conditions outside, or other than, its own.

Conversely, as we have seen, the theatrical is taken up by theorists of the postmodern as a positive refusal of the frozen abstraction of the idea of the work-in-itself in favour of the idea of the work-as-process. For the German critic Hans Georg Gadamer, the apparent distinction between forms of art that exist in themselves and forms that require a transition from text to performance, like theatre and music, is false. In fact, he argues, all works of art only exist in the occasions of their reception in different historical circumstances. Performability is the guaranteee of the necessary temporal extension of any work of art. As Joel C. Weinsheimer writes, in his analysis of Gadamer:

> Performance is not something ancillary, accidental, or superfluous that can be distinguished from the play proper. The play proper exists first and only when it is played. Performance brings the play into existence, and the playing of the play is the play itself . . . Thus the work cannot be differentiated from the representations of it since it exists only *there*, only in the flesh. It comes to be in representation and in all the contingency and particularity of the occasions of its appearance.[1]

As one might expect, postmodern theories of drama have laid great stress upon this contingency of performance; indeed, Michel Benamou sees performance as 'the unifying mode of the postmodern'.[2] Postmodern theatre is often dated from the upsurge of performance art during the decade of the 1960s, with its happenings, spectacles, dance-theatre, etc. One strain of radical theatre theory at that time and afterwards sought to free performance from its degrading subservience to the pre-existing script. Patrice Pavis argues, for example, that postmodern theatre such as the work of the American Robert Wilson, is characterized by its disposability, its disdain of the score or text which guarantees the survival and repeatability of a performance at the cost of cramping its spontaneity. What matters according to this aesthetic of impermanence is not the bourgeois-repressive qualities of memory, inheritance and repeatability, but the liberating qualities of immediacy and uniqueness:

> The only memory which one can preserve is that of the spectator's more or less distracted perception, or the more or less coherent and concentrated system of its reprises and allusions. The work, once performed, disappears forever. Paradoxically, it is during the age in which technical reproducibility is nearing perfection, that one becomes aware of the nonreproducible and ephemeral nature of theatre, and the futility of trying to reproduce the score so as to reproduce the performance.[3]

However, this embrace of the transient might also be said to be modernist in that it springs from or conduces to an ambition to restore the theatre to itself, to its own intrinsic conditions. In the influential work of Antonin Artaud the theatre is seen as a colonized or dispossessed cultural form, dominated as it is by written language. Artaud argues that the theatre should abandon its fealty to the authority of Text and learn to speak its own intrinsically theatrical language of light, colour, movement, gesture and space. This is not to say that language should be banished from the theatre, though Artaud anticipates a return to 'popular, primal theatre sensed and experienced directly by the mind, without language's distortions and the pitfalls in speech and words', but language is to be made physical too, communicating as pure sound and sensation rather than through abstract correspondence.[4]

The result of this is a theatre theoretically coiled in upon itself, in which work, performance and audience-effect fission together in a powerfully externalized unity. For Artaud, the characters and events on a stage must not gesture outside themselves, or otherwise distract the audience from their absorption in the dramatic experience: 'We might say the subjects presented begin on stage. They have reached such a point of objective materialization we could not imagine them, however much one [sic] might try, outside their compact panorama, the enclosed, confined world of the stage.'[5] In this, Artaud seems to stand at the opposite extreme from Brecht, despite some apparent similarities. Although he was no more interested than Artaud in a theatre which simply reflected or represented the world, and looked to a theatre which frankly acknowledged itself as such, Brecht's dramatic theory demanded not that the audience and actors plunge themselves into the sensual immediacy of a performance, but that the play should be performed and received in a mood of detachment. Artaud's formulation, which has been extremely influential, especially on the work of Peter Brook during the 1960s and 1970s, can be called modernist in so far as it provides a programme for closing off all the uncertainties and formal duplicities of theatre. Oddly, Artaud's pure theatricality comes down to something like what Fried might applaud as the work's absorption in itself. Where Fried and Greenberg complain that art has been contaminated by the non-artistic, Artaud complains that theatre has been contaminated by the non-theatrical; and where Greenberg and Fried aim to restore art to itself by detheatricalizing it, so in equivalent terms, Artaud can be seen as attempting to detheatricalize theatre.

One early and influential formulation of the principle of theatrical self-sufficiency is that of Bonnie Marranca, co-editor of the *Performing Arts Journal*. Her introduction in a book published in 1977 on the experimental theatre of the 1970s characterized the movement in Artaudian terms as a turn away from the word, or from the 'literary' theatre. The new theatre of Richard Foreman, Robert Wilson and Lee Breuer, associated with avant-garde theatrical companies like the Ontological–Hysteric Theater, the Mabou Mimes, the Living Theater and the San Francisco Mime Troupe, is promoted as a 'theatre of images', produced by artists who 'exclude dialogue or use words minimally in favour of aural, visual and verbal imagery that calls for alternative modes of perception on the part of the audience'. It is a theatre, she claims, which 'voids all considerations of theater as it is conventionally understood in terms of plot, character, setting, language and movement. Actors do not create "roles." They function instead as media through which the playwright expresses his ideas; they serve as icons and images. Text is merely a pretext – a scenario.'[6]

In a similar way, Bernard Dort has celebrated what he calls the emancipation of performance. Where the enemy of theatre for Artaud was the text, Dort sees the real agent of repressive power in the theatre as the director who 'has not only gained authority over all the other workers in the theatre, but left them helpless and impotent, and in some cases reduced them almost to slavery'.[7] New forms of theatre reduce the control of the director by emphasizing improvization and group authorship. The emancipated performance allows the foregrounding of things which traditional theatre ignores or suppresses. Dort writes interestingly, for example, about new uses of theatrical space, which refuse simply to subordinate such space to the demands of the drama. Here is his description of the autonomy of place in the kind of drama he calls 'performance-installation':

> Here the performance site (which is usually not a theatre, but a building or even a landscape with an identity and a history completely unrelated to the script and to all theatrical activity) is not selected to correspond to a preconceived idea or to certain potential themes in the text; nor is it built or used to give an account of them. Instead it constitutes an autonomous and permanent element of the performance, in the same way as the text (or lack thereof), and the actors' gestures, movements, and delivery. The site adds its own identity and history, and the weight of its meaning to the performance.[8]

This stress on the immediacy of performance can even encompass reflexivity, that form of metatheatre in which a play reflects upon and represents its own procedures. Bonnie Marranca acknowledges this as a symptom of a 'crisis' in the relationship of theatre to itself, but represents this crisis in terms that loop back into a celebration of the intensified *presence* of theatre:

> This focus on process – the producedness, or seams-showing quality of a work – is an attempt to make the audience more conscious of events in the

theatre than they are accustomed to. It is the idea of *being there* in the
theatre that [produces the] emphasis on immediacy in the relationship of the
audience to the theatrical event.[9]

The rest of Marranca's account of the 'Theater of Images' stresses
Friedian detheatricalization, sometimes with critical claims about the
painterly and sculptural qualities of performance which seem to derive
from dominant trends in modernist art criticism: 'Like modern painting,
the Theater of Images is timeless . . . abstract and presentational . . . It is
the flattening of the image (stage picture) that characterizes the Theater of
Images, just as it does modern painting.'[10] This belief in the absorption
and immediacy of the performance is shared by other writers about
contemporary avant-garde theatre. Xerxes Merhta, in a review of recent
performance art, argues openly that 'far from being a "post modern"
phenomenon, Performance Art . . . is, in its insistence on flatness and
abstraction, and in its profound indebtedness to every major modern art
movement since Cubism, firmly in this century's great tradition of
modernist formalism'.[11]

Here, no attempt is being made to characterize absorption as postmodernist, but even accounts that adopt the postmodernist designation and
paradigm tend to reproduce such ideas of immediacy and formal self-sufficiency. Robert W. Corrigan identifies the postmodernist strain in contemporary theatre in its exhilarating dissolution of every kind of traditional
dramatic coherence, plot, character, setting, and so on. But this radical
indeterminacy is recouped by the familiar emphasis on the compensating
plenitude and immediacy of the act of performance: 'Unable to create
representations of human beings in action (and not believing in their
validity anyway) . . . presentation replaces *re*-presentation and performance
is increasingly about performance itself.'[12] Again, painterly images are to
the fore in Corrigan's account, which stresses the creation in postmodernist drama of 'patterns in space', 'icons' and 'tableaux'.

Interestingly, the stress on the theatrical as the prime embodiment of an
art of process has led to a new privileging of the theatre in other cultural
modes. In an extremely interesting meditation on the lessons of post-structuralist theory for teaching, Greg Ulmer draws on Artaud and Derrida for
a theory of 'applied grammatology' in the classroom.[13] Ulmer argues that,
like the actor or performer, the teacher must unlearn the structure of
opposition in which he or she is represented as merely the transmitter of
a discipline or knowledge that lies prior and elsewhere, and the classroom
as merely the setting or stage for that knowledge. Ulmer draws on
avant-garde performance theory, and especially that of Artaud as glossed

by Derrida, for his model of the post-pedagogical classroom, arguing that teaching should become the active production of meaning rather than simply its replication. Ulmer is interested in the overlaps between performance and pedagogy and devotes a good deal of attention to the work of the artist Joseph Beuys. In one of Beuys's rituals, known as *Fat Corner*, a lump of fat, usually margarine, is packed in the shape of an inverted cone in a corner. The ritual involves simply leaving the fat to spread and stink over the course of days. The piece consists of all the elements brought into being in this process, the deposit of the fat, its slow spreading, and the viewer's response. In another ritual, Beuys smeared his face with honey and gold and had himself locked into a museum which he walked around, carrying a dead hare in his arms while explaining his pictures to it. Beuys's insistence on performance as process rather than object and his refusal of abstract theory or interpretation runs together theatre, theory and interpretation.[14] But even Ulmer's sophisticated analysis reproduces in tendency what it often disclaims in fact, the idea that there can be such a thing as an absolute, self-sufficient performing instant, either in the theatre or in the classroom, unmarked by the shadow of previous knowledge, theory or experience. Ulmer calls for a heightened awareness of the various forms of 'situatedness' of stage and classroom, but remains constrained by a nostalgic belief that this situatedness amounts to a kind of presence.

Other forms of postmodern theatre and postmodern theories of theatre have their point of origin in a break with Artaud's pure theatre, and their embrace of the conditions of theatricality in Fried's unfriendly sense. For many, this break is marked by two essays of 1968 by Jacques Derrida, both written about Artaud, 'The Theater of Cruelty and the Closure of Representation' and 'La Parole Soufflée'.[15] Derrida's discussions enact a complex relationship with Artaud's work, for the most part shadowing it in commentary, but culminating with a demonstration of the contradictions at the heart of Artaud's beliefs. Derrida sees Artaud's work as a desperate struggle against logocentrism, that is, the belief in the possibility of full and perfect embodiment of thought in language, and the structures of repetition that guarantee it, with the stage always acting as the supplementary shadow of original full speech. Artaud's Theatre of Cruelty is a refusal of this secondary status, a refusal of its role as repetition:

> The stage will no longer operate as the repetition of a *present*, will no longer *re*-present a present that would exist elsewhere and prior to it, a present whose plenitude would be older than it, absent from it, and rightfully capable of doing without it: the being-present-to-itself of the absolute Logos, the living present of God. (*WD*, 237)

Artaud's embrace of the particularity of performance is, therefore, a powerfully subversive act, 'the hand lifted against the abusive wielder of the logos, against the father, against the God of a stage subjugated to the power of speech and text' (*WD*, 239). When Derrida praises Artaud's theatre of cruelty as 'the art of difference and of expenditure without economy, without reserve, without return, without history' (*WD*, 247), he comes strikingly close to Michael Fried's distrust of the theatrical. Both writers want to deny the operations of repetition and therefore purge a given art form from contamination, although their denial takes different forms. Where Fried wants to guard against the corrupting effects of time and context on the pure objecthood of art, Derrida represents Artaud as denying the dependence of theatrical repetition on any originary essence; so where Fried wants to protect essence from repetition, Derrida wants to strip repetition of its dependence upon essence. The end-point is curiously similar for both writers – an idea of 'pure presence as pure difference' (ibid.).

But Derrida's essay goes a step further than this, to point out that Artaud's theatre of cruelty is, in fact, an impossibility. No matter how intensely spontaneous, or unpreconditioned, any act of theatre might seem, it must always to some degree involve representation and repetition, by virtue of the fact of being theatre. 'Artaud', writes Derrida, 'knew that the theater of cruelty neither begins nor is completed within the purity of simple presence, but rather is already within representation, in the "second time of Creation," in the conflict of forces which could not be that of a simple origin' (*WD*, 248). Derrida leaves Artaud and his reader with this paralysing but perhaps also energizing prospect: that, in digging back to the primitive essence of theatre, one is always going to encounter the fact of difference, the fact that theatre is a derivation, a representation, a fiction. In this apprehension, Derrida is more than the simple antagonist of Fried, for he implicitly works Fried's antitheatricalism back to the point where it recoils upon itself, revealing the presence of the theatrical within every imaginable form of pure 'objecthood'.[16]

One of the most interesting responses to Derrida's critique of Artaud is Chantal Pontbriand's. Like many other writers about performance, she begins with a refusal of Michael Fried's refusal of theatricality, but also recognizes that the privileging of performance is implicitly a privileging of 'presence'. She is concerned to discriminate two different kinds of presence in performance. The classical theatre (and Pontbriand seems to include in this category modern theatre too) gives the sense of presence by making the theatre the shadowing forth of some ideal truth that lies somewhere behind or before it; the theatre acknowledges its fallen or secondary nature, the better to confirm the absolute status of this occluded, timeless meaning. This is to say that performance establishes presence through repetition or re-presentation, the acting out in time and in a specific place of truths that are essentially timeless and placeless.

Pure performance, which Pontbriand takes to be characteristic of postmodern theatre, refuses to be ashamed of its contingency. It embraces, even insists upon its situational, occasional nature, underlining the sense of the here and now. In its temporal 'coming into being', postmodern performance presents rather than represents.[17] We can say, then, that postmodern performance, or postmodern performance theory, relies upon an idea not of a 'full' presence, the evidencing or visibility of a sense of truth or Being, but an empty presence, which is always vulnerable to time and contingency, a presence which is always porous to its situation rather than aloof from it. Henry Sayre has called this kind of performance theory the 'aesthetics of absence', as opposed to the aesthetics of presence announced in Fried's 'Art and Objecthood':

An aesthetics of presence seeks to transcend history, to escape temporality. An aesthetics of absence subjects art to the wiles of history, embraces time . . . An aesthetics of presence defines art as that which transcends the quotidian; an aesthetics of absence accepts the quotidian's impingement upon art. For the one, art is absolute; for the other, it is contingent.[18]

It is for this reason that postmodern 'presence' can be represented as conducing to the disruption of expectations and the displacement of forms of identity. Presence-as-process is evidenced in a theatre that refuses to deliver itself as a commodity, refuses to satisfy the viewer who seeks to abstract or translate the performance. This sort of presence is always on the point of becoming something else, consisting not in emotional states, but in drives, pulsions, energies. It is a theatre which 'rejects form, which is immobility, and opts, instead, for discontinuity and slippage'.[19] Jean-François Lyotard, in an essay on Artaud, looks forward to such a theatre of pure, formless energies, whose characteristics will be 'not the concordance of dance, of music, of mimicry, of speech, of season, of time, of public, and of nothingness, but rather the independence and simultaneity of sound-noises, of words, of body-figures, of images'.[20]

This theme has been a common one, especially in contemporary French accounts of the postmodern theatre. Josette Féral sees the specificity of postmodern theatre in its refusal of narrative and, along with this, of 'the symbolic organization dominating theatre'. Theatre should consist of 'continuous displacements of the position of desire', never allowing its audience anything to grasp, 'except for flows, networks and systems'.[21] Similarly, Régis Durand speaks of a theatre whose organizing forces 'are no longer narrative impetus and coherence but rather superimposition or "layering," "tracking" (Lee Breuer), quotation, repetition, tracing and erasing, doubling, "ghosting" (Herbert Blau), translation, transference, etc.'[22] The kind of theatre which is taken to exemplify these requirements is the Ontological–Hysteric Theater of the American dramatist Richard Foreman. The experience of one of his performances is described by Chantal Pontbriand:

> in his productions neither the eye – nor the ear – is able to find a fixed point on which to rest. The spectator at Foreman's plays is bombarded by a multiplicity of visual and auditory events. At the visual level, there are continual changes of the geometrical stage set, even within an act. The displacement of pieces of furniture and parts of the set alter the context, either by giving it greater depth or by creating various levels stacked in depth or in height. The lighting also changes continually; its transformations may occur slowly or rapidly and may affect stage and house alike: the spectators may suddenly find themselves bathed in light when the spotlights are turned on them without warning. As for the sound, everything is recorded: car horns, sirens, whistles, bits of jazz, as well as the dialogue itself. The script is fragmented, made up of short, aphoristic, unconnected sentences.[23]

The work of Richard Foreman instances a principle of dramatic exorbitance, a refusal of continuity so absolute as to compel a ceaseless mobility of subject, purpose and perspective. Foreman represents a kind of limit-case of postmodernist performance, in his absolute refusal of the consolations of closure, and desire to open the theatre to the experience of unmasterable difference, or what he has called 'the web of everything interrupting everything else'.[24] Foreman's plays, of which the published texts are not so much the scores as the residues, are experiences of flux, in which lines of plot and situations can be abruptly derailed and rerouted at any moment, settings and sets can transform arbitrarily, and in which the traditional organising privilege given to characters and their speech is dissolved. The language in a Foreman play, for instance, which is recorded as well as live, circulates between actors rather than emanating from and defining characters, and must in any case make its way against many kinds of auditory distraction, including music, whistles and sirens. Foreman's account of the nature and purpose of this kind of theatre presents it as a kind of Becoming, or continuous emergence of significance rather than a fixing or manifestation of Being:

[W]hen it seems that my plays, line by line, are changing the subject, that
is true – but that changing of subject is the ground of the real subject, an
openness and alertness resulting from a 'non-human' (post-humanistic)
wandering over the whole field of everything-that-is-discoursing to us. . . .
To create that field (rather than allowing the consciousness to be hypnot-
ized) my plays keep 'changing the subject'. But is it changed? Since the
subject is the field, not spoken of directly, but articulated, layed [sic] out,
by the writing of 'things'.[25]

Interestingly, Foreman's account of his work includes an awareness that
the work can never be pure performing without performance, action
without enaction. Foreman thus makes explicit what remains implicit in
other postmodernist writers interested in exploring the Artaudian intensities of performance, namely, that despite his hostility to the referential
function of theatre, his work is a kind of reflection of, or mimetic
approximation to what is taken to be the real, but hidden, ground or
condition of our being. This ground is paradoxically groundlessness itself,
and the work is said to be a specimen of that condition rather than a
referential reduction of it. But such performance, in the accounts that
Foreman offers of it and that it offers of itself, cannot avoid some element
of the referential: 'What I am trying to do', Foreman tells us, 'is get to the
grain of thought and feeling . . . I try in my work to take dictation from
the non-coagulated, still granual source: paradise'.[26]

It is for this reason that Foreman's work must proceed and represent
itself not as a pure mobility of appearances, but as a series of self-contra-
dictions or self-interruptions, in which the tendency of performing to
coagulate into performance is everywhere at work and everywhere resisted:

The pleasure I take (writing) is the pleasure of undercutting: interrupting:
an impulse I want to (and do) make. The impulse is registered, but allowed
to twist, turn, block itself, so that blockage, that reaction to its energy,
produces a detour, and the original impulse maps new, contradictory
territory.[27]

The resistance to traditional referential performance, as the acting out of
some other scene, or the actualisation of some pre-existing condition, can
never be total, since it so easily and necessarily precipitates into an
exemplification of another truth, the truth of performance-in-itself. The
pure process of performing can never be, as Herbert Blau puts it, 'the
designated site of the extermination of the mimetic', since, as Blau goes on
to observe, performing always involves to some degree a representation of
itself *as* performance.[28] Foreman's work differs from that of other post-

modernist writers for the theatre in its acknowledgement that there is always a kind of declension of performance into truth-telling, and its determination therefore to try to continue showing a truth beyond truth-telling in the sheer fact of its own failure to inhabit the truth:

> [T]he need of the theatre to be effective, to be convincing, to testify to 'truth' . . . is the heart of the corruption and vulgarity of theatre . . . One reason I believe this is because I find myself, in my own work, imprisoned, hypnotized, fooled whenever I do something well, whenever I am (to myself) convincing in my mastery. Because at that point I sense I am, myself, hiding from truth behind the facade of the well-built artistic edifice. So my work has been, over the past few years, to document my failure to really live up to the rigors of that impossible situation where one must show that all mastery is anti-truth.[29]

Richard Foreman's work for the theatre and reflections on that work (the title of the essay, 'Notes on the Process of Making It: Which Is Also the Object', observes the nondifferentiation of these two) is perhaps the most powerful example that can be imagined of the exorbitance of postmodern performance.

These accounts of theatre link back to another aspect of Fried's critique of theatricality. For Fried, we will remember, 'presence' was only achievable in an art which remained thoroughly and perfectly itself. 'What lies between the arts', he wrote, 'is theatre.'[30] Theories of postmodern theatre have sought to embrace and explore this in-betweenness, drawing together and setting in opposition different constituents of performance, sound, light, language, setting, movement, music, and so on. Bernard Dort includes in his history of the emancipation of performance an account of the move from the notion that theatre was, or should be, an ideal synthesis of all its elements – as in Wagner's project for a *Gesamtkunstwerk*, or collective work of art. Where the ideal of the unified work of art concentrated upon the figure of the author–director, postmodern theatre dissolves this unity; and with the surpassing of the authority of the single director goes the notion of the unified production. Where Roland Barthes could define theatre as a cooperative 'density of signs', none of them having the same meaning, or working in the same code, but all gathering together for one purpose, more contemporary theatre and theatre theory abandon this synoptic sense.[31] 'If staging means putting into signs', writes Bernard Dort, 'then acting means shifting those signs and setting them in motion with clearly defined limits of space and time – perhaps even setting them adrift.' Theatricality becomes, therefore, 'the drifting of these signs, the impossibility of their union, and finally their confrontation before the spectator of the emancipated performance'.[32]

Richard Schechner, like many other theorists of postmodern performance, accepts Fried's designation of theatre as that which lies between the arts, but goes even further. Performance, he argues, lies always on the threshold between life and theatre itself. Once theatre acknowledges itself, recognizes the gap between reality and representation – and all theatre to some degree acknowledges this gap – then a complex layering of levels can come into being:

> A person sees the event; he sees himself; he sees himself seeing the event; he sees himself seeing others who are seeing the event and who, maybe, see themselves seeing the event. Thus there is the performance, the performers, the spectators; and the spectator of spectators; and the self-seeing self that can be performer or spectator or spectator of spectators.[33]

So Schechner is interested in a form of performance that subjects the thresholds between theatre and non-theatre to scrutiny, for example the performances of the New York theatre group Squat. Their 'theatre' was on the ground floor of a store-front building and performances took place against the backdrop of the plate-glass window through which passers-by could see into the theatre, though often without realizing that they were thus being drawn into the spectacle.

Perhaps extending Fried's diagnosis of the differential force of theatricality, as it creates and recrosses thresholds, Schechner moves his discussion outwards to encompass forms of non-theatrical performance, arguing that the mode of the theatrical is actually dominant in Western culture today. Television news programmes, for example, seem to abide by theatrical conventions; whether they be 'Ibsenite naturalistic drama in a burlesque or variety show format' or the more melodramatic and cinematic mode of national TV news, life is constructed as a series of performances.[34] Far from wanting to separate off the realms of 'life' and 'performance', Schechner looks forward with relish to a proliferation of liminalities, 'between literature and recitation, between religion and entertainment, between ritual and staged shows. Also the in-between among cultures: events that can't be easily located as belonging to this or that culture but which appear to extend into several cultures, like the national news, which is neither national nor news.'[35]

There is obviously a libertarian flavour to this celebration of the 'in-between', but it is not immediately clear why such a state of affairs should necessarily seem desirable or emancipating. The situation might be said just as much to resemble Debord's or Baudrillard's account of the society of the spectacle or the era of simulations – in which the dissolution of distinctions between the real and what stands in for it may destroy the possibility of political critique. As Herbert Blau puts it, a trifle mystically: 'Over the global village falls the veil of Maya. Amazement sits upon the brow. We are not only talking about play, but in the galaxy of the Imaginary, the immanence of World-Play.'[36]

But another strand of postmodern dramatic theory sees political possibilities in the disruption or complication of strict boundaries and the coherent distinctions they maintain. In a world in which performance and spectacle dominate, it is necessary to be suspicious of structures of representation in themselves, in order to begin to refuse the myth of presence which dominates this world theatre:

> The suspicion of presence and of simple presentation of performer to audience that suffuses postmodern experimental theatre derives . . . from the anxiety created by recent historical demonstrations of collusion between presence as charisma or salesmanship and repressive power structures. In theatre, presence is the matrix of power; the postmodern theatre of resistance must therefore both expose the collusion of presence with authority and resist such collusion by refusing to establish itself as the charismatic Other.[37]

In his discussion Philip Auslander does not propose a radical theatre which simply breaks with the language and experience of conventional theatre. His account of the production *L.S.D. (. . . Just the High Points . . .)* by the Wooster Group in New York in 1984–5 stresses the ways in which the group used innovative technique in order to undermine the theatre of presence from within. The Wooster Group's performance ran together passages from Arthur Miller's *The Crucible* and a representation of the trial of the 1960s drug-guru Dr Timothy Leary. These were intercut with many other items, including quotations from recent public debates between Timothy Leary and G. Gordon Liddy, excerpts from *Miami Vice* and a section in which the cast re-enacted its attempts to rehearse *The Crucible* while under the influence of LSD. The point of this, Auslander argues, is to take apart Miller's text and view it in different contexts and from different angles – pointing up, for instance, the issues of racial and sexual difference which seem to be occluded in or absent from Miller's play.

This, then, is not liberation, but a form of theatrical deconstruction, a critique that risks a certain complicity with the structures it subjects to critique, in the interests of rooting out deeper or more unconscious conventions or assumptions. Auslander writes that 'it was not a question of declaring, with Artaud, "No more masterpieces", but of simultaneously occupying and resisting the given structures'.[38] One example of this in Auslander's approving account is the way that the Wooster Group denied the immediacy of the performance by having the actors reading, sometimes as themselves, sometimes in character, from texts which were physically present on stage. This resulted in character becoming 'a problematic, not a given . . . By asserting their dependence upon text yet radically problematizing their relationship to it, the Group dissected the major structure of authority in traditional theatre.'[39]

Similar claims have also been made recently for the work of women performance artists and groups. Jeanie Forte writes of the ways in which performance theatre can work within and outside the structures of representation which, no less than apparently 'harder' political structures, are said to constitute patriarchy. Forte's largish claim is that discourse depends upon the construction of woman as object, as that sign in language which is always spoken about, while never achieving the status of a full speaking subject. This means that women occupy the space of an absence within the dominant culture and can only speak through falsity or simulation. The response to this in women's postmodern performance is simultaneously to foreground and refuse this suppression of the female voice. The 'deconstruction' described by Forte seems to be a rather different thing from that evoked in Auslander's account of the Wooster Group, for, rather than the difficult negotiation of a set of representational conventions which must be accepted and rejected at once, it offers the more immediately satisfying prospect of a discovery and intimate enactment of women's identities as 'speaking subjects'. One, not terribly cryptic, performance piece that she describes as a vivid 'refusal of Otherness' involved Ulrike Rosenbach, dressed in a white leotard, shooting arrows at a madonna and child.[40] An odd example that Forte gives is a piece called 'Interior Scroll' (1975), in which Carolee Schneemann stood naked in dim lighting and read from a narrow rope-like text which she extracted from her vagina (the text itself being the discourse of a male film-maker). Given the bizarre division of language between male and female, body, voice and text in 'Interior Scroll', or in Forte's description of it, it seems odd simply to say that in such pieces 'women performance artists thus challenge the symbolic order by asserting themselves as "speaking subjects," in direct defiance of the patriarchal construction of discourse.'[41] Undeniably, the kind of theatre being described here is political and in many ways it is also in some sense subversive, but it is not easy to see how it exemplifies the elaborate claims of the deconstruction and postmodern theory that are ranged behind it.

The difficulty of achieving the simple step 'outside' conventional dramatic structures and their supposed apparatus of authority, repression and exclusion, is rarely considered in postmodern theories of performance. One of the few writers to have meditated upon the worrying paradoxes involved in postmodern theatre while remaining faithful to the desire for a theatre of deconstruction, is Herbert Blau. In an essay entitled 'Universals of Performance', Blau argues that what characterizes contemporary theatre is a simultaneous desire to deny theatricality and the necessary and unavoidable return of the fact of theatricality:

> As we become enamored of the unifications which we project upon 'primitive' cultures, we tend to forget that even performances which are presumed to be outside representation exist within its enclosure . . . None of us . . . has ever seen a performance which, in the revulsion against the mimetic, the desire to banish seeming, has not (the more effective it is) radically increased the quotient of *pre*tense, the disruption of time by seeming.[42]

For Blau, the claims of the theatre to immediacy, with the apparent subversions of the authority of the text, the author, or the director, are always vitiated or restrained by the fact of theatricality, since 'the machinery of the theater quickly disables the appearance and marshals itself around a space of subversion, so long as there *is* a performance'.[43] Even the theatrical effect of the suspension of time is a framed, or projected effect, which always exists within, and is legislated by, the structures of social-habitual time; in this sense, the suspension of time 'on borrowed time'. This metaphor leads Blau to the central claim of his essay, that no performance can ever really hope to open up a truly autonomous space for itself; every performance takes place within an institutional context, and every return to an origin (like Peter Brook's actors performing elemental dramas in aboriginal villages) is always caught up within structures of cultural difference and expectation. To step outside history is always an historical act. For this reason, Blau says that every performance is in some way 'amortized' or mortgaged; never immediately self-sufficient, but always owing to its multiple contexts the possibility of its appearance of contextless immediacy:

> No seeming self-denial on the part of an actor, no pretense of immediacy, however momentarily powerful or time-effacing, can amplify the privileged instant, for it is only for the instant timeless – and once again the theater

suffuses the truth with its presence, the only *presence* which is there. It is then that we realize that approval has been, in our very assent to the transgression of performance, institutionalized, historicized, *on borrowed time*.[44]

What is distinctive about Blau's deconstructive critique is the way that it investigates the structures which embody a critical response to the drama and to performance. Many other accounts of postmodern theatre and performance uncritically reproduce a single, simple model of the dramatic, which projects an absolute split between fixity on the one hand, identified as it may be with authorship, the dictatorship of the director, the dead hand of the text; and process on the other, in all the variability and allegedly 'free' contingency of performance.

Dance

These tensions have been particularly evident in the area of dance and in theoretical reflections upon it, especially those of Sally Banes, who has done more than any other writer to account for the evolution of dance in terms of the modernist and postmodernist analytic paradigms. Modernism in dance – in the work of Isadora Duncan, Loïe Fuller and Martha Graham – began with a rejection of academic formality and an embrace of the values of individual expressiveness. Isadora Duncan strove to reproduce the natural forms and movements of wave and wind in dancerly movement, rejecting the formality of costume and choreography. The dancer became, not the instrument, but the source of the meaning of the dance. Modernism in dance was identified above all with the expressive freedom of the body and with the body's expression of that freedom, as urged by Isadora Duncan in declaring that 'the dancer of the future will be one whose body and soul have grown so harmoniously together that the natural language of that soul will have become the movement of the body'.[45] Declarations of this kind, whether concerning modern dance, or enacted through it, involve a certain, undetected paradox. If the untrammelled body became the centre and source of the meaning of modern dance, its very role as a symbol, if only a symbol of its own expressive powers, bracketed and derealized it. The body could never be wholly *itself* as long as its role was to bodyforth its authentic selfhood. The stage became – or remained – a theatre, in Michael Fried's derogatory sense, a field of representation which divided the viewer's attention between the visible and the intelligible, what was seen and what was meant. Not surprisingly, the allegedly free celebration and expression of the spiritual body in Duncan's dance gave way to an increasingly stringent formalization of expressivity, in the work especially of Martha Graham and Doris Humphrey, which was both intensely personal, and yet also highly disciplined, insisting on the growing autonomy of technique and dance-language.

During the 1960s, this way of understanding dance and the practices and institutions which had become sedimented around it, began to be challenged. This challenge was centred in the ferment of avant-garde activity which took place in New York during the 1960s, and most particularly in the activities of the dancers and choreographers who became known as the Judson Dance Theater, who included Yvonne Rainer, Steve Paxton, Simone Forti and Lucinda Childs. These dancers sought at once to widen and to clarify the nature of dance. In opposition to the traditions of modernist dance associated with Martha Graham, they attempted to open dance up to different styles, activities and dynamic vocabularies. However, as Roger Copeland has observed, the nature of this opening would be oddly determined by the fact that the institutionalized modernism in dance that was being reacted against was not so obviously formalist as the stylistically impersonal work of Mies van der Rohe in architecture, or the avant-garde technicism promoted by Clement Greenberg in painting. The fact that modernism in dance was definitionally 'hot', expressive and individualist, meant that a postmodern reaction to it would have to take forms that paradoxically combined stylistic expansion with the curbing of expressive excess.[46] For the dancers and choreographers of the Judson Dance Theater, dance should and could include activities like breathing, bending, yawning and walking, and the manipulation of everyday objects. Collaborative, exploratory, and improvisatory, the work of the Judson Dance Theater was also heavily influenced by the work and ideas of Merce Cunningham and John Cage, who had evolved a form of music-dance collaboration in which there was no attempt to blend music and dance into purposive unity. The preference for coincidence over cohesion is evident in the fact that Cunningham and Cage would often work apart, the two parties in the collaboration coming together only with the actual performance of a particular piece. The suffocating effects of artistic intention were further protected against in the use of chance procedures by both Cunningham and Cage to generate the structures and rules of combination of the discrete elements of movement and sound.

Where the deformalization and multiplication of means characteristic of modernist dance were tied to and driven by an ethic of expressiveness, the equivalent deformalization effected by the Judson Dance Theater and the work that developed from it during the later 1960s and 1970s was opposed to expressiveness. What was seen and heard in the dance was not to be the allegorical sign of anything else (freedom, power, the striving human spirit); it was to be itself, without allowing itself to become the symbol either of some other thing, or even the symbol of that being itself. For all its proliferating versatility, this work is founded upon a refusal, the refusal of interpretation, or interpretability urged by Susan Sontag in her influential 1964 essay 'Against Interpretation':

> Ideally it is possible to elude the interpreters ... by making works of art whose surface is so unified and clean, whose momentum is so rapid, whose address is so direct that the work can be ... just what it is ... Our task is not to find the maximum amount of content in a work of art, much less to squeeze more content out of the work than is already there. Our task is to cut back content so that we can see the thing at all.[47]

But interpretation is not something arbitrarily and illegitimately added on to artistic practice, from which one might by a simple decision or act of will refrain. The possibility of reflection upon the nature and meaning of works of art is built into them, if only by dint of the fact that artistic works must always propose or enact their difference from everyday activities of a nonartistic kind (not least and especially in self-consciously denying this difference). This means that an 'an-interpretative' art is not something to be discovered or retrieved before or beneath the inauthentic accretions of reflection, but an achievement brought about by an elaborate and knowing subtraction of interpretability from the work. It is the work of Yvonne Rainer that best embodies this subtractive aspiration to the intrinsic, though that work has probably become emblematic of this phase of postmodern dance as much for her quotable declarations about it as for the work's own qualities. In 1965 she wrote:

> NO to spectacle no to virtuosity no to transformations and magic and makebelieve no to the glamour and transcendency of the star image no to the heroic no to the anti-heroic no to trash imagery no to involvement of performer and spectator no to style no to camp no to seduction of spectator by the wiles of the performer no to eccentricity no to moving or being moved.[48]

There was one dance in particular which embodied this orientation. It began as a dance for three simultaneous solo performers performed in January 1966, when it was given the title *The Mind is a Muscle Part 1*. This dance evolved into a number of different versions, which were performed

by Rainer and her associates on different occasions and in different
contexts, usually under the title *Trio A*. The dance lasted only about four
and a half minutes, and was composed of a complex, unbroken sequence
of different movements. It was difficult for the viewer to read not only
because of the absence of any repeated movements, but also because of the
deliberate avoidance of any kind of cadence, or structuring pattern. It
aimed not to restructure or transform the time and space of its occurrence,
but merely, entirely to coincide with them. Despite the variety of different
kinds of movement displayed in it, the piece also eschewed virtuosity or
the suggestion of extreme effort; there was very little extended floor work
or work in the air. In contrast to the sharp defining contrasts of traditional
ballet, as expressed in particular in the use of the jump and the pirouette,
and in the alternation between the extremes of arrest and motion,
prostration and elevation, revelation and concealment, *Trio A* consists of a
constant movement of making apparent. In the course of her detailed
analysis of the dance in *Terpsichore in Sneakers*, Sally Banes describes it as
'a post-modern answer to the pirouette, a denial of classic dance that is
also its expansion'. In it, 'the body never stops, never conceals its up and
downness, its in and outness . . . The beauty of *Trio A* lies not in ideas of
grace, elegance, dramatic expression, or even of nature, but in the material
truth of its coexistent presence and distance.'[49]

Trio A precipitated from Yvonne Rainer another manifesto in 1966, 'A
Quasi Survey of Some "Minimalist" Tendencies in the Quantitatively
Minimal Dance Activity Midst the Plethora, or an Analysis of *Trio A*',
which offered a tabulation of contrasts between elements of traditional or
modernist dance that were to be minimized or eliminated and the qualities
of postmodern dance that she proposed to substitute. In place of phrasing,
and dynamic variation resulting in development and climax, she proposed
to substitute 'found' movements, discrete events and a repetitive equality
of parts. In place of the dance as expressive performance or enactment of
character, she proposed to substitute the neutral performance of tasks or
task-like activity. In place of the complexity of the spatial field, she
proposed to substitute the singular event, action and tone in a simplified
spatial field. And in place of the virtuosic display of the fully extended
body, she wanted to devise dances on a human scale.[50]

It is for this reason that the stylistic diversification of 1960s and 1970s
dance which was documented and celebrated by the first, and still perhaps
the definitive announcement of postmodernism in dance, Sally Banes's
Terpsichore in Sneakers, had elements which seemed so unmistakably
modernist. The austerity of the desire to explore and assert the nature of
dance in itself, the desire for simplicity, purity and abstraction, and the

cultivation of a certain abstract coolness and lightness of tone over the dangerous fluidities of intense feeling, all associated dance with the self-conscious assertion and purification of the medium demanded by Clement Greenberg. (Not the least of the ironies attaching to Greenberg's requirement for each art to attend to the specificity of its own technical nature is its success as a generalizable rule of nongeneralizability, which is taken to be applicable indifferently to all the arts.)

The title of one of Steve Paxton's performances, which has been documented in detail by Sally Banes, nicely expresses this aesthetic convergence. *Flat*, first performed in 1964, is a piece organized around simple, prosaic movements and actions: walking, sitting, standing, getting dressed and undressed. The action and effect of the piece correspond precisely and without overflow to its levelling title. And yet the title cannot be seen as simply continuous with the piece. Whether by design or significant accident, the flatness of Paxton's dance alludes to the demand for painterly flatness which had been proclaimed by Greenberg twenty years before. The ideal of dancerly flatness is offered as an imitation of and equivalent to the ideal of painterly flatness, in a move that allows the work illegitimately to distend into interpretative depth and dimension. Sally Banes's analysis of the piece, which derives significantly not from its original performance, but from its restaging by Paxton in 1980, comically acknowledges the unachievability of the flatness it advertises and attempts to enact, in her subtitle ('Steve Paxton's *Flat* in Perspective') and in the poker-faced offer in her opening sentences to 'perform an in-depth analysis' of the piece (*WDAP*, 227). For the point of her detailed description (which is itself as deliberately flat and unmarked by affect as its object) is to demonstrate, not the horizontal self-sufficiency of the work but the fact that 'postmodern dances not only *are* but also *mean*' (*WDAP*, 227). In this case, the work is interpreted as a narrative about social flatness, as 'a small tragedy about a man who is bound and inhibited by his social role', and a self-conscious reflection on the limits and possibilities of dance, which 'illustrates the proposition that a dance can consist of movement organised poetically, familiar movements made strange by virtue of a new context' (*WDAP*, 239). Here, one kind of claim to postmodernism has been replaced by another. Where *Terpsichore in Sneakers* had affirmed a postmodernism of absolute, self-sufficient performance, *Writing Dancing* subjects that account to a rereading which suggests the importance of rereading as such to definitions of the postmodern. The postmodernism of such a work as *Flat* is shown to inhere precisely in its failure of self-identity, its failure to correspond to the previous definitions of postmodernism.

This goes along with a new stylistic richness and variety in dance during the 1980s. The emphasis on lightness, immediacy and purification in what Banes calls the 'postmodern analytic choreography' of the 1960s and 1970s began to give way to a desire for collaboration and mixing of modes. Choreographers who had previously worked to discover and display the autonomy of dance, began to work with dramatists and musicians, Trisha Brown with Robert Rauschenberg and Laurie Anderson, and Lucinda Childs with the painter Sol LeWitt, the composer Philip Glass and the dramatist Robert Wilson. What previous decades had suspected of being inessential distractions and distortions of dance's purposes and possibilities – lighting, decor, costume – took on a new expressive purpose.

The American choreographer and dancer Jim Self, who trained with Merce Cunningham, but grew weary of the technical austerity of the Cunningham style, expressed the new expansiveness of the later phase of postmodern dance in a response to Yvonne Rainer's defining vetos: 'Yvonne Rainer's thing was saying no . . . .And I felt like saying yes to all those things. So I did. I said yes to theatricality, yes to costumes, yes to virtuosity, yes to staging works on a big scale, yes to creating ballets, yes to everything I could think of to say yes to' (quoted in *WDAP*, 334). Styles of dance from different traditions and cultures, African, Asian and Latino, began to collide and coalesce. The extraordinary rise in popularity of popular dance culture through the 1980s and 1990s, in which dance began to drive and determine the nature of popular music, as it had from the 1920s to the 1950s, rather than being determined by it, as it had been during the 1960s and 1970s, with the arrival in turn of disco, breakdance, bodypopping, hiphop and rave culture, has impacted upon serious and avant-garde dance. At the same time, dance has turned back to its own history, in order to reimagine and reenact its relations with classical ballet. The closed reflexivity of works that drew attention to their 'dancerliness' has developed into the more complex reflexivity of work that ironically parodies the traditions of dance, especially with respect to projection of gender difference, as for instance in the work of the British female dance group, the Cholmondeleys, and also alludes to its coincidences and cooperations with other media. The increasing visibility and availability of dance on TV and video has brought about an interpenetration of performance and representation, evidenced both in the interest in choreographing TV productions and in the 'videotizing' of dance style itself.[51] All these developments are summed up by Sally Banes as the expression in and by dance of

That multidisciplinary, cosmopolitan, internationalist culture [which] is inspired by – and appropriates in jarring juxtapositions from – the fusion of the arts we have come to think of as disparate, in cultures distant from our own high-art notions of separation and specialization either geographically (e.g. West Africa or Japan), temporally (eighteenth-century Europe or pre-Christian Russia as interpreted in Diaghilev's Paris), or in terms of class stratification (the Bronx or Chicago's Milwaukee Avenue). (*WDAP*, 324)[52]

In postmodern dance, or in the contemporary convergence of dance with postmodernism in general, the naming of the postmodern is thus not an afterthought, but a constitutive part of its nonself-identical nature. Sally Banes's enthusiastic first report on the condition of contemporary dance in her *Terpsichore in Sneakers* named the new dance postmodern, but did not seek to name its own act of naming. The title of her more recent collection of reports upon aspects of contemporary and postmodern dance reflects a new inability or unwillingness to partition off the activities of performance and reflection upon performance from each other. *Writing Dancing in the Age of Postmodernism* suggests, first of all a new fluidity of relations between authentically 'postmodernist' dance and more general postmodern cultural conditions – notably the interference and interfusion of styles and traditions consequent upon and characteristic of multiculturalism – and secondly the continuity of dance with writing on dance. Under these conditions, it may no longer be absurd to see writing as a kind of dancing and dancing as a kind of writing. The move from the first postmodernism of Sally Banes's *Terpsichore in Sneakers* centred on the experimental choreographers of the 1960s in the US, to the second postmodernism evidenced more diffusely but more unignorably in the styles of choreography and performance reported on in *Writing Dancing in the Age of Postmodernism* may perhaps be understood as a move from the genealogical to the analogical postmodernism defined in my preface. What now appears to matter most is not the interior history of dance, but its mobile attentiveness to other kinds of artistic practice and social function.

Mime

The art of mime also participates in this rhythm of modernist purification, followed by postmodernist aggregation. As Thomas Leabhart has suggested, the idea of wholly silent performance is itself a relatively recent development in theatre. In earlier periods, theatrical miming or mimesis was rarely silent; it would be accompanied by song, incantation and music and might well involve spoken text. The dumb-show of mime would have been part of a cooperative distribution of the functions of speech, sound and movement across the theatrical spectacle as a whole. Sometimes, for example in oriental theatre such as the Bharata Natyam of Southern India, or the Noh drama of Japan, this was the result of the intense virtuosic specialization of the vocal and kinetic aspects of performance, to the point where they became the responsibility of separate performers. Purely silent performance, in which words are suppressed entirely, seems to have had its origin in the legal restrictions placed on the Italian Players, a rival company to the Comédie Française and the Opéra, which Louis XIV expelled to the Left Bank and allowed to perform only on condition that the actors did not speak. Restrictions of a similar kind were maintained in many French theatres throughout the eighteenth century, leading to the development and refinement of silent pantomime.[53]

Even here, however, it was the actors who were silent, not the piece as a whole, which might supply words on accompanying cards, or in the form of songs and choruses sung by the audience. The development of pure 'corporeal mime', in which bodily movement is not only dissociated from but also wholly independent of speech and sound took place as part of a twentieth-century movement to purify or detheatricalize performance. The French actor, teacher and theorist of drama Jacques Copeau trained actors in a strictly formalistic expressiveness of pose and gesture, separating movement from speech in order to make both available for fuller analysis. During the 1930s and 1940s, these ideas were carried forward by his student Etienne Decroux in collaboration with the actor Jean-Louis Barrault. Decroux proposed in 1931 that theatre should be purified by a complete ban on ordinary speech for a period of thirty years, after which time it was to be allowed back in under strictly controlled conditions. The critic and historian of mime Jean Dorcy reported rapturously of a performance by Decroux and Barrault in 1945 in Paris:

> Let us understand that the corporeal mime wants a bare stage, nude actors, and no variation in lighting. For once, the theatre is no longer a cross-roads of all the arts, but the triumph of one art only: that of the body in motion.[54]

Rather than belonging to this austere tradition of theatrical purification, the work of the most famous mime artist of recent decades, Marcel Marceau, actually looks back to the stagy, sentimental, storytelling traditions of nineteenth-century pantomime, mediated as these probably were for twentieth-century audiences by silent film. But Marceau's work also looks forward to the diversification or retheatricalization of mime which has taken place since the late 1960s. This has brought about a collapse of pure corporeal mime, and the hyphenation of mime with other styles and media. The autonomous, silent body of modernism gives way to the fragmented, but aggregated body of postmodern performance, in which mime is once again intermittent rather than continuous, one element in a theatrical whole which coordinates features such as dance, music, storytelling, clowning, acrobatics, juggling and illusionism. Those contributing to this dedifferentiation of mime during the 1970s and 1980s included the San Francisco Mime Troupe, the Bread and Puppet Theatre, the Mabou Mimes, Bill Irwin, Paul Zaloom and other practitioners of 'new vaudeville' in American performance.[55] Curiously, it may be suspected that the diversification of mime may have freed it more effectively from a subordination to the word than the absolute suppression of extraneous elements in modernist corporeal mime, in which the body tended to become a symbol for the absent word. As Thomas Leabhart remarks:

> The post-modern mime transforms and shapes his body not as a sign or symbol for some word he has chosen not to speak, or as a complement to a word he had [sic] chosen to speak, but as a metaphor for some other transformation, some other shaping, that can not be seen, but which can be hinted at through the visible.[56]

Where modernist theatrical silence yearns and substitutes for fullness of the word, postmodern silence cooperates in a discontinuous clamour of different modes of theatrical display and address.

Music

Modernist music was defined by the same rhythm of dissolution followed by reconstitution as is evidenced in the fields of art and literature. The shock of the new associated with the coming of modernism in music had been particularly penetrating and traumatic. Modernism arguably has its beginnings in the newly complex harmonic structures to be found in the work of Wagner, Bruckner and Mahler in the late nineteenth century. In the work of these composers, the dense overlayering of harmonies and ever more intricate cooperation of elements complicated the previously defining contrast between melodic foreground and harmonic background, and the clear articulation of successive narrative elements. The use of leitmotif and the construction of networks of anticipation and recurrence, has the effect of compelling the awareness of simultaneous rather than progressive structures. If such music is expressive, it is, so to speak, structurally expressive; increasingly it expresses, not some idea or experience or body of feeling lying behind or before the music, but the drama of its own evolving composure or composedness. At the same time, musical aesthetics began to insist more and more upon the idea of music as the absolute art, which was unrelated and irreducible to the vulgarity of discourse and meaning.[57]

Twentieth-century avant-garde composers asked much more extreme questions of music, enlarging and transforming its conventions and vocabularies, pushing to the edge and beyond of what had seemed musically possible and legitimate. Stravinsky opened up the possibility of a music organized around percussion and rhythm in *The Rite of Spring*. Bartók sought new structural and expressive possibilities in Hungarian folk music. Scriabin, Berg, Schoenberg and Webern went even further, leaving behind the harmonic basis of Western music and exploring the possibilities of atonality. There was a widespread sense of acoustic enlargement and exhilaration, a desire to match and encompass the new clamour and dissonance of modern life in the temporal arts of the ear which seemed to many to be the necessary expression of modernity as such. The Italian futurist painter, inventor and composer Luigi Russolo called for an 'art of noises' which would liberate the musical form and potential in factory sirens, traffic noise and the hubbub of the modern city. After his move to the USA, the French composer Edgard Varèse strove, in pieces such as *Hyperprisms* (1923) and *Ionisation* (1931) for a new epic inclusiveness, which would both register the new compelling auditory overload of modern life, and use its technologies to make available and manipulable new timbres and harmonies. In later years, Varèse was one of the first to experiment with the possibilities of electronic music.

But the centrifugal forces of expansion and dissolution in modern music quickly produced their own kind of anxious recoil, parallel to the classicizing of the artistic avant-garde brought about by the work of Clement Greenberg and Michael Fried. In 1921, Arnold Schoenberg announced the discovery of a principle which would give order and disciplined purpose to the hitherto free-floating and intuitive exercise of atonal composition. Schoenberg proposed that composition be governed not by the Pythagorean symmetries of traditional Western harmonics, but by variations on patterns derived from the twelve notes of the octave, arranged in a simple series which came to be known as the twelve-tone row. This series would provide the basis for a theme or sequence of notes, which would then be used to programme permutations and transformations, subject to the principle that the sequence must always be completed before another is begun. The serialist principle provided as tight a means of organization as any Bach fugue, with the notable difference that it would in most cases be wholly inaudible to the listener. Modernism had begun in an attempt to rematerialize music, to make composing more responsive to the dynamic actualities of listening, and to open up the expressive possibilities of sound. Serialism offered the opportunity of dematerializing music, separating the ideal or essentially composed work from the contingencies of its performance. Modern music began with an exhilarated sense of the centrality of the ear to modern life; high modernist music made hearing beside the point.

Schoenberg's work, and that of his follower Anton Webern, who applied serialist principles even more unbendingly than his master, came to be characterized by an autonomy based on negation of the raucous contingencies of modern life as such. If modern art found its great champion and impresario in Clement Greenberg, modernist music found its interpreting Aaron in the figure of Theodor Adorno. Schoenberg's music provided for Adorno the basis of an aesthetic theory which emphasized the necessity of the autonomy of art, in a severe, but always incomplete refusal of the degraded conditions of advanced commodity capitalism. In musical terms, Adorno insisted on a modernism against modernity.

For Adorno, organized musical sound is a kind of 'noise' or excess, which cannot be wholly assimilated to the ordered cacophonies of contemporary cultural life. Jacques Attali similarly identifies modernity, not with the deafening increase in toxic noise, but with a systematic drowning out of the possibility of noise, in the regime of what he calls 'repetition'.

> Power, in its invading, deafening presence, can be calm: people no longer talk to one another. They speak neither of themselves nor of power. They hear the noises of the commodities into which their imaginary is collectively channeled, where their dreams of sociality and need for transcendence dwell. The musical ideal then almost becomes an ideal of health: quality, purity, the elimination of noises; silencing drives, deodorizing the body, emptying it of its needs, and reducing it to silence. Make no mistake: if all of society agrees to address itself so loudly through this music, it is because it has nothing more to say, because it no longer has a meaningful discourse to hold, because even the spectacle is now only one form of repetition among others, and perhaps an obsolete one. In this sense, music is meaningless, liquidating, the prelude to a cold social silence in which man will reach his culmination in repetition.[58]

Modernism began with the 'desacralization of musical matter, the advent of the nonformal, the noninstituted, the nonrepresentative', but the 'code of dissonance' into which modernism developed in fact becomes 'a more efficient channelization of the productions of the imaginary . . . forming

the elements of a code of cybernetic repetition, a society without signification – a repetitive society'.[59]

However, not all of the possibilities opened up in the early days of
modernist experimentation proved possible to discipline in the austere
technicism of serialism. The great drive of the musical avant-garde in the
later twentieth-century has been towards the liberation and autonomization
of noise from the formalizations of musical sound. Perhaps the great
initiating impulse of this tradition, which runs through the work of Edgard
Varèse, Pierre Schaeffer, Pierre Boulez and John Cage, was Luigi Russolo's call, in his manifesto of March 1913, for a liberation of the musical
possibilities of noise in general, especially the diverse and unsynthesizable
complexity of sound in the city:

> The ear of the Eighteenth Century man would not have been able to
> withstand the inharmonious intensity of certain chords produced by our
> orchestra (with three times as many performers as that of the orchestra of
> his time). But our ear takes pleasure in it, since it is already educated to
> modern life, so prodigal in different noises. Nevertheless, our ear is not
> satisfied and calls for ever greater acoustical emotions.[60]

> Noise . . . arriving confused and irregular from the irregular confusion of
> life, is never revealed to us entirely and always holds innumerable surprises.
> We are certain, then, that by selecting, coordinating, and controlling all the
> noises, we will enrich mankind with a new and unsuspected pleasure of the
> senses. Although the characteristic of noise is that of reminding us brutally
> of life, the Art of Noises should not limit itself to an imitative reproduction.
> It will achieve its greatest emotional power in acoustical enjoyment itself,
> which the inspiration of the artist will know how to draw from the
> combining of noises.[61]

The pleasures of the arts of noise are the pleasures of enlargement, of
an amplification of attention to the sounds of everyday experience. This
amplified attention involves two kinds of enrichment; first of all, there is
the expansion of the limits of the audible, as previously unheard events
and aural objects become available to be heard; secondly there is the
thickening of attention required of the modern subject, the capacity to hear
the complex simultaneity of modern auditory existence. The postmodernist expansion of audition may be achieved by a drastic emptying out of
the opulent, omnicompetent plenitude of modernism, for example in the
harmonic desiccation and the contraction of single tones evidenced in the
work of Morton Feldman, La Monte Young's *The Tortoise, His Dreams and
Journeys* (1964) or Tom Johnson's *Four Note Opera*, works which aim, not

to purify auditory attention so much as to disquiet it. It can also take the form of a thickening of harmony and timbre, for example in the strange, shifting soundmasses of a work such as Gyorgi Ligeti's *Atmosphères* Minimalism, as embodied in the 1970s and 1980s in the work of Terry Riley and Steve Reich, seems to bring together the ambitions of impoverishment and enlargement; minimalist works such as Riley's *In C* or Steve Reich's *Clapping* deliberately reduce the range of technical resources available to music only to proliferate from this reduced range of elements a kind of overload.

This combination of the principles of reduction and expansion in music written since the Second World War derives enormous impetus from the work of John Cage, who trained with Arnold Schoenberg in California, but led his teacher to declare 'He's not a composer – he's an inventor'. Cage aimed to liberate the materiality of sound from the objectifying, organizing, spatializing powers of the eye and the ear that has come to be modelled upon it. This entailed the extension of the Russoloan ambition of an art of noises – in the notorious silencing of the music in the piece *4'33"*, in order that we be no longer deafened to the rich phenomenality of ambient sound. If this renewed acquaintance with sonorous materiality, it also involved an immaterialization of sound, a refusal of the impulse to treat sounds as replicable and manipulable objects, and a determination to open himself to the unmasterable temporality of sound. As Cage himself put it: 'A sound possesses nothing, no more than I possess it. A sound doesn't have a being, it can't be sure of existing in the following second. What's strange is that it came to be there, this very second. And that it goes away. The riddle is the process.'[62]

In one sense, music may be said to be the defining art of modernism, in its push towards an absolute autonomy, uncompromised by the desire to represent, express, or be associated with any other art form. Curiously, music, or, more broadly, the arts of sound, have come to have a defining centrality in postmodernist aesthetics and philosophy of art, but for entirely opposite reasons. Thomas Docherty writes that 'aurality . . . in postmodernism replaces specularity as a dominant determining mode of perception', and suggests that, since temporality is of the essence of aurality, the postmodernist appellation of the ear implies a destabilizing work of temporal passage beyond the fixed condition of a Work: 'aurality is thus also marked by a tendency to heterogeneity or alterity, for its major transgression is its tendency to hear what is not there, to make the work which is the object of its aural perception different from itself'.[63]

Jean-François Lyotard has also turned to the arts of sound in order to express the ambition of an art that would put its own competence powerfully into question, arguing for a 'music as *Tonkunst* [which] tries to rid itself of music as *Musik*'.[64] Such an art characteristically does not manipulate or exercise mastery over its materials; rather it engineers its own exposure to them. The (immaterial) material of sound is both elementary, actual, 'here and now', and also an always transient happening, which resists every attempt to capture and synthesize it. Music provides the possibility for the condition Lyotard calls 'impassibility', the determinate presiding over one's own evacuation: 'the essential features of what there is to be "liberated" in sound, and in particular the essential features of what music aided by contemporary technologies is trying to free in sound [are] its authority, the belonging of the spirit to the temporal blowing-up involved in the "being-now" of the heard sound.'[65]

Modernism began in the dissolution of musical propriety, the shattering of its inherited and defining languages through an openness to the sounds of modern life and its musics, especially ragtime and jazz, but ended in the impossible attempt to bend that noisily heteroglot language back to its own technical and aesthetic purposes. The undermining of the authority and givenness of the 'work' in postmodernist music has led, from the 1970s onwards, to a promiscuous mingling of the substance of classical or 'serious' music with popular forms of music of all kinds, as well as with musics from other cultural traditions. The music of John Zorn is one of the most striking examples of what might be called critical hospitality to popular musical styles. Rather than effecting smooth fusions of classical and popular music, Zorn effects noisy, abrasive disjunctions of sounds and styles. A work for chamber ensemble such as *Cobra* 'not only uses conventional orchestral instrumentation including harp, brass, woodwind and percussion, but also incorporates electric guitar and bass, turntables, cheesy organ, telephone bells and industrial clanging'.[66] Elsewhere, Zorn has combined classical scoring with the use of punk thrash, heavy metal and jazz. Kevin McNeilly suggests that such music 'politicizes the aural environment . . . [involving] the creation of a new form of attention, of listening' (though one would perhaps wish to know what, in the absence of an authoritative set of listening instructions intrinsic to the music, guarantees this political effect).[67]

The movements of association and hybridization that have come to be known as 'world music' began in modernism, with Debussy's incorporation of the structures of Indonesian gamelan music, and the turn to various folk traditions by other composers. But such musical styles and influences tended to be treated by modernist composers as raw material to be incorporated and transformed, thus confirming the self-identity of western music, rather than providing occasions for its disturbance. Although it is evident that 'world music' has now become a particular meta-style of western commodity-music, whose undemanding and unsurprising blendings are instantly recognizable as a specific kind of style, there have been much richer more unpredictable effects from the meeting of musical traditions, such as those systematically promoted by Peter Gabriel for his annual WOMAD festivals.

As in other arts, the postmodernist transformation in music has resulted in more than the diversification of style. It has also led to the breaking open of the closure of music as a form, and a determined effort to read its social meanings and effects. Particularly important here have been the readings of the relations between music and larger regimes of socio-technological power, such as Jacques Attali's *Noise*, and of the relations between musical theory and the construction of gender at different moments in the West, such as Catherine Clément's *Opera, or the Undoing of Woman* (1988) and Susan McClary's *Feminine Endings* (1991).[68]

What underlies much postmodern performance theory is often not a dissatisfaction with form, or fixity, or identity, but rather the suspicion that these are the means used to trap and exploit artistic work in the form of commodities for the market. If art must always seek to protect itself from the threat of this commodification by art galleries, theatres, TV networks and universities, then the logical extreme of this attitude is to refuse to be art at all, to refuse to embody oneself in stable or reproducible forms; this as part of a desire, says Henry Sayre, 'to counter not merely art's exploitation in the marketplace, but also the authority and privilege with which the marketplace self-interestedly invests it'.[69] This is rendered all the more difficult and all the more necessary in a situation in which, far from attacking or expelling alternative culture, official media culture preys parasitically upon it. The crisis for the avant-garde, and the push towards the postmodern as it is described by Bonnie Marranca, comes from the fact of a bourgeois culture which 'imitates modernist aesthetics and attitudes so openly in its obsession for self-expression and the new that the concept of "avant-garde" has been drained of its original meaning'.[70]

The dread of being frozen into a commodity brings about the contradictory response described by Henry Sayre as the 'mythology of presence' with which performance and such things as the oral poetry movement have surrounded themselves.[71] To highlight the fugitive intensity of the 'liberated' performance is to deny and downgrade any attempt to provide documentary records of such performances in galleries, museums and books, even as it simultaneously creates an ever more intense desire for such records (and opportunities for different kinds of packaging and display, in tapes, photographs and archives of performance). Sayre is right to emphasize as he does the parasitic relationship between free performance and exploitable commodity, for it is in fact never possible to abstract one pole of the opposition and simply set it against the other, to insist on performance against text. For our intuition of the immediacy of performance is always a second-degree intuition, itself formed within a context of habits and expectations. What is more, the desire for noncommodifiable immediacy, for free theatrical experience, is no more immune from the operations of commodification than practices which yield an obvious object. In fact, the fixation of much postmodern performance theory upon the opposition of the commodity and of free experience draws, in an oddly anachronistic way, upon the language and concepts more appropriate to an earlier period in the development of capitalism. Late capitalism, organized in new ways around vastly enhanced networks of information, communication and reproduction, seems effectively to have dissolved the simple opposition of dead commodity-as-thing and live performance-as-process. The problem may then be not so much that performance always risks falling into the dead residue of objecthood in reproduction (photographs, audio-and video-recordings) as that performance and reproduction have become intertwined in complex ways.

This can best be exemplified, not in the more restricted field of avant-garde drama and performance, but in the much larger and culturally more pervasive area of rock music.[72] (This is not to deny the significant forms of connection between the two realms in the work of artists like Andy Warhol, Peter Gabriel, Tom Waits and Laurie Anderson, of course.) Rock music, with its recurrent display of the values enshrined in performance, along with its extraordinary generation of new reproductive technologies, instances in a particularly powerful way the mutations undergone by those conceptual opposites, performance and text. The late 1970s and 1980s saw a return in rock music to the 'primitive' value and vitality of 'live' performance, after the retreat of the largest and most influential bands like The Beatles and Pink Floyd into the technological delights of the studio. It is striking that the most powerful and successful artists over the last twenty years have all felt obliged to demonstrate their capacity to engage with audiences in the direct contact of live performance as well as via albums and video recordings – the most familiar examples being Bruce Springsteen, Dire Straits, Madonna and Michael Jackson. It is perhaps Springsteen whose career projects most unassailably the values associated with live performance, and because of this, the Springsteen

mythology provides the most useful and interesting place to begin analysing the problematic status of the concept of the 'live' in postmodern mass
culture. It needs to be said at this point that not many people would be
inclined to see Bruce Springsteen's work as itself postmodernist in style or
expressive content; but, the ways in which his work is taken up, dispersed
and distributed provide a way of understanding the contemporary conditions with which a theory of postmodern culture has to deal.

The most important part of the Springsteen mythology has always been
his reputation as a live performer, one who works hard to give himself with
energy and enthusiasm to his enormous audiences. To see Springsteen live
is to be in the presence of a mythical figure, to enjoy a certain erotic
closeness. Springsteen is most authentically 'himself' when he is on stage,
and the ecstasy generated by the sudden shrinking of distance between fan
and star is at its most extreme in live performance. This ecstasy of desired
identification is a comparatively recent phenomenon in mass culture and
turns out to depend oddly upon the technology of mass reproduction and
communication; for it is only when the means exist to provide audiences
with various kinds of substitute for the presence of the star – films,
records, tapes, pictures – that this ecstatic yield of pleasure can be obtained
from being in his actual presence. In fact, the success of the rock industry,
which has taken over from the film industry in the business of star-manu-
facture, depends upon the kinds of desire that high fidelity reproduction
stimulates, the itch for more, and for more faithful reproductions of the
'real thing', the yearning to move ever closer to the 'original'.

There is a drama of possession and control acted out through this. To
own a record is, in a limited sense, to be able to control the music that it
encodes, for, with certain exclusions, one purchases with the record the
freedom to reproduce and replay it wherever and whenever one wishes, at
home, in the street, in the car. This repeatability is what seems to
guarantee the consumer's possession and control of the commodity; but it
also encloses a hidden deficiency. If recorded music is infinitely repeatable,
then this is precisely because it is a form of copy, which must always stand
at one remove from its original. So paradoxically, at the moment of its
greatest yielding, the commodity always holds something back; the more
the record is played, the more it confirms the possession and control of
the consumer, the more it displays its failure to be the real thing. What
guarantees the possibility of the consumer's control is an intrinsic shortfall
in the commodity, the fact that it can never be the original of itself.

These factors connect with the more general issues which have been the
subject of intensified debate within postmodern cultural theory in recent
years. As Deleuze, Derrida and others have argued, we continue to depend

upon an opposition between things which are felt to be immediate, original and 'real' on the one hand, and the representations of those things, which we conceive of as secondary, derived and therefore 'false' on the other. Repetition plays a crucial part in sustaining our sense of the real, since repetition is always, as Deleuze argues, tied to the conception of a return of the Same, and the threat posed by repetition and replication to the authority of original and universal ideas is only ever a temporary threat, which customarily reverts to the service of origins.[73]

In the light of the fantastic proliferation of processes for the replication of products, texts and information, many cultural theorists, from Walter Benjamin to Jean Baudrillard, have seen a diminution in the authority of ideas of originality, Benjamin arguing that the 'aura' of the original work of art is lost with the predominance of mechanical reproduction, and Baudrillard proclaiming that the very opposition between original and copy has been lost in an age of simulacra, or repetitions without originals.[74] At the same time, it is possible to see how the proliferation of reproductions actually intensifies the desire for origin, even if that origin is increasingly sensed as an erotic lack rather than a tangible and satisfying presence. In Baudrillard's terms, the real is ceaselessly manufactured as an intensified version of itself, as hyperreality.

For the rock fan, it is above all the live show which seems to offer this unfalsifiably real corporeal presence, for here – apparently – are to be found life, music, the body themselves, naked and unignorable, unobscured by barriers of reproduction or representation. But what kind of live experience characterizes contemporary rock music? In the case of Bruce Springsteen it is an experience of manufactured mass closeness. Whereas audiences at the great pop festivals of the 1970s had to make do with the sight of tiny figures performing inconsequentially on a stage half a mile away ('Is that Dylan in the hat?'), and a sound system that worked efficiently only with a following wind, Springsteen's appearances on his world tour in 1985, which were rarely to fewer than 50,000 people, made sure that no member of the vast audience could escape the slightest nuance of music or voice. Behind him, an enormous video screen projected claustrophobically every detail of his agonized facial expressions in a close-up which at one and the same time abolished and re-emphasized the actual distance between him and his audience.

Intimacy and immediacy on this scale can only be achieved by massively conspicuous acts of representation. Enormous amplification, hugely expanded images; these are the forms which reproduction takes in the context of the live. Sound and image are simultaneous with the 'real' music that is being performed (although, of course, in the case of most contemporary music the 'original' sound is usually itself only an amplified derivation from an initiating signal), even if it remains obvious that what is most real about the event is precisely the fact that it is being projected as mass experience. The normal condition for Springsteen's performances is an ecstatic, somatic excess that spills over into and is constituted by an excess of representations at the very heart of the live experience.

It is for this reason that audiences of 80,000 or more now regularly attend concerts to watch videos, albeit 'live' videos; the ecstasy of experience is turned into what Baudrillard calls an 'ecstasy of communication', a fantastic, barely-controllable excess of images and representations.[75] This was well borne out during the Live Aid concerts in 1985 when Phil Collins, after playing in London, absurdly travelled across the Atlantic on Concorde in order to play in Philadelphia later that day, during the same global transmission of the concert, in a monstrously inflated version of the prank in which a schoolchild runs from one end to the other of a serial school photograph in order to be photographed in two places. But Phil Collins travelled 3,000 miles not in order to be visible in the flesh, but to provide an image to be projected on to the video-screen which projected close-up images of him to the audience in the stadium and round the world.

During the Live Aid concerts, video screens allowed the easy incorporation of other, recorded material into the live spectacle. David Bowie and Mick Jagger had originally planned to sing 'Dancing in the Street' simultaneously in Philadelphia and London, but the unavoidable half-second delay in transmission made this impossible; so they came together in a video recording which was fitted seamlessly into the experience of the live concerts – and the fact that the song and the dance routines in the video exemplified the theme of spontaneous, *en plein air* celebration only added ironic piquancy to the blending of the real and the represented. The audience were also closely involved in this process of willed simulation. Often, the viewer of the spectacle at home was shown the audience watching an image of themselves on the giant video screen, so that when we at home subsequently saw shots of the audience, we were not sure whether it was the audience itself that we were seeing, or the image of the audience projected on to the video-screen at the event – whether we were watching them, in other words, or watching them watching themselves.

What emerges from all this is not so much the abolition of the desire for originality and presence in the performing instant, as the inversion of the structural dependence of copies upon originals. In the case of the 'live' performance, the desire for originality is a secondary effect of various forms of reproduction. The intense 'reality' of the performance is not something that lies behind the particulars of the setting, the technology and the audience; its reality consists in all of that apparatus of representation.

We should not be surprised, therefore, at the success of that postmodernist oxymoron, the 'live recording'. Of course many of the protocols of live performance derive from the familiarity of audience and performer alike with representations of other live performances. This is confirmed by the aesthetic conventions that determine the ways in which live recordings, in that evocative contemporary term, are 'produced'. After recording a live album, most artists have to spend considerable amounts of time in the studio, reworking sections, altering the balance, overdubbing vocals, adding instruments, correcting mistakes and, indeed, sometimes, roughing up a sound that may be too smooth in actual performance. (Once this becomes known, it can produce a primitivist reflex, as with Dire Straits' *Alchemy* album, which made a selling point of the fact that the 'original' sound had not been tampered with in any way.)

Increasingly, then, the experience of the 'live' is itself being commodified, 'produced' as a strategic category of the semiotic, even though its function *within* semiotic systems may be to embody that which remains authentically and dangerously outside the distortions of the commodity and of signification itself. The live is always in a sense the quotation of itself – never the live, always the 'live'. Paradoxically, the desire for original and authentic experience exists alongside the recognition that there can never be any such thing, at least in contemporary rock music. The increasing sophistication of studio technology, and the consequent multiplication of versions of a single song, in remixes and extended twelve-inch versions, combined more recently with the cult of 'sampling', or the appropriation and re-editing of snatches of music from other songs, means the loss of a sense that there can be such a thing as an original version of a song. Nowadays, the title of a song names a diverse and theoretically endless range of embodiments and performances, or versions of performances, since one performance may be mixed and reassembled in any number of ways. This means that the opposition between the live and the reproduced which is sustained within studio recordings themselves – promotional videos often show the studio as a sort of substitute scene of the 'live', discovering in the instant of recording a kind of immediacy which the technology of recording disseminates – is jeopardized. This recalls Walter Benjamin's argument that the abandonment of 'real time' continuity in film-making with the chopping up of the narrative into discontinuous segments for the purpose of filming, results in a loss of 'aura', since the narrative that is eventually synthesized has never been acted out anywhere all at once. Something similar happens in the modern studio recording, which assembles a performance which has never had any existence all at once anywhere except on the producer's console.

These points may be considerably generalized. Everywhere the world of the mass media holds out the possibility and desirability of 'live' experience, and embraces 'process' while discrediting fixity of definition. The economics of mass culture, far from requiring the freezing of freely contingent human experiences into commodifiable forms, consciously promotes these forms of transient intensity, since it is, in the end, much easier to control and stimulate demand for experiences which are spontaneously (nothing of the kind, of course) sensed as outside representation. From rock music to tourism to television and even education, advertising imperatives and consumer demand are no longer for goods, but for experiences.

Here, as elsewhere, postmodern theory has a complicated and ambivalent relationship to this process. Postmodern theories of performance, whether inversive (asserting the presence of performance against the inauthenticity of representation) or deconstructive (examining the mutual implications of performance and text) simultaneously stand aside from and form part of this semiotic terrain. In the attempt to think through the complexities of performance, and the ways in which it reproduces authoritative structures of thought, postmodern theory aligns itself with what it describes, and perhaps secretly designates itself in its descriptions of the subversive mission of avant-garde art. But, at the same time, it can function as an imaginative and institutional filtering of its own vision of the subversive sublime of pure performance. The more successful the intellectual paradigm of postmodern performance becomes, the tighter is the circuit of exchange between the self-acknowledging and unmistakable energies of performance and the exemplary or demonstrative function that such free energies perform for the paradigm. The freedom of performance, of the 'live', is mortgaged to the theory and, of course, the cultural codes and assumptions, which accredit it in advance as freedom. The postmodern theory of a performance that escapes the museum, the script, or the recording, is the discursive form which precisely legislates the conditions of that escape.

Notes

1 Joel C. Weinsheimer, *Gadamer's Hermeneutics: A Reading of 'Truth and Method'* (New Haven and London: Yale University Press, 1985), pp. 109–10.
2 'Presence as Play', in *Performance in Postmodern Culture*, ed. Michel Benamou and Charles Caramello (Milwaukee: Center for Twentieth Century Studies, 1977), p. 3.

3 'The Classical Heritage of Modern Drama: The Case of Postmodern Theatre', trans. Loren Kruger, *Modern Drama*, 29: 1 (1986), p. 16.

4 Antonin Artaud, 'The Theatre of Cruelty: Second Manifesto', *The Theatre and Its Double*, trans. Victor Corti (London: Calder and Boyars, 1970), pp. 82–3.

5 Ibid., p. 118.

6 Introduction to *The Theatre of Images*, first published 1977, reprinted in *Theatrewritings* (New York: Performing Arts Journal Publications, 1984), p. 78.

7 'The Liberated Performance', trans. Barbara Kerslake, *Modern Drama*, 25:1 (1982), p. 62.

8 Ibid., pp. 64–5.

9 Marranca, *Theatrewritings*, p. 79.

10 Ibid., p. 80.

11 'Some Versions of Performance Art', *Theatre Journal*, 36:1 (1984), p. 165.

12 'The Search for New Endings: The Theatre in Search of a Fix, Part III', *Theatre Journal*, 36:1 (1984), p. 160.

13 *Applied Grammatology: Post(e)-Pedagogy from Jacques Derrida to Joseph Beuys* (Baltimore and London: Johns Hopkins University Press, 1985).

14 Ibid., p. 229.

15 *Writing and Difference*, trans. Alan Bass (London: Routledge and Kegan Paul, 1978), pp. 232–50. References hereafter to *WD* in the text.

16 For a particularized reading of the consequences of this postmodern view of performance see my *Samuel Beckett: Repetition, Theory and Text* (Oxford: Basil Blackwell, 1988), pp. 115–69.

17 ' "The eye finds no fixed point on which to rest . . ." ', trans. C. R. Parsons, *Modern Drama*, 25:1 (March, 1982), p. 155.

18 'The Object of Performance: Aesthetics in the Seventies', *Georgia Review*, 37: 1 (1983), p. 174.

19 Josette Féral, 'Performance and Theatricality', *Modern Drama*, 25:1 (1982), p. 175.

20 'La Dent, la Paume', in *Des dispositifs pulsionnels* (Paris: UGE, 1973), quoted in Régis Durand, 'Theatre/SIGNS/Performance', in *Innovation/Renovation: New Perspectives in the Humanities* ed. Ihab and Sally Hassan (Madison, Wis.: University of Wisconsin Press, 1983), p. 219.

21 Féral, 'Performance and Theatricality', pp. 177, 179.

22 Durand, 'Theatre/SIGNS/Performance', p. 220.

23 Pontbriand, ' "The eye finds no fixed point . . ." ', p. 159.

24 Richard Foreman, 'Notes on the Process of Making It: Which Is Also the Object', *Reverberation Machines: The Later Plays and Essays* (Barrytown: Station Hill, 1985), p. 191.

25 Ibid., pp. 191–93.

26 Ibid., p. 191.

27 Ibid., p. 193.

28 Herbert Blau, 'Universals of Performance', *The Eye of Prey: Subversions of the Postmodern* (Bloomington and Indianapolis: Indiana University Press, 1987), p. 167.

29 'How Truth . . . Leaps (Stumbles) Across Stage', *Reverberation Machines*, p. 199.

30 'Art and Objecthood', in *Minimalist Art*, ed. Geoffrey Battcock (New York: E. P. Dutton, 1968), p. 142.

31 'Literature and Signification', in *Critical Essays*, trans. Richard Howard (Evanston, II.: Northwestern University Press, 1972), pp. 261–2.

32 Dort, 'The Liberated Performance', p. 67.

33 'News, Sex, and Performance Theory', in *Innovation/Renovation*, p. 191.

34 Ibid., pp. 207–8.

35 Ibid., p. 209.

36 'The Remission of Play', in *Innovation/Renovation*, p. 162.

37 Philip Auslander, 'Toward a Conception of the Political in Postmodern Theater', *Theatre Journal*, 39:1 (1987), p. 26.

38 Ibid., p. 29.

39 Ibid.

40 'Women's Performance Art: Feminism and Postmodernism', *Theatre Journal*, 40:2 (1988), p. 221.

41 Ibid., p. 224.

42 *The Eye of Prey: Subversions of the Postmodern* (Bloomington and Indianapolis: Indiana University Press, 1987), p. 167.

43 Ibid., p. 170.

44 Ibid.

45 Quoted in Sally Banes, *Writing Dancing in the Age of Postmodernism* (Hanover, NH: Wesleyan University Press/University Press of New England, 1994), p. 248. References hereafter to *WDAP* in the text.

46 Roger Copeland, 'Is It Post-Postmodern?' in 'What Has Become of Postmodern Dance: Answers and Other Questions by Marcia B. Siegel [etc.]', in *TDR – The Drama Review*, 36, (1992), p. 66.

47 'Against Interpretation', in *A Susan Sontag Reader*, ed. Elizabeth Hardwick (Harmondsworth: Penguin, 1983), pp. 102, 104.

48 'Some Retrospective Notes on a Dance for 10 People and 12 Mattresses Called "Parts of Some Sextets," Performed at the Wadsworth Atheneum, Hartford, Connecticut, and Judson Memorial Church, New York, in March 1965', *Tulane Drama Review*, 10 (1965), p. 178.

49 *Terpsichore in Sneakers: Post-Modern Dance* (Boston: Houghton Mifflin, 1980) p. 51. For a detailed analysis of *Trio A*, see pp. 44–54.

50 'A Quasi Survey of Some "Minimalist" Tendencies in the Quantitatively Minimal Dance Activity Midst the Plethora, or an Analysis of *Trio A*', in *Work 1961–73* (Halifax, Nova Scotia: Press of the Nova Scotia College of Art and Design; New York: New York University Press, 1974), p. 63.

51 For an account of one such production, Margaret Williams's and Lea Anderson's *Perfect Moment*, broadcast by Britain's Channel 4 in 1992, see

Valerie A. Briginshaw, 'Postmodern Dance and the Politics of Resistance', in *Analysing Performance: A Critical Reader*, ed. Patrick Campbell (Manchester: Manchester University Press, 1996), pp. 125–32.

52 For reports on these and other characteristics of what Banes now sees as a second postmodernism in dance, see the essays in section V of *Writing Dancing in the Age of Postmodernism*, 'Postmodern Dance: From the Sixties to the Nineties', pp. 207–352.

53 Thomas Leabhart, *Modern and Post-Modern Mime* (London: Methuen, 1989), pp. 1–16.

54 Quoted ibid., p. 49.

55 See the issues of *Mime Journal*, 1980–2 and 1983 devoted to 'New Mime in North America' and 'New Mime in Europe'.

56 Leabhart, *Modern and Post-Modern Mime*, p. 146.

57 See Robert P. Morgan, 'Secret Languages: The Roots of Musical Modernism', in *Modernism: Challenges and Perspectives*, ed. Monique Chefdor, Ricardo Quinones and Albert Wachtel (Urbana and Chicago: University of Illinois Press, 1986), pp. 33–53.

58 *Noise: The Political Economy of Music*, trans. Brian Massumi (Manchester: Manchester University Press, 1985), p. 122.

59 Ibid., pp. 82, 83.

60 Luigi Russolo, *The Art of Noises*, trans. Barclay Brown (New York: Pendragon Press, 1986), p. 24.

61 Ibid., pp. 27–8.

62 Quoted in Daniel Charles, *For The Birds* (London: Marion Boyars, 1981), p. 150.

63 Thomas Docherty, *After Theory: Postmodernism/Postmarxism* (London: Routledge, 1990), p. 30.

64 Jean-François Lyotard, *The Inhuman: Reflections on Time*, trans. Geoffrey Bennington and Rachel Bowlby (Cambridge: Polity Press, 1991), p. 173.

65 Ibid., p. 179.

66 Kevin McNeilly, 'Ugly Beauty: John Zorn and the Politics of Postmodern Music', *Postmodern Culture*, 5:2 (1995), p. 3.

67 Ibid., p. 7.

68 Catherine Clément, *Opera, or the Undoing of Woman*, trans. Betsy Wing (Minneapolis: University of Minnesota Press, 1988); Susan McClary, *Feminine Endings: Music, Gender, and Sexuality* (Minneapolis: University of Minnesota Press, 1991).

69 Sayre, 'The Object of Performance', p. 185.

70 *Theatrewritings*, p. 133.

71 Sayre, 'The Object of Performance', p. 177.

72 In this book, I use the term 'rock music' to distinguish the popular music of the 1960s onwards from the larger field of popular music this century; the former would begin with rock and roll, Elvis Presley and the Beatles, the latter would include artists like Bing Crosby and Frank Sinatra and would extend back at least until the 1920s.

73 See Gilles Deleuze, *Différence and Repetition*, trans. Paul Patton (London: Athlone, 1994).

74 Walter Benjamin, 'The Work of Art in the Age of Mechanical Reproduction', in *Illuminations*, trans. Harry Zohn (London: Fontana, 1970), pp. 219–54; Jean Baudrillard, 'The Precession of Simulacra', in *Simulations*, trans. Paul Foss, Paul Patton and Philip Bleitchman (New York: Semiotext(e), 1983), pp. 1–80.

75 'The Ecstasy of Communication', in *Postmodern Culture*, ed. Hal Foster (London and Sydney: Pluto Press, 1985), pp. 126–34.

6
Postmodern TV, Video and Film

TV and Video

It is hardly surprising that TV and video should have attracted such attention from theorists of postmodernism. Like film (with which, of course, TV overlaps more and more closely), TV and video are mass-cultural media which employ techniques of technological reproduction. As such, they seem structurally to embody a surpassing of the modernist narrative of the individual artist struggling to transform a particular physical medium. Uniqueness, permanence and transcendence (the medium transformed by the artist's subjectivity) seem in the reproducible arts of film and video to have given way irrevocably to multiplicity, transience, and anonymity. At the same time, both film and video seem to offer certain possibilities of a reawakened radical impetus, and the emergence of avant-garde video art is evidence of this. As such, TV and video encompass, like film, the two worlds of mass culture and minority avant-garde culture. Another way of saying this is that video exemplifies in a particularly intense way the postmodern dichotomy between avant-garde disruptive strategies and the processes whereby such strategies are absorbed and neutralized. It is the very familiarity of TV, and the global spread of TV expertise, both in production and consumption, that make this question of transgression and incorporation recur with such violent persistence.

Accounts of postmodern TV and video take two forms, identified respectively with the 'transgressive' or 'incorporative' hypotheses. The first form aims to identify postmodernist traits within television, or to identify and promote progressive possibilities within postmodern video texts. Such an approach is demonstrated by John Wyver in his article 'Television and Postmodernism'.[1] Wyver takes as his starting point

Stephen Heath's and Gillian Skinner's claim that the dominant mode of TV is the 'relay' – the transmission of reality direct and in real time to the viewer, without apparent selection, control or mediation. Against this mode, which derives from, but is not limited to, live broadcasts of news and sport, Wyver sets the postmodernist mode of TV, which freely acknowledges the play of the visual signifier, making no pretence to be transmitting the 'real'. The oddly-assorted group of examples which he gives includes the TV series 'About Time', in which, he says, the unquestioned ascendancy of the image over the word is challenged as images and arguments are used against each other to open up questions; a group of 'Arena' documentaries first shown on BBC2, including 'My Way' and 'The Private Life of the Ford Cortina', which were highly-structured collages centred around a theme or object, whose mixing of forms and strategies Wyver sees as a resistance to the dominant relay form; and rock promotional videos, whose indulgence of non-realistic fantasy worlds amounts to 'a full liberation of the signifier'.[2]

In fact, rock video is also the TV form favoured by other theorists of the postmodern, notably E. Ann Kaplan, who has devoted a whole book to the discussion of MTV, the American station which at its inception, showed rock videos 24 hours a day. The central section of Kaplan's book divides rock videos into five types, the 'romantic', the 'socially conscious', the 'nihilist', the 'classical' and the 'postmodernist'.[3] A chart maps out for us the, rather elementary, distinctions between them, largely in terms of theme and content. So, for instance, 'romantic' videos are said to rely on narrative, on the themes of loss and reunion, along with the projection of 'normal' sexual relationships, while 'nihilist' videos, associated with artists like Billy Idol and Van Halen, are non-or anti-narrative and stress an exotic blend of sadism, masochism, homoeroticism and androgyny. 'Classical' videos, on the other hand, either employ the characteristic Hollywood structure of the (male) gaze directed voyeuristically at female figures who are turned into objects of desire by that gaze, or employ or parody Hollywood genres like horror, suspense and science fiction (Michael Jackson's 'Thriller' and Peter Gabriel's 'Shock the Monkey' are examples here). As we might anticipate, what Kaplan calls 'postmodernist' videos are those which are unwilling to adhere to these lines of distinction:

> What characterizes the postmodernist video is its refusal to take a clear position vis-à-vis its images, its habit of hedging along the line of not communicating a clear signified. In postmodernist videos, as not in the other specific types, each element of a text is undercut by others: narrative is undercut by pastiche; signifying is undercut by images that do not line up

in a coherent chain; the text is flattened out, creating a two-dimensional effect and the refusal of a clear position for the spectator within the filmic world. (*RATC*, 63)

This definition is not much use for the humble spotter of postmodernist videos, since it depends so unstably upon negatives – postmodernism as (not) narrative, (not) centred, offering (no) position for the spectator. A similarly negative definition of the functions and effects of postmodernist rock video is given by Dick Hebdige in his discussion of Talking Heads' 'Road to Nowhere':

the pop promo video becomes a form designed to 'tell an image' rather than to 'tell a story' . . . At the most 'developed' end of this video aesthetic, a tape like *Road to Nowhere* establishes a narrative or rather non-narrative space – a space of sub-liminal narrative *suggestions* which is neither 'realist' nor 'modernist' . . . encouraging neither identification nor critical reflection.[4]

What is more confusing, however, is the fact that, in a sense, the whole field of contemporary rock music is in itself postmodern; certainly, Kaplan wants to claim something like this with respect to the output of MTV as a whole. This comes about because of MTV's self-conscious recycling of the whole history of rock music. Like Fredric Jameson, Kaplan posits a stylistic chronology in rock music via its videos; 'romantic' videos derive from to the commercialized soft rock of the 1960s, 'socially conscious' videos (which she mysteriously calls 'modernist') derive from the artists of the 1960s and 1970s who took oppositional stances towards established values, and 'nihilist' videos derive from the heavy metal bands who dominated the 1970s. But the postmodernist era of rock music is characterized not so much by any particular identifying style as by the multiplication of styles, which are now projected as a set of production options. As we move further into the postmodernist 1980s, the different types of video 'begin to reflect merely a different "look" rather than specifically to embody what we may loosely call different "ideologies" ' (*RATC*, 56).

This flattening of rock's history into an undifferentiated present comes to characterize the output of MTV as such, which encapsulates and recirculates as stylistic commodities the styles of different periods of rock music. As a result, the distinct forms and audiences of rock music are forcibly impacted into one amorphous, if hermeneutically versatile mass. It is an intriguing indication of the grip of postmodernism. One can be a thoroughly modernist viewer one minute watching an archival text from the very allegorical heart of rock music's modernist phase, a Beatles promotional film, say; and a postmodernist viewer the next, as a sophisticatedly ironic Talking Heads video slips on to the screen; but it is not a matter of simply choosing one's stylistic affiliation, as one would choose a hat or a hotel room, for, of course, in one's very capacity to wind in and out of these different modes of response and interpretation, one has been a postmodernist all along.

But Kaplan also wants to assert the ways in which rock video, in a Derridean or deconstructive fashion, also embodies an attack on what she calls 'bourgeois signifying practices', that is to say, challenges the status of representation as 'natural' or 'true' and exposes the illusion of a speaking position which is outside or above structures of representation (*RATC*, 147). Like John Wyver, Kaplan seems to believe that this tall order is fulfilled by means of the simple fact of stylistic versatility. Postmodernist rock videos have implications for feminism, because 'the breaking up of traditional realist forms sometimes entails a deconstruction of conventional sex-role representations that opens up new possibilities for female imaging'. In a further leap that is neither explained nor easily explicable, Kaplan also gives, as another recommendation of postmodernist video for the feminist, the fact that it 'offers the female spectator pleasure in sensation – color, sound, visual patterns – and in energy, body movement; it also opens up possibilities for expression of female desire' (*RATC*, 150). Quite apart from the extraordinary and insulting infantilization of female spectators here – they are made to sound like the excitable natives of the colonial imagination with their childish delight in colours and patterns – this definition seems to owe much to the desire to proclaim at all costs the transgressive possibilities of MTV, this powerful and entirely typical product of late capitalist cultural commodification, in order to lend the analysis itself a credible level of chic commitment.

In another, more circumspect account, Pat Aufderheide argues similarly for the productive potential of rock videos. Despite the fact that the modes of rock video have already penetrated so far into advertising and public spectacle, even into political promotion, the strength of this 'powerful, if playful, postmodern art' derives from the process which music videos embody, echo and encourage, 'the constant re-creation of an unstable self'.[5] This theme is a common one in many contemporary accounts of rock music video, but rarely is it accompanied by any analysis of how one might isolate these allegedly progressive purposes from the self-evident banalities and narrow stereotyping within rock videos, as well as the absolute saturation of the form by the crassest kind of commercialization.

The problem of separating the transgressive from the incorporated is one that is encountered sooner or later by many theorists of the postmod-

ernist video-text. It comes to the fore, for instance, in Susan Boyd-Bowman's description of the Institut National de la Communication Audiovi-
suelle (INA) in France.[6] The INA was formed in 1975 and was required
to supply the three French broadcasting channels with about 60 hours a
year of innovative or experimental programmes, as well as to maintain a
vast national archive of film and video material. This partly fortuitous
coincidence of role no doubt had a large part to play in the programmes
produced by the INA since 1975, including 'Hieroglyphs' (1975), 'Rue des
archives' (1978) and 'Juste une image' (1982), for they are characterized by
a now familiar postmodernist aesthetic of montage, repetition, jump-cut,
and discontinuity. This is Boyd-Bowman's description of the sixth episode
of 'Juste une image', which was a montage of a day's transmission on the
second State broadcasting channel:

> A digital clock in the corner of the frame records the time of day. To further
> complicate the montage, the programme is interspersed with a few 'para-
> sites': pieces of video art, mostly North American, such as Joan Logue's
> *Advertisements for Artists*. So, overlaid with the deconstruction of main-
> stream television is a flaunting of oppositional practice. Thus, a witty
> re-editing of *Apostrophes*, the intellectual chat-show, in which the sound is
> speeded up over a montage of cutaways which foreground the participants'
> body language, is in turn interrupted by *T-Women*, a video of lesbian
> love-making by an experimental German film-maker.[7]

In the output of the INA the actual museum of archives is turned into
an ever-changing, de-narrativized, imaginary museum-in-process. The
pillaging and recycling of the televisual and film history of France here
advertise its avant-garde status, in a refusal of closure, narrative, etc.
which is designed to upset the customary coherences of prime-time TV.
In this respect, it is very different from MTV; but in another respect, it
surely resembles it, since its 'subversive' recycling of materials also mimics
by intensification the form of mainstream TV output, with its running
together of disparate forms, genres and viewing pleasures. Once again, it
is difficult to be sure of being able to distinguish on purely stylistic terms
a 'good' postmodernism which, sitting on 'the postmodern gilt market' of
the national archives, can 'return those images to the world of social
relations', from a 'bad' postmodernism, which will merely 'leave its
viewers gazing at the flat screen'.[8]

By far the most extended consideration of the radical claims of postmodernist video is Fredric Jameson's. For Jameson, video and TV represent in
their very forms challenges, not only to the hegemony of modernist
aesthetic models, but also to the contemporary dominance of language and

the conceptual instruments associated with linguistic and semiotic sciences.[9] Central to Jameson's argument is an insistence on the absolute
assimilation of the viewing subject to the mechanical structure of the video
medium. By this he means that, whereas other representational media like
novels or films are committed to producing the effects of 'real time', while
actually distorting it (by foreshortening, telescoping, extending, varying
the focus, and so on) video – or at least non-narrative avant-garde video –
locks the viewer into the time of the video, which is in the end nothing
more than the 'real time' of the machine itself, spooling to its end. In
Jameson's account, avant-garde video is taken to be the essential form of
video, with commercial television, which patently does imitate film in
producing narrative effects, as its strange, bastard offshoot; he finds cause
for wonder, therefore, not in the fact that commercial TV imitates other
temporal visual media, but in the way that such TV manages to produce
the impression of fictive time out of what he believes to be 'the rigorously
non-fictive languages of video' ('Postmodernism and the Video-Text',
206). But there is, of course, no reason to suppose that the particular
practices or representational structures characteristic of (some forms of)
experimental video art are any more intrinsic to the medium than those
practices or structures which video shares with film, or even novels.
Jameson seems over-anxious here to ground his analysis of specific video
effects in what might pass for a 'materialist' argument about the physical
form of video, but does not really offer anything to characterize that
physical form or its effects.

The consequence of the revolutionary abandonment of the dimension of
fictive time for Jameson is an art without boundaries – an art characterized, in the terms influentially suggested by Raymond Williams, not so
much by individual units or separable elements, but by 'total flow',
without breaks or distinctions.[10] Williams uses this term to describe the
experience of broadcast TV, which works over the course of an evening or
period of viewing, rather than being organized into clearly separated
'programmes', but Jameson uses it to define the particular recalcitrance of
a certain kind of avant-garde video-text, which presents itself as 'fragments
in flight', as a kind of pure and empty duration, rather than a modernist
'work', which suspends and reshapes the experience of time. Even to select
one of these vanishing fragments for analysis is a guilty act of theoretical
violence, says Jameson, for it is 'fatally to regenerate the illusion of the
masterpiece or the canonical text, and to reify the experience of total flow
from which it was momentarily extracted' ('Postmodernism and the
Video-Text', 208). To this implausibility, Jameson adds another; such a
selection 'turns the anonymous video-maker back into a named artist or

"auteur", opens the way for the return of all those features of an older modernist aesthetic which it was in the nature of the new medium to have precisely effaced and dispelled' ('Postmodernism and the Video-Text', 209). The mesmerically imperative language slides the reader over the obvious questions here. Why should exemplification necessarily bring with it this dreaded relapse into the discredited modernist heroics of the author? (And, perhaps, why shouldn't it?) To be sure, analysis etymologically and practically requires the isolation of separate parts, but it does not automatically bring with it the whole collection of mystifications which Jameson so terrifyingly invokes. For why might analysis not be used precisely to demonstrate the fact of 'total flow'?

But the rhetorical strategy here turns out to be *occupatio*. Having established as an undemonstrated given the sublimely uncontainable flow of TV (although the differences and similarities between avant-garde and scheduled TV are nowhere explored in his account), Jameson has succeeded in discrediting analysis in advance, in order to guarantee that the subject of the enquiry will slip through the grip of his theory. But, of course, a theory that can so benignly encompass its own discomfiture in the end only increases its claims to interpretative command. Appropriately enough, then, Jameson's essay goes on to do precisely what it has said should not be done, which is to analyse a particular video-text, in this case, a video called 'AlienNATION', produced in 1979 by Edward Rankus, John Manning and Barbara Latham of the Chicago School of Art. The video lasts a mere 29 minutes, but is a furiously thick collage which, in Jameson's description, includes science fiction footage (drawn from a Japanese film of 1966 called *Godzilla vs. Monster Zero*), reproductions of classical paintings, a woman lying down under hypnosis, ultra-modern hotel lobbies with escalators moving busily, close-ups of children's building blocks, Beethoven sonatas, flying saucers over the Chicago skyline, advertisements for 1950s kitchens and much more. The video offers us no hierarchy of connotation, writes Jameson, by which we might be able to tell how one part or sequence 'interprets' or metaphorically translates any other part, and so the video will always elude any attempt to understand or decipher it, in the flood of its 'beginnings and thematic emergences, combinations and developments, resistances and struggles for dominance, partial resolutions, forms of closure leading on to one or another full stop' ('Postmodernism and the Video-Text', 211). As before, Jameson instances these effects by apparently contradicting himself, describing how a sequence featuring experimental music intersects with passages of vocational or psychological counselling heard on the soundtrack, to yield 'predictable messages about the hidden programming and conditioning mechanisms of bureaucratic society' ('Postmodernism and the Video-Text', 216). But Jameson then repeats his warning that to identify such themes is an artifical and culpable blocking of the text's total flow, which is 'a ceaseless rotation of elements such that they change place at every moment, with the result that no single element can occupy the position of "interpretant" (or that of primary sign), for any length of time; but must be dislodged in turn in the following instant' ('Postmodernism and the Video-Text', 218).

But finally, in what seems like a last effort to countermand the imperative of total flow, Jameson identifies the 'real meaning' of this piece, in its cryptic reference to the assassination on 27 November 1978 of the San Francisco city supervisor Harvey Milk, the evidence for this being the presence of shots of an upset milk carton and an apparent visual reference to hostess twinkies (a type of American biscuit) – Harvey Milk's murderer, Jameson tells us, 'entered the unforgettable plea of not guilty by reason of insanity, owing to the excessive consumption of hostess twinkies' ('Postmodernism and the Video-Text', 220). The note of triumph is unmistakable (perhaps it is ironic, but, in that case, the irony itself seems like a masking device): 'Here, then, at last the referent is disclosed; the brute fact, the historical event, the real toad in this particular imaginary garden' ('Postmodernism and the Video-Text', 220). A moment later, Jameson backs down again from this particular ascription of meaning; we cannot be sure, he mopes, whether this discovery documents 'the persistence and stubborn all-informing gravitational charge of reference' or shows what a pitiful remnant of meaning is left after reference has been 'systematically processed, dismantled, textualized and volatilized' ('Postmodernism and the Video-Text', 221).

Jameson's account ends with a fable of the gradual detachment of signs from their referents through history, with postmodernist video as characteristic of late capitalism in its absolute separation between the two. But where modernist art forms of the early twentieth century could derive a certain critical power from their detachment from the 'real', postmodernist video offers no such possibility of critique of a cultural order with which it seems banally identical. Jameson's attempts to fan his dialectic back into life by proclaiming contemporary video as the 'strongest and most original and authentic form' ('Postmodernism and the Video-Text', 223) of the logic of postmodernist culture, seem like a nostalgic revival of the language of modernist masterpiece-aesthetics which he has previously dismissed so sadly.

With its uncertainty of focus between commercial TV and avant-garde video, and its final wavering oppositionality, Jameson's account presents in a particularly pure form a recurrent struggle within theories of contemporary postmodernist forms. Theories of contemporary culture express a dual allegiance: firstly, to the democratic impetus to close the gap between elitist high culture and mass or popular culture, and secondly, to a lexicon of cultural subversion and deconstruction which is partly inherited from modernist culture and its avant-garde theorists. For many theorists of the contemporary, mass culture is no longer the deadening antagonist of individual creativity that it was for Q.D. Leavis or Theodor Adorno, and the effort within much of this criticism is to find ways of crediting mass culture with subversive or progressive potential. In the specific case of TV, this struggle is particularly intense, since TV works in so many obvious ways to trivialize cultural innovation. In much of the work of such theorists, the struggle to provoke flares of resistance or subversive potential out of the fading coals of contemporary culture is matched by an internal struggle of terms and concepts, in which a theory of the encyclopaedic powers of incorporation of contemporary culture vies with a desire to promote forms of resistance – and to advertise the place of theory in that process.

In some accounts of contemporary TV, however, the capitulation to the technological seductions of TV and video is rather less complicated. Lawrence Grossberg, whose work on the sociology of rock music has sometimes evidenced a Jamesonesque distaste for the moral emptiness of mass culture, has recently shown a change of attitude in his work on postmodernist TV. Grossberg defines contemporary TV in terms of its deliberate superficiality, its multiplication of empty, merely interreferential images. Like many other theorists, he uses the 1980s police series 'Miami Vice' as an example of this:

> *Miami Vice* is, as its critics have said, all on the surface. And the surface is nothing but a collection of quotations from our own collective historical debris, a mobile game of Trivia . . . The narrative is less important than the images . . . Narrative closure becomes a mere convenience of the medium. And the spectator as subject all but disappears in the rapid editing and rather uncomfortable camera angles.[11]

But more important for Grossberg than these specific forms of textual evidence are the patterns and processes whereby TV is produced and consumed. Arguing along Jameson's lines, he suggests that TV theory must learn to accommodate itself somehow to the intense variability of the contemporary electronic media and the ways, and even places, in which they are experienced. This variability seems to frustrate any critical attempt to speak normatively about any TV 'text' or its postulated viewer:

The text is located, not only intertextually, but in a range of apparatuses as well, defined technologically but also by other social relations and activities. One rarely just listens to the radio, watches TV or even goes to the movies – one is studying, dating, driving somewhere else, partying, etc. Not only is it the case that the 'same' text is different in different contexts, but its multiple appearances are complexly intereffective.[12]

Add to this the increasing capacity for fragmentation and interruption, with the growing habit of channel-jumping, along with the intensifying absorption of TV in its own forms and history (what Umberto Eco has called 'neo-TV', TV which takes itself and its participants as its own subjects, as in chat shows, or award ceremonies),[13] and we seem to have arrived at a view of TV as constituting the postmodern psycho-cultural condition – a world of simulations detached from reference to the real, which circulate and exchange in ceaseless, centreless flow. Grossberg's infatuation with this prospect is mitigated by his tough-sounding call for a 'mapping' of this complex and shifting affective field, and he draws back from the depressingly common position that because TV forms subjectivity, its forms are *identical* with subjectivity. But elsewhere, his infatuation with the paradoxes of TV's pleasures and effects ('to put it most bluntly, TV is in-different to differences, even as it constitutes differences out of the very absence of difference')[14] testifies to the strangely defeatist sense in postmodernist TV theory that its object has already outstripped and neutralized all of the deconstructive theories and procedures which are available to that theory.

The arch-theorist of this outflanking of theory, the writer whose shadow hovers like a nightmare over accounts of postmodern film, TV and video, is Jean Baudrillard, particularly in his influential essay, 'The Ecstasy of Communication'.[15] In that essay, Baudrillard does not so much write about TV as a specific cultural form as evoke TV and its technologies as a metaphor for the regime of simulation in contemporary Western cultures. Baudrillard argues that in these societies the psychical structuring of social life has been fundamentally transformed. Previous eras had required and reproduced a set of related and equivalent contrasts between private and public life, and between the subjective self and the objective world. In contemporary times these relationships have been neutralized, so that, for example, an older conception of the self or psyche as projecting itself into objects in a relationship of mastery and possession (as in status symbols, like cars, houses and swimming-pools), has given way to a flat, interchangeable equivalence of subject and object. Baudrillard uses the example of driving a car. Progressively, he says, driving has had less to do with the

aggressive affirmation of subjective will over a resistant but finally
compliant material object, and more to do with a cooperative interface
between what are newly experienced as correlative mechanisms. Now the
road or landscape is not an antagonist or obstacle to be penetrated with
effort and power, but something that unrolls smoothly before the
driver/spectator like images on a television screen; and with modern cars
that actually talk to their occupants, the collapse of the distinction between
man and mechanism is complete. (Baudrillard ought to try driving my car
through London traffic some time.) Baudrillard's metaphor for this
collapse of the subject-object dichotomy is the screen. A TV screen or
computer monitor cannot be thought of simply as an object to be looked
at, with all the old forms of psychic projection and investment; instead,
the screen intersects responsively with our desires and representations, and
becomes the embodied form of our psychic worlds. What happens 'on' the
screen is neither on the screen nor in us, but in some complex, always
virtual space between the two.

This accomplishes the neutralization of another opposition, that between
the 'invisible' world of feeling and fantasy and the 'visible' world of public
representations. The sheer bulk of representations, in film, TV and
advertising, and the exponential expansion of information not only
threaten the integrity of the private world, says Baudrillard, they actually
abolish the very distinction between the private and the public. Just as the
private worlds of actual individuals are relentlessly pillaged by TV, with
the multiplication of intimate explorations of private lives and fly-on-the-
wall documentaries, so the private world comes to enfold or be inhabited
by the public world of historical events, which are made available instantly
in every living-room by the agency of TV. The public possesses the
private, the private encompasses the public. What typifies this situation
above all is an explosion of visibility, to a point of excess that Baudrillard
calls 'obscenity': 'Obscenity begins precisely when there is no more
spectacle, no more scene, when all becomes transparence and immediate
visibility, when everything is exposed to the harsh and inexorable light of
information and communication' (Ecstasy of Communication', 130). In
this situation, it hardly even seems possible to speak of being alienated by
or from the mass media – for this would require the reinstatement of a
whole structure of thought, including the clear distinction between authentic individual existence and inauthentic false consciousness, which this
explosion of visibility makes impossible. You cannot be misrepresented, or
misconceive yourself, in a situation in which there are no longer any
positives or negatives, but only ever the feverish production of more signs,
more meanings, 'ecstasy of communication'. If alienation is superseded,

then so is the very idea of repression, since, with the collapse of the idea of the private self, there is no longer anything to repress, or any space in which to repress it; this is 'no longer the traditional obscenity of what is hidden, repressed, forbidden, or obscure; on the contrary, it is the obscenity of the visible, of the all-too-visible . . . of what no longer has any secret, of what dissolves completely in information and communication' ('Ecstasy of Communication', 131).

This situation seems, interestingly, to reproduce or resemble the models of performance developed in theories of postmodernist drama. Here, the electronic media, though initially conceived as instruments of mere reproduction, have become liberated from this subservient function. Like the performance text, the TV network does not aim to represent the world, but enacts itself, its own forms and languages, in a pure performing present. But Baudrillard's analysis does not carry the same exhilarating charge as most accounts of the 'liberated' performance. This world of communicational saturation is, in fact, emotionally empty, or 'cool', and its representative psychic state is not hysteria, a condition in which the body and its symptoms are made the externalized 'text' of internal feelings and desires, but schizophrenia, which, Baudrillard reminds us, is the condition not so much of a retreat from the external world, as of the overintense advance of that world upon the consciousness of the sufferer, which painfully dissolves through lack of distance; it is 'the absolute proximity, the total instantaneity of things, the feeling of no defense, no retreat. It is the end of interiority and intimacy, the overexposure and transparency of the world which traverses him without obstacle' ('Ecstasy of Communication', 133). Above all, it is the TV screen which provides the metaphor for all of these themes: absolute visibility, the loss of interiority, the proliferation of information and communication; the schizoid subject of this 'obscenity' becomes 'a pure screen, a switching center for all the networks of influence' (ibid.).

In this situation, it is less than ever the case that one can discriminate between a particular postmodernist text and its non-postmodernist context. Although Baudrillard himself never uses the term 'postmodernism', TV is in and of itself always a representative part of the postmodern scene of simulation, ecstasy and obscenity. The 'Ecstasy of Communication' essay comes from a transitional point in Baudrillard's writing, between the grounded structural-Marxism of *For a Critique of the Political Economy of the Sign* (1972) and the more ecstatic revellings in the world of simulation that have characterized his later work. Yet even here the tone of his writing, poised midway between relish and despair, leaves no real possibility of distinguishing, within the saturated and curiously unified field of postmodern communications, different, even 'progressive' forms of postmodernist cultural effect. This kind of totalizing vision is common among many adherents of Baudrillard, and often manifests itself particularly in discussions of TV. A striking example is the work of the Canadian sociologists Arthur Kroker and David Cook, both associated with *The Canadian Journal of Political and Social Theory*. For Kroker and Cook, TV is 'in a very literal sense, the real world . . . of *postmodern* culture, society and economy . . . of real popular culture driven onwards by the ecstasy and decay of the obscene spectacle', such that anything which has not been submitted to the ontological test of being processed by TV becomes 'peripheral to the main tendencies of the contemporary century'.[16]

Kroker and Cook's work shares the tonal ambivalence of Baudrillard's. On the one hand, TV is dismissed *in toto* as an instrument of oppression and intellectual deprivation; it transforms actual individuals into passive, though perfectly functioning, media machines, by 'implanting a simulated, electronically monitored, and technocratically controlled identity in the flesh'; it degrades socially cohesive groups into the amorphousness of 'packaged audiences held hostage to the big trend line of *crisis moods* induced by media elites for an audience which does not exist in any *social* form, but only in the form of digital blips on overnight rating simulacrums'; and it substitutes a world of flat images for a world of experience, in 'the triumph of the culture of signification'.[17]

So, for Kroker and Cook, postmodern TV represents neither the subversive dissolution of cultural and aesthetic norms, nor the progressive rewriting of the classic-realist Hollywood text, but rather the last moment before our culture vanishes into the absolute and total dominion of the image. This moment is simultaneously one of 'ecstasy' and 'decay', because it involves a feverish intensification of differences and intensities, in an attempt to compensate for the slipping away of the real, which nevertheless always ends up consolidating the power of the spectacle. Faced with this situation, Kroker and Cook have no response to offer except simultaneously to yearn for the lost and entirely imaginary 'old world of society' and to fling themselves into the maelstrom of the spectacle they appear to despise. Their perfervid prose invests in the glamorous apocalypse it invokes: 'an electronically composed public of serial beings which, smelling the funeral pyre of excremental culture all around it, decides of its own unfettered volition to celebrate its own exterminism by throwing its energies, where attention is the oxygen of TV life, to the black hole of television'.[18] Like the 'imploding supernova' to which they compare TV itself, the thrashing, hypertrophied excitement of

Kroker's and Cook's writing masks a fundamental argumentative inertia, which deprives their work of the capacity or grounds to criticize, condemn, or condone.

Perhaps Kroker and Cook's account represents one form of extreme of a postmodern theory of contemporary culture, whose impetus, like that of the culture it describes, seems always to be towards totalized, all-inclusive narratives. Again, at this point, the strength of the postmodern hypothesis turns out to be its weakness; the capacity to offer expansive explanations of the 'complete' inversion, 'simulation', 'satellization' of social and cultural life is what gives such theory its force and prestige, even as it is an obedient echo of the grandiose enlargement and globalization of technological culture itself. But this pulls damagingly against that other strain of postmodern cultural theory, which asserts difference, multiplicity and centrelessness. For all its attempts to foster or describe a culture of resistance, the rhetorical-institutional demands of postmodern theory can turn it damagingly into a mere celebration and legitimation of the situation it describes.

Film

The most frequently-cited analytic account of the effect of modern electronic media, and one that has been referred to already in this study, is Walter Benjamin's 'The Work of Art of the Age of Mechanical Reproduction'.[19] This essay offers simultaneously an intimation of the progressive possibilities of modern technology, aligning it in various ways with the experiments and challenges of modernist art, and a structure for defining the postmodern cultural universe. As we have seen, the possibility of making multiple reproductions of any given work suggests to Benjamin a threat to the 'aura' of a work of art, that is to say, our sense of its uniqueness in space and time, with the associated myths of its absolute permanence and transcendent distance from the material world. Above all, it is film which breaks down or dissolves this sense of aura for Benjamin. This has to do, first of all, with the emotional effect of film, which depends upon motion and viewer-involvement, rather than with stasis and contemplation; for Benjamin, the constant interruptions of film shockingly disallow any point of rest for the viewer, preventing any easy recognition of a familiar world. Film also allows for the analysis of that familiar world, in much the same way as psychoanalysis analyses the structures of dreams and everyday life, for, with its repertoire of techniques like variable speed, shifts of focus and setting, film substitutes for a space which is simply experienced a space which is actively explored.[20] The destruction of the otherwordly aura of art is carried through even in the forms of film production, Benjamin argues. Where an actor in the theatre gives a performance all at once and in one place, a film, while giving the illusion of a single performance, actually requires of the actor that his or her performance be broken up in time and space. The effect of unity is achieved by technology and not by the immediacy of the human presence on the stage.[21]

Benjamin's account of the vulnerability of artistic aura to mechanical reproduction is parallel in some respects to Michael Fried's account of the way that the 'theatrical' awareness of the particular spatial, temporal and social contexts of art threatens its essential self-absorption. This equivalence between theatricality and mechanical reproduction is made particularly clear in Benjamin's insistence on the necessarily enhanced role of the responsive and evaluative spectator in contemporary mass culture. Mechanical reproduction offers the prospect of an art which may be brought back into relationship with the world in which it is produced and received. It is not surprising, therefore, that Benjamin's essay has been the starting point for many accounts of postmodernism in contemporary electronic media and particularly in film, although this is sometimes achieved by means of a certain shifting of terms; where, for Benjamin, film was the representative form of the modern, in its assault on artistic aura, for most adherents of the postmodernist hypothesis, Benjamin's argument predicts the movement from a modernist epoch (now seen as thoroughly committed to safeguarding the idea of the aura of the work of art) to a postmodernist epoch.

For what Benjamin seems to have discounted was the capacity for modern cinema itself to create and sustain artistic aura, or myths of aura. This is not to say, of course, that all cinema before the postmodernist break (during the 1960s, perhaps) can easily be called modernist in this respect. Rather, the dominant form of cinema as mass-cultural entertainment is what has been called the 'classic-realist' text of the Hollywood cinema, derived as it is from the adoption of the realist techniques and assumptions of the · nineteenth-century novel and theatre.[22] Alternative practices in the cinema need, therefore, to be defined against the dominating model of Hollywood and the narrative conventions it maintains. In their history of classical Hollywood cinema, David Bordwell and Janet Staiger distinguish three forms of such variant practice: the 'art film' associated with directors such as Fellini, Bergman, Truffaut and Visconti, which is typified by the exploration of psychological complexity and its suffusion of narrative by a sort of authorial expressivity; the 'avant-garde' film, which is characterized by various forms of rejection of narrative causality; and the 'modernist' film, in which 'spatial and temporal systems come forward and share with narrative the role of structuring the film' – Bordwell and Staiger instance here the work of such film-makers as Eisenstein, Ozu, Tati, Godard, Duras and Bresson.[23] This account of modernism clearly rejoins and depends on the descriptions of artistic modernism provided by Greenberg and Fried, in that it seems to emphasize the film's formal exploration of its own medium as against its domination by the mode of narrative.

Christian Metz has suggested an expanded account of the modernist cinema in an essay published in 1974 called 'The Modern Cinema and Narrativity'.[24] Metz gathers together some of the more influential claims about the modernist cinema, including the authority of the director as *auteur* rather than as studio functionary, and the attack on theatrical conventions in film, with the emergence of a cinema which stresses contemplation rather than involvement, and concentrates upon the structure of the individual shot rather than on the dramatic sequence. All of these have in common the presumption that the modernist cinema rejects or moves beyond narrative. Metz's characterization of theories of modernist cinema is more expansive than Bordwell and Staiger's, therefore, though he is correspondingly more sceptical than they are about the claims for a distinctively modernist art of the cinema. For Metz, the denial of narrative is a fantasy-projection on the part of critics of the modern, since cinema, by its nature a temporal medium, must always depend on and revert to structures of narrativity (though these do not have to be of the same kind as Hollywood realist narrative). Metz argues, for example, that the often-renewed avant-garde emphasis on the individual framed shot, as against the aggregative energy of the sequence in realist cinema, ignores the combinative structures whereby distinct shots are related and contrasted in extended temporal structures.

Although Metz does not use the vocabulary of postmodernism, this essay, as well as his subsequent work, may be seen as an attempt to resist the formation of a Greenbergian model of the cinema as self-sufficient art, whose destiny is to purify itself of everything that is extrinsic to it. Metz insists on the necessary impurity of cinema, its unavoidable and energizing overlappings with different media and genres. The projection of the modernist cinema in the way that Metz describes here may be seen as the operation of a critical will to restore the qualities of aesthetic aura – self-sufficiency, transcendence, universality – to a cultural practice whose specific nature it is to dissolve aura.

Fredric Jameson has given an equivalent account of the modernist inheritance in cinema. The great monuments of twentieth-century film, he says, are all distinguished by the intensity with which they display and explore their artistic natures. Like modernist painting, music and literature, modernist films simultaneously resist and exhibit their status as commodity, by means of stylistic self-reference. On the one hand, the cultivation of 'style' is the way in which the artefact seems to acknowledge that it exists in the market-place, as something to be bought and exchanged, and has lost its more immediate functions within, and relationship to, collective social structures. On the other hand, this style is the means by which the commodity holds itself aloof from the market-place; by a kind of intensification of the logic of division and specialization which brought it into being as a commodity in the first place, the extreme assertion of individual style outbids the market and immunizes the artefact-commodity against absorption by it.[25] Jameson claims that the modernist emphasis on style is an insistence on the agonized expressiveness of the individual, speaking in the uniqueness of his or her personal idiom simultaneously of potency and alienated helplessness:

> The great modernisms were . . . predicated on the invention of a personal, private style, as unmistakable as your fingerprint, as incomparable as your own body . . . This means that the modernist aesthetic is in some way organically linked to the conception of a unique self and private identity, a unique personality and individuality, which can be expected to generate its own unique vision of the world and to forge its own unique, unmistakable style.[26]

Although Jameson does not make it clear just how this works in the field of film, one might point to the influential *auteur* theory of the 1970s as an instance of the modernist outlook that organizes the stylistic analysis of a film around the figure of the author-director.[27] What replaces such an outlook in postmodernist culture and theory is not the absolute absence of style, but its detachment from the concept of the powerful originating author. As in other areas of contemporary culture, the collapse of the modernist ideology of style, therefore, brings with it a culture of multiple styles, which are combined, set against each other, rotated and regenerated in a furious polyphony of decontextualized voices. This brings about a flattening of the sense of historical origins, so that what are circulated in this art of pastiche are not only stylistic individualities, but also dislocated histories.

The sign of this in postmodern cinema is the nostalgia or 'retro' film, like *American Graffiti, Star Wars, Chinatown* or *Body Heat.* These are all films, Jameson writes, which set out to recreate not a particular historical setting but the cultural experience of a particular period, so that, in the cases of *Star Wars* and *Raiders of the Lost Ark*, what is being evoked is not an actual past, but rather the kinds of narrative experience – the adventure story, the science-fiction movie – that seem to typify the experience of the 1950s.

Postmodernist cinema is characterized, for the many writers who have approved and extended Jameson's analysis, by different forms of pastiche or stylistic multiplicity. Sometimes this is internal to one film, as in *Kiss of the Spider Woman*, with its parodies of Hollywood romance and melodrama set into the narrative of the developing relationship of two political prisoners. A more complex example is Terry Gilliam's strange film *Brazil*, which Linda Hutcheon sees as postmodern because of its 'ironic rethinking of history', with its parodic recalls of other films like *Star Wars* and *Battleship Potemkin*, along with the undecidable mix of different historical periods in the film; futuristic sets mingling with drably 1930s clothes and presentation of a world dominated by computers and advanced automation whose archaic design and unreliability suggest that they too belong to the 1930s.[28] Perhaps *Brazil* is another example of Jameson's *retro* mode, since what is being evoked here is not any actual phase of machine styling, but rather the imaginary technology of mid-century science fiction. Along with these forms of temporal discontinuity goes the film's generic heterogeneity, with its unsettling lurches between comedy and tragedy, utopia and dystopia, adventure story and satire.

But, as with postmodern TV, stylistic multiplicity is also a characteristic of the entire field of contemporary film culture, with the increasing availability of old films on video and their continuing visibility on TV. Indeed, as with theories of postmodernist TV, it often seems as though postmodernism in film is not a matter of a new dominant style so much as the corrosion of the very idea of such a dominant. As James Collins argues:

What distinguishes the postmodernist context is the simultaneous presence of that style alongside modernist, pre-modernist, and aggressively non-modernist styles, all enjoying significant degrees of popularity with different audiences and institutions. *Diva* may indeed be a postmodernist detective text, but what individuates the postmodernist context is the appearance of this film on a cable film channel while *The Maltese Falcon*, *Death of an Expert Witness* and *Miami Vice* run on opposing channels the same evening.[29]

This aspect of postmodernist film theory clearly corresponds very closely to architectural theories of postmodernism, in which the supersession of modernist 'univalence' is similarly announced in an architecture of fragmented citation, in which stylistic hierarchies are abolished. The difference between the two fields is striking, however. Put simply, film is a much more socially-diffused medium than architecture, its audiences much larger and more expert in its codes, languages and history. (Ironically, it is the growth of TV and, latterly, the arrival of video technology which has assisted this.) This means that stylistic heterogeneity is both more prevalent, and less noticeable in TV and film than in architecture; in the former, heterogeneity is actually a form of homogeneity. Another interesting symptom of the postmodern in film, and one that is frequently commented upon, is its erasure of the historical boundaries between high and low culture; postmodernist films may evoke the complexities of high theory but this is at odds with the apparent accessibility and box-office success of such impeccably postmodernist films as *Blade Runner*, *True Stories*, *Diva*, and *The Draughtsman's Contract*.

All this would pose no problems if theory of postmodernist cinema were simply a stylistic matter. But, as with postmodernist TV, more is at stake, for here, as elsewhere, theorists have been concerned with trying to identify an oppositional practice in film and film criticism. Questions of the power and effect of individual postmodernist texts and the postmodernist theoretical field itself become much more apparent in this sort of context. This may be demonstrated in a comparison of two postmodernist 'readings' of films – Norman Denzin's account of David Lynch's *Blue Velvet* (1986) and Patricia Mellencamp's study of Yvonne Rainer's *The Man Who Envied Women* (1985).[30] Denzin sees *Blue Velvet* as postmodernist on a number of counts. Firstly, the film provides an improbable and disturbing stitching-together of different genres and genre-expectations. The plot concerns Jeffrey and Sandy, two middle-class kids living in the small and conventional town of Lumberton, USA, who are gradually drawn into a world of violence and perverted sexuality, revolving around Dorothy Vallens, a disturbed night-club singer, and her sadistic lover Frank. The mystery, which seems to involve the kidnapping of Dorothy's son and husband (this apparently occasioning the severed ear which Jeffrey discovers at the beginning of the film), is never really resolved; at the end of the film Frank has been killed and Jeffrey and Sandy have reverted to normal suburban married existence. Denzin argues that *Blue Velvet* runs together in a postmodernist fashion the tradition of the small-town film (exemplified by Frank Capra's work in the 1940s) with the pornographic cult film (Denzin, 466–71). Postmodernist too, according to Denzin, is the way that the film mixes the 'unpresentable' (rotting ears, sexual excess, brutality, insanity) and the commonplace, thereby challenging the boundaries that separate the two realms (Denzin, 462).

But the central point of Denzin's analysis concerns the film's treatment of time. The film refuses to allow the viewer to identify its period with any security. The first shot shows red roses blooming with hallucinatory intensity against a white picket fence and a blue sky, while a 1940s fire-engine glides slowly down a tree-lined suburban street. The primary colours seem to frame the shot as a quotation by insisting ironically on the childish simplicity of this world, even as the colour-quality summons up memories of the gaudy technicolour process used in American films of the 1940s and 1950s. But this temporal coding is upset in the next few minutes by the appearance of cars, technology and dress from the 1950s, 1960s and 1980s. 'This is a film', writes Denzin, 'which evokes, mocks, yet lends quasi-reverence for the icons of the past, while it places them in the present' (Denzin, 469).

Denzin enlists the vocabulary and apparatus of postmodernist analysis to give a sort of libertarian allure to the film, while recognizing at the same time that it has voyeuristic and sadistic elements that make it seem very far from a liberal or progressive film in any obvious way. If *Blue Velvet* searches for new ways 'to present the unpresentable, so as to break down the barriers that keep the profane out of the everyday' (Denzin, 471), it also reproduces ruthlessly and apparently without irony the narrowest cultural stereotypes, particularly in its presentation of male and female sexuality. The clutch of related postmodernist concepts which Denzin deploys allow him to present the film as in some way culturally resistant, even as he acknowledges its political barrenness. With a final insouciant shrug, Denzin concludes that 'postmodern individuals want films like *Blue Velvet* for in them they can have their sex, their myths, their violence and their politics, all at the same time' (Denzin, 472). This analysis neatly demonstrates the difficulty of maintaining a position in which postmodernism is both a set of identifiable stylistic features and a cultural dominant, for in such a model the relationship between forms of resistance and critique on the one hand and the reduction of these to stylistic gesture on the other, is always hard to theorize.

Patricia Mellencamp's reading of Yvonne Rainer's *The Man Who Envied Women* sees the film as an investigation of the gender-power protocols of aspects of postmodernist film theory itself. The film has as its central character Jack Deller, who is such a film theorist. The film shows Deller's well-intentioned narcissism – he is 'a perfect caricature masquerading as a feminist – in theoretical drag which cannot conceal his powerful patriarchy' (Mellencamp, 91) – but also challenges his easy assumption of control through theoretical language. Mellencamp focuses on the way Jack Deller is shown to be oblivious of the various forms of unregulated and chaotic discourse which surround him, sitting in front of a film screen, proceeding smoothly with his interminable talk while fights break out in the audience; wearing headphones in the street, while around him street talk and jokes bustle and jostle. So the film sets against the deadening monolith of male theory the decentring force of women's language; it is as though an actual postmodern multiplicity of voices displaces the 'official' postmodernism represented by Deller and his endless explications of Foucault. This gendered technique provides a way of understanding the other instances of postmodernist style which Mellencamp describes in the film; there is the setting of the verbal against the visual, as in the matter-of-fact account of a woman's difficult week which is spoken over the opening shot showing the famous slitting of the woman's eye in Bunuel's *Un Chien Andalou*: 'It was a hard week. I split up with my husband and moved into my studio. The hot water heater broke . . . I bloodied up my white linen pants; the Senate voted for nerve gas; and my gynecologist went down in Korean Airlines Flight 007' (quoted, Mellencamp, 91). This is elaborated by other postmodernist disruptions, among them the following: 'denying dichotomies, bipolarities, the ontology of media boundaries; dissolving binary oppositions, including the great cultural fault, the divide between the sexes . . . challenging modern culture's definitive premises – the centrality of the usually masculine author/genius, the uniqueness of the precious object of Art, and the entrenched, sacred distinction between it and mass or popular culture' (Mellencamp, 98).

The strength of Mellencamp's analysis in this essay is that it overlaps in a complex way the postmodern strategies of the film and the official-sounding postmodernist theory which actually stands as its own counter-part in the film, embodying, not play and heterogeneity, but fixity and authority. For Mellencamp, the film demonstrates how 'feminism becomes the repressed, managed rupture of postmodernism – marginalized and thus contained, like "primitivism" earlier, *outside* the debate as the unknowable, appropriated other, along with other races and cultures, through the convoluted benevolence of local colonialism' (Mellencamp, 99). In other words, taking Rainer's film as her starting point, Mellencamp uses the occasion of analysis to initiate a self-reflective account of postmodernist theory itself, and the strategies of containment that it can develop. If postmodernist theory is in a sense the cultural custodian of postmodern film, then it will need to acknowledge its complicity in the projection and circulation of stylistic norms in criticism and in film itself. This is to say that the development of a postmodernist 'culture of resistance' depends to a large degree upon the willingness of cultural theory to acknowledge and explore its own role in the creation of that culture, for such a theory can produce a culture of indifference as well as bringing out productive differences.

Notes

1 *Postmodernism: ICA Documents 5*, ed. Lisa Appignanesi (London: ICA, 1986), pp. 52–4.
2 Ibid., p. 53.
3 *Rocking Around the Clock: Music Television, Postmodernism and Popular Culture* (London and New York: Methuen, 1987), pp. 49–88. References hereafter to *RATC* in the text.
4 *Hiding in the Light: On Images and Things* (London: Comedia, 1988), p. 237.
5 'The Look of the Sound', in *Watching Television*, ed. Todd Gitlin (New York: Pantheon, 1986), p. 135.
6 'Imaginary Cinematheques: The Postmodern Programmes of INA', *Screen*, 28:2 (1987), pp. 103–17.
7 Ibid., p. 115.
8 Ibid., p. 117.
9 'Reading Without Interpretation: Postmodernism and the Video-Text', in *The Linguistics of Writing: Arguments Between Language and Literature*, ed. Derek Attridge, Alan Durant, Nigel Fabb and Colin McCabe (Manchester: Manchester University Press, 1987), pp. 198–223. References hereafter in text.
10 Williams elaborates his account of 'total flow' in *Television: Technology and Cultural Form* (London: Fontana, 1977), pp. 78–118.
11 'The In-Difference of Television', *Screen*, 28:2 (1987), p. 29.
12 Ibid., p. 34.
13 Umberto Eco, 'A Guide to the Neo-Television of the 1980s', *Framework*, 25 (1984), pp. 18–25.
14 Grossberg, 'The In-Difference of Television', p. 41.
15 In *Postmodern Culture*, ed. Hal Foster (London and Sydney: Pluto Press, 1985), pp. 126–34. References hereafter in the text.
16 *The Postmodern Scene: Excremental Culture and Hyper-Aesthetics* (New York: St. Martin's Press, 1986), p. 268.
17 Ibid., pp. 274–5.
18 Ibid., p. 279.
19 In *Illuminations*, trans. Harry Zohn (London: Fontana, 1970), pp. 219–54.
20 Ibid., pp. 238–9.
21 Ibid., pp. 230–2.

22 See, for instance, Colin McCabe's influential 'Realism and the Cinema', *Screen*, 15:2 (1974), pp. 7–24.

23 David Bordwell, Janet Staiger and Kristin Thompson, *The Classical Hollywood Cinema: Film Style and Mode of Production to 1960* (London: Routledge and Kegan Paul, 1985), pp. 373–4, 381–2.

24 *Film Language: A Semiotics of the Cinema*, trans. Michael Taylor (New York: Oxford University Press, 1974), pp. 185–227.

25 See Jameson, 'Postmodernism and the Video-Text', pp. 222–3.

26 'Postmodernism and Consumer Society', in *Postmodern Culture*, ed. Hal Foster (London and Sydney: Pluto Press, 1985), p. 114.

27 For theories of the *auteur*, see *Film Theory and Criticism: Introductory Readings*, ed. Gerald Mast and Marshall Cohen, 3rd edn (Oxford: Oxford University Press, 1985), pp. 521–675.

28 Linda Hutcheon, 'Beginning to Theorize Postmodernism', *Textual Practice*, 1:1 (1987), pp. 11–12.

29 'Postmodernism and Cultural Practice: Redefining the Parameters', *Screen*, 28:2 (1987), p. 12.

30 Norman Denzin, '*Blue Velvet*: Postmodern Contradictions', *Theory, Culture and Society*, 5:2–3 (1988), pp. 461–73; Patricia Mellencamp, 'Images of Language and Indiscreet Dialogue: *The Man Who Envied Women*', *Screen*, 28:2 (1987), pp. 87–102. References hereafter in the text.

7

Postmodernism and Popular Culture

Recent years have seen an explosion of interest in a whole range of cultural texts and practices which had previously been scorned by, or remained invisible to, academic criticism. Contemporary cultural critics, following the inspiring lead of Richard Hoggart, Raymond Williams, Roland Barthes and Stuart Hall, take as their subjects sport, fashion, hairstyles, shopping, games and social rituals, and unabashedly bring to bear on these areas the same degree of theoretical sophistication as they would to any high cultural artefact. In a sense, this is itself a postmodern phenomenon, for it is the mark of that levelling of hierarchies and blurring of boundaries which is an effect of the explosion of the field of culture described by Jameson in which the cultural and the social and the economic are no longer easily distinguishable one from another.

Many of these popular cultural forms and practices have a claim to be representatively postmodern in themselves, even though they may be forms and practices which never passed through any recognizably modernist phase. Such forms apparently do not need the legitimation of postmodern theory to enjoy their postmodern status. But this is not to say that there are not significant forms of transference and parallel among and between other forms of postmodern cultural theory. In popular culture as elsewhere, the postmodern condition is not a set of symptoms that are simply present in a body of sociological and textual evidence, but a complex effect of the relationship between social practice and the theory that organizes, interprets and legitimates its forms.

Rock Music

In one sense, of course, rock music as a specific cultural form can only be called postmodern by analogy. Arguably, rock music has undergone an accelerated internal genealogy which imitates, or can be construed as imitating, narratives of the emergence of the postmodern sensibility in other cultural areas. Fredric Jameson hints at this when he instances the Beatles and the Rolling Stones as the 'high modernist moment' of rock music.[1] The kind of narrative this implies might be as follows: after its rebellious insurgence in the 1960s rock music became canonized and incorporated by the culture industry in the 1970s, even as its most advanced representatives seemed to be exploring experimental or mock-experimental styles associated with contemporary avant-garde aesthetics; this producing a contradictory but, arguably, 'modernist' amalgam of the experimental and the institutionally incorporated. This was followed in the late 1970s by punk and new wave music, associated with groups like The Clash, The Sex Pistols and others who aimed to purify the aristocratic 'stadium rock' which had grown up by returning to the primal energies and origins of rock music in the experiences of working-class and disaffected youth. This is then succeeded by the rapid diversification (and unerring recurrence) of styles characterstic of the 1980s and 1990s – gothic, new wave, grunge, rap, hip-hop, techno, house and rave.

The analogy works only partially, of course. It cannot easily be claimed that, even in its 'modernist' phase, rock music ever really explored the nature of its own medium, conventions or institutions in the way that the literary and artistic modernisms of the early part of this century did; nor is there much resemblance between the opposition to mass industrial society instanced in literary and artistic modernism and the near-absolute identification of rock music with the energies of capitalist expansion in the 1960s, and again in the 1980s. Nor can it easily be argued that a decisive postmodern mutation has taken place in rock music since punk and new wave. Rather, what seems to have happened is that the cycle of inclusion, in which new forms and energies are incorporated, tamed and recycled as commodities, has accelerated unimaginably, to the point where authentic 'originality' and commercial 'exploitation' are hard to distinguish.

Of course one definition of cultural postmodernism fits this perfectly – Jameson's notion of a movement beyond history to a flat present without depth or extension, in which styles and histories circulate interchangeably. Along with the fashion industry, the rock industry is the best example of the elastic saleability of the cultural past, with its regular recyclings of its own history in the form of revivals and remakes, comebacks and cover-versions. In recent years the development of new forms of technology has accelerated and to some degree democratized this process, to the point where the cultural evidence of rock music can be physically dismantled and reassembled in the form of pastiche and collage, much more quickly and uncontrollably than ever before. The present cult of 'sampling', the use by musicians of audio technology to appropriate and manipulate recordings by and performances of other musicians, provides the clearest exemplification of the postmodernist aesthetic of the fragment, as well as showing rock music's willingness to live off its own history and forms.[2]

In larger terms, of course, rock music has a claim to be the most representative of postmodern cultural forms. For one thing, it embodies to perfection the central paradox of contemporary mass culture, in the fact of its unifying global reach and influence on the one hand combined with its tolerance and engendering of pluralities of styles, media and ethnic identities on the other. Although rock music has a clearly visible and easily-evidenced history it is also characterized by a congenital impurity of means and nature. From the very beginning the importance of rock music lay in the potency of its amalgams with youth culture as a whole; with fashion, with style and street culture, with spectacle and performance art in the work of artists like The Who, Genesis, Talking Heads and Laurie Anderson, with film, and with new reproductive technologies and media – the most recent and obvious example being the rock video.

Most accounts or celebrations of postmodern rock or popular music stress two related factors: firstly, its capacity to articulate alternative or plural cultural identities, of groups belonging to the margins of national or dominant cultures; and secondly (often, though not invariably, related to this) the celebration of the principles of parody, pastiche, stylistic multiplicity and generic mobility. For Dick Hebdige, writing about Caribbean music, the important thing about styles like ska, dub, rap and hip-hop are the opportunities they give for affirmation of the cultural identity of subordinated social groups in the West Indies and in Britain. Hebdige stresses the spontaneously eruptive character of this music, which has often been kept invisible and inaudible by official white rock (though in certain forms has, of course, always been massively popular and influential), and celebrates the power of such subcultural forms simultaneously to bind together social groups and to express the plurality of cultural and ethnic experience. For Hebdige, there is no clear dividing line between the products of black music and the techniques and technologies involved in producing them: the record decks, 'ghetto-blasters' and sound systems, all of them appropriate for such forms of cultural improvisation and innovation as sampling or scratching.[3] This is a music which runs together the modes of the live and the recorded, by incorporating and manipulating recorded material in live performance. Hebdige approves of the unofficial nature of this technology, which can be used, he says, to decentre and redistribute cultural power. Towards the end of his book, Hebdige celebrates the healthy cosmopolitanism of the airwaves, in a passage that makes the radio the very embodiment of postmodern cultural mobility:

> There are no age or dress restrictions with a radio. You don't have to get past burly bouncers to get to the music. All you have to do is switch the radio on and turn the dial. And you don't have to stay in one place all the time. You can travel up and down the wavelengths from Cape Town to the Caribbean via Brooklyn and Clapham Junction. (*Cut 'N' Mix*, 156)

Hebdige stakes his claims for cultural value on the aesthetic of the 'version'; where official culture values originality, identity and uniqueness, black music culture in Hebdige's account insists on repetition and plural identity: 'no one owns a rhythm or a sound. You just borrow it, use it and give it back to the people in a slightly different form. To use the language of Jamaican reggae and dub, you just *version* it' (*Cut 'N' Mix*, 141). The aesthetic of the version gives a popular-cultural equivalent to the much-celebrated principle of intertextuality. Versioning, says Hebdige, is 'a democratic principle because it implies that no one has the final say. Everybody has a chance to make and contribute. And no one's version is treated as Holy Writ' (*Cut 'N' Mix*, 14).

Rather than simply expressing a single cultural identity this aesthetic principle allows the expression of heterogeneous cultural experience, the 'negotiation of mixed or transitional cultural identities' (*Cut 'N' Mix*, 159). Angela MacRobbie presents a similar case for the constitution of provisional identities in popular culture, arguing for the cultural potency of camp, or the art of pastiche, in the work of pop musicians like Frankie Goes to Hollywood, Bronski Beat, Marc Almond and Boy George. Taking issue with Fredric Jameson's diagnosis of the emptiness of postmodern pastiche, she sees radical possibilities for the construction of new, fictional identities by means of the invocation of multiple texts and images: 'Black urban music has always thrived on fake, forged identities, creating a façade of grand-sounding titles which reflect both the 'otherness' of black culture, the extent to which it is outside that which is legitimate, and the way in which white society has condemned it to be nameless.'[4]

Similar claims are made in a study by George Lipsitz of Mexican rock music originating in Los Angeles. He argues that ethnic minority cultures are key performers in the postmodern world, because their exclusion from official culture allows them 'to cultivate a sophisticated capacity for ambiguity, juxtaposition, and irony'.[5] Chicano rock and roll music is characterized therefore by a stylistic multiplicity, which mixes Mexican street song and Latin-American rhythms and instruments together with blues and rock and roll melody. Like Hebdige and MacRobbie, Lipsitz stresses the versatility of the cultural identity embodied and displayed in this music:

> The dominant culture – and its popular culture industry – often treated ethnicity as a discrete and finite entity, but Chicano musicians treated it as plastic and open-ended. For them, ethnicity was as much a dynamic construct as an inherited fact, as much a strategic response to the present as an immutable series of practices and beliefs derived from the past.[6]

There is a worrying ambivalence in the claims made for cultural marginality in these accounts, which comes from the fact that all of them are dealing with capitalist success stories, with forms of culture that are not hidden, invisible, marginal and ineffective, but widely-circulated and often highly profitable. This dichotomy is most visible in Lipsitz's account, which can romanticize the cultural marginality of Mexican musicians even as it accords them a centrally representative status within contemporary 'society':

> Because their experience demands bifocality, minority group culture reflects the decentered and fragmented nature of contemporary human experience. Because their history identifies the sources of their marginality, minority group cultures have a legitimacy and connection to the past that distinguishes them from more assimilated groups. Masters of irony in an ironic world, they often understand that their marginality makes them more appropriate spokespersons for society than mainstream groups unable to fathom or address the causes of their alienation.[7]

Here, marginality and centrality have somersaulted into exact inversion, as the alleged outsider becomes the representative 'spokesperson for society'. It is very difficult to see who this mainstream society consists of (dominant culture?, Chicano culture?, dominant plus Chicano culture?, all cultures everywhere all at once?), since the Chicano has been made theoretically more mainstream than any other group in its coolly ironic self-awareness. In this account, allegedly dominant groups turn out to be somehow *more* alienated than those in the margins; being not only alienated in the first place (but how, and from what, if they are so mainstream and so dominant?) but alienated from their own alienation, in being so feebly tongue-tied about it.

And yet this paradox is actually only the intensified form of a duality which inhabits theory of contemporary popular culture. This theory is locked into an oppositional logic of dominant and marginal which does not allow for the blending of the two categories. For, after all, what is dominant in contemporary culture is the projection of a universe of multiple differences. If it is the case that the rock music industry requires a stable and reproducible product, it is equally the case that this industry depends upon the periodic invasion of difference and innovation. Indeed, the rock music industry is probably the best example of the process by which contemporary capitalist culture promotes or multiplies difference in the interests of maintaining its profit-structure. If there is a dominant in contemporary rock music, it is the dominance of multiple marginality. In this sense, Hebdige, Lipsitz and MacRobbie are right to celebrate marginal rock music as representatively postmodern, but wrong to assume that its energies are necessarily in a liberalizing direction. For from decentring or undermining the structures of the rock industry, each eruption of cultural difference only serves to stabilize this culture, by spreading and diversifying its boundaries. As we have seen repeatedly, theories of the postmodern can participate in and replicate this process. To celebrate the marginal or aberrant in rock music is to assert an emergence which is constantly denied or at least contained by the institutional forms and conventions in which this marginality has become such a valorized term. This form of cultural commentary can easily itself become a quasi-commodity, forming part of a ritualized exchange in an institutional and commercial economy of ideas and intellectual styles.

More recently, Lawrence Grossberg has offered an equivalent analysis of what he calls the 'rock formation', by which he means the patterns of meaning, identification and affect configured by and around popular music since the late 1950s in the US.[8] Grossberg suggests that cultural studies needs to develop a theoretical vocabulary of sufficient suppleness and bite to remain true to the complexity and mobility of the 'lines of flight' in contemporary cultural life while also maintaining the possibility of bringing to light the forms of its organization. Central to Grossberg's analysis is the notion of what he calls a 'structured mobility' in contemporary social life, a framing or constraining, with specific effects and purposes, of the very patterns of change and movement that seem to deny the possibility of any such constraint. Also central to the book's argument is a focus upon feeling and affect, which Grossberg believes has played too little part in a cultural studies restricted by its definition of culture as made up of signifying practices, or the communication of ideological meanings and beliefs. An account of the present must learn to attend to what Grossberg calls the 'maps of mattering' of which every individual's life is made up. Like 'structured mobility', this phrase attempts to hold together the force and the form of social life, without subordinating one to the other, or losing the sense of their dynamic opposition.

Grossberg elaborates a complex and powerful case about the relationship between rock music, postmodernity and cultural conservatism. Unlike other critics who content themselves with enquiring whether rock music, or certain forms of it are, or are not, authentically postmodern. Grossberg sees rock music as in a sense articulated both against and within postmodernism. This is because rock music, and its associated forms, styles and practices come into being as a way of simultaneously exceeding and anchoring identity.

> Rock was always about the transitions between investments and differences. It was not only a territorializing, but a differentiating machine as well. . . . Rock was about the control one gained by taking the risk of losing control, the identity one had by refusing identities. Its only stability was the investment one made into the formation itself. It reified its own transitional status, locating itself as the permanent 'between'. (p. 180)

If rock music, defined in these terms as a form of 'structured mobility', is in one sense itself a symptom of postmodernism, in another sense, it is vulnerable to a postmodernity which, Grossberg tells us, threatens 'the historical collapse of specific relations within everyday life, the "fact" that certain differences no longer matter' (p. 221). Rock music continues to offer intensity, transcendence and transgression, but in a form that is now exactly coincident with the multiple and manufactured intensities of postmodern consumptionism. Where other such analyses can only crackle around the intricate circuitry of this cultural defeat, Grossberg's sensitivity to the unevenness and mobility of cultural meanings and affects leads him to recognize in the rock formation a continuing principle of resistance or at least indigestibility.

Here, however, another irony prowls. Grossberg argues that, precisely because of the possibility of transgression it represents, and the reservoirs of intensity to which it gives access, the rock formation has been the subject of a concerted attempt at appropriation for the purposes of the political right. Grossberg notes that it is important for the new conservatism to appropriate rather than to attack rock music and its energies precisely because the former 'has been built on an affective politics, on sentimentality and passion, in which meaning and political positions have become secondary' (p. 269). The appropriation involved here is not a crude matter of translation or impersonation, as though the presidential press office were to sign up its own rock bands and insist on its own political agenda in the lyrics of their songs (though something of this kind is perhaps not completely unimaginable either). Rather, it is an appropriation of something like the logic of intensity itself, since the new conservatism in the USA 'does not need to deploy specific commitments or beliefs, but it has to foreground the need to believe in belief, to make a commitment to commitment' (271). Achieving control over the meaning and experience of intensity and desire makes it possible to depoliticize them, to disconnect affect from political interests or motivations. Far from being contained, channelled or regulated in the older, cruder forms of social discipline, affective intensity is controlled precisely by being un-fixed, by means of a heightened mobility which prevents affect from settling into any stable form of effectivity. Where earlier regimes of power worked by keeping us in our places, postmodern neoconservatism – and the advanced global capitalism which works its purposes through it – achieves the same effect by keeping us on the move. If all goes well for the new conservatism, the carceral society will become the evicted society, meaning will dissolve into feeling, the semantic will slide into the somatic and politics will be banalized into spectacle. The 'disciplined mobilization' of rock music is essential to this process:

> By rearticulating rock's structured mobility to a specific hegemonic struggle, it has constructed a different territorialization of everyday life. In this new apparatus of power, the homelessness of the rock formation is normalized. And more importantly, the rock formation's lines of flight are disciplined so that they can no longer point to another space. They must always return into everyday life, reterritorializing themselves without becoming lines of articulation. It is simply that their flight now has to be enclosed within the space of everyday life. (p. 296)

What distinguishes Grossberg's analysis from the elaborate defeatism of much contemporary analysis of the effects of incorporation is his conti-nuing conviction that if analysis can explain social process, it can also evaluate it, and intervene to change it. The final section of Grossberg's study is a friendly, but unflinching criticism of the failures of the cultural left either to acknowledge the successes of the right, or to engage with them. Central to this failure is a willingness to allow left critique to be disaggregated into the politics of identity, in which any suggestion of a horizon of common interest risks being howled down as incipient fascism. Just as disabling, Grossberg believes, is the failure to acknowledge the importance of the affective in forming and sustaining political identifica-tion and purpose. Grossberg's commanding study ends with a call for a left politics that would accept the challenge of imagining and forming an open or nondominative totality, that would neither dissolve differences nor dissolve its own responsible authority in the idolatry of absolute difference.

The achievement of Grossberg's book lies not just in the force of its analysis of contemporary conditions, nor even in the power of its political imagination, but in its exemplification of the very mode of attention to cultural life that would be necessary to such an open totality.

Style and Fashion

One of the most striking and representative areas of postmodernist theory of popular culture is fashion. Although it remains unorganized in any institutional sense, the study of fashion as cultural practice has produced some striking analyses of the effects of postmodernism in this, the most intimate and general and widely-experienced area of socio-cultural life. Roland Barthes's *Système de la Mode* was perhaps the first sustained attempt to understand the workings of fashion as a language, with its own rules and structures, and subsequent work has attempted to build on Barthes's insights in accounting for the specific forms of fashion in the contemporary postmodern world.[9]

Of course, the history of fashion does have a significant and well-attested modernist phase. The insistence on purity and function, along with the hatred of superfluous ornament, that are expressed in the work of architects like Mies van der Rohe, artists like Piet Mondrian and theorists like Alfred Loos, resulted in attempts to rationalize dress, and figures like Victor Tatlin, Kasimir Malevich, Sonia Delaunay, Walter Gropius and Jacobus Oud were all interested in extending the modernist revolution in the arts to matters of clothing. It is even possible to conceive of the invention of something like a 'modernist body', the slim and functional female figure of the 1920s, liberated from the corset and the paraphernalia of female ornament, but also compelled to pay continuous attention to the body via the internalized artifice of diet and exercise. The predictable form of postmodern departure from this would of course be a return to ornament, decoration and stylistic eclecticism, and it is indeed possible to see this in the abundant multiplicity of styles and accelerated rhythm of fashion from the prosperous years of the 1960s onwards. Elizabeth Wilson, one of the few historians of fashion in modernity, sees a particular congruence between the 'fragmented sensibility' evidenced in contemporary fashion, with its 'obsession with surface, novelty and style for style's sake' and a postmodernist aesthetic of fragments.[10]

However, this account has also been challenged by Peter Wollen, who argues that there is an alternative history of dress design to be discerned in modernism, a history of a continuing infatuation with decorative excess

and stylistic extravagance, instanced in the work of the designer Paul
Poiret and traceable in part to the influence of the voluptuous spectacle of
the Russian Ballet in the early years of the century.[11] This strain in early
modernism anticipates the revival of the decorative and the extra-vagant
in postmodernist culture. Indeed, Wollen suggests that there may be an
important link between the Russian Ballet and punk, between 'the radical
excess of the last years of the *ancien régime* and that of postmodern street
culture, complete with its own scenography of bondage, aggressive display
and decorative redistribution of bodily exposure'.[12]

But most accounts of postmodern style do not rely on the developmental
account that Wollen offers, preferring instead to constitute the notion of
postmodernist fashion by analogy with other accredited symptoms of
postmodernism, and most particularly the mode of bricolage, or the
improvised juxtaposition of incompatible or heterogeneous fragments,
often for ironic or parodic effect, as opposed to the principle of unity or
'match'. Dick Hebdige sees this sort of bricolage at work, for instance, in
the theft and transformation by 1950s teddy boys of the revived Edwardian
style then being made popular by Savile Row, the incorporation and
connotative inversion of the conventional suit, collar and tie of the
businessman by 1960s 'mods', and the more radical 'collage aesthetic' of
1970s punks, with their angry recycling of the detritus of metropolitan life
(safety-pins, dustbin liners) alongside defiled scraps of school uniforms,
kilts and ballerinas' tutus.[13] All of these groups were concerned with an
implicit politics of style, using fashion to quote, invert and distort dominant
meanings, but Hebdige's sympathies are with the Dadaist strategies of punk,
rather than the smoother and more uniform projection of group identity by
groups like the teddy boys: behind punk's favoured mode of the cut-up, he
writes, 'lay hints of disorder, of breakdown and category confusion: a desire
not only to erode racial and gender boundaries but also to confuse chronological sequence by mixing up details from different periods'.[14]

Indeed, Hebdige sees punk as pressing its avant-garde undermining of
meaning still further, to the point at which the ironic setting of one style
against another becomes the accelerated dissolution of any style in the
expressive sense at all (though the ultra-anarchist extremity of Hebdige's
claims about punk is in curious contrast to the impeccable academic
credentials with which he provides it):

> Whereas the teddy boy style says its piece in a relatively direct and obvious
> way, and remains absolutely committed to a 'finished' meaning, to the
> signified, what Kristeva calls 'signification', punk style is a constant state of
> assemblage, of flux. It introduces a heterogeneous set of signifiers which are

liable to be superseded at any moment by others no less productive. It invites the reader to 'slip into' 'signifiance', to lose the sense of direction, the direction of sense. Cut adrift from meaning, the punk style thus comes to approximate the state which Barthes has described as 'a *floating* (the very form of the signifier); a floating which would not destroy anything but would be content simply to disorientate the Law'.[15]

Contemporary postmodernist theory has turned increasingly in this way to popular cultural practice for its models of cultural plurality and resistance. As with postmodern rock theory, one of the most important themes in this form of work has been the experience of relegated or excluded ethnic groups, and theorists have drawn increasingly on post-modern categories and concepts to evoke and understand this experience, which will often seem to require a more expanded focus than previous forms of sociological enquiry. Kobena Mercer, for example, has recently extended the postmodern analysis of contemporary culture to the subject of black hairstyles, arguing that 'the question of style can be seen as a medium for expressing the aspirations of black people excluded from access to "official" social institutions of representation and legitimation in the urban, industrialized societies of the capitalist First World'.[16] For Mercer, black hairstyle should not be seen as simply or naturally ex-pressive of black cultural identity, for in the contemporary urban scene, the dominant features are bricolage and intercultural exchange. Writing against the promotion of the 'natural' Afro style, as against styles like the curly-perm style (which some have condemned as a sell-out because it requires the hair to be straightened), Mercer urges that

> the curly-perm is not the 'one' uniformly popular black hair-style, but only one among many diverse configurations of 'post-liberated' black hair-styles that seem to revel in their allusions to an ever wider range of stylistic references . . . Black practices of stylization today seem to exude confidence in their enthusiasm for combining elements from any source – black or white, past or present – into new configurations of cultural expression. Post-liberated black hair-styling emphasizes a 'pick' 'n' mix' approach to aesthetic production, suggesting a different attitude to the past in its reckoning with modernity.[17]

But it is at precisely this point, with the accelerated parade of empty style in punk, or the insouciant sophistication of the 'pick' 'n' mix' aesthetic, that, as elsewhere, oppositional critique can switch over into something like the furious rush of images which is the fashion industry itself. Hebdige is indeed much concerned by the problems of incorporation which attend every subcultural challenge to a dominant cultural regime, for, as he acknowledges, contemporary capitalist culture, far from depending upon the ceaseless replication of the same products, actually feeds off the dissident energies of marginal or oppositional cultural forms. Codifying, simplifying, and sometimes even diversifying subcultural styles for the market-place (the appearance in the fashion houses of a sedate form of punk is one example), the fashion industry simultaneously stimulates its own markets and drains the energy from its subcultural prey.

The benign view of incorporation sees it as a fate which is difficult for any successful cultural innovation to avoid; but there is, among some commentators on the contemporary cultural scene, a much more sinister story to be told, of functional interdependence, or even identity of resistance and incorporation. Julia Emberley writes gloomily that 'while anti-fashion may have sporadic and intermittent success at exposing the dominant and repressive fashion discourse or "life-style," the reproductive tendencies of postmodern late capitalism effectively neutralize and dissolve its potential through an inevitable re-creation of its process'.[18] Gail Faurschou, writing in the same issue of the *Canadian Journal of Social and Political Theory*, is even more pessimistic. Fashion, she believes, is the purest and most developed form of commodity capitalism, in its compulsive desire to produce innovation for the sake of innovation, and to stimulate and multiply desire than can never be satisfied. Faurschou rewrites Hebdige's vision of the fugitive and subversive instability of punk, construing it as the official mode of late capitalist consumer culture, in its nightmare of interchangeable surfaces:

Fashion *is* the logic of planned obsolescence – not just the necessity for market survival, but the cycle of desire itself, the endless process through which the body is decoded and recoded, in order to define and inhabit the newest territorialized spaces of capital's expansion. A line of escape at one moment, fashion is recaptured in the network of images the next; frozen in the mirror of the media-scape, we gaze forever at our suspended moment of flight.[19]

The paradox is a familiar one, and it recalls the difficulties encountered, and often evaded, by analysts of other popular cultural forms. The possibilities for a 'disruptive' cultural practice based upon an aesthetic of excess, discontinuity, bricolage and pastiche depend upon the idea that what these things challenge is a set of official or dominant cultural norms, which are anxiously monolithic and committed, whether by design, or structural consequence, to the suppression of diversity. But what allows and creates the conditions for the very politics of diversity which speaks for this kind of cultural resistance is not so much a sudden access of revolutionary consciousness or critical nerve, as a relaxing of the grip of authoritarian uniformity, and an expansion and diversification of official norms. It is not that the postmodern hypothesis is wrong; it is that it is righter than it knows, and seems unable in many cases to think through the contradictions of a logic of the simulacrum in which it is possible simultaneously to be subversive and to be the official mode of postmodern capitalism.

The problem becomes a little clearer when seen in the terms suggested by Baudrillard in 'The Ecstasy of Communication', that is to say in terms of the question of a new form and function of visibility. Theoretical schemes which depend upon the idea of dominance and suppression often involve a sense that the dominant excludes the suppressed term by simply making it invisible. In fashion, in music, in art, in writing, the obvious way to resist this condemnation to invisibility has seemed to be for the marginal group to insist on *being seen* (and heard). Hence, cult or subcultural style is a means of attaining or proclaiming forms of group visibility, which depend for their radical or unsettling effect on their brazen openness to view. Such an analysis encounters difficulties when faced with the fact that this visibility of diverse and stylistically distinct groups is part of the official or dominant mode of advertising and the media in the West. It is not that the fashion industry somehow captures and fossilizes the previously free and self-directing energies of subcultural style; rather the fashion industry, greedy as it is for new and diverse images, functions as part of an economy which depends more and more upon forms of visibility as commodity, upon 'publicity' and less and less upon the exchange of actual goods, or even services. Under these circumstances, visibility and self-proclamation may have become a market requirement rather than a mode of liberation.

This argument can be extended outwards to the question of cultural or ethnic identity. Here, too, visibility and audibility can function simultaneously in ways that affirm cultural identity and in ways that yield it up to appropriation. Stuart Hall has spoken in these terms of the example of Aboriginal Australian culture, which has undergone a considerable and heartening revival recently:

> In the last ten or fifteen years, marginality has become a very productive space. People are speaking up from the margins and claiming representation in ways in which perhaps they didn't twenty or thirty years ago. But now the problem is that the price of putting your head up above the parapet, so

to speak, is to be instantly swept up by this global culture which precisely because it is more sensitive and positively oriented towards difference, diversity, pluralism, eclecticism sweeps you in. Whatever new voice, they say, yes, you can be a part of the global culture. And before you know where you are an Aboriginal painter is just one slot in somebody else's heroic portrait and has lost the sense of a relationship to a culture.[20]

Once again, the twist in the tail of this conceptual spirochaete is the role of cultural analysis in this situation. Much contemporary cultural theory presents itself as a partisan endeavour, speaking for the dignity and value of a whole range of practices and experiences which may be ignored by dominant accounts of elite culture. At the same time, it is conventional to regard the work of the cultural analyst in something of the same way as that of the anthropologist, as somehow always a kind of intrusive alien in the culture that is being studied and brought to light, and perhaps even in the end destructive of that culture. Dick Hebdige employs this model when, at the end of *Subculture*, he mourns the necessarily excluded condition of the cultural analyst, who is 'in society but not inside it, producing analyses of popular culture which are themselves anything but popular'.[21] But this is to assume that there exist spaces of pure sociality which, like some brooding, primitive wilderness, fragilely preserve the principles and experiences of real life; and that once explored, once understood, this unreflective and spontaneous life may be extinguished. Hebdige laments that the study of subcultural style which seemed at the outset to draw the academic world back to the real world, reuniting it with the people, ends by merely confirming the distance between the text and its reader, between everyday life and the 'mythologist' whom it surrounds, fascinates and finally excludes.[22] But this kind of remorse may be the reverse of a kind of hubris, in promoting the cultural analyst to the real condition of existential hero, marginalized as s/he is even from the subcultural margins, and condemned to a life of intellectual wandering.

In a different response to this reflexive discomfort, much theory of contemporary culture cultivates a deliberately less authoritative, more autobiographical mode, in the attempt to disclaim abstract academic authority and to saturate the analysis in the materials that it aims to analyse. Some of Dick Hebdige's recent work provides a good example of this, with its intercutting of theory and autobiographical journal (it will be discussed in more detail in the next chapter). But, like the complaint of outsiderdom, this mode of theoretical modesty conceals or leaves out of account the way that academic criticism and commentary of this kind can be closely involved in the process of social externalization, or bringing to visibility, which is increasingly the only mode in which local or popular culture can be experienced at all – that is to say, in the images and narratives in which 'authentic' or non-theorizably quotidian existence is reflected back to its participants by the media and associated forces (of whom perhaps the ostensibly maverick academic may be one). It is nothing as crude as the anthropological model, in which the academic is solely responsible for uncouthly thrusting the relics of popular culture into the withering light of scientific visibility; but the relationship of postmodernist culture and popular culture in general to the postmodernist theory which speaks via its forms and on its behalf is unavoidably part of that larger and even more complex process by which no popular culture may now be said to exist without being publicly visible as representation, and therefore mediated and administered by the structures and rhythms of spectacle and consumption which attend visibility.

This is not the same thing as claiming that popular culture can never be anything other than what the multifarious forms of cultural management make of it. One of the most important developments within theories of the relation between postmodernism and popular culture has been the development of a more precise language for evoking the multiplicity of meanings, values, practices and purposes which make up the field of popular culture. In his *Uncommon Cultures* (1989), Jim Collins warily navigates between the two kinds of generality which have often afflicted accounts of popular culture; the generalized denunciation of popular culture as the obedient mechanism of ideology and the generalized celebration of popular culture. Collins argues, through a series of admirably detailed readings of cultural examples ranging from musicals and Westerns to detective stories and rock music, that, while it is true that popular culture in postmodernism involves fragmentation and discontinuity, it is important to grasp the particular and determinate forms that such fragmentation takes. 'The Post-Modernist aim . . . is not haphazard "pastiche," motivated only by perversity, but specific juxtapositions for particular purposes', he cautions.[23] Collins avoids defining the popular in terms of particular genres or practices which can be set against other, equally particular high-cultural genres or practices; romance-reading and horse-racing, say, as opposed to opera and point-to-point. Popular culture is to be located not as a particular level in a stable hierarchy of cultural representations, but rather in the field of potential choices, juxtapositions and amalgamations made by increasingly active and ironically self-aware subjects in coping with the semiotic overload of contemporary culture. Popular culture therefore inheres in these combinatory activities, not in particular objects.

It is not quite clear where this leaves the cultural critic. Collins is clear that he finds the idea of the critic as cultural legislator or curator both distasteful and fatuous, but he seems unwilling to face what might be taken to be one consequence of his argument, namely that, if subjects (people) neither need rescuing from popular culture nor instruction from it, then there may be no role for the cultural critic or analyst at all. But then, in the last pages of his book, Collins stages a dramatic, though not wholly convincing rescue of the critic, who is now to act as a kind of exemplary *bricoleur*:

> The function of the critic cannot be limited to showing his or her readers the error of their culture's ways; it must instead sensitize readers and students to the processes involved in the production of subjectivity. Unless we emphasize the active role all people may play in that production, criticism remains a "spectator sport" for an increasingly smaller audience. The activity of the critic, then, must be directly linked to the activity of subject production; the critic's activity, undertaken in a specific cultural context, should serve as a model for the latter.[24]

A substantial cake is being had and eaten here. Having subjected the arrogance and blindness of legislative cultural theory to such marvellously comprehensive mauling, Collins reinstates the legislative impulse in the rather absurd idea that the critic could be a technician or consultant for the production of subjectivity. This is perhaps more evidence, where one would least expect to find it, of the inseparability of the critique of cultural authority from the continuing impulse to cultural management within postmodernist theory.

John Frow argues along similar lines in his astute and judicious unfolding of the problem of value in *Cultural Studies and Cultural Value* (1995). He focuses sharply on the question of the popular, arguing that it is no longer possible for cultural studies simply to identify itself with the study and promotion of popular culture, and assembling a number of strong objections to the Manichean distinction between high culture and low culture which once seemed to have such commanding clarity for cultural studies. Patterns of cultural distinction no longer map regularly – if they ever did – on to patterns of social domination and advantage, so that it is no longer plausible to see popular culture as the integrated expression of a singular and homogeneous politico-cultural will. Frow submits the influential work of Pierre Bourdieu to a slow, respectful, but unsentimental roasting, making it clear that his own intellectual affiliations are with work such as that of Ernesto Laclau and Stuart Hall who have been stressing since the 1980s the essential mobility and unevenness of patterns of cultural taste and identification. Crucial to this vision is a strengthened sense that value does not merely inhere objectively and permanently within particular texts or artefacts; so there is nothing about either Mantovani or Mozart's *Requiem* which associates them inevitably with one social position or another. What counts for much more, Frow argues, are the increasingly unpredictable patterns of what is done to and with such objects; the strategies of cultural use, as Michel de Certeau has insisted in *The Practice of Everyday Life*, as opposed to the crude distribution of cultural goods.[25]

Having argued along similar lines to Jim Collins about the diversity and unpredictability of cultural choices and uses, Frow turns to the question of what, in the light of these transformed conditions – or at least transformed assumptions – cultural studies ought to be and do. One option might be to try to develop an ethnomethodological neutrality, which aimed simply to collect and tabulate the workings of culture in general. Another might be the 'happy relativism' of postmodernism, which would surrender all claims either to totalize the field of the cultural or to give a privilege to any particular kinds of evidence or experience within that field. Neither of these options appears satisfactory to Frow, founded as they both appear to be on a worrying indifference to the intensity with which competing claims of value are made, and a numbing of the sense of how much value *matters*. Moreover, and more importantly, both attitudes appear to embody a self-contradiction insofar as they offer to take into account every perspective but that of the cultural analyst, whose own values and interests are mysteriously and suspiciously evaporated away. Putting it at its rawest: if it is no longer possible for cultural studies to identify itself with a simple affirmation of the value of the popular, it is equally implausible for it to try to function as pure and disinterested description.

For cultural studies to proceed without amputating either its critical–evaluative or its descriptive–analytic aspirations, it is necessary, Frow argues, to suppress the suppression of the interests of the observer; to include in the picture a self-portrait of the observer as a cultural intellectual. Frow begins this work by providing an impressive argument about the steady expansion of what he calls the category of cultural capital, and the role of cultural intellectuals of all kinds in mediating and managing cultural knowledge. This includes not only the deepening bureaucratization of the arts, along with the sedimenting of the functions of cultural criticism in institutions of education, but more generally the huge expansion in what Fritz Machlup has described as the 'knowledge-producing occupations'.[26] Frow's conclusion is that cultural studies should learn to be less other-fixated (and therefore other-fixating) in its dealings with culture. This is to say that cultural studies should give up its ventriloquizing co-optation of the value of the popular ('the' value of 'the popular') and learn to affirm a cultural politics which should be 'openly and without embarrassment presented as their politics, not someone else's'.[27]

This vision of cultural studies as a kind of pressure-group, jostling for cultural elbow-room alongside the campaign for euthanasia and the tobacco lobby, is rather a queasy one. But Frow appears to press further than other surveyors of the postmodern cultural scene to the conclusion that it may not be possible for exponents of cultural studies both to prosecute the postmodern delegitimation of cultural theory and to retain their position as unacknowledged legislators of the delegitimation.

Notes

1 'Postmodernism: Or, the Cultural Logic of Late Capitalism', *New Left Review*, 146 (1984), p. 54.
2 See Andrew Goodwin, 'Sample and Hold: Pop Music in the Age of Digital Reproduction', *Critical Quarterly*, 30:3 (1988), pp. 34–49.
3 Described in *Cut 'N' Mix: Culture, Identity and Caribbean Music* (London: Comedia, 1987), pp. 138, 141. References hereafter in the text.
4 'Postmodernism and Popular Culture', in *Postmodernism: ICA Documents 5*, ed. Lisa Appignanesi (London: ICA, 1986), p. 57.
5 'Cruising Around the Historical Bloc – Postmodernism and Popular Music in East Los Angeles', *Cultural Critique*, 5 (1986–7), p. 159.
6 Ibid., pp. 169–70.
7 Ibid., p. 160.
8 Lawrence Grossberg *We Gotta Get Out of This Place: Popular Conservatism and Postmodern Culture* (New York and London: Routledge, 1992). References hereafter in the text.
9 Roland Barthes, *Système de la mode* (Paris: Editions du Seuil, 1967).
10 *Adorned in Dreams: Fashion and Modernity* (London: Virago, 1985), p. 11.
11 'Fashion/Orientalism/The Body', *New Formations*, 1 (1987), pp. 5–33.
12 Ibid., p. 28.
13 *Subculture: The Meaning of Style* (London: Methuen, 1979), pp. 46–71.
14 Ibid., p. 123.
15 Ibid., p. 126.
16 'Black Hair/Style Politics', *New Formations*, 3 (1987), p. 34.
17 Ibid., p. 51.
18 'The Fashion Apparatus and the Deconstruction of Postmodern Subjectivity', *Canadian Journal of Political and Social Theory*, 11:1–2 (1987), p. 49.

19 'Fashion and the Cultural Logic of Postmodernity', *Canadian Journal of Political and Social Theory*, 11:1–2 (1987), p. 72.

20 Interview With Stuart Hall, *Block*, 14 (1988), p. 13.

21 *Subculture*, pp. 139–40.

22 Ibid., p. 140.

23 Jim Collins, *Uncommon Cultures: Popular Culture and Post-Modernism* (London and New York: Routledge, 1989), p. 138.

24 Ibid., p. 146.

25 Michel de Certeau, *The Practice of Everyday Life*, trans. Stephen Rendall (Berkeley: University of California Press, 1984).

26 Fritz Machlup, *Knowledge and Knowledge Production* (Princeton, NJ: Princeton University Press, 1980).

27 John Frow, *Cultural Studies and Cultural Value* (Oxford: Clarendon, 1995), p. 169.

Part III
Consequences

8

Post-Modesty: Renunciation and the Sublime

The last few chapters have concentrated upon the narratives of postmodernism built through the work of critics and theorists across and between different disciplines and cultural areas, and so have necessarily focused mostly on what is said about these different forms of postmodernism in and by such narratives. But we have frequently needed to remind ourselves of the fact that the phrase 'postmodern theory' speaks in a complex and reflexive way not only of the object of theorization but also of the responsive self-transformations of theory itself. 'Postmodern theory' names the ambition of theory to attempt to examine and transform itself as part of the same logic or movement of ideas in 'culture' itself. It is this transformation of the perceived and traditional role of criticism which is the mark of what I have taken to be the most significant and central determinant of the postmodern debate – namely the recasting of the relationship between the sphere of culture and the different spheres of cultural reception, management, mediation and transmission.

The most obvious sign of this – obvious in its symptoms and ideology, though not in its more complex determinants and effects – is the apparent collapse of criticism into its object, the much-discussed blurring of the 'critical' and 'creative' functions. A common argument is that, given that one can no longer depend upon the principle of metalanguage, language that can be seen to comment reliably and as it were at a higher level upon another language without being contaminated by its terms, criticism is always implicated in the literature it mediates. Like the language of literature, critical language is composed of different voices, registers, points of view, figures of speech, forms of dramatization, rhythm, style and so on and is finally not to be distinguished from literary language as such. These claims have been taken up and extended by the American literary critics, Geoffrey Hartman and J. Hillis Miller. Hartman's view, voiced in his *Criticism in the Wilderness* (1980), is that critical discourse must give up its attempts to master literary discourse, and should allow or even foster a sharing of substance between the two realms, such that criticism may find itself 'within literature, not outside of it looking in'.[1] J. Hillis Miller, although his own critical language has much less metaphorical and pseudo-poetic effervescence than Hartman's, has similarly argued for the interchangeability of literature and criticism, defending criticism against the charge of being a parasite upon the life of literature by an ingenious explication of all the etymological indeterminacies and reversals buried within the history of the word and concept of the 'host' and its derivatives.[2]

These developments in literary criticism intersect with developments in other fields, such as the absorption of critical discourses into avant-garde practices of various kinds, in the high theoretical 'literacy' displayed by artists like Victor Burgin, Martha Rosler and Mary Kelly. Fredric Jameson has similarly specified the blurring 'of the disciplines and discursive styles of history, philosophy, social theory and literary criticism into an "undecidable" amalgam that must simply be called "theory" ' as one of the prime features of the postmodern intellectual scene.[3] An account of the regroupings of theory, criticism and culture ought to encompass all the different forms and effects of this 'de-differentiation' of spheres; but I hope it will be a tactical advantage to focus on just one aspect, the implicit political claims of stylistic mutation in academic or institutional forms of criticism.

What underlies the present preoccupation with the forms of theoretical language is a generalized mistrust of the capacity of any language (let alone critical language) to render truths about the world or other forms of language in a simply transparent or objective way. This has general and particular determinants; in general terms we may point to the gradual discrediting of traditional forms of transhistorical authority, with the dissolution of Empire, and the diffusion of small class elites in the name of a nominally more inclusive democracy·of culture. This goes along with such particular amplifying effects as the development of perspectivism in science, which casts doubt on the possibility of generating means of measurement or observation which do not in themselves impinge upon and perhaps distort the nature of the results to be derived, and the widespread rise of theories of 'discourse' to replace theories of 'language' – that is, theories that emphasize the embeddedness of every utterance in its particular social contexts, rather than the authority of abstract rules and systems. Perhaps the most influential formulations of this last position are in the work of Ludwig Wittgenstein and Mikhail Bakhtin, both of whom deny that language has any abstractably essential nature, and argue that it must be thought of instead as a diverse range of social games and practices.[4] Added to these has been the influence of Michel Foucault, whose work gives the word 'discourse' – often used flabbily to signal no more than a general awareness of language in social use rather than as a system of rules and structures – a more precise rooting in relations of power and, in particular, the forms of power embodied in specialized and institutionalized languages.[5] In much recent criticism, Foucault's influence has reinforced that of Bakhtin. Where Foucault's work is often read as the analysis of the diffuse but mighty operations of power in strategies of containment, Bakhtin is usually read as a theorist of forms of cultural resistance. For Bakhtin, power is embodied in the urge to centralize or unify language, pressing it inwards towards regularized and dominant forms which exclude eccentric or unorthodox voices. Against this, Bakhtin affirms the 'dialogic' conversation of multiple voices, or the cacophonic subversiveness of the 'carnivalesque' in language, in which the careful social hierarchies and boundaries of language are inverted or effaced.[6]

These particular influences underlie the assault upon the politics of representation in cultural discourse. With the growing awareness of the ways in which power is lodged and reproduced in dominant forms of discourse, criticism has repeatedly caught itself with its own hands in the till, and been forced to convict itself of participation in the same or similar conjunctures of knowledge, power and language as it investigates and (perhaps) condemns elsewhere, in the languages of science, medicine, law and high cultural accomplishment. This guilty awareness produces two principal responses. The first is a willed renunciation of authoritative forms of language, and an attempt to develop more open, democratically inclusive forms of critical discourse; this will often involve the promotion of alternative, 'unofficial' or private forms within or alongside critical writing. The second is an intensified form of the first, but with the emphasis on the undermining of critical authority from within, by forms of stylistic excess or heightening. The result is often a kind of stylistic overload, which asserts simultaneously the impossibility of maintaining objective authority and the omnicompetence of a criticism which pushes itself towards this sublime self-defeat. These two modes, which it seems reasonable to call the modes of 'renunciation' and of 'sublimity', share elements of a common purpose and have a powerful reciprocity.

The renunciatory mode is illustrated very well by the work of Ihab Hassan, the most consistent promoter of the idea of the 'postmodern turn'.

His early works, like *The Dismemberment of Orpheus* (1971) are written in a recognizably detached and authoritative, if allusive and metaphorically active, academic style and indeed he has continued to publish scholarly discussions in this mode. But his work has also shown signs of a move towards much less traditionally authoritative critical styles. In 1975 he produced *Paracriticisms: Seven Speculations of the Times*, and in its opening essay Hassan proposes a criticism that will be prepared, against an academy that always prefers the fixities of doctrine, precedent and formula against the shock of the new, to 'improvise on the possible'.[7] This improvisation aims to recreate criticism according to the image of the literature that it serves, because, as Hassan says, 'the theoretical solemnity of modern criticism ignores the self-destructive element of literature, its need for self-annulment' (*P*, 9). Criticism must learn to acknowledge and to humble itself to the forces of undoing and decreation which Hassan believes typify postmodern literature and the modernist 'literature of silence' that precedes it, in their tendencies toward self-cancellation, self-reflective acuity, disorganization and the refusal of meaning. If this renunciation of authority seems in one sense to make criticism an even more arcane procedure than ever before, it may also serve, Hassan claims, to bring criticism back into a cultural mainstream, for it involves a movement 'beyond the control of the art object, toward the openness, and even the gratuitousness – gratuitous is free – of existence. Perhaps it is even a movement toward the generalization of our attitudes in an age that heralds universal leisure, the end of specialization – a movement, therefore, that seeks to adapt the literary response to new conditions of survival' (*P*, 27–8). And the relaxation of its academic/theoretical grip on procedures and protocols is in the interests of a new, epochal purpose for criticism, which may embody 'a desire for life', may 'envision a new man' (*P*, 28).

The opening three-part essay of *Paracriticisms* provides a useful template for this critical movement. Entitled 'Frontiers of Criticism: 1963, 1969, 1972', it begins with an elegant, but stylistically conventional essay about the need for criticism to expand its frontiers and thus harness itself to the destiny of man. The next section, dating from 1969, moves into a rather darker consideration of the ways in which criticism must begin to encompass forms of silence and denial. Here the language of judicious authority begins to be shredded by digressions, intermissions and interventions, quotations, short inset anecdotes, often highlighted by typographic means, emboldening, indentation, and so on. Hassan's own question, 'How will criticism speak when humanism ceases to breathe?' (*P*, 18) is answered not so much in the text as in its discontinuous mode of argument, its offering to the reader of 'empty spaces, silences in which he can meet himself in the presence of literature' (*P*, 25). The name that Hassan offers for this self-demonstrating practice is 'paracriticism', a criticism which is the 'attempt to recover the art of multivocation' (ibid.).

The process is developed even further in the last section of the opening essay. 'Frontiers of Criticism: 1972' concerns the writing of and responses to Hassan's own earlier volume *The Dismemberment of Orpheus*. The essay is strung between a network of different dramatized voices, 'The Reviewer', 'The Professor' and 'The Literary Cynic', who discuss and dispute the themes of the earlier book when they are not setting and answering riddles for each other – the Literary Cynic asks the Professor, for example, to write a FORTRAN program to prove the theory that the sum of the first *n* terms of the progression 1,3,5,7,9,11 . . . 99 is equal to n^2 (*P*, 35). This triologue is itself crossed by the quotation of actual reviews of *The Dismemberment of Orpheus* by named (notable) reviewers, and framed by a cynical condemnation of the exclusive reviewing practices of the *New York Times Review of Books*.

The mode of 'multivocation' persists and is made even more various through *Paracriticisms*. The point is to multiply the voices of criticism in order to free the critic from the responsibility or guilty pleasures of the single authoritarian voice (a favoured trick is to conduct autobiographical musings in a distanced third person). Hassan has The Professor say at one point in the third essay of 'Frontiers of Criticism': 'Writing a book is an act of aggression . . . Writing a book, then, one enters the endless cycle of Victimizer and Victim' (*P*, 30). Accordingly, we have a critical discourse that displays abrupt leaps between different forms or accents of academic and quasi-academic language, the dead enthusiasm of the book-blurb, the stiff violence of the formal denunciation, the 'authorless', reasoning style of progressive argumentation and the demonstrative citing of authorities – itself made a prime example of the functioning of collage in Hassan's work, which stitches together authorities as diverse as Claude Lévi-Strauss and Jimi Hendrix. The essay 'The New Gnosticism' begins with a cocktail of quotations from, among others, *The Tibetan Book of the Dead*, Blake's *Jerusalem*, Henri Bergson, Teilhard de Chardin and Marshall McLuhan, which is followed immediately by this blunt disclaimer: 'But what do twelve epigraphs prove? Surely they do not answer an appeal to authority since few of us now accept the same authorities . . . epigraphs become a kind of preparation for failure' (*P*, 122). On the same page, critical language suddenly lurches into free verse, giving a sense of curious, limping rapture:

```
The theme of this
               paracritical essay
                        is              the growing
                        insistence of Mind
     to apprehend reality im-mediately
     to gather more and more mind
                             in itself:
                             thus to become
                             its own
                             reality
```

                                                            (*P*, 122–3)

In Hassan's next collection of essays, *The Right Promethean Fire* (1980), the paracritical mode of multivocation is at its most mischievously insistent.[8] The five essays that make up the book are interspersed with fragments from a journal which Hassan tells us he kept during a sabbatical year at the Camargo Foundation in a small fishing village near Marseilles. This enables him to fill out his speculations regarding the theme of the book, the purpose and destiny of human imagination, with what are mock-modestly described as 'queries, musings of a reading man between idleness and work . . . a variety of voices patterned disjunctively' (*RPF*, 31), which turn out to consist of vapid descriptions of the sea and the stars, of restaurants where he has eaten with his wife (complete with menus), of cats – we are solemnly informed that 'they neither write nor speak' (*RPF*, 37) – accounts of his attempts at watercolour painting, bathetic meditations such as 'Our windows face south in Cassis. I also face my fiftieth year' (*RPF*, 33), and sentimental sketches of picturesque local characters, like the bent old woman he sees struggling up the hill 'her mouth working at her dog in some toothless speech' (*RPF*, 41) – all ornamented with glittering chips struck off his (admittedly impressive) casual reading in Bataille, Deleuze, Gödel and Giordano Bruno.

The final section of the book is subtitled 'A University Masque in Five Scenes' and consists of a conversation between eight characters, including 'Mythotext', who keeps telling the story of Prometheus, 'Heterotext', whose only function is to quote from other scholarly authorities, 'Metatext', who comments on the other voices and 'Postext' 'who vainly attempts to conclude the nonaction' (*RPF*, 189). Again, this apparent self-indulgence – deconstruction in cartoon form – is carefully justified by the intention 'to play voice against voice and text against text, hoping thus to perform the indefinitions of a posthumanist moment' (ibid.).

But all the way through the archly-performed shifts or intercuttings of discourse, the sense is not so much of the surrender of self or the undermining of academic discourse, as the display of versatility. We watch Hassan quick-change through his wardrobe of critical costumes without feeling that this is anything but fancy-dress. This is partly due to the fact that Hassan insists on telling us in advance, and repeatedly thereafter, what his stylistic strategies are *for*, and how we are meant to receive them. The journal is there, he alerts us owlishly, because it 'avows a degree of subjectivity, even of intersubjectivity, which I hope can modify the incantatory abstractions of the Promethean theme' (*RPF*, xvii). But although Hassan claims to be allowing a multiplicity of voices to speak through him ('Who, indeed, is the critic? How many in him speak?', he muses oratically (ibid.)), but these are not voices that ever seem likely to enter into serious argument with their governing text, or even with each other. All this is more like a séance than a seminar, more like an orchestra than an argument, more like a referendum than a vote.

Hassan is most convincing when he sheepishly acknowledges the meekness of his gestures of deformation (*RPF*, xviii) and least convincing when claiming the status of renegade. Hassan likes to suggest that his typographical versatilities represent a kind of political intervention, and upbraids the journal *College English* for attempting to carry through its left/liberal editorial policies without challenging any of the 'social or technical or sensuous conventions of its own medium' (*RPF*, 21). Although he mentions material factors like editorial policies, printing rules, advertising practices and distribution procedures, what he really finds reactionary in *College English* is the fact that 'its arguments appear invariably in serried double columns of an unvarying typeface' (ibid.). Here, what Hassan proclaims as the 'politics of the page' is no suggestive synecdoche for the range of material factors that undoubtedly form part of the 'discourse' of English studies, but simply, well, what you see on the page. Seemingly a radical materialism, Hassan's 'politics of the page' is really a reification of one particular aspect of the material production of criticism. There might indeed be some point in seriously considering changing the discursive forms of critical writing, but a politics of the page might turn out to have more to do with who reads criticism, and where, and how, and for what purposes, than with the attractiveness of typeface and binding.

In fact, although he keeps pointing to the 'calculated duplicity' of his 'ruptures and diremptions' (*RPF*, xviii), Hassan also seems aware of the way that these allegedly multiple voices actually blend into easy, mystical conjuncture. Explicitly, Hassan's desire is to imagine forms of unity, models of universality, in which 'thought finds its identity . . . in language, in mind, ubiquitously' (*RPF*, xviii). This universality is achieved, as perhaps all such universalities are, by a refusal or glossing over of actual resistances or forms of incommensurability. Despite his awesome range of reading and responsiveness, and his undoubtedly sincere concern about the parochial separation of criticism from important contemporary issues, and for all of his willingness to acknowledge the close imbrication of the political with the critical, Hassan's project is in the end not to rethink the role of criticism within an expanded and complex postmodern sphere of values and commitments, but to find some way of subsuming such contexts in a new universal frame. Especially in his most recent work, he pays lip service to the accommodating pragmatism of William James, with its insistence simultaneously on the demand for moral, political and cognitive engagement and its sense of the world as 'gravid and stubborn with its differences'.[9] But Hassan's tendency of mind is fundamentally idealist in gazing beyond the jagged particularities of engagement and difference to the glossy transcendences of Mind or Imagination. His work moves us closer to the world of particular responsibilities and commitments only to accelerate past it towards the 'blessed region', where 'Life truly matters' and where 'power and its human psychomachias dissolve' (*RPF*, xxi). Declaring that 'politics is what we must work politically to make obsolete' (*RPF*, xx) is a form of utopianism with a venerable socialist ancestry, but it also colludes dangerously with that vacating of the political that is so powerfully at work in the contemporary West. Hassan's critical direction grotesquely mimics the movement of the postmodern world towards hyperreal generality when he declares that 'the struggling must always be double: to struggle and *at the same time* struggle to empty all struggle' (*RPF*, 23).

The mode of renunciation of authority found in Hassan's writing has also become popular in some areas of the social sciences, and perhaps particularly among writers associated with the study of forms of popular culture under the conditions of postmodernism. Examples of the renunciatory mode of social analysis may be found in the buoyant field of Australian, Canadian and British sociology, in work that seeks to context, complicate or dissolve the detachment and authority of academic discourse. Some of the effects of this can be seen in a collection of essays entitled *Future*Fall: Excursions Into Post-Modernity*, the record of a conference of the same name held at the Power Institute of Fine Arts in the University of Sydney in 1984.[10] The collection runs together traditional explorations of academic themes and readings of texts with critical performance pieces which play with and reflect upon scholarly conventions and intersperse unofficial or casual forms like the journal with academic modes.[11] The theme that runs through these speculations on the present and the future is the willed humility of the cultural analyst. It is articulated well by George Alexander, who introduces his wide-ranging aphoristic meditation on science-fiction, semiotics, city life and African musical rhythms with the disclaimer 'I had no strategy for the essay, no particular position to defend, no territory to add to, no place to stockpile gains: scientific, political, theoretical or even military'.[12] As we have already noticed, the search for modes of critical openness is also commonly to be found in postmodern social theory in Britain, especially in the work of Angela MacRobbie and Dick Hebdige. In his evocations of popular culture, street life and subcultural forms, Hebdige in particular has been increasingly concerned to heal the gap between social theory and its object that he lamented at the end of his *Subculture*.[13], by allowing academic discourse to be invaded by a number of other cultural forms, rhythms and influences. Hebdige's study of Caribbean music, *Cut 'N' Mix* (1987) is divided into three sections which, borrowing the argot of the West Indian DJ, he calls the 'Original Cut', the 'Dub Version' and the 'Club Mix', to evoke the idea that the book is 'three separate books or three tracks on a single rhythm'.[14] Another, more absorptive kind of bricolage is to be found in his later article entitled 'A Report on the Western Front: Postmodernism and the "Politics" of Style', which sets off illustrations, from Mickey Mouse to contemporary advertisements, against a text that cites authoritative worthies such as Jameson and Baudrillard alongside literary figures like Borges and the science-fiction writer Philip K. Dick.[15] Like Hassan, Hebdige announces his intention to 'address the problematics of postmodernism . . . in the form in which I shall pose questions rather than in the arguments I shall incidentally invoke'. The pop-cultural filter this time is not music, but 'the flow and grain of television discourse switching back and forth between different channels', and the intention is 'to induce in the reader that distracted, drifting state of mind we associate with watching television'.[16]

Such stylistic immersion in the shape, texture and rhythms of everyday life is in Hebdige's work an affirmation of solidarity, as well as a gesture of humility, the humility imagined by Iain Chambers, when he argues that 'the traditional semantic chains that once tied "truth" and "meaning" to the powers of an intellectual priesthood, and their exclusive institutions (the academy, the university, the scholarly journal, academic publishing) are snapping under the expansion of the contemporary world.' Given this situation, Chambers follows Foucault in arguing for the supersession of the 'universal' intellectual, who speaks imperiously on behalf of Humanity, by the 'specific' intellectual, who is immersed inescapably in the particular conditions of his or her time: 'the intellectual can no longer be considered as a dispenser of the Law and Authority, the Romantic poet–priest–prophet, but is rather a humble detective, living, like all of us, under authority and the law, inside the contemporary metropolis'.[17] It is always possible, of course, that this humble self-effacement may be performing other functions, for example, restoring credibility to the work of an intellectual formation that believes it may be losing its hold on the cultural world. The slackening of the will-to-power in academic discourse may turn out to have been a form of adaptive mimicry which has the effect of maintaining or extending the field of academic competence. The result of this may be less to fling open the windows of critical discourse to the vibrant clangour of the contemporary carnival than to capture and assimilate these influences within critical discourse and screen them (in the senses both of, displaying and approving) silently as guarantees of the continuing integrity of critical discourse. To the degree that this interpretation runs together postmodernist criticism indistinguishably with the mass media, in its appropriation and sterilization of popular culture, it is a violent overstatement. But where there is not exact identity of purpose and function, there may still be forms of functional equivalence; and a critical discourse that is content merely to aestheticize its own forms and procedures, squandering energies that might be directed at more tangible enlargements of forms of critical exclusion, invites the accusation that it is retaining or even enlarging its versatile authority in seeming to surrender it.

Passive renunciation is not the only mode in which the foregrounding of style works in postmodern theory. A later article of Dick Hebdige's gives a hint of its more active mode. In 'The Impossible Object: Towards a Sociology of the Sublime', Hebdige intercuts a scholarly meditation on the dominance of a Kantian model of the sublime with reflections on living in his street in North London; reflections which centre especially on his neighbour Mr H and his infatuation with his imported Thunderbird car. But, although there is little doubt that Hebdige enjoys the lurches between the aesthetic sublime and the quotidian grime, he is concerned in this article less to celebrate diversity for its own sake than to attempt a kind of unification: 'This weaving together of incommensurable levels, tones, objects represents an attempt to . . . alternate between on the one hand the personal, the confessional, the particular, the concrete, and on the other the public, the expository, the general, the abstract: to walk the flickering line between vertigo and ground.'[18]

Hebdige's concern is to respond to the reappearance of what he calls the 'asocial sublime' in contemporary cultural theory – the apocalyptic inheritance from Nietzsche and more obviously from Kant, which suggests that the only form of value is to be found in the embrace of theoretical extremity. One influential example of this is Lyotard's postmodern aesthetics of the sublime. For Lyotard, the collapse of metanarrative leaves only one option for a postmodern culture, to reactivate an art of the sublime, which testifies to the impossibility or impotence of art, or representation in general, when faced with certain kinds of extremity or vastness, in nature or beyond it. This kind of art goes beyond the limited and citizenly ambitions of an art of the real, says Lyotard. In common with the art of the modernist avant-garde, postmodernist art gestures to those things which lie beyond the possibility of representation. But where modernist art still allows pleasure in the capture of the sublime in artistic form, postmodernist art, says Lyotard, goes further towards the sublime, in destroying form itself:

> The postmodern would be that which, in the modern, puts forward the unpresentable in presentation itself, that which denies itself the solace of good forms, the consensus of a taste which would make it possible to share collectively the nostalgia for the unattainable; that which searches for new presentations, not in order to enjoy them but in order to impart a stronger sense of the unpresentable.[19]

Hebdige emphasizes the Kantian/Nietzschean inheritance of the will to the sublime across the influential writers of post-structuralism, Derrida, Lacan, Foucault, Kristeva and Barthes, all of whom extend in various ways the 'aspiration towards the ineffable' and consequently convert asociality into an absolute value ('Impossible Object', 67). Despite its apparent resemblances to the pursuit of decentred non-form, Hebdige's critical mode in this article aims to earth the abstraction of this mode of sublimity in local and provisional forms of value in ordinary collective life. The essay ends with a very odd return to the mode of the sublime in its final, camp, vision of Mr H's fetish, the Thunderbird, flooded and destroyed by an apocalyptic downpour, while a covenantal apparition of Mr H himself in the sky, transfigured bizarrely into Walter Benjamin's Angel of History, flies free ('Impossible Object', 74). But the real strength of the essay lies in Hebdige's diagnosis of and resistance towards the aesthetics of the sublime in contemporary theory.

The mode of sublimity which Hebdige writes against here induces in critical writing a strange dialectic which pushes renunciation of authority and of unified form to a point of absolute impotence, which may then loop back into a renewed assertion of nihilistic power. Hebdige suggests that this apocalyptic strain in postmodern writing signals, not so much the actual collapse of values and political meanings, as the terminal convulsions of a certain intellectual formation:

> Rather than surrender mastery of the field, the critics who promulgate the line that we are living at the end of everything (and are *all* these critics men?) make one last leap and resolve to take it all – judgement, history, politics, aesthetics, value – out of the window with them . . . The implication seems to be that if they cannot sit at the top of Plato's pyramid, then there shall be no pyramid at all. ('Impossible Object', 70)

This double position, of relinquishment and suicidal prerogative, is to be found not only in the stylistics of much contemporary criticism, but also, framing or 'territorializing' them, increasing numbers of works of metacriticism. One such work is Greg Ulmer's 'The Object of Post-Criticism', one of the earliest and most influential disquisitions upon the subject of the styles of postmodern criticism. In common with other commentators, Ulmer argues that modern criticism has taken over many of the subversive devices of modern art.[20] Ulmer specifies two particular forms of avant-garde strategy apparent in 'post'-criticism, the use of various forms of collage and montage and the revival of a specific form of allegory. The characteristics of collage are the severing of materials from their original contexts and the assemblage of fragments into new arrangements, although Ulmer predictably stresses the fact of severance and discontinuity rather than the fact of renewed unity ('Object of Post-Criticism', 84–7). His principal example of such critical collage is the work of Derrida. Collage is used in Derrida's work, says Ulmer, to assist and embody Derrida's critique of representation, of the belief or claim that signs can refer directly to their referents; it does this by demonstrating the necessary intertextual weavings of texts one with another, and the breakdown of the clear distinctions between text and commentary. Thus, in his 'reading' of Philippe Sollers' novel *Numbers*, Derrida grafts his commentary on to a number of quotations from the novel, in a process that allows the two texts to penetrate and echo each other: 'the two texts are transformed, deform each other, contaminate each other's content, tend at times to reject each other, or pass elliptically one into the other and become regenerated in the repetition . . . Each grafted text continues to radiate back toward the site of its removal, transforming that, too, as it affects the new territory.'[21] In other critical readings by Derrida, the principle is carried even further. In his reading of Shelley's 'The Triumph of Life', Derrida carries out a stereophonic discussion of Shelley's poem and Maurice Blanchot's novel *L'Arrêt de mort*, as well as grafting together two critical discussions; one, a speculation on Shelley and Blanchot, the other, carried on in a continuous undercommentary at the bottom of the page, a meditation on translation.[22]

This kind of collage also furnishes an example of Ulmer's second category of critical innovation, the reworking of allegory. Ulmer does not have in mind here the usual meaning of the term (a text which means something different from what it appears to mean, and calls upon the reader to decipher this concealed meaning). He calls the kind of criticism which treats literary texts in this way 'allegoresis'. 'Allegorical' criticism seeks instead to dramatize or enact the possibilities inherent in the linguistic material of the object-text, and does so not by cancelling or excavating the surface of the text in search of deeper meanings, but by improvising on the material of the original text.[23] Allegorical criticism therefore 'favors the material of the signifier over the meanings of the signifieds' ('Object of Post-Criticism', 95). This sort of allegory will often involve direct and 'parasitic' incorporation of the work of others, and it is exemplified very well in John Cage's appropriations and reworkings of sections of Thoreau's *Journals* and his celebrated reassemblages of Joyce's *Finnegans Wake* in the form of 'mesostics', columnar arrangements of chance-generated phrases from the novel held together by a spine of highlighted letters spelling out 'JAMES JOYCE'.[24]

Again, it is Derrida who furnishes the most extreme example of this kind of critical reading, whose works of commentary never simply comment on the texts they discuss, thereby fixing the distance between text and commentary, and freezing the play of language within the original texts, but always attempt to prolong the energies of association at work in those original texts. In this situation, criticism does not aim to tell the truth about the texts it criticizes, but to use those texts as generative machines for new texts. A good example of this sort of generative machine is a chance note made about an umbrella in Nietzsche's notebooks, which Derrida seizes on for his elaborate account of the sexual metaphors by which we conceive the idea of 'style'.[25] In his later work, *Applied Grammatology*, Ulmer gives an extended analysis of Derrida's adoption of a number of such metaphorical generators in different works, including a postcard, boots, flowers, and even a coffin. Ulmer insists that in Derrida's use of these objects, they are never symbols, carrying their own meanings hidden behind their backs, but are 'models of the inventive process itself, productive and restrictive at once, of any exemplarity whatever'.[26]

Perhaps the most astonishing example of criticism as avant-garde practice is Derrida's *Glas*.[27] The text consists of two columns running continuously on the left and right of the page, the left hand column conducting a disquisition around the work of Hegel and Hegelian themes, the right hand column dominated by a discussion of the work of Jean Genet. The visual splitting of the text, with the discussions of the themes of wholeness, knowledge, philosophy, abstraction and the spirit on the left and of literature, sexuality, castration and excess on the right, along with the domination of two textual-machine metaphors – the idea of the eagle (resulting from a French pun on the name of Hegel (Hegel/aigle) and the idea of flowers (stemming from the fact that Genet's name recalls the *genet*, the gorse or broom flower) – is itself undercut by the variable passage of themes and puns between the two columns and the irregular breaking up of the typeface and spatial arrangement of the page.

Glas has been taken as the object- or limit-text of postmodern criticism, standing in the same relationship to traditional criticism as *Finnegans Wake* does to literature; indeed, *Glas* imitates Joyce's text in the circularity of its beginning and ending, for the first sentence asks 'What remains today, for us, here, now, of a Hegel?', a question which is answered by, and itself serves to complete, the fragment which ends the text, 'today, here, now, the debris of'.[28] It is the critic Geoffrey Hartman who has meditated most deeply on the lessons and problems set by *Glas*. Hartman reacts to the book with fascination as well as a fair degree of horrified recoil, noting that 'there is, it seems, no knowledge except in the form of a text – of ecriture – and that is devious and dissolving, very unabsolute, as it leads always to other texts and further writing'.[29] What captivates Hartman in Derrida's writing is its contamination of text and commentary and, in acknowledgement of this, Hartman's own engagement with the text takes the form of a struggle to comment on *Glas* without being drawn into its orbit of puns, neologisms and metaphorical machines. As he works through *Glas*, we sense the impulse to allegoresis, the desire to distance, formulate and interpret the original text, fading before the desire to replicate and extend its structures. This struggle summons up the sense of the sublime, as Hartman hangs over the abyss of meaning apparently opened up by Derrida's text, horrified and excited by its yawning immeasurabilities. For other writers, too, *Glas* stands as the final fulfilment of the project of deconstruction; Vincent Leitch's description of it is a good example of the imitative overreach to which (meta)criticism can be prompted by this prospect:

> Derrida's verbal play here is to foreground the materiality or physicality of language: language's wicked asemia and wit, generating relentless disruptive surfaces, continually surpass the reader and the author. More than the excess of themes, or the surplus of interruptions, or the multiplying

bifurcation of compositional units, this textual play of signifiers presses home the interminable qualities of writing and analysis. Or rather, it arrests and checks any passage beyond language.[30]

The argument here is conducted entirely via the invocation of sublimity, insisting as it does, with its absolute terms ('relentless', 'continually', 'interminable') and its gathering rhythms, on the complete lack of boundaries or limits in Derrida's work, even as it swerves round in the last sentence to the blunting awareness of restriction. Such statements or evocations commonly attend accounts of Derrida's style, and are the principal mode in which the postmodern politics of sublimity are formulated.

As with the renunciatory mode, to pin one's faith in this absolute way upon the subversive sublime enacted in critical language requires crucially the privileging of language as the arena of all power. Many claims about the subversive power of critical style depend upon the barely legitimate intensification of the view that language is an embodiment or enactment of forms of power to the point at which language is seen as the secret vibrating heart of all power whatsoever – as though all that were really objectionable about, say, US imperialism, were its syntactic habits and choice of metaphor. This absolute collapse of language and power leads to (or allows) the grandiose, usually self-mortifying claim that the most radical form of politics consists of turning languages of authority (criticism, for example) against themselves. The difference between the renunciatory and the sublime modes of postmodern criticism is in this sense only one of degree; where renunciation tries to give away authority, the sublime mode authoritatively evicts authority from its own language. Both modes involve the implicit claim that everything may be done in terms of language itself, and may be regulated by an intention which is actualized in and through the language alone.

Well, this certainly is not to say that *nothing* changes when critical languages are subjected to the extraordinary strains and complications that they are in Derrida's writing. Derrida's writing characteristically mingles a canny note of reserve with its abstract sweeps into sublimity, and when he turns his attention to the functioning of language within institutions of power, he is carefully particular in his judgements. Nevertheless, there is a strain in Derrida's work of a generalizing will-to-sublimity, and, as Hartman observes of *Glas*, the exercise of will may be a residual production of every nihilism; the nihilist's vision is cold, he writes, but 'luxurious in its expressive strength', and what propels the apparent vault into absolute relinquishment of mastery is an inverted will-to-power:

The surprising power, even richness of language in Nietzsche, Stevens, or Derrida betrays the inner relation of what is now called 'deconstruction' to the very nature of writing. And that is Derrida's point, his understanding of Nietzsche's yea-saying within a suicidal nihilism. Language itself, nothing else, or the Nothing that is language, is the motivating residue. Despite obsolete and atrophied words, and falsifiable, disputable, or undecidable meanings, the will to write persists.[31]

This will to write, when taken up and institutionalized in intellectual procedures, as Derrida's work has been, is disindividuated. The repetition and recirculation of Derrida's deconstructive strategies as formulae bring about in criticism that peculiarly postmodern situation in which the yearning for absolutes of difference or undecidability beyond every form of containment is itself territorialized, that is to say, channelled, filtered, concentrated and routinized. And the most insidious form of this territorialization is the restriction of the alleged 'play' of deconstruction to repeatable gestures like the alternation of typefaces or the glamorizing of critical languages. When Vincent Leitch upbraids the Gilles Deleuze and Félix Guattari of *Anti-Oedipus* (1974) for 'relying on smooth and safe language', which encourages us 'to believe in the accuracy and truthfulness of their representations', while praising the 'poetics and practice of fracture' in Derrida and others, he enacts precisely this kind of critical framing.[32] Nothing, nobody is seriously or more than momentarily unsettled by a critical style that comes so surrounded with the marks of critical prestige and legitimacy and circulates in contexts that so reliably muffle its subversive effects. There is nothing in such rhetorical ultra-leftism to suggest the likelihood of any shift or complication in the institutional-economic structures of academic research, communication and publication, or the powerful apparatus of exclusion, hierarchy and certification which is higher education in advanced Western countries.[33]

So, although postmodern theory may begin with the attempt to politicize the realm of the aesthetic, it can invert easily into the distracting and self-promoting aestheticization of politics. It is not surprising to find the same effects at work in the arch-theorist of this very phenomenon, Jean Baudrillard. As we have seen, Baudrillard describes a postmodern world in which everything has been reduced – or rather, perhaps, extended and intensified – into representations and simulacra, a world in which, so complete is the identification between power and representations of power, that power must be said effectively to have disappeared. (This, brutally shorn of its argumentative detail, is the burden of Baudrillard's *Forget Foucault*.)[34] For Baudrillard, there is no earthly point in a deconstructive criticism that multiplies languages and styles, or employs the mode of allegory to undercut onto-theological certainties, since this is only to trail feebly in the wake of a world mass-media which does the same thing with infinitely more finesse. Under these conditions, the only role for theory is to mimic the furious energies of simulation in a (necessarily) futile attempt to outdo them. Baudrillard's early works convey the sense of a certain disapproval, a minimal 'tut tut' beneath their floods of analysis, but the complete draining of value or ameliorative possibility from his later work, with its catalogues of apocalypses and semiotic finalities and seemingly absolute refusal to judge, contorts into a sort of counter-value of its own, in which nothing succeeds like excess. Baudrillard's hectic prose, with its mesmeric concentricities and clotted inclusiveness, compulsively attempts to hasten the world to oblivion, even to outrun it. It is a 'strategy', if so it may be called, of immunizing overdose. Baudrillard's metaphors furiously mingle science fiction and the pop sciences of relativity and particle physics with the staider functional or organic metaphors of philosophy and social science to create an exciting but empty friction of intensification. This is matched in a passage like the following by what Meaghan Morris has wittily called 'the technique of adjectival escalation':

Deterrence of all real potentiality, deterrence by meticulous reduplication, by macroscopic hyperfidelity, by accelerated recycling, by saturation and obscenity, by abolition of the distance between the real and its representation, by implosion of the differentiated poles between which flowed the energy of the real: this hyperreality puts an end to the system of the real, it puts an end to the real as referential by exalting it as model.[35]

Those who read Baudrillard for clues as to how to analyse contemporary society, or who miserably protest that his argument is not susceptible to 'ratification by measurement against any currently popular or plausible conceptions of actuality' have spectacularly missed the point.[36] If Baudrillard's aim is to represent the real, then he does so only by imitating the way that the postmodern real so suavely disposes of itself. This mode of the sublime is at the opposite pole from the renunciatory mode that I began this chapter by considering, for it involves a Faustian determination to outdo appearances, upping the stakes, not only on the object of analysis, but on theory itself. Its mode is infectious. This is Sylvère Lotringer reverently characterizing Baudrillard's practice during an interview with him, and using something like Baudrillard's own mode:

You've cut yourself off from every system of reference, but not from referentiality. What I see you describing is not a challenge to the real, but a challenge internal to theory. You don't criticize the genealogical attitude or the libidinal position, you send them spinning away like tops. You wholly embrace the movement that animates them, you amplify their concepts to the maximum, pulling them into the vortex of your own dizziness. You draw them into an endless spiral which, like the treatment of myth by Lévi-Strauss, leads them bit by bit to their own exhaustion.[37]

A similar sort of glee attends writers like Arthur Kroker and David Cook, who take dark delight in complex, but ethically vacant enlargements of despair, highly-flavoured by the language of fatality and epochal compulsion: 'Our fate now is to live in that dark region where power suddenly passes over into its opposite, the plunging downwards of society into the last cycle of the Nietzschean regression, the hyper-materialist side of nihilism . . . The "thinking subject" and the concept museum of the "lifeworld" are last outbursts of modernist nostalgia before the relational play of disembodied power and sliding bodies in hyperspace.'[38] Kroker and Cook's desperately and deliberately hyped catch-phrases, 'excremental culture', 'panic sex', 'sign crimes', 'theory in ruins' are the academic roué's attempts to extort a last fetishistic *frisson* from a glazed language that has gone dead on him. The point is not so much that Kroker and Cook and Baudrillard suffer too much from a nostalgia for the real, as Michael Ryan suggests, as that they do not suffer *enough* from it.[39] Witnessing these arch displays of decadence, one wants to murmur feebly, 'how can things be this bad without this person caring more?'

A similar kind of exhilarated gloom permeates Stephen Pfohl's extended Baudrillardian meditation on the apparently lethal conditions of contemporary global cyberculture, *Death at the Parasite Café: Social Science (Fictions) and the Postmodern* (1992). There was once a time – call it modernity, perhaps – when the political authority of the white male middle class was secured, in the order of fact and of representation alike, by iron binarisms, which defined, expelled and excluded 'others' of all kinds. If this was once the case, then political power has undergone a bizarre contortion in the epoch of what Pfohl calls 'ultramodernity'. For the contemporary explosion of information and means of reproduction – along with the growth of the society of the spectacle and the arrival of a libidinal economy of ephemeral intensities as the dominant mode of capitalism – has made excess not the abjected other of contemporary society, but its organizing principle.

Excess is being reduced to the self-same realm of access. . . . Those experiences which had previously exceeded or fractured the social constructed 'commonsense' of the modern order, are today being manufactured in a simulated form and then fed back for our consumption without their once disturbing potential for creating a critical difference.[40]

The problem which the book poses to itself is the traditional one of incorporation: with what principles of dissent or difference should a critical social theory line up, in a situation in which dissent and difference are not only disarmed, but are the very engine that drives an oppressive system? The 'parasite café of Pfohl's title is his metonymy for the 'commanding communicative circuitries . . . of ultramodernity itself' (*DAPC*, 20). It is 'a terrifying place where a simulated return of the repressed does little but fuel desires for continuous consumption and where the ideal purity of fascist mastery might be terminally realized in the telecommunicative aestheticization of everyday life' (*DAPC*, 35).

Things are obviously not looking too good. Nevertheless, the book does identify itself with the possibility of subversion, of a resistance to a system that appears to become more total and more monolithic the more it decentres and differentiates itself. It is the varieties of critical postmodernism which Pfohl pits against the protean adaptability of ultramodernism: ethnographic postmodernism, drawing on early twentieth-century criticisms of anthropological reason; sex/gender postmodernism, mounting challenges to heterosexist patriarchy; multicultural postmodernism, involving resistance to white hegemony in colonial and postcolonial contexts. So convinced is Pfohl of the corruption or superannuation of any kind of political critique, whether in a liberal or Marxist tradition, which would derive its validity from the reasoned and unconstrained negotiation of interests, rights and values, that he is forced towards a Dionysian or ecstatic politics the legitimacy of which would be grounded not in reason but in the ecstatic intensity of transgression.

Of course, given the defeatist totalization of Pfohl's initial account of the ultramodern culture of accessible excess, there is absolutely nothing, apart, perhaps, from a faith in the principle of extremity itself, to guarantee such corporeal counter-discourses against incorporation. If the book manages to convey accurately something of the power of modern capitalism to include everything which it once seemed imperative for it to exclude, it deliberately cuts itself off from the kinds of intellectual resource needed to analyse such a situation and disclose any kind of auspicious flaw in it. For all its passionate hostility to political violence and exclusion of all kinds, the book is too mesmerized by the principles of extremity, violence and excess to develop plausible or human-shaped political arguments, values and alternatives. Given its principled (though unargued) certainty that the traditions of reasoned critique are the tools of the oppressor, this is condemned to be an argument governed not by the movement of dialectic, but by arbitrary mood swings.

This is appropriate, perhaps, in a book where the argument is conducted as much through the form as through the subject of its discourse. Throughout, exposition and argument are interrupted by images seemingly derived from a video-text by the author on the same theme and with the same title, passages of autobiography, real and fictionalized, dream-sequence, fantasy, self-dramatization, and enlivened throughout with prankish typography. Stephen Pfohl hands over authorship of his book to imagined characters, notably the crackpot alter-ego, Professor Jack O. Lantern, and a figure who acts as the carefully correct good conscience of the book, the mythic female figure of Black Madonna Durkheim, who breaks in at intervals to deliver reproofs to its author, slapping his wrist for indulging in male fantasy and nagging him (though wholly in his own idiom and cadence) about his narcissism.

When it comes to its own form, this is a book that emphatically, even oppressively, knows its own mind. At regular intervals, it breaks off the fun and games to deliver strict little lectures about their form and purpose: 'Methodologically this text may be read as an effort to deconstruct the dominance of a positivist aesthetics in the (w)riting of contemporary social science', we are instructed at one point (*DAPC*, 75). The kind of social theory which this book aims to exemplify will have avoided the vicious and guilty reduction of the world to a mere theme for knowledge, and abandoned theory's fond dream of being able to subtract itself from the scene which it surveys. Social theory of this kind must not repress awareness of its own forms of historical positioning, and its practitioners must 'open ourselves to questions and methods falling between the forced fields of philosophy, literature, linguistics, HIStory, economics, women's studies, psychoanalysis, the iconic or performing arts, and even theoretical physics, (*DAPC*, 78).

Following the hint of James Clifford and some other postmodern ethnographers, Pfohl looks to the 'ethnographic surrealism' of Georges Bataille for a model. The purpose of all this is to allow social theory to unpick itself from the political oppression with which it has for so long been wickedly complicit. The book wants to describe and exemplify 'a language that dissolves itself festively. A language that opens out to and materializes itself in a dialogue with others' (*DAPC*, 14). And if it knows what it wants, it knows how to get it, too:

The text you are reading stupidly mixes *social-psychoanalysis* with *collage– (w)riting, deconstructive ethnography*, and a *genealogical approach to HIStory*. . . . I am trying to construct a reading environment that disinFORMs as much as it shares knowledge. Hopefully this will offer an experience closer to the uncertainties of *dialogical research* than the more masterful pleasures of dialectical analysis. (*DAPC*, 95)

Like other such come-on-in declarations in postmodern writing, this manages to sound, not hospitable, but hectoring and cocksure. The problem seems to be partly in the assumption that a text can be dialogic or monologic as a matter of simple authorial or stylistic choice. But if the condition of all texts is to be only partly aware and in charge of the conditions of possibility that make them readable in different contexts, then to embrace that condition of partial mastery as part of a conscious programme is always going to be futile – since the text will continue to be readable and be read in terms of constraints and contingencies that are not entirely in its ken. Consciously embracing or bracing itself against such contingencies will make them neither more nor less operative, since they are by definition a matter of what exceeds the text's intentions with respect to itself. Indeed, it might be said that the will to self-unmaking that this book so voluptuously indulges is anyway no depletion of the masterful intentionalism that it finds so revolting, but a stock item in its repertoire.

In a sense, the Baudrillardian outbidding of simulation is the end-point of the postmodern stylistics of the sublime, but it is an end-point that demonstrates a potentially dangerous paradox; if the prime responsibility of criticism and theoretical knowledge is not to represent the representable, but to become awed witnesses of the unpresentable, then what is there to guarantee the subversive effects of that work except its own inevitably institutionalized forms of self-legitimation? A self-legitimating sublime that denies its positioning by the exigencies of its own material production becomes a mere sublime simulation, a cool professional fiction of subversion which paradoxically brings into being the very effects of simulation, unreality and deterrence which its discourse evokes, but in the passive or negative mode of routine and rationalization.

Notes

1 *Criticism in the Wilderness: The Study of Literature Today* (New Haven: Yale University Press, 1980), p. 1.

2 'The Critic as Host', in Harold Bloom et al., *Deconstruction and Criticism* (New Haven and London: Yale University Press, 1979), pp. 217–53.

3 'Postmodern Culture and Consumer Society', in *Postmodern Culture*, ed. Hal Foster (London and Sydney: Pluto Press, 1985), p. 112.

4 See Mikhail Bakhtin, *The Dialogic Imagination*, trans. Caryl Emerson and Michael Holquist (Austin: University of Texas Press, 1981); Ludwig Wittgenstein, *Philosophical Investigations*, trans. G. E. M. Anscombe (Oxford: Basil Blackwell, 1958); V. Volosinov, *Marxism and the Philosophy of Language*, trans. L. Matejka and I. R. Titunik (New York: Seminar Press, 1978).

5 See, for example, Foucault's *The Archaeology of Knowledge*, trans. A. M. Sheridan Smith (London: Tavistock Press, 1972), and 'The Order of Discourse', in *Untying the Text: A Post-Structuralist Reader*, ed. Robert Young (London: Routledge and Kegan Paul, 1981), pp. 48–78.

6 For a representative use of Bakhtin, see Allon White and Peter Stallybrass, *The Politics and Poetics of Transgression* (London: Methuen, 1986).

7 *Paracriticisms: Seven Speculations of the Times* (Urbana: University of Illinois Press, 1975), p. 3. References hereafter to *P* in the text.

8 *The Right Promethean Fire: Imagination, Science, and Cultural Change* (Urbana: University of Illinois Press, 1980). References hereafter to *RPF* in the text.

9 Ihab Hassan, *The Postmodern Turn: Essays in Postmodern Theory and Culture* (Columbus: Ohio State University Press, 1987), p. 230.

10 *Futur* Fall: Excursions Into Postmodernity*, ed. E. A. Grosz, Terry Threadgold, David Kelly, Alan Cholodenko and Edward Colless (Sydney: Power Institute, 1986).

11 See, for instance, David Wills's essay on Derrida in imitation of Derrida's philosophical style, 'Post(e)s', ibid, pp. 146–58.

12 'Les Maîtres Fous: The Signifying Monkey on the Planet of Post Modernism', ibid., p. 40.

13 See discussion above, pp. 218–19.

14 *Cut 'N' Mix: Culture, Identity and Caribbean Music* (London: Comedia, 1987), p. 14.

15 'A Report from the Western Front: Postmodernism and the "Politics" of Style', *Block*, 12 (1986/7), pp. 4–26.

16 Ibid., pp. 7–8.

17 Iain Chambers, 'Maps for the Metropolis: A Possible Guide to the Present', *Cultural Studies*, 1:1 (1987), p. 20; Michel Foucault, 'The Political Function of the Intellectual', *Radical Philosophy*, 17 (1977), p. 12.

18 'The Impossible Object: Towards a Sociology of the Sublime', *New Formations*, 1:1 (1987), p. 48. References hereafter to 'Impossible Object' in the text.

19 *The Postmodern Condition: A Report on Knowledge*, trans. Geoff Bennington and Brian Massumi (Manchester: Manchester University Press, 1984), p. 81.

20 Foster, *Postmodern Culture*, pp. 83–110. References hereafter in the text. Vincent Leitch also suggests that contemporary criticism 'catches up with and

surpasses avant-garde literature', *Deconstructive Criticism: An Advanced Intro-duction* (London: Hutchinson, 1983), p. 224.

21 Jacques Derrida, *Dissemination*, trans. Barbara Johnson (London: Athlone Press, 1981), p. 355.

22 'Living On: Border Lines', in Bloom et al., *Deconstruction and Criticism*, pp. 75–176.

23 For further consideration of 'allegory' in this sense, see Craig Owens, 'The Allegorical Impulse: Toward a Theory of Postmodernism. Part 2', *October*, 13 (1980), pp. 59–80, and Stephen Melville, 'Notes on the Re-emergence of Allegory, the Forgetting of Modernism, the Necessity of Rhetoric, and the Conditions of Publicity in Art and Criticism', *October*, 19 (Winter, 1981), pp. 55–92.

24 See John Cage, *Empty Words* (Middletown: Wesleyan University Press, 1981).

25 *Spurs: Nietzsche's Styles*, trans. Barbara Harlow (University of Chicago Press, 1979).

26 *Applied Grammatology: Post(e)-Pedagogy from Jacques Derrida to Joseph Beuys* (Baltimore and London: Johns Hopkins University Press, 1985), p. 114.

27 *Glas* (Paris: Galilée, 1974).

28 Ibid., pp. 7, 291.

29 *Saving the Text: Literature/Derrida/Philosophy* (Baltimore and London: Johns Hopkins University Press, 1981), p. 24.

30 Leitch, *Deconstructive Criticism*, p. 209.

31 *Saving the Text*, p. xxiv.

32 Gilles Deleuze and Félix Guattari, *Anti-Oedipus: Capitalism and Schizophre-nia*, trans. Robert Hurley, Mark Seena and Helen Lane (London: Athlone, 1984); Leitch, *Deconstructive Criticism*, p. 249.

33 Despite Derrida's frequent lapses into the modes of the vatic and the sublime, his work probably needs to be excepted from this rather sweeping and unforgiving characterization of deconstruction. Another honourable exception might have to be Greg Ulmer, who focuses in his *Applied Grammatology* on the pedagogic effects which might follow from a practice of grammatology 'in which knowing and knowledge are oriented, not by the *results* as aftereffect, known in advance and to which presentation must conform, but to creativity, innovation, invention, change' (p. 152).

34 *Forget Foucault*, trans. Nicola Dufresne (New York: Semiotext(e), 1987).

35 Meaghan Morris, 'Room 101 Or A Few Worst Things in the World', in *The Pirate's Fiancée: Feminism, Reading, Postmodernism* (London: Verso, 1988), p. 189; Jean Baudrillard, *In the Shadow of the Silent Majorities . . . Or The End of the Social and Other Essays*, trans. Paul Foss, Paul Patton and John Johnston (New York: Semiotext(e), 1983), pp. 84–5.

36 R. Gibson, 'Customs and Excise', in *Seduced and Abandoned: The Baudrillard Scene*, ed. André Frankovits (New York: Semiotext(e), 1984), p. 46.

37 'Forget Baudrillard: An Interview With Sylvère Lotringer', trans. Philip Bleitchman, Lee Hildreth and Mark Polizzotti, in *Forget Foucault*, pp. 131–2.

38 *The Postmodern Scene: Excremental Culture and Hyperaesthetics* (New York: St. Martin's Press, 1986), pp. 131, 265–6.

39 Michael Ryan, 'Postmodern Politics', *Theory, Culture and Society*, 5:2–3 (1988), pp. 569–71.

40 Stephen Pfohl, *Death at the Parasite Cafe: Social Science (Fictions) and the Postmodern* (Basingstoke and London: Macmillan, 1992), p. 15. References hereafter to *DAPC* in the text.

9
Postmodernism and Cultural Politics

Spaces of Resistance

Postmodernism holds out simultaneously possibilities for the revival and widening of a cultural politics and for its neutralization. Much postmodern aesthetic theory concerns itself precisely with the denial of the modernist separation of the sphere of art from other social activities and concerns, and attempts to restore the repressed political dimensions of aesthetic and cultural activity of all kinds. With the explosion of culture into every aspect of life, and the aestheticization of the social, political and economic realms, as it is evoked by Fredric Jameson, comes the opportunity for a left cultural politics which would concentrate not so much, as traditional Marxisms have done, on relating cultural forms to the more 'fundamental' socio-economic foundations which determine and produce them, as on investigating the whole realm of culture considered as in itself a form of material practice. In a global situation in which the production of 'culture' in the widest sense, of signs, representations, images, even 'life-styles' has begun to outstrip the older modes of production of tangible and calculable amounts of goods and services, this approach may seem more than ever imperative. The later work of Michel Foucault and other theorists of discourse like Michel Pêcheux, has assisted the development of a postmodern cultural politics in two ways. Firstly, it suggested that culture could no longer be considered simply as the sphere of representations, hovering immaterially at a distance from the brute facts of 'real' life, since discourse theory sees the forms and occasions of representations as in themselves power (rather than merely the reflection of power-relations that exist elsewhere). Secondly, it suggested that power is best understood not in the macropolitical terms of large groupings or monolithic blocs, of class or State, but in the micropolitical terms of the networks of power-relations subsisting at every point in a society. This outlook is in accord with the movement away from the all-encompassing global narratives of history and politics, and a countervailing stress on the local and particular forms of difference and struggle.

Clearly, this situation promises a reinvigoration of cultural politics in allowing for the articulation of interests and concerns which cut across or intersect irregularly with the classical Marxist theory of class – issues concerning race, gender, nuclear and green politics and, less commonly, of the aged and of animal rights. In all of these spheres, the investigation of cultural forms as the producers and bearers of meaning, value and power has proved central. In some forms of contemporary postmodern politics, it is precisely the liberation of culture and signification generally from economic necessity that offers opportunities for wider, freer forms of self-determination than have been possible in eras in which culture and representation have been tied more closely to the economic. Michael Ryan evokes this freedom thus:

> Rather than being expressive representations of a substance taken to be prior, cultural signs become instead active agents in themselves, creating new substances, new social forms, new ways of acting and thinking, new attitudes, reshuffling the cards of 'fate' and 'nature' and social 'reality'. It is on this margin that culture, seemingly entirely autonomous and detached, turns around and becomes a social and material force, a power of signification that discredits all claims to substantive grounds outside representation and this discrediting applies to political institutions, moral norms, social practices and economic structures.[1]

This analysis rests on the principle of catastrophic intensification, and seems to be invoking the works of Lyotard and Deleuze and Guattari. According to this account, capitalism, whose processes of standardization and rationalization initially function to repress significatory freedom, may end up in a 'post-Fordist' phase, in which diversification rather than standardization is the norm, suicidally promoting that freedom.[2] It depends on a faith that capitalism itself is centred around the logic of progressive commodification, through alienation and specialization, which will in the end produce (perhaps already has produced) a situation in which the alienation of signs from things will enable a dissolution of capitalism itself. It is in this sense that Ryan can promise that 'in the cultural scene that high capitalism admittedly makes possible . . . the positive lineaments of a post-capitalist world can be glimpsed'.[3] This is obviously rather a cheerful view in many respects, but also involves a certain degree of conceptual risk, in that it seems to surrender the possibility of a critique of capitalism on any other ethical grounds than its own, requiring as it does a benign interpretation of the operations of the 'free' market in signs and representations; according to which, you can become free, simply by thinking yourself into freedom.

But this expansion and decentring of politics also brings with it the possibility of a disastrous decompression; if everything can be said to be political, then, for a politics of opposition, this can often be equivalent to saying that nothing is really or effectively political any more. With the movement away from clearly-defined and universally-acknowledged grounds of legitimation, indeed, with the discrediting of such beliefs as inherently metaphysical, politics may simply dissipate itself, like a river spilling its propulsive strength into the marshes and rivulets of a delta. Jean Baudrillard believes that, in a sense, this has already happened, arguing that the techniques and strategies of a molecular micropolitics, far from tactically outflanking the authoritarian centres of social power, mimic the operations of a situation that is itself already imperturbably molecularized. Baudrillard's chilling suggestion is that the spread of power away from conspicuous centres of control, like the State or the armed forces (hard to persuade the population of North Korea or Burma of this tendency, though), is not a diffusion but a consolidation of control, a spiralling of power into a system that can resist any resistance, can predict and encompass every form of challenge, because such challenges take place in an empty world of controlled simulations. Such a world, far from promising freedom or change, is 'metastable', because it has succeeded in conventionalizing subversion, turning disruption into a stabilizing principle:

> This time we are in a full universe, a space radiating with power but also cracked, like a shattered windscreen still holding together. However, this 'power' remains a mystery – starting from despotic centrality, it becomes by the half-way point a 'multiplicity of relations' . . . and it culminates, at the extreme pole, with *resistances* . . . so small and so tenuous that, literally speaking, atoms of power and atoms of resistance merge at this microscopic level. The same fragment of gesture, body, gaze, and discourse encloses both the positive electricity of power and the negative electricity of resistance.[4]

The problem for a postmodern politics, then, is this dual prospect, on the one hand of a transformation of history by a sheer act of imaginative will, and on the other, of an absolute weightlessness, in which anything is imaginatively possible, because nothing really matters.

This difficulty often plays itself through in postmodern cultural theory in the metaphorical-topographical terms of space and territory, in the imagery of centre and margin, inside and outside, position and boundary. This system of metaphors can conjure up an oddly antique-seeming map of the world and global political relations, when struggles for power and conquest could be represented in much more reassuringly visible terms; *here* is power, *there* is exploitation and resistance. In their mimicking of this easy but vanished territorialization of power relationships, these metaphors also seem to embody a nostalgia for what has been lost with that sort of map of the world.

In recent years there has been a huge expansion of interest in questions relating to the social and political mapping of space; indeed, one might almost say that space has become the dominant concern not only in the now consolidated postmodern geography associated with Edward Soja and David Harvey, but across the range of theories dealing with the postmodern. David Harvey's *The Condition of Postmodernity* (1989) argues that postmodernity is to be identified with a fundamental transformation in the politico-economic regime of space. The technologies and social transformations of modernity took the form of a dialectic: on the one hand there was the spatial disruption caused by the rapid accelerations and new spatial impermanence of modern life; on the other there were the spatializing aesthetics of modernism and the nostalgia for rootedness and human dwelling expressed for instance in the work of Martin Heidegger. The cooperation of modern technologies and primitivist appeals to racial essence in Nazism is perhaps the most sinister form of this dialectic.

Postmodernity represents an intensification of the process whereby the solidity, specificity and historical resistance of particular places are dissolved, in a process that Harvey calls 'time–space compression'.[5] During the period of modernity, time had been distributed and solidified in space. The new urban spaces became identified with rapid movement into the future, while other, less developed regional, provincial or colonial spaces either marked out earlier stages in universal evolution or development, or stood outside time altogether. These spatial asymmetries, or this spatialization of asymmetry, were confirmed in the economic relations between the Western metropolitan producers of wealth, and those who provided its raw products and markets.

Harvey agrees with Fredric Jameson in seeing postmodernity as the intensification rather than the supersession of capital, but sees this intensification as bringing about a dissolution of the global world-picture set up during the nineteenth and early twentieth centuries. Postmodernity is characterized, not by the seized sedimentations of power of the nation-state, or the national corporation (Ford, Volkswagen), but by the restless circulation and exchange of spaces and places. In modernity, the movement of goods, values and meanings still occurred within space and place; in postmodernity, also called the era of post-Fordism, or of 'flexible accumulation', this movement has become so rapid and so incessant as no longer to be visualizable or placeable. If modernity had spatialized time, therefore, postmodernity retemporalizes space; the solidity of space and place yields to the uncentred mobility of information and investment.

Modernity's relentless colonization of space also expressed itself through space, which had the effect of giving the victims of its power a sense of where they were, and thus the possibility of grounding their resistance: one thinks of the tradition of the revolutionary occupation of city spaces, from the Paris Commune to Tiananmen Square. In the era of multinational capitalism, with its restless relocations and forced redistributions of labour and resources, it is no longer clear where the centres of power or sites of struggle are. For, as Fredric Jameson suggests, the means to orientate oneself spatially may be precisely what are missing from the postmodern world, in which, to take one instance, power seems not to reside in nation states but is relayed and distributed across a global network of multinational corporations and communicational structures.[8]

For Harvey, space is abolished, and replaced by the increasingly rapid turnover times of international finance capital. Paul Virilio goes even further to suggest that it is not so much time which governs the postmodern production and reproduction of space, so much as speed – the time, so to speak, taken by time itself. For Virilio, modernity was expressed through the increasing speeds of physical movement achieved by cars, trains and aeroplanes; postmodernity manages to move even faster than modernity in a paradoxical abolition of physical movement itself. It now proves to be more efficient to stand still, and accelerate images and information past ourselves than to travel sluggishly through actual physical space. The era of 'extensive time', in which the elapsing of time was related to movement across actual space, has given way to the 'intensive time' of telecommunications:

> If automotive vehicles, that is, all air, land, and sea vehicles are today also less 'riding animals' than *frames* in the optician's sense, then it is because the self-propelled vehicle is becoming less and less a vector of change in physical location than a means of representation, the channel for an increasingly rapid optical effect of the surrounding space. The more or less distant vision of our travels gradually recedes behind the arrival at the

destination, a general arrival of images, of information that henceforth stands for our constant change of locations.[6]

The filling of the intervals of actual travel with the 'audiovisual speed' of images and information exchange – the in-car computer and CD player, the in-flight movie, the multiplication of mobile phones and laptops on planes and trains – turn 'the means of long-haul transport into a means of transport in place', providing more and more occasions for the telematically-permeated sedentariness of contemporary life.[7]

Again, the distinguishing postmodern problem is one of reflexivity, or of the involvement of the activity of theory in the very field which it is attempting to theorize. For a map, at least the kind of map that we are used to in the advanced West, presupposes a position outside or suspended placelessly above the field that is being surveyed. The problem for a postmodern cultural theory is to construct a map of the world from inside that world. One response to this reflexive problem has been to turn to the theoretical equivalent of the mediaeval *periplus*, a map that projects the stages of a journey in terms of a temporal narrative. It is clear that the sort of map that allows one, as it were, to feel one's way through history has certain disadvantages (not knowing where you are going, or why you are going there, to name two), but is also more responsive to the small-scale intimacies and complexities of political life. Jameson suggests that a postmodern map of the world must do two contradictory things at once, rendering the sense of placelessness even as it suggests ways of orientating ourselves to that placelessness:

> The new political art – if it is indeed possible at all – will have to hold to the truth of postmodernism, that is to say, to its fundamental object – the world space of multinational capital – at the same time at which it achieves a breakthrough to some as yet unimaginable new mode of representing this last, in which we may again begin to grasp our positioning as individual and collective subjects and regain a capacity to act and struggle which is at present neutralized by our spatial as well as our social confusion.[9]

David Harvey similarly insists that the geographical understanding of the dispositions of space and place must grasp the nature of changes in economic, political and cultural life, and their impact upon and concretion in spatial relationship. In this his work belongs to a broader current in postmodern geography and spatial theory. This work, represented by Edward Soja's *Postmodern Geographies* (1989), Gillian Rose's *Feminism and Geography* (1993) and Derek Gregory's *Geographical Imaginations* (1994), strives to understand and represent the dynamic complexity of space and place as well as its socially-produced nature.[10] This contemporary current of thinking derives in turn a great deal of its impetus from the work of the French social and political theorist Henri Lefebvre, who, in the years after the Second World War, waged a single-handed campaign against what he saw as the complicity of Marxist theory with industrial capital in enforcing a 'police space' of abstract structures imposed over the irregularity and complexity of space in everyday life.[11] Against this, Lefebvre urged a study of the local and the quotidian production and transformation of meanings, and especially the meanings of, and expressed through, place. Although Lefebvre has little to say about the possibilities for a specifically postmodern regime of space, his *The Production of Space*, first published in 1974, does provide some warrant for the idea of a critical reoccupation of space; for a corporeal productiveness of space which might be made to emerge from within the oppressive production of constrained, abstracted and commodified space characteristic of the modern.[12]

David Harvey deploys Lefebvre's insights against the further intensified abstraction and delocalization of space, but his work cleaves to what may be called a modern desire for synoptic grasp, for a critical 'overview' which will restore the totality which is fragmented, or dissimulated in the postmodern dissolution of space. Harvey's reading of the economic processes of postmodernity offer to provide that 'conceptual map' of postmodernity's dissolution of spatiality looked for by Jameson. Perhaps encouraged by Harvey's example, Jameson's more recent work has been more willing to name and characterize those remorseless, and ever more impersonal processes of global commodification towards which his earlier characterizations of the condition of postmodernity could only mutely, mysteriously gesture. The 'ultimate referent' of discussions of the dialectic of sameness and difference in the contemporary world is a modernist spatialization that provides the basis for a postmodern topophagy, or rage to consume place itself. It is

the power of commerce and then capitalism proper . . . to seize upon a landscape and flatten it out, reorganize it into a grid of identical parcels, and expose it to the dynamic of a market that now reorganizes space in terms of an identical value. The development of capitalism then distributes that value most unevenly indeed, until at length, in its postmodern moment, sheer speculation . . . now reigns supreme and devastates the very cities and countrysides it created in the process of its own earlier development.[13]

Jameson insists that the despatialization of the world must be grasped as an effect of modernist spatialization, since 'all such later forms of abstract violence and homogeneity derive from the initial parcelization, which translates the money form and the logic of the commodity production for a market back onto space itself'.[14] Others have criticized the lingering will-to-mastery of this desire for total picturing. Meaghan Morris, for example, criticizes the concept of a 'master-mirroring' of postmodernity in the work of David Harvey, which, modernist and masculinist at once, austerely refuses to implicate spatial theory itself in the decentred, implicated spaces of postmodern existence.[15] Derek Gregory proposes a different kind of social mapping of space, in a 'critical human geography' which would resist the modernist relapse into the map or master-mirror, and would itself be more firmly situated within the fields it charts:

> Different people in different places are implicated in time-space colonization and compression in different ways. . . . A critical human geography must not only chart the differential locations and the time-space manifolds that are created through these processes – a project for which some of the concepts of spatial science might still be retained – but also draw out the multiple, compound, and contradictory subject–positions that they make available. The production of space is not an accidental by-product of social life but a moment intrinsic to its conduct and constitution, and for geography to *make* a difference – politically and intellectually – it must be attentive *to* difference.[16]

These problems of spatial imagination, and the imagination of space have affected much postmodern thinking regarding cultural politics. To articulate questions of power and value in postmodernity is often for example to identify centralizing principles – of self, gender, race, nation, aesthetic form – in order to determine what these centres push to their silent or invisible peripheries. The project can be seen as one of bringing the consciousness of those peripheries back into the centre. This metaphorical–topographical dynamic is a powerful imaginative strategy which also carries with it some risks, of which the most important is the romance of the marginal. It is articulated in one form by the video artist and theorist Martha Rosler:

> It is only through a 'guerrilla' strategy which resists a deadly universalization of meaning by retaining a position of marginality, that the production of critical meanings still remains possible. It is only on the margins that one can still call attention to what the 'universal' system leaves out.[17]

The romance of the marginal is to be found throughout postmodern cultural politics. Work on youth style and subculture, such as Dick

Hebdige's, derives its authority from this embrace of the marginal. Hebdige takes up as an embodiment of the subcultural subject the French writer Jean Genet, who is, he says, 'a subculture in himself'. Genet retains his position as a thief, liar and outsider *par excellence*, and it is his refusal to be contaminated by the dominant orders that preserves intact the subversive potential of his marginal condition:

> He becomes, like his fictional Maids, the 'unwholesome exhalation' of his Master. He turns a system on its head. He 'chooses' his crimes, his sexuality, the repugnance and outrage he arouses on the streets, and when he looks at the world, 'nothing is irrelevant': the stock-market quotations, the style of the judiciary, the flower beds have a meaning – his Otherness, his Exile.[18]

This form of subcultural study takes its place within a cultural/critical frame which explores the possibilities of inverting conventional mappings and distributions of power.

However, the new complexity of spatial relations in the postmodern world renders the very coherence of this kind of inside/outside, centre/margin model suspicious. Perhaps the most important and troubling aspect of the new systematic placelessness of the postmodern is the rapidly increasing development of information technology and, in particular, the move towards networked and distributed rather than localized systems for the exchange of images and information. Optimistic readings of these developments suggest that they make it possible to develop new and diverse forms of virtual collectivity, using global electronic mechanisms to pluralize forms of cultural belonging. Interestingly, as with the video revolution, it is the very standardization of computing protocols and software, with the ubiquity of Windows, and the World Wide Web browser Netscape, and the hypertext markup language that it reads, which makes it possible for such interest groups to be established and flourish, homogeneity proving to be the very engine of difference. The creation of such mobile forms of collectivity seems to cut across the frontiers and spatial limits established within modernity. And yet, as I write, the internet is itself the object of a massive attempt at commercial colonization and regulation, its very heterogeneity making it an irresistible target for commodification. These developments give the problem of analytic or critical perspective a new complexity and urgency. Where in the web of international communications and information exchange is the vantage point supposed to be that would enable one to grasp the internet, and the associated networks of finance and information for which it metonymically stands, as a whole and judge of their shape, nature, and direction?

Cyberspace and its possibilities have become a compulsive and fascinating topic for postmodern cultural theory, not to mention its elective medium, with the development of electronic journals such as *Postmodern Culture*.[19] Because postmodern theory operates within as well as upon these new conditions, there is a curiously intimate relationship between theory and its object. Cyberspace, the term deriving from the work of William Gibson, suggests a new expanded kind of locale or situation for the operations of consciousness and communication. Evocations of cyberspace often seem to combine the fantasy of an unexplored blankness, in a postmodern reinstatement of the modernist challenge and exhilaration of the uncharted wilderness, with that of a nurturing envelope or matrix.

Cyberspace appears to offer a stage within which to enact an ecstatic drama of the transcendence of limits, even as it continues, if only in the terms of its 'consensual hallucination', to provide that transcendence with defining limits. Perhaps the reason that it has proved impossible to provide any stable account of the nature and possibilities of cyberspace is that it lies so indeterminately between the conditions of the produced and the given. Moving around a virtual electronic 'site', navigating from place to place, or level to level in the World Wide Web, one is neither wholly inventing, nor wholly inhabiting its spaces and trajectories. The difficulty of reflecting analytically upon the notion of cyberspace is that it may already itself be a kind of metaspatial phenomenon, the result of a transformative reflection upon space, or its absence.

The very notion that information might form or be formed into a spatial environment is perhaps the precipitated form of a defence against a condition of topographic vertigo. In a three-dimensional version of the process suggested by Freud, in which the ego is formed, not as a kernel from the inside out, but as a defensive, semi-permeable membrane maintaining the boundary between what does and does not belong to the self,[20] the very notion of cyberspace may be a reparative hallucination, a mobile home, generated to compensate the electronically evicted or unbodied self for the absence of spatial coordinates. But, if cyberspace is neither given, nor produced space, but the production of its own givenness, it will not be possible for postmodern theory merely, neutrally to reflect upon it, from some other place. Scott Bukatman suggests that cybernetic science-fiction 'constructs *a space of accommodation* to an intensely technological existence';[21] it may be that postmodern spatial theory itself also constitutes just such a defence against a threatening placelessness. Postmodern theory of cyberspace will continue to be forced to inhabit and produce the space it reflects on, and in.

Feminism and Postmodernism

The exploration of the marginal in feminist writing projects the female as the place of patriarchy's Other, identified with the dark and discredited negative side of every polarity, as body to mind, nature to culture, night to day, matter to form and madness to reason. For Alice Jardine, modernity in philosophy and literature is definable as the attempt to explore and articulate these marginal spaces, in a movement she calls 'gynesis':

> To give a new language to these other spaces is a project filled with both promise and fear . . . for these spaces have hitherto remained unknown, terrifying, monstrous: they are mad, unconscious, improper, unclean, non-sensical, oriental, profane. If philosophy is truly to question these spaces, it must move away from all that has defined them, held them in place: Man, the Subject, History, Meaning.[22]

Julia Kristeva similarly argues for the potent marginality of feminist critique which, as Toril Moi says, 'undermines our most cherished convictions precisely because it situates itself outside our space, knowingly inserting itself along the borderlines of our own discourse'.[23] Kristeva's work has been extremely concerned with the issue of the 'place' from which women may speak or represent themselves, struggling, like much feminist theory of this kind, to articulate the subversive potential of a marginal discourse, while avoiding a repetition of the gesture of patriarchy in lodging woman immovably in position *as* the marginal. The real drive of Kristeva's thought is the attempt to undermine the very concept of intrinsic identity, and thus of intrinsic position, the attempt 'to locate the negativity and refusal pertaining to the marginal in "woman", in order to undermine the phallocentric order that defines woman as marginal in the first place'.[24]

All this might seem to suggest a close relationship between the leading concerns of feminism and the recurrent themes of postmodern criticism. This is certainly the view of Craig Owens who sees feminism as a representatively postmodern phenomenon in its assertion of difference, its refusal of totalizing meta-('master-')narratives and, above all its critique of the structures of power involved in representation. In this account, woman emerges as the very energizing force of the marginal and the sublime:

> It is precisely at the legislative frontier between what can be represented and what cannot that the postmodernist operation is being staged – not in order to transcend representation, but in order to expose that system of power that authorizes certain representations while blocking, prohibiting or invalidating others. Among those prohibited from Western representation, whose representations are denied all legitimacy, are women. Excluded from representation by its very structure, they return within it as a figure for – a presentation of – the unrepresentable.[25]

More recently, Jane Flax has agreed that 'feminist theorists enter into and echo postmodernist discourse as we have begun to deconstruct notions of reason, knowledge, or the self and to reveal the effects of the gender arrangements that lay beneath their "neutral" and universalizing facades', and identified feminism as a discourse of the marginalized Other, whose destiny lies 'with those who seek to further decenter the world'.[26]

But, despite the alleged potencies of the marginal position, it appears that the forces of marginalization reappear even in postmodern theory. Craig Owens acknowledges, for instance, that the issue of sexual difference has been notably absent from the modernism/postmodernism debate,[27] and the darker possibilities in store for feminism within postmodern theory are portended by Alice Jardine's incisive account of the turn to the female Other in modern and postmodern philosophy and art. 'Such rethinking', she writes, 'has involved, above all, a reincorporation and reconceptualization of that which has been the master narratives' own "non-knowledge", what has eluded them, what has engulfed them.'[28] The turn towards this space of 'nonknowledge' which has always been marked as feminine, is therefore to be understood as an attempt to retrieve control, to reterritorialize, by forms of reasoning and intellectual competence that are progressively losing their own authority. This is to say that feminism may find itself, not as the vibrant voice of postmodernism, but, as 'the repressed, managed rupture of postmodernism', merely a part of speech within it.[29] This strange tendency of authoritative marginality to flip over into its own dark side, the exploited and managed Other, may in a sense be programmed by the conceptual map of centre and margin, which often lacks the particularity or flexibility to encompass all the worrying irregularities of actual political alignments and cultural practices.

Postmodernity and Post-Coloniality

Some of the same complexities can be seen at work in another important area of cultural politics, that having to do with colonialism and post-colonialism. From the beginning, the mapping of centre and periphery has had an obvious fit to this topic, since the semiotics of mapping as an actual expression and fulfilment of forms of imperial domination make the question of imagined conceptual political space a particularly important one. The exploration of colonial cultural politics exemplified in the work of Edward Said, Gayatri Spivak and Homi Bhabha, and in publications like *Cultural Critique* in the US and *Third Text* in the UK, has concerned itself accordingly not so much with the raw materiality of power, but with the workings of power-in-representation, in colonial images and languages, and in the question of the language of the oppressed.[30]

The postmodern condemnation of universalizing metanarratives provides in this context a riposte to that oppressive story of the unfolding of a unified destiny for Man (as alibi-figure for Western civilization) which ruthlessly expunges particular or local or national histories in its drive towards universal rationalization, industrial progress and the global expansion of markets. Modernism in the arts and modernity in social and economic terms are collapsed in complex but, in the end, mutually confirming ways in this model. Nelly Richard writes:

> With regard to its economic programme and its cultural organisation, this concept of modernity represents an effort to synthesize its progressive and emancipatory ideals into a globalizing, integrative vision of the individual's place in history and society. It rests on the assumption that there exists a legitimate centre – a unique and superior position from which to establish control and to determine hierarchies.[31]

For Jean-François Lyotard, as we have seen, this domination of the centre is similarly expressed as a linguistic subordination of every grammatical person into the inclusive but repressive person of a universal 'we'.[32] Simon During takes up Lyotard's argument in his 'Postmodernism or Post-Colonialism Today'; refusing the illusory and repressive narrative of progressive universal emancipation, During joins with Lyotard in affirming that reason and justice can survive only in the delegitimated openness of postmodernity (though gives little hint of what might guarantee or necessarily conduce to such generous openness, other than the benevolence of the individuals involved).[33] In terms of the imperialism of representation, this domination of universal narrative may bring about the

projection from the 'civilizing' imperial centres of fetishized images of
Africa, the 'Orient', Latin America, etc. as civilization's Other, in ways
that simultaneously bring these regions into being for Europe, fulfil its
need for psychological and political centring, and silence any attempts at
self-representation by these people and their post-colonial descendants.
'The Orient', writes Edward Said, 'was not Europe's interlocutor, but its
silent Other'.[34]

The response to this in postmodern cultural theory has been to assist
the exploration of the centrist metropolitan myth of universal history by
opening theories of discourse to the voices of those constituted as the
Other. As with subcultural studies and feminist cultural theory, the
emphasis is on articulating the margins, or what has been projected as
marginal. It is a matter of taking hold not only of actual power, but also
of the languages, systems of metaphors and regimes of images that seem
designed to silence those whom they embody in representation. As Edward
Said observes, feminism and women's studies, black and ethnic studies,
socialist and anti-imperialist studies, all rest similarly upon one ethico-dis-
cursive principle, 'the right of formerly un- or misrepresented human
groups to speak for and represent themselves in domains defined, politically and intellectually, as normally excluding them, usurping their signifying and representing functions, over-riding their historical reality'.[35]

The articulation of the margins has taken different forms, of which the
most direct is a model of simple inversion. In Frantz Fanon's prescient
Black Skin White Masks (1952), the struggle is to find a form of
self-definition for the black man that is not the obedient reproduction of
Western paranoiac projections. Although Fanon's work consists very much
of the articulation of that struggle to define its own voice, rather than the
easy leap into rhetorical self-possession, his work makes it clear that the
end-point is the desire to be and to be able to speak on his own terms and
not as the ventriloqual echo of some other, to declare 'I am not a
potentiality of something. I am wholly what I am. I do not have to look
for the universal. No probability has any place inside me. My Negro
consciousness does not hold itself out as a lack. It is. It is its own
follower.'[36]

More recent theorists of the need to articulate the margins have become
suspicious of the binary models which such a desire for full speech and
identity seems to require. This suspicion is grounded in the belief that
such oppositional models themselves may derive from and reproduce
colonial structures of thought – so that to proclaim oneself as a marginalized or silenced people is implicitly to accept and to internalize the
condition of marginality. Such theory tends in some of its forms to

stigmatize the desire to affirm the being and articulate self-identity of oppressed colonial groups as a 'nativism' which inhabits and perpetuates repressive structures of thought.

This position, which may be conveniently demonstrated in the work of Gayatri Spivak and Homi Bhabha, argues the need for the careful deconstruction of the very structures of dominant and marginal. One of the forms which this takes is an analysis which, instead of obediently adopting a marginal place itself, brings the margins into the centre by applying deconstructive critique to the dominant self-histories of the West. The aims and results of this important work are to demonstrate the inner principles of weakness within Orientalism, or racist ideologies of blackness, in order to challenge the Western claims to serenely self-aware rationality and to show their existential dependence upon the forms of the Other that they expel beyond their boundaries of rationality. Thus, Homi Bhabha characterizes racial stereotyping as a fetishistic projection of those things which are disavowed by the colonial self. To objectify the frightening forms and forces of irrationality, perversity, femininity and evil in the shapes of subjugated races is reassuringly to distance those forces, but it is by the same token to give them a positive existence and thus to risk recontamination by or 'reversion' towards them. The exercise of power in these kinds of representation is therefore always problematically composed of 'both fixity and fantasy', and provides a sense of colonial identity 'that is played out – like all fantasies of originality and origination – in the face and space of the disruption and threat from the heterogeneity of other positions'.[37] Other studies like Edward Said's *Orientalism* similarly place their emphasis, not on the exterior, countervailing strength of a marginal position, but on the internal contradictions within dominant Western forms of knowledge. This strategy brings the margins into the centre in order to question the very map-making which projects the centre and margins as such – by suggesting that the margins inhabit the centres which expel them from consciousness.

Powerful though this rhetorical strategy may be, it runs the risk of discrediting the energies of self-affirmation that provide the impetus to revolt against exclusion and oppression. This can take different forms; but some of the most important of them have to do with the growing dominance in Western academic institutions of a theory of the postmodern condition that, in diagnosing the decline of the metanarratives of authority in the West, also high-mindedly evaporates the legitimacy of national emancipatory struggles, which may depend crucially on these very shop-soiled ideals of universal freedom and justice. For Nelly Richard, the dominance of postmodern theory offers Latin American post-colonial politics a distinctly two-edged sword. First of all, postmodern theory legitimates the evacuation of the centre or the idea of the centre, splintering it into 'dissident micro-territories', 'constellations of voices' and 'plurality of meanings', allowing and promoting 'specificity and regionalism, social minorities and political projects which are local in scope, or surviving traditions and suppressed forms of knowledge'. But these differences are mortgaged to a theoretical coding which always reaffirms the primacy of the (postmodern) knowledges of the West:

> The fact is . . . that no sooner are these differences – sexual, political, racial, cultural – posited and valued, than they become subsumed into the meta-category of the 'undifferentiated' which means that all singularities immediately become indistinguishable and interchangeable in a new, sophisticated economy of 'sameness'. Postmodernism defends itself against the destabilising threat of the 'other' by integrating it back into a framework which absorbs all differences and contradictions. The centre, though claiming to be in disintegration, still operates as a centre: filing away any divergences into a system of codes whose meanings, both semantically and territorially, it continues to administer by exclusive right.[38]

Gayatri Spivak has similarly pointed to the ways in which the cult of global, ahistorical difference may constitute a new form of colonialism.[39] But Spivak has herself recently been criticized as the representative practitioner of a form of theory which closes off the possibilities of discursive self-determination among oppressed or marginalized groups in what the West designates as the 'Third World'. Benita Parry characterizes the deconstructive project of Spivak, Bhabha and Abdul JanMohamed as an attempt to

> decentre the native as a fixed unified object of colonial knowledge through disclosing how colonialism's contradictory mode of address constitutes an ambivalently positioned colonial subject . . . [which] . . . then reveals for analysis the differential, variously positioned native – for some critics a self-consolidating other, for others an unconsenting and recalcitrant self – and in place of the permanently embattled colonial situation constructed by anti-colonialist theory, installs either a silent place laid waste by imperialism's epistemic violence, or an agonistic space within which unequally placed contestants negotiate an imbalance of power.[40]

Undoubtedly, Spivak's and Bhabha's complex model of negotiation and mutual dependence between colonizer and colonized yields a greater theoretical richness and flexibility; but its disadvantage is that it seems to have surrendered an ethical imperative in disallowing the idea of a fully-formed consciousness and language of victimage. Such a theory threatens to fall into the very error that it seeks to correct, that is to say, fixating upon and duplicating a binary model of the centre versus the margin, the voiced versus the entirely voiceless. Parry's charge against Spivak is that she pushes the theory of the enforced collusion of the native 'in its own subject(ed) formation as other and voiceless' to the point where the theory duplicates the original silencing, such that 'while protesting at the obliteration of the native's subject position in the text of imperialism, Spivak in her project gives no speaking part to the colonized, effectively writing out the evidence of native agency recorded in India's 200-year struggle against British conquest and the Raj – discourses to which she scathingly refers as hegemonic nativist or reverse ethnocentric narrativization'.[41]

This critique may seem a little misplaced considering Spivak's early and consistently-maintained sensitivity to the neo-colonial dangers of Western theory, but it nevertheless coheres suggestively with Nelly Richard's charge that some forms of postmodern 'decentring' can reproduce forms of the centre/margin hierarchy at the level of the cultural manufacture and administration of ideas.[42] Postmodern theory may be impelled by a centrifugal pull to the periphery, but if that movement is not prepared to surrender its sense of its own territorial right to codify and manage the margins, determining the conditions under which speech from the margins is possible, then the map remains unchanged. Indeed, one could argue that what impels theory towards this kind of impasse is precisely the tenacious persistence of the centre-margin cartography. Useful as an analytic mechanism, the model has gathered in some postmodern theory a kind of absolute ethical force, in which the demand for absolute marginality and its concomitant refusal to countenance any form of occupation of the centre creates a Manichean universe of absolute opposites which is barely responsive to the actual complexities and overdeterminations of the situation under consideration.

The romance of the marginal takes many other forms in postmodern theory, forms which may in the end suggest more about the troubled status of theory itself than about its objects. For what is to be discerned functionally, if not intentionally, in much postmodern theory is the desire, not for legitimation by inclusion or identification with dominant forms, but the desire for legitimation by opposition, by 'disidentification'. This term, drawn from the work of Michel Pêcheux, is one of a trio of terms embodying a spectrum of responses to the power of institutions, discourses, or structures of knowledge. Identification with a discourse means living within its terms; 'counteridentification' is the mode of the trouble-maker who stays within a governing structure of ideas, but reverses its terms; while 'disidentification' is the attempt to go beyond the structure of oppositions and sanctioned negations supplied by a discourse. One might instance an industrial conflict in which a workforce would identify with the conventions of labour relations if they accepted no pay rise in the interests of increased productivity, would counter-identify if they struck for higher wages and then negotiated a settlement, and would disidentify if they demanded that the factory be turned into a cultural centre, in the interests of overcoming the ideological separation of work and leisure. The rhetoric of disidentification which characterizes most contemporary cultural theory actually reverts to a complicitly counteridentifying mode to the degree that it fails or declines to transform itself and its relations to the interests that it serves, education as certification and professional advancement, the sustaining of structures of cultural privilege, and so on.[43]

In recent years, different forms of cultural politics have attempted to deal with this kind of difficulty by undertaking the investigation and acknowledgement of their own positions, histories and interests. This work of reflexivity has been given considerable impetus by the call issued by Donna Haraway for 'situated knowledges'.[44] Knowledge has been wedded for too long, suggests Haraway, to the ideal of disembodied, disinterested and universal reason. Claims to objectivity, neutrality and disinterest are delusions at best and hostile ruses at worst. All knowledge, including scientific knowledge, is partial, embodied knowledge, produced by particular groups and persons for particular purposes within particular contexts. We should give up claiming to speak on behalf of the universal, along with the aspiration to attain the 'view from nowhere'. An acknowledgement of our situatedness will lead not only to greater plurality and tolerance of the other, but also to the possibility of critical transformation. Haraway does not align herself in any simple way with arguments about modernity and postmodernity, but her insistence on the local and plural nature of knowledge seems to set her firmly against the kinds of Enlightenment universalism that are often identified with modernity, in either its utopian or dystopian characterizations. Haraway speaks to and for a general mood (though I am about to remark on the oddity of this notion) in which the modernist 'view from nowhere' gives way to inhabitation, by turns cheerful and uneasy, of partial perspectives and the fostering of 'local knowledge' in the parallel phrase coined by the ethnographer Clifford Geertz.[45]

Clifford Geertz's work inaugurated what now must be called a wave of postmodern ethnography, in which the situatedness of anthropological knowledge, which had hitherto aspired to the loftiness, distance and disinterest of the view from nowhere in its dealings with other cultures, presses into view. Paul Rabinow, for example, insists that, for a postmodern ethnography, it is necessary to see epistemology 'as a historical event – a distinctive social practice, one among many others', as well as to 'anthropologize the West: show how exotic its constitution of reality has been; emphasize those domains most taken for granted as universal . . . make them seem as historically peculiar as possible.'[46] Stephen A. Tyler has suggested that the collapse of the distance between anthropological observer and his or her observed, and the acknowledgement of their mutual implication will produce a different kind of ethnographic writing, which will privilege the situatedness of 'discourse' over the abstractions of 'text'. Postmodern ethnography

> foregrounds dialogue as opposed to monologue, and emphasizes the cooperative and collaborative nature of the ethnographic situation in contrast to the ideology of the transcendental observer. In fact, it rejects the ideology of 'observer-observed', there being nothing observed and no one who is observer. There is instead the mutual, dialogic production of a discourse, of a story of sorts.[47]

In postmodern ethnography, as in postmodern cultural politics in general, the idea of situated knowledges, and associated ideas of provisional values, and mobile or strategic identifications and affiliations, do a great deal of work; they act as a kind of immuno-suppressive device to protect the continuing desire to be involved in transformative political critique from the toxicity of the challenge mounted against foundational or universal reason in modernity.

However, there is a lurking incoherence in the idea of situated knowledge. For what Haraway proclaims or at least enacts is something more than the advantage of situatedness as such. It is the advantage of recognising and declaring yourself to be situated, the epistemological edge conferred by knowledge *about* the situatedness of knowledge. The injunction issued by Haraway and repeated by those who follow her is not 'Be ye situated', but 'Know and acknowledge thy situatedness'. The question that then arises is where this knowledge of the situatedness of one's knowledge comes from, and what its status is. Is the knowledge of the partiality of one's knowledge itself partial? If not, what is it that allows one to see round one's situatedness in order to grasp it, as it were from the outside? Does the honouring of situatedness mean declaring one's interest, or does it involve the exhortation to be *more* situated (but what could this possibly mean?) The idea of situated knowledge can be rescued from incoherence only at the cost of weakening the idea of situatedness, as though in acknowledging one's history and partial perspective one were to be conceding no more than the person who recognizes that they are not very good at sums or speak with a Bronx or Cockney accent. But, if situatedness is to have any stronger way – if it is really to imply that your sex, ethnic background, upbringing, class position, age and professional affiliations in some fundamental way define what it is possible for you to know and how it is possible for you to know it – then the knowledge of your situatedness is either unattainable or completely beside the point. In the end, the ethical and political force of Haraway's critique depends upon a significant weakening of the claim for the situatedness of all knowledge, since she believes that the embrace of the 'detailed, active, partial way of organizing worlds' should lead to 'elaborate specificity and difference and the loving care people might take to see faithfully from another's point of view'.[48] The 'and' in this last phrase leaps an enormous ethical and political gap. 'Elaborate specificity and difference' are where we are; knowing that does not seem in itself to offer any obvious route to seeing 'faithfully from another's point of view'.

The objections I have been articulating so far resemble those brought forward in other contexts by Stanley Fish against the ideas of critical self-consciousness and 'anti-foundationalist theory hope'.[49] At this point, Fish would tend simply to break off the discussion, having demonstrated the impossibility of grounding a new universal theory on the theory of the universal absence of grounds, and the fundamental irrelevance of the knowledge of one's situation to the situatedness of one's knowledges. Curiously though, one might say that both Haraway and Fish share an inability to include, or tolerate the element of time in these processes. The utopian claims for the power of the knowledge of situatedness and the sceptical reading of that claim have in common a tendency to try to see the issue all at once, and in the round, measuring and taking account of all its consequences, or (for Fish) failures of consequence. Haraway argues against the spatializing of the world, its reduction by universalist reason to an object for sight. But the desire to see and take account of the corporeal situatedness of all angles of vision is itself a kind of visualising, an aspiration to see the act of seeing. Postmodern cultural politics must continue its work of self-acknowledgement, but cannot do so authentically without giving up its modernist desire to hold the nature and outcomes of this self-acknowledgement in its fist. Including the element of time would mean precisely not including it, not attempting to compress the unfolding and contingent futurity of one's actions and values in the domain of one's spatial competence.

Postmodernism, the Avant-Garde and Ethical Possibility

One of the most important of the ways in which postmodern theory tries to develop postures of disidentification is by means of a revival of the role and function of the avant-garde. The concept of the cultural avant-garde is, of course, a prime element in most narratives of modernism and the emergence of postmodernism out of it. Most accounts of modernism stress the progressive narrowing of focus of the avant-garde; beginning as a politically-engaged force, concerned to involve or subsume the products of art to some larger or more inclusive programme (for example in the artists of the Paris Commune of 1871, or the Russian avant-garde of the revolutionary period), the avant-garde gradually withdrew to a position of detachment, in a fatal splitting of the aesthetic and political realms, with the result that the political challenges of the early avant-garde could be contained in the controlled explosions of experiment with artistic form alone.[50] The two most extreme justifications of this willed and violent separation of the political and cultural spheres are Theodor Adorno's concept of the 'negative dialectic' of an art whose political force consists of its obstinate denial of the alienating influences of mass culture and bourgeois rationalization by insisting on its own untranslatable, abstract specificity of form; and Clement Greenberg's cognate praise of the avant-garde's leap into abstraction, in order to maintain a world of absolute, self-legitimating value amid the degradations of kitsch and the barbarities of fascism and capitalism alike.[51] The terms of the avant-garde's seclusion from the dust and heat of history proved to be exactly the means by which art could be commodified and absorbed into professional structures of cultural publicity and management. In no time, the negative dialectic had been safely museumized and the drive for aesthetic purity and renovation reduced by critical procedures to precisely-calculable rhythms of novelty and repetition.

As we have seen, postmodernist art and, along with it, postmodernist theory appear in reaction to this institutionalization of the energies of modernism. This reaction takes two different forms. Firstly, the pose of aristocratic aloofness from the mass culture that had always functioned as the avant-garde's despised opposite, is put aside.[52] This means the embrace of kitsch and popular culture, for example in the work of artists like Andy Warhol and Roy Lichtenstein and writers like Kurt Vonnegut. One representative of this view of postmodernism is Charles Jencks, who believes that the institutionalization of the avant-garde only shows that 'Modernism is the natural style of the bourgeoisie (even if disguised in blue jeans and I-beams)' and that 'the avant-garde which drives Modernism forward directly reflects the dynamism of capitalism, its new waves of destruction and construction, the yearly movements and "isms" which follow each other as predictably as the seasons'.[53] Given this, however, Jencks apparently has nothing better to offer than an uncritical acceptance of this merging of culture into fashion.

But there is a second mode in postmodern theory and art practice, which actually seeks to recapture and purify avant-garde strategies and ideals. For those writers and artists, most notably those associated with the journal *October*, what enabled the modernist avant-garde to bed down so safely in the institutions was its willingness to ignore and leave untransformed its material conditions and setting. For these writers, a purified or invigorated avant-garde practice is to be found in an art which breaks out of its mutely self-mirroring trance to reflect upon institutional contexts and functions. Marjorie Perloff, for example, praises the 'situational' and 'participatory' art of Robert Smithson, Joseph Kosuth, Laurie Anderson and John Cage, all of whom produce work which requires of the viewer not the mere adoration of an object, but an active reflection upon its nature as a work of art. In this, she says, the postmodernist avant-garde recovers much of the energy of its primal begetters at the beginning of modernism, the Russian and Italian Futurists and the early work of collage artists like Braque and Picasso, all of whom promote the collapse of the distinction between the artistic and the non-artistic.[54]

Modernism seen in this way can therefore provide a precedent for a pure moment of avant-garde refusal which postmodernist art may hope to recapture. It is in these terms that Lyotard stakes his association between the avant-garde and the aesthetics of the sublime, praising Marcel Duchamp for his undermining of the very idea of the art-object, with his ready-made sculptures, and Daniel Buren for his questioning of the place in which the work of art can be presented. Postmodernism, as the reprise of those energies, is 'not modernism at its end, but in the nascent state, and this state is constant'.[55] Lyotard writes of the internal interrogation of the principles of modernism itself which is mounted by avant-garde artists like Cézanne, Picasso, Delaunay, Kandinsky, Klee, Mondrian, Malevich and Duchamp, stating that 'the real process of avant-gardism has been a long, obstinate, highly-responsible labour of research into the presuppositions of modernity'.[56]

In contrast, against this, a writer like Rosalind Krauss repudiates the terms and ambitions of the modernist avant-garde *tout court*, canvassing instead the superior credentials of the postmodernist avant-garde. As we saw earlier, the principal feature of modernist aesthetics that she wishes to discredit is its cult of originality – the belief in the possibility and necessity of an absolutely new beginning in art or culture, combined with the cluster of associated beliefs in the absolute, self-grounding singularity, uniqueness and authenticity of the true work of art. Against this, she sets the 'discourse of the copy', practised by artists like Robert Rauschenberg and photographers like Sherrie Levine, in whose work the ideas of origin and originality are subverted. But despite this rejection of the absolutism embedded in the cult of originality, Krauss's own evocation of the new critical possibilities for art partakes of a modernist mode of utopian yearning:

> What would it look like not to repress the concept of the copy? What would it look like to produce a work that acted out the discourse of reproduction without originals, that discourse which could only operate in Mondrian's work as the inevitable subversion of his purpose, the residue of representationality that he could not sufficiently purge from the domain of his painting?[57]

This is a critical language that thrills to the prospect of the apocalyptic return of what has been darkly repressed. Krauss explicitly aligns 'demythologising criticism' with the 'truly postmodernist art' which will ride the back of this vengeful monster of repressed content. Although she rejects the language of new birth and self-ordaining origin in the manifestos of modernism, this language exactly recurs in her evocation of the new world of postmodernism, in its desire to 'void' and 'liquidate' the basic propositions of modernism, and in its paradoxical vision of an absolute gulf between the past and the future: 'it is from a strange new perspective that we look back on the modernist origin and watch it splintering into endless replication'.[58]

This gesture of disidentification therefore conceals and reverts to a simple replication of the concepts which Krauss claims to be revoking. The rhetoric of this criticism claims what its aura of cultural prestige negates – that it is spoken from a position of authority which is, as it were, transcendently marginal, whose refusal of the 'centring' principles of originality and authenticity and embrace of the repressed 'other' of modernism is absolute. This gesture in postmodern theory, especially when it is combined with a heady whiff of the sublime like this, identifies that theory as the new inheritor of the mantle of the avant-garde, in a gesture whose bad faith is redoubled by the fact that it occurs in the context of a repudiation of the very concept of the avant-garde.

A third strain within postmodern cultural politics has attempted to resist this glorified return of the avant-garde. In a powerful reading of Lyotard's work, John Tagg has suggested that accounts of the postmodern condition have become fixated upon the vision of the artist as Promethean outsider, or cultural guerrilla. What identifies this romantic appropriation as desire rather than strategy is its manifest anachronism, its refusal to acknowledge that the role of the avant-garde is always produced in different ways in different sets of historical conditions – in Paris in the 1850s and 1870s, in Zurich during the First World War, in New York in the 1940s – and that the avant-garde is therefore not an historically generalizable category. In sliding into the posture of the avant-garde, postmodern theory perpetuates a falsely absolute view of the sealed totality of 'society' on the one hand, and the wintry, heroic exposure of the 'outsider' on the other. 'This exclusive mission', he writes, 'is . . . only an elitist or utopian fantasy. Marginality guarantees nothing.'[59] A radical and progressive cultural politics will have to accept its necessary implication in what it opposes, will have to accept the fact of the collapse of critical distance and so will need to develop a tactically supple range of responses to different situations:

> Cultural practices always involve the mobilization of determinate means and relations of representation within an institutional framework whose organization takes a particular historical form . . . There is no meaning outside this framework but it is not monolithic. The institutions which compose it offer multiple points of entry and spaces for contestation – and not just on the margins.[60]

This call to abandon the scenario of centre and margin, or the 'imaginary threshold between incorporation and independence', as Tagg puts it, is to be heard as well in Hal Foster's idea of a postmodern 'culture of resistance'. Foster proposes, instead of the glamour of avant-garde 'transgression', the more modest ambition of 'counterhegemony', consisting of resistance and interference, which requires us 'to see in the social formation not a "total system" but a conjuncture of practices, many adversarial, where the cultural is an arena in which active contestation is possible'.[61] And Victor Burgin has argued for a similarly 'immanent' cultural politics, arguing that there is no point to the avant-garde debate about whether to work inside or outside the institutions of art, since 'quite simply there *is* no 'outside' to institutions in contemporary Western society'.[62]

There is much to be gained from this cooling-down of the self-aggrandizing rhetoric of marginality, outsiderdom and transgression in postmodern theory, and from the movement beyond the concept-metaphors of centre and margin which so insistently reproduce absolute polarities and, more importantly, disguise the complicity of postmodern theory in the construction of the totalizing global systems which it fantasizes about getting 'outside' of. But for a cultural politics, indeed, for any kind of politics, there is something crucially missing in the prospects offered by Tagg, Foster and Burgin. All of them seem to accept the necessity of doing without the forms of absolute legitimation produced by metanarratives such as human progress towards universal liberty, and attempt to imagine a postmodern cultural politics consisting of provisional counterhegemonic 'tactics'. In this sense, they share the point of view of Stuart Hall, who suspects that 'there isn't . . . one "power game" at all, more a network of strategies and powers and their articulations – and thus a politics which is always positional'.[63] But this ignores the full force, firstly, of the collapse of critical distance announced by Jameson, the loss of an obvious ethico-political position outside the play of social relationships from which to ground a theory of counterhegemony, and secondly, of the discrediting carried through by Lyotard and others, whose object is not tactics, but ends and values. Burgin attempts to argue that these values can survive the transition to decentred pragmatics undamaged:

> Moral certainty and political necessity is [sic] not, of itself, dissolved in the 'restless flux' of postmodernism's 'anything goes'. We should first remember that the 'postmodern' is a 'first-world' problematic – thus, for example, the moral certainty and political necessity that black South Africans should democratically participate in the government of their own society, will not be swept away by any amount of breathlessly fashionable gush about postmodernism . . . The end of 'grand narratives' does not mean the end of either morality or *memory*.[64]

But Burgin is underestimating the effect of the postmodern abandonment of the universal horizon of value and morality. It will not do simply to assume the continuation of value and morality, in the hope that these will naturally persist among postmodern persons of good will who will automatically agree about what value and morality are. Burgin indicates that he thinks the erosion of certainty in 'first world' postmodernism is contradicted by the persistence of local struggles on moral principles elsewhere in the world, but this could only ever stand as an argument about the cultural relativity of certain values, and does not cope with the a priori denial of the possibility of any universal value in Lyotard's postmodernism. The point is not whether or not the South African black population believed in the legitimacy of their struggle – Hitler's Nazis believed in the legitimacy of *their* struggle, after all – but whether we did as well, and whether grounds can be said to exist to validate this collective belief. Put another way, the question is not, how do you persuade people to agree with you who are already inclined to do so, but how do you persuade (or how do you justify forcing) people to agree with you who do not already do so?

All this is to say that if tactics, strategies and forms of political organization and expression can be locally and historically variable, then the principles and values that might impel one to any kind of political action in the first place cannot easily survive such splintering. For what principle, other than a collective one, indeed, a universal one, is going to guarantee the possibility of free negotiation between these multiple centres of interest, or Lyotard's heterogeneous language-games? It is certainly the case that a postmodern cultural politics must beware of systems that impose uniformity oppressively through the rhetoric of universality – including its own. But the postmodern critique of totality has only ever amounted to the demonstration that totality and universality are regularly claimed dishonestly in the names of structures of power that are neither total nor universal; they nowhere build convincingly into an argument against the desire for a universal application of the principles of freedom and justice. Indeed, when inspected closely, it becomes apparent that the postmodern critique of unjust and oppressive systems of universality implicitly depends for its force upon the assumption of the universal right of all not to be treated unjustly and oppressively – otherwise, who would care whether metanarratives were false or not, oppressive or not, and what reason might there be for their abandonment when they no longer compelled assent? Seen in these terms, the very 'incredulity towards metanarratives' that Lyotard writes about is not a symptom of the collapse of general or collective ethical principles, but a testimony to their continuing corrective force.

The evacuation of the horizon of universal value leads in the end either to an irrationalist embrace of the agonistics of opposition – to put it more simply, the adoption by default of the universal principle that might is right; or to the sunny complacency of pragmatism, in which it is assumed that we can never ground our activities in ethical principles which have more force than just saying 'this is the sort of thing we do, because it suits us'. (In the end, in fact, the pragmatic option will always turn into the agonistic, since it will only work satisfactorily until somebody refuses to agree with you, or refuses to allow you to disgree with them.) Postmodern cultural analysis and cultural politics certainly mark an important, indeed, probably an epochal stage in the development of ethical awareness, in the recognition of the irreducible diversity of voices and interests. But, as this study has attempted to show, this cultural analysis always risks falling into complicity with the increasingly globalized forms which seek to harness, exploit, and administer – and therefore violently to curtail – this diversity. The task for a theoretical postmodernity of the future must be (without dissipating its energies in fantasies of potently defeated marginality, or narrowing into self-promoting professionalism, or acting as the cultural legitimation of the alienating effects of the 'information society' of late capitalism) to forge new and more inclusive forms of ethical collectivity. There will be those who will see this as just another spineless relapse into universalism, but it is no such thing. It is a call for the creation of a common frame of assent which alone can guarantee the continuation of a global diversity of voices.

Afterculture: Postmodern Ecology

The contemporary problem of value is thus the problem of how to speak with rationality as well as mere enthusiasm or good intentions of value or values in the peculiar condition of afterculture that we inhabit – culture, that is to say, formed and defined in terms of its own belatedness, and our necessary ironic half-residence in identities, traditions and values that are at once there and not there, ours and not ours. In this condition, the past is neither alive nor dead, neither present to us, nor separable from us. Our condition is one of uncompleted mourning, in which reliable distinctions between self and other, inner and outer, now and then, are not easily to be precipitated. After cultural value, we must negotiate 'aftercultural value': the condition, and quality of living in, and as, an afterculture.

Certain kinds of contemporary thinking have begun to measure the consequences of a radical decentring not just of the authority of certain kinds of culture, but of the authority and centrality of 'culture', indeed, the human, as such. In particular, certain styles of ecological thinking, in philosophy and in artistic practice, require a much more radical evacuation of culture, as Paul de Man calls it, an emptying of culture towards its others, than has hitherto had to be conceived.[65] Seen from this perspective, the afterculture of the postmodern does not name the question or condition of value in a certain stage of culture, but frames a question about the very possibility of there being value beyond or without culture; value after, beyond, or in the remission of the human.

Hitherto, ethical and aesthetic thought has been governed by two related, but distinct theories of the relationship of culture and nature. In the first, the role of culture is to reflect, fulfil, or actualize the truths of nature; cultures that produce themselves on this model look to the natural as validation. Such a model depends upon the mutually confirming identity of nature and culture. If such a model survives into the period of social modernity – which is perhaps to say, into the Renaissance in Europe – then it is in the form of idealized compensation for the loss of this sense of union between man and nature.

This contrasts with those forms of society and forms of social theory which regard culture and nature as adversaries. According to this second view or tendency, culture is the product of a more or less traumatic self-extrication from nature. This view both produces and reflexively depends upon the idea of culture as the formation of consciousness or subjectivity out of the primitive unconsciousness of matter. Such a view is dramatized in a number of different forms and dimensions: psychoanalytic, anthropological, economic and theological. In this view, culture may still be held to actualize the truths of nature, but only as the result of appropriation, struggle and transformation. Much of the history of Western aesthetics can be aligned with this view of the relations between culture and nature, insofar as the category of the aesthetic comes to depend upon the curbing, purging, or sublimatory transformation of the body and its natural appetites. Lynda Nead shows how this model operates in the history of Western art through the centrality of the female nude. In an obstinately renewed allegory, the female nude enacts the transformation of formless 'female' matter into the clarity, intelligibility and purposiveness of 'male' form. As an allegory of the process of art itself, the female nude is also an allegory of the more or less violent transformation of nature into culture.[66]

Where, in the first model, nature and culture reciprocally requite each other, in the second, nature's meaning, value and existence are requisitioned by culture. In certain forms, however, these two contrasting views of the relation between culture and nature can cooperate strangely; as for example in theories that suggest that nature completes itself precisely through the internal dehiscence of consciousness, culture and history. Indeed, we might say that, insofar as any theory of the relationship of culture and nature depends upon a prior apprehension that their relationship is in some way problematic, some kind of dehiscence, or traumatic caesura must always be operative in any theory of the plenary reciprocity of culture and nature. Subject to this naturally very considerable proviso, it might be said that the first model of mutuality predominates in archaic and premodern societies, while the second, adversary model is characteristic, or even definitional of modern societies. In societies or epochs in which nature and culture exist in symmetrical plenitude, time is recurrent and nonprogressive. It is only with the experience of the split between material and cultural existence that memory and the possibility of human innovation can come about. History, in fact, can arise only from this split between the self-evidence of nature and the orientation towards uncompleted possibility that is culture.

It has been variously claimed that ecological thought is postmodern thought, in that it enjoins us to imagine the relations between culture and nature as relations neither of identity, nor of subordination and antagonism, but as dynamic, differential relations of exchange. Ecological theory proposes a move from a 'restricted economy' of value, which suggests that the natural world is available as raw material to be transformed into use-value for humanity, to a 'general economy', which assumes that value is not produced out of, but is rather in some sense immanent in the relations between the natural and the human.

My distinction between a 'restricted' and a 'general' economy derives from Jacques Derrida's reading of Georges Bataille's work in *Writing and Difference*, and is meant to signal something like the following contrast. A restricted economy is a system of exchanges governed by and directed towards certain specified outcomes, measured typically according to one dominant scale of value. A restricted economy is therefore always a bounded economy, one which enables one to discern clearly what lies inside and outside its scope. A general economy, by contrast, is one in which the process of exchange is neither end-directed nor bounded. A general economy is characterized by process without production or outcome. For Bataille, any economic system geared towards production, profit and the conservation of value is restricted. Seen in the widened perspective of a general economy, which would place Western economic systems in relation to other forms of economic exchange – up to and including the cosmic economy formed by the gathering, exchange and expenditure of energy in the total physical universe – production and conservation do not seem like economic ends, but only stages in some larger, less easily constrained process.[67] In the restricted economy formed by the 'modernist' model, value is strenuously exacted from the antagonism between culture and nature; in the general economy said to be proposed by postmodern ecology, value circulates between them. In the former model, value is

concentrated and appropriated from externally-regulated systems; in
the latter it is dispersed and distributed throughout self-regulating
systems.

All these forms of general economy depend upon the drastic curtailing
of the sovereignty of the human subject, and a correlative remission of the
force of the association between culture and subjectivity. Seen in this way,
an ecological ethics would be an ethics of alterity, rather than an ethics
which aimed to preserve and enlarge the *ethos* or the *ethnos*; an ethics not
of being, but of letting be.

I want here to register some of the implications of this situation for
ethical and aesthetic thought and for the relations between them. Among
the necessary questions thrown up by the ecological turn might be the
following: What kind of ethics might it be that was not founded upon
human life and its preservation, or, was even directly founded upon its
secondariness? How can such an ethics be instituted and enacted? Is a 'wild
philosophy' imaginable? What kind of artistic practice, what kind of
aesthetic theory, might typify and actuate this new relationship? Insofar as
it might be said to depend upon a violent appropriation of the natural, for
example, how does the Western tradition of the aesthetic need to be
enlarged or transformed by ecological thinking? What new relations
between the ethical and the aesthetic need to be conjectured by ecological
theory? Does the decentring of human interests and concerns result in or
in some way require an aestheticization of ethics and politics, whereby
these latter would be validated and governed not by questions of truth and
justice, but by activities of imagination, identification, projection; not by
the regulation of the world, but by activities of world-making?

Central to much recent postmodern ecological thinking has been what
one might call a corporealization of the work of Heidegger. Heidegger
provides the principal impetus in particular behind one of the most
emphatic recent statements of postmodern ecology, David Michael Levin's
The Opening of Vision: Nihilism and the Postmodern Situation (1988). Here,
Levin elaborates what has become quite a familiar assault on the modernist
centring of man as the legislating source of all things, a centring which is
imaged and enacted principally through the development of perspective in
the Renaissance and the prestige of sight in the Cartesian rationality which
it prefigured and empowered. Levin follows Heidegger in construing the
emancipatory dream of the Enlightenment as bringing about a certain
violence of lucidity, in which the possibility of a scientific and perspicuous
knowledge of the world depends upon an alienating split between the
knowing and all-seeing subject and the known and perceived object. For
Levin, as for many others writing in what Martin Jay has characterized as

the 'anti-ocularcentric' tradition of twentieth-century thought, there is an oppressive synonymity between looking, knowing and power.[68]

Against the closure and violence of this system of thought, Levin proposes a Heideggerian movement of opening, writing that 'the ego, the *ego cogito* of modern metaphysics, cannot let itself be open to (the question of) Being without being decentred, cast out, in a kind of exile, into the dimensionality of a wider, more open field'.[69] The nonviolent recollection of Being for Levin involves crucially a regathering of the sense of the body, which is held to be violently suppressed or abstracted in modernity:

> Our critical task therefore consists in a process of recollection which begins in the body, retrieving that pre-ontological understanding of Being which, whenever it is recognized as such, is always to be found already schematized for us corporeally, and therefore . . . deeply inwrought in the structural flesh of our visionary being-in-the-world.[70]

This return to the body has become a marked feature of a certain strain of postmodern ecofeminism as well. The assumption here is that the Cartesian partition of the self-legislating ego from the clinging illusions of matter, sensuality, and nature, is to be seen principally as a denial and privation of the female. To recapture the possibility of a mutuality between reason and matter means disavowing this disavowal of the female. Charlene Spretnak, whose work is representative of the style of feminist critique I am here characterizing, is untroubled by the charge of essentialism, or even just plain old sentimentality which she anticipates from what she calls a deconstructive criticism. Indeed, she argues that this charge is precisely the sign of the complicity of 'deconstructive postmodernism' with the metaphysical tradition of the rationalist disavowal of the body.

> The female, like other cosmological life-forms, consists of a flux of microevents rather than stasis, or a fixed essence, yet to deny the particularities of the female body is to serve the interests of patriarchy. Deconstructive postmodernism promises freedom for all, but elements of its internal logic continue the patriarchal project by authoritatively declaring NO! to the female body, the Earthbody, and the larger reality that is the cosmological scope of existence.[71]

Both Levin and Spretnak dream of a healing saturation of intellect in the body, an achieved corporeal innocence that in claiming to go beyond, or get back to, a condition before the dismembering dualisms of Western metaphysics, is itself an extension and effect of the tradition it wishes simply to surpass. For such dreams are the co-operating obverse of modernity's traumatic split from the natural. Its absolute abolition of violence is itself a kind of violence, its healing of the despoliatory history of the modern is a replication of it. The dream here is of a life lived through and in the body, in a Romantic-aesthetic ideal of the union of the sensuous and the intelligible which is precisely produced as the effect and complement of a modernist privation of the body. The redemptive merger of categories – the self and the other, the intellect and the body – and the inversion of categories – the other in preference to the self, the body in preference to the intellect – are both derived from and continue to support the categorial partitions they claim to supersede. The ecological dream of redemption from metaphysics is an originary supplement of the primal rending of metaphysics. Only metaphysical thought of the most profoundly uninspected or somnambulistic kind is capable of such a naïve hope of turning the page on metaphysics.

In *The Middle Voice of Egological Conscience* (1991), John Llewelyn also co-opts Heidegger, in association with Emmanuel Levinas, in order to mount an argument that outflanks some of the more usual ethical problems that attend upon the question of the responsibility that we may owe to the nonhuman animate and even inanimate worlds. Llewelyn reads Levinas back into the Heidegger whom Levinas is so concerned to distinguish himself from, arguing for the reciprocity of the Heideggerian principle of 'letting be' and the Levinasian recommendation of a catastrophic opening of the self to the primary ethical obligedness of the face-to-face relation. Like Derrida, Llewelyn sees a link between Heidegger's ethics-before-ethics of letting be and the 'proto-ethical' relationship he sees characterized by Levinas, that absolute, terrifying, demanding and dilapidating proximity of the Other. Llewelyn is anxious with Heidegger to prevent the question of ethics from slipping back into questions of economics, or prudential calculation of benefit: 'To suppose that appraisal is the primary business of ethics is to confuse ethics with economics, with business. It is a devaluation of ethics to ground it on valuation and questions of comparative worth'.[72] Grafting this version of Levinas on to this version of Heidegger allows Llewelyn to get over the difficulty that, for all its alleged hostility to the 'egological' violence of metaphysics and ontology, even in their Heideggerian form, Levinas does not anywhere elaborate, or perhaps even allow for an account of an ethical relationship to the nonhuman world, to an alterity that is in no respect the 'same'. Llewelyn has an ideal of an absolute transcending value in the absolute transcendence *of* value – in a kind of primary responsibility that is prior to all systems of morality, and philosophical categories of all kinds insofar as they are themselves blind to their own necessary investments in structures of value.

The problem is that nothing can be wholly outside such structures of value, which is to say structures of relative estimation, least of all a claim such as Llewelyn's to which so much value and prestige is attached. In fact, Llewelyn's postmodern ecology joins with Spretnak's and Levin's, in that they all attempt to heal, cancel, or surpass the condition of division. All attempt to purge entirely the guilt of rationality, and of a culture founded upon rationality's disavowal and objectification of its opposites. All attempt to transcend and transfigure the human, by a paradoxical evocation of the absolute value of what lies beyond the reach of human evaluation. All attempt to open the restricted economy of cultural value to a form or dream of a general economy. In this, all three fall back into the very anthropomorphic error they set out by denouncing, by the very intensity of their desire, or compulsion to evade that error. The paradox and the danger that their work reveals is that by founding ethics on a radical evaluation of the human, they necessarily remain autistically on the interior of the human, insofar as it is constitutive of the human to define itself in its own capacity for self-transcendence. The complete dispossession of the subject, the complete abandonment of reason and its alleged violence restore the subject intact to itself, for the abandonment of egological interests and motivations is a resource drawn from the structure of egological thought.

Here, I am profoundly at one with Gillian Rose in her recent attacks on the ethics of alterity in *The Broken Middle* and *Judaism and Modernity*, especially as these are focused in the dream of some *wholly* other, more ethically responsive form of rationality, allegedly instanced in a Judaic tradition of thought rather than in the oppression of Greek metaphysics and its wicked historical accomplices and legatees – Enlightenment, modernity, science, Marxism. Rose argues that such a view profoundly misrecognizes the self-exteriorizing force of modernity and its Enlightenment, its constitutive capacity to put itself at risk through exposure to alterity.[73] Derrida, too, though his work is often subjected to a skim-reading that suggests he is in some simple way *against* Enlightenment rationality and the Hegelian dialectic, also draws attention tirelessly to the inseparability of the Hegelian will-to-mastery over the contingencies of history and the principle of alterity that is the very shape and purpose of the Hegelian story of spirit. To be postmodern in the simple or factitious sense of dreaming of some self-evident and fully-determinate beyond or outside to rationality, is actually to be, in the worst sense, modern.

The paradox here is that the ecological imperative comes about – perhaps could only ever have come about – at a moment when the powers of appetitive, appropriative, technologistic rationality seem to have become total. From this time onwards, only a fully conscious and self-conscious programme can govern the process whereby humanity contracts with itself to constrain itself and its needs. Only a hitherto unprecedented expansion of the powers and responsibilities of the sovereign subject can inform the necessity of its gratuitous self-dispersal. Only a willed mutation of the field of value can bring about the muting of the will-to-power that has hitherto governed its thinking. It is only after nature has effectively ceased to exist – which is to say precisely at the crisis-point at which humanity seems to have the choice as to whether nature continues to exist or not – that nature can be produced.

The failure to acknowledge this continuing, paradoxical necessity of the subject and the ethical modes of its egological preservation results oddly in ecological programmes which are themselves sentimentally primitivist or violently anthropocentric. Postmodern ecology requires rather the paradoxical feat of inventing the modes of our inherence in the world, determining the nature of our determination by the natural, bringing about the condition of our givenness. For theory to become, or construe itself as ecological must involve, not any simple move from the alleged violence and abstraction of male instrumentalist thought to the generous 'letting be' of ecological thought, nor any simple move from transcendence to immanence, but rather some as yet unthinkable and unthought transformation of the nature of thought itself, that would enable it to be unconscious and self-conscious, willing and acquiescent, determining and determined at once. This would require, for example, not a move beyond rationality, nor any kind of relaxation of, or reversion from it, but the incitement of a condition of permanent, responsibly conserved catastrophe within it and the ethics and politics founded upon its norms.

Notes

1	'Postmodern Politics', *Theory, Culture and Society*, 5: 2–3 (1988), pp. 560–1.
2	For an account of 'post-Fordism' in late twentieth-century industrial organization, see Robin Murray, 'Life After (Henry) Ford', *Marxism Today* (October 1988), pp. 8–13.
3	Ibid., p. 566.
4	*Forget Foucault*, trans. Nicola Dufresne New York: Semiotext(e), 1987), p. 37.
5	David Harvey, *The Condition of Postmodernity: An Enquiry Into the Origins of Social Change* (Oxford: Blackwell, 1989), p. 116–26.
6	Paul Virilio, 'The Last Vehicle', in Jean Baudrillard et. al., *Looking Back On The End of the World*, ed. Dietmar Kamper and Christoph Wulf, trans. David Antal (New York: Semiotext(e), 1989), p. 114.

7   Ibid.

8   'Postmodernism: or, The Cultural Logic of Late Capital', *New Left Review*, 146 (1984), p. 91.

9   Ibid., p. 92.

10 Edward Soja, *Postmodern Geographies: The Reassertion of Space in Critical Social Theory* (London: Verso, 1989); Gillian Rose, *Feminism and Geography: The Limits of Geographical Knowledge* (Cambridge: Polity, 1993); Derek Gregory, *Geographical Imaginations* (Oxford: Basil Blackwell, 1994).

11 Henri Lefebvre, 'Space: Social Product and Use Value', in *Critical Sociology: European Perspectives*, ed. J.W. Freiburg (New York: Irvington, 1979), p. 293.

12 Henri Lefebvre, *The Production of Space*, trans. Donald Nicholson-Smith (Oxford: Blackwell, 1991).

13 Fredric Jameson, *The Seeds of Time* (New York: Columbia University Press, 1994), p. 25.

14 Ibid.

15 Meaghan Morris, 'The Man in the Mirror: David Harvey's "Condition" of Postmodernity', *Theory, Culture and Society*, 9 (1992), pp. 253–79.

16 Gregory, *Geographical Imaginations*, p. 414.

17 Notes for a televised discussion of 'Art After Modernism', *Voices*, 11 April 1984, on British Channel 4, quoted in John Tagg, 'Postmodernism and the Born-Again Avant-Garde', *Block*, 11 (1985/6), p. 4.

18 *Subculture: The Meaning of Style* (London: Methuen, 1979), pp. 137–8.

19 http://www.village.virginia.edu/pmc/contents.html

20 Sigmund Freud, 'The Ego and the Id' (1923), *The Standard Edition of the Complete Psychological Works of Sigmund Freud* (London: Hogarth Press, 1953–74), trans. James Strachey, Vol XIX, p. 26 and n.1.

21 Scott Bukatman, *Terminal Identity: The Virtual Subject in Postmodern Science Fiction* (Durham NC: Duke University Press, 1993), p. 10.

22 *Gynesis: Configurations of Woman and Modernity* (Ithaca and London: Cornell University Press, 1985), p. 73.

23 *Sexual/Textual Politics: Feminist Literary Theory* (London: Methuen, 1985), p. 150.

24 Ibid., p. 163.

25 'Feminists and Postmodernism', in *Postmodern Culture*, ed. Hal Foster (London and Sydney: Pluto Press, 1985), p. 59.

26 'Postmodernism and Gender Relations in Feminist Theory', *Signs*, 12:4 (1987), pp. 626, 642.

27 'Feminists and Postmodernism', p. 59.

28 *Gynesis*, p. 25.

29 Patricia Mellencamp, 'Images of Language and Indiscreet Dialogue: "The Man Who Envied Women" ', *Screen*, 28:2 (1987), p. 99.

30 See, for example, Edward Said, *Orientalism* (London: Routledge and Kegan Paul, 1978) and Gayatri Chakravorty Spivak, *In Other Worlds: Essays in Cultural Politics* (London and New York: Methuen, 1987); and collections

such as *Europe and Its Others, Vol. 1, Proceedings of the Essex Conference on the Sociology of Literature* (Colchester: University of Essex, 1985); *Critical Inquiry*, special issue on ' "Race", Writing and Difference', 12:1 (1985), and *Oxford Literary Review*, special issue on 'Colonialism', 9:1–2 (1987).

31 'Postmodernism and Periphery', *Third Text*, 2 (1978/9), p. 6.

32 *Le Postmoderne expliqué aux enfants: Correspondance 1982–1985* (Paris: Galilée, 1986), pp. 48–9. See discussion above, chapter 2, pp. 31–3.

33 'Postmodernism or Post-Colonialism Today', *Textual Practice*, 1:1 (1987), pp. 32–47.

34 'Orientalism Reconsidered', in *Literature, Politics and Theory: Papers From the Essex Conference, 1976–1984*, ed. Francis Barker, Peter Hulme, Margaret Iversen and Diana Loxley (London: Methuen, 1986), p. 215.

35 Ibid., p. 212.

36 *Black Skin White Masks*, trans. Charles Markmann (London: Pluto Press, 1986), p. 135.

37 'The Other Question: Difference, Discrimination and the Discourse of Colonialism', in *Literature, Politics and Theory*, p. 164.

38 'Postmodernism and Periphery', p. 11.

39 'The Production of the "Post-Modern": The Minimalist Aesthetics of Rei Kawakuba', paper given at 'Futur*Fall' conference, Power Institute, University of Sydney, 26–29 July, 1984. The paper does not appear in the collection of papers from the conference, but is briefly summarized in E. A. Grosz's introduction; see *Futur*Fall: Excursions into Postmodernity*, ed. E. A. Grosz, Terry Threadgold, David Kelly, Alan Cholodenko and Edward Colless (Sydney: Power Institute of Fine Art, 1986), p. 3.

40 'Problems in Current Theories of Colonial Discourse', *Oxford Literary Review*, 9:1–2 (1987), p. 29.

41 Ibid., p. 35.

42 Spivak discusses different aspects of the politics of postmodern theory in 'Imperialism and Sexual Difference', *Oxford Literary Review*, 8:1–2 (1986), pp. 225–40 and 'The Politics of Interpretations' and 'French Feminism in an International Frame', in *In Other Worlds*, pp. 118–33, 134–53.

43 For 'identification', 'counteridentification' and 'disidentification', see Michel Pêcheux, *Language, Semantics and Ideology: Stating the Obvious*, trans. Harbaas Nagpal (London: Macmillan, 1982), pp. 156–9, and the discussion of these terms in Diane Macdonell, *Theories of Discourse: An Introduction* (Oxford: Basil Blackwell, 1986), pp. 39–42, 112–14, 128–9.

44 Donna Haraway, 'Situated Knowledges: The Science Question in Feminism and the Privilege of Partial Perspective', in *Simians, Cyborgs and Women*, (New York: Routledge, 1991), pp. 183–201.

45 Clifford Geertz, *Local Knowledge: Further Essays in Interpretive Anthropology* (New York: Basic Books, 1986).

46 Paul Rabinow, 'Representations Are Social Facts: Modernity and Post-Modernity in Anthropology', in *Writing Culture: The Poetics and Politics of*

Ethnography, eds. James Clifford and George E. Marcus (Berkeley, Los Angeles and London: University of California Press, 1986), p. 241.

47 Stephen A. Tyler, 'Post-Modern Ethnography: From Document of the Occult to Occult Document', ibid., p. 126. The rethinking of anthropology and ethnography in the light of postmodern thought is also carried forward influentially in James Clifford's, *The Predicament of Culture: Twentieth-Century Ethnography, Literature, and Art* (Cambridge, MA: Harvard University Press, 1988). I discuss these developments in my *Theory and Cultural Value* (Oxford: Basil Blackwell, 1992), pp. 231–59.

48 'Situated Knowledges', p. 190.

49 See the discussion above, chapter 2, pp. 66–9.

50 See Renato Poggioli, *The Theory of the Avant-Garde*, trans. Gerald Fitzgerald (New York: Harper and Row, 1971) and Matei Calinescu, 'The Idea of the Avant-Garde', in *Five Faces of Modernity: Modernism, Avant-Garde, Decadence, Kitsch, Postmodernism* (Durham, NC: Duke University Press, 1987), pp. 95–148.

51 Theodor Adorno, *Ästhetische Theorie* (Frankfurt am Main: Suhrkamp, 1970); Clement Greenberg, 'Avant-Garde and Kitsch (first published, 1939), in *Art and Culture* (London: Thames and Hudson, 1973), pp. 5–6. See, too, Peter Bürger, *Theory of the Avant-Garde*, trans. Michael Shaw (Manchester: Manchester University Press, 1984).

52 On the close relationship of modernism and mass culture, see Andreas Huyssen, *After the Great Divide: Modernism, Mass Culture, Postmodernism* (Bloomington: Indiana University Press, 1986) pp. 3–64.

53 'The Post-Avant-Garde', in *The Post-Avant-Garde: Painting in the Eighties*, ed. Charles Jencks (London: Academy Editions, 1987), p. 17.

54 Marjorie Perloff, *The Futurist Moment: Avant-Garde, Avant Guerre, and the Language of Rupture* (Chicago and London: University of Chicago Press, 1986).

55 *The Postmodern Condition: A Report on Knowledge*, trans. Geoff Bennington and Brian Massumi (Manchester: Manchester University Press, 1984), p. 79.

56 *Le Postmoderne expliqué aux enfants*, p. 125.

57 *The Originality of the Avant-Garde and Other Modernist Myths* (Cambridge, MA.: MIT Press, 1986), p. 169.

58 Ibid., p. 170.

59 'Postmodernism and the Born-Again Avant-Garde', p. 5.

60 Ibid., pp. 6–7.

61 *Recordings: Art, Spectacle, Cultural Politics* (Seattle: Bay Press, 1985), p. 149.

62 *The End of Art Theory: Criticism and Postmodernity* (London: Macmillan, 1986), p. 192.

63 'Brave New World', *Marxism Today* (October 1988), p. 28.

64 *The End of Art Theory*, p. 198.

65 Paul de Man, 'Dialogue and Dialogism', *Poetics Today*, 4 (1983), p. 103.

66 Lynda Nead, *The Female Nude: Obscenity, Art and Sexuality* (London: Routledge, 1993).

67 See Jacques Derrida, 'From Restricted to General Economy: An Hegelianism Without Reserve', *Writing and Difference*, trans. Alan Bass (London: Routledge and Kegan Paul, 1978), pp. 251–77; Georges Bataille, *The Accursed Share*, trans. Robert Hurley (New York: Zone Books, 1988).

68 Martin Jay, *Downcast Eyes: The Denigration of Vision in Twentieth-Century French Thought* (Berkeley: University of California Press, 1993).

69 *The Opening of Vision: Nihilism and the Postmodern Situation* (New York and London: Routledge, 1988), p. 24.

70 Ibid., p. 41.

71 Charlene Spretnak, *States of Grace: The Recovery of Meaning in the Postmodern Age* (San Francisco: Harper San Francisco, 1991), p. 126. See too, Somer Brodribb, *Nothing Mat(t)ers: A Feminist Critique of Postmodernism* (Melbourne: Spinifex Press, 1992).

72 John Llewelyn, *The Middle Voice of Ecological Conscience* (Basingstoke: Macmillan, 1991), p. 260.

73 Gillian Rose, *The Broken Middle: Out of Our Ancient Society* (Oxford: Blackwell, 1992); *Judaism and Modernity* (Oxford: Blackwell, 1993).

Bibliography

It is customary to apologize for the incompleteness of bibliographies, and such a precaution is particularly necessary for a bibliography of postmodernism, which moves so quickly and continues to expand at such a prodigious rate. A bibliography of this kind can only ever be a snapshot of a literature that is still in convulsive growth.

Nevertheless, I have tried to be as complete as possible in the bibliography that follows, and to cast my net as widely as possible over the different cultural areas in which the idea of postmodernism has taken root. This is not to say that the reader will find listed here every text that is relevant to the postmodernism debate. As this is an introduction to postmodernism, I have adopted the principle of only including texts which offer definitions of postmodernism, summarize or oppose other definitions, exemplify its characteristics, consider the problems arising from, or otherwise contribute consciously and directly to the debate about postmodernism, usually by naming it specifically.

Bibliography

Postmodernism in Philosophy, and Political and Cultural Theory

Adair, Gilbert. *The Postmodernist Always Rings Twice: Reflections on Culture in the Nineties*. London: Fourth Estate, 1992.

Agger, Ben. *The Decline of Discourse: Reading, Writing and Resistance in Postmodern Capitalism*. London: Falmer, 1990.

Ahmed, Akbar S. *Postmodernism and Islam*. London and New York: Routledge, 1992.

Anon. 'Intellectual Journalism, Postmodernism and Cultural Theory'. *New Formations*, 2 (1987): 3–5.

Arac, Jonathan, ed. *Postmodernism and Politics*. Manchester: Manchester University Press, 1986.

Baudrillard, Jean. *Le Système des objects*. Paris: Gallimard, 1968.

——. *Le Miroir de la production: ou l'illusion critique du matérialisme historique*. Tournai: Casterman, 1973. Trans. Mark Poster, as *The Mirror of Production* (St. Louis: Telos Press, 1975).

——. *La Société de la consommation: ses mythes, ses structures*. Paris: Gallimard, 1974.

——. *Pour une critique de l'économie politique du signe*. Paris: Gallimard, 1976. Trans. Charles Levin, as *For a Critique of the Political Economy of the Sign* (St. Louismo: Telos Press, 1981).

——. *L'Echange symbolique et la mort*. Paris: Gallimard, 1976.

——. *L'Effet Beaubourg: implosion et dissuasion*. Paris: Galilée, 1977.

——. *Oublier Foucault*. Paris: Galilée, 1977. Trans. Nicola Dufresne, as *Forget Foucault* (New York: Semiotext(e), 1987).

——. *De la séduction*. Paris: Galilée, 1980.

——. *Simulacres et simulation*. Paris: Galilée, 1981. 'The Precessions of Simulacra' and 'The Orders of Simulacra', trans. Paul Foss, Paul Patton and Philip Bleitchman, in *Simulations* (New York: Semiotext(e), 1983).

——. *Les Stratégies fatales*. Paris: Grasset, 1983.

——. *A l'ombre des majorités silencieuses*. Paris: Denël, 1983. Trans. Paul Foss, Paul Patton and John Johnson as *In the Shadow of the Silent Majorities . . . or the End of the Social and Other Essays*. (New York: Semiotext(e), 1983).

——. *La Gauche divine: chroniques des années 1977–1984*. Paris: Grasset, 1985.

——. *Amérique*. Paris: Grasset, 1986.

——. *L'Autre par lui-même*. Paris: Galilée, 1987. Trans. Bernard and Caroline Schutze as *The Ecstasy of Communication* (New York: Semiotext(e), 1988).

——. *Cool Memories*. Paris: Galiliée, 1987.

——. *Selected Writings*. Various translators. Ed. Mark Poster. Oxford: Polity Press, 1988.

——. *Fatal Strategies*. Ed. Jim Fleming. Trans. Philip Beitchman and W.G.J. Niesluchowksi. London: Pluto, 1990.

——. *Revenge of the Crystal: Selected Writings on the Modern Object and Its Destiny, 1968–1983*. Ed. and trans. Paul Foss and Julian Pefanis. London: Pluto, 1990.

——. *Baudrillard Live: Selected Interviews*. Ed. Mike Gane. London: Routledge, 1993.

Bauman, Zygmunt. *Legislators and Interpreters: On Modernity, Postmodernity and Intellectuals*. Cambridge: Polity Press, 1987.

——. *Intimations of Postmodernity*. London: Routledge, 1992.

——. *Postmodern Ethics*. Oxford: Blackwell, 1993.

——. *Life in Fragments: Essays in Postmodern Morality*. Oxford: Blackwell, 1995.

Bell, Daniel. *The Coming of Post-Industrial Society*. New York: Basic Books, 1973.

——. *The Cultural Contradictions of Capitalism*. New York: Basic Books, 1976.

Benhabib, Seyla, 'Epistemologies of Postmodernism: A Rejoinder to Jean-François Lyotard', *New German Critique*, 33 (1984): 103–26.

Benjamin, Andrew, ed. *Judging Lyotard*. London: Routledge, 1992.

Bennington, Geoff. *Lyotard: Writing the Event*. Manchester: Manchester University Press, 1988.

Berman, Marshall. *All That Is Solid Melts Into Air*. London: Verso, 1982.

Berman, R. A. 'The Routinization of Charismatic Modernism and the Problem of Post-Modernity', *Cultural Critique*, 5 (1987): 49–68.

Bernstein, Richard, ed. *Habermas and Modernity*. Cambridge, Mass.: MIT Press, 1986.

——. *The New Constellation: The Ethical–Political Horizons of Modernity/Postmodernity*. Cambridge: Polity, 1991.

Best, Steven, and Kellner, Douglas. *Postmodern Theory: Critical Interrogations*. London: Macmillan, 1991.

Bertens, Hans. *The Idea of the Postmodern: A History*. London: Routledge, 1995.

Blocker, H. Gene. 'Autonomy, Reference and Post-Modern Art'. *British Journal of Aesthetics*, 20:3 (1980): 229–36.

Bové, Paul. 'The Ineluctability of Difference: Scientific Pluralism and the Critical Intelligence'. In J. Arac, ed., *Postmodernism and Politics*, pp. 3–25.

Boyne, Roy, and Attansi, Ali, eds. *Postmodernism and Society*. London: Macmillan, 1990.

Bradbury, Malcolm. 'Modernisms/Postmodernisms'. In Hassan and Hassan, eds., *Innovation/Renovation*, pp. 311–28.

Calinescu, Matei. 'Avant-Garde, Neo-Avant-Garde, Post-Modernism: The Culture of Crisis', *Clio*, 4 (1975): 317–40.

Calinescu, Matei. 'From the One to the Many: Pluralism in Today's Thought'. In Hassan and Hassan, eds., *Innovation/Renovation*, pp. 263–88.

——. *Five Faces of Modernity: Modernism, Avant-garde, Decadence, Kitsch, Post-modernism*. Durham, NC: Duke University Press, 1987.

Callinicos, Alex. 'Poststructuralism, Postmodernism, Postmarxism?' *Theory, Culture and Society*, 2:3 (1985): 85–102.

——. *Against Postmodernism: A Marxist Critique*. Cambridge: Polity Press, 1989.

Chambers, Iain. *Border Dialogues: Journeys in Postmodernity*. London: Routledge, 1990.

Chefdor, Monique, Wachtel, Albert and Quinones, Richard, eds. *Modernism: Challenges and Perspectives*. Urbana and Chicago: University of Illinois Press, 1986.

Chow, R. 'Rereading Mandarin Ducks and Butterflies: A Response to the Postmodern Condition', *Cultural Critique*, 5 (1987): 69–93.

Collins, James. 'Postmodernism and Cultural Practice', *Screen*, 28:2 (1987): 11–27.

Connor, Steven. *Theory and Cultural Value*. Oxford: Blackwell, 1992.

Cook, David and Kroker, Arthur. *The Postmodern Scene: Excremental Culture and Hyper-Aesthetics*. New York: St. Martin's Press, 1986.

Crowther, Paul. *Critical Aesthetics and Postmodernism*. Oxford: Clarendon Press, 1993.

Dallmayr, F. R. 'Democracy and Post-Modernism'. *Human Studies*, 10:1 (1987): 143–70.

Debord, Guy. *Society of the Spectacle*. First published 1967. Trans. Exeter?: Rebel Press, 1987. No translator named.

Derrida, Jacques. *Glas*. Paris: Galilée, 1974.

——. *Spurs: Nietzsche's Styles*. Trans. Barbara Harlow. Chicago: University of Chicago Press, 1979.

——. *Dissemination*. Trans. Barbara Johnson. London: Athlone Press, 1981.

Docherty, Thomas. 'Theory, Enlightenment and Violence: Postmodern Hermeneutic as a Comedy of Errors'. *Textual Practice*, 1: 2 (1987): 192–216.

——. *After Theory: Postmodernism/Postmarxism*. London: Routledge, 1990.

Eagleton, Terry. 'Capitalism, Modernism and Postmodernism'. In *Against the Grain: Essays 1975–1985* London: Verso, 1986, pp. 131–48.

——. *The Illusions of Postmodernism*. Oxford: Basil Blackwell, 1996.

Enzensberger, Hans Magnus. *The Consciousness Industry: On Literature, Politics, and the Media*. New York: Seabury Press, 1974.

Featherstone, Mike. *Consumer Culture and Postmodernism*. London: Sage, 1991.

Fekete, John, ed. *Life After Postmodernism: Essays on Value and Culture*. London: Macmillan, 1988.

Ferraris, Maurizio, *Tracce: Nichilismo, moderno, postmoderno*. Milan: Multhipla, 1983.

——. 'Problemi del postmoderno'. *Cultura e scuola*, 97 (1986): 106–18.

Foster, Hal, ed. *The Anti-Aesthetic: Essays on Postmodern Culture*. Port Townsend: Bay Press, 1985. Reprinted as *Postmodern Culture* (London and Sydney: Pluto Press, 1985).

Frankovits, André, ed. *Seduced and Abandoned: The Baudrillard Scene*. New York: Semiotext(e), 1984.

Fraser, Nancy. 'The French Derrideans: Politicizing Deconstruction or Deconstructing Politics'. *New German Critique*, 33 (1984): 127–54.

Gane, Mike. *Baudrillard: Critical and Fatal Theory*. London: Routledge, 1991.

Giddens, Anthony. 'Modernism and Post-Modernism'. *New German Critique*, 22 (1981): 15–18.

——. *The Consequences of Modernity*. Cambridge: Polity Press, 1990.

Grosz, E. A., et al., eds. *Futur*fall: Excursions Into Postmodernity*. Sydney: Power Institute of Fine Art, 1986.

Haber, Honi Fern. *Beyond Postmodern Politics: Lyotard, Rorty, Foucault*. London: Routledge, 1994.

Habermas, Jürgen. *Legitimation Crisis*. Trans. Thomas McCarthy. London: Heinemann, 1976.

——. 'The French Path to Postmodernity: Bataille Between Eroticism and General Economics'. *New German Critique*, 33 (1984): 79–102.

——. 'Modernity – An Unfinished Project'. In Hal Foster, ed. *Postmodern Culture* (London and Sydney: Pluto Press, 1985), pp. 3–15.

——. *The Philosophical Discourse of Modernity*. Trans. Frederick Lawrence. Cambridge, Mass.: MIT Press, 1987.

Hassan, Ihab. 'Abstractions'. *Diacritics*, 2 (1975): 13–18.

——. *The Right Promethean Fire: Imagination: Science and Cultural Change*. Urban, Ill.: University of Illinois Press, 1980.

——. 'Desire and Dissent in the Postmodern Age'. *Kenyon Review*, 5 (1983): 1–18.

——. *The Postmodern Turn: Essays in Postmodern Theory and Culture*. Columbus: Ohio State University Press, 1987.

——. , and Hassan, Sally, eds. *Innovation/Renovation: New Perspectives on the Humanities*. Madison: University of Wisconsin Press, 1983.

Hjort, A. M. 'Quasi-Una-Amicizia: Adorno and Philosophical Postmodernism'. *New Orleans Review*, 14: 1 (1987): 74–80.

Hoesterey, Ingeborg. 'Die Moderne am Ende? Zu den ästhetischen Positionen von Jürgen Habermas und Clement Greenberg'. *Zeitschrift für Ästhetik und allgemeine Kunstgewissenschaft*, 29:1 (1984): 19–32.

——. ed. *Zeitgeist in Babel: The Postmodernist Controversy*. Bloomington: Indiana University Press, 1991.

Hoffmann, Gerhard and Hornung, Alfred, eds. *Ethics and Aesthetics: The Moral Turn of Postmodernism*. Heidelberg: Universitätsverlag C. Winter, 1996.

Honneth, Axel. 'An Aversion Against the Universal: A Commentary on Lyotard's *Postmodern Condition*'. *Theory, Culture and Society*, 2:3 (1985): 147–57.

Hutcheon, Linda. 'The Politics of Postmodernism: Parody and History'. *Cultural Critique*, 5 (1987): 179–207.

Hutcheon, Linda. *The Politics of Postmodernism*. London: Routledge, 1988.

Huyssen, Andreas. 'The Search for Tradition: Avant-Garde and Postmodernism in the 1970s'. *New German Critique*, 22 (1981): 23–40.

——. 'Mapping the Postmodern'. *New German Critique*, 33 (1984): 5–52.

——. *After the Great Divide: Modernism, Mass Culture, Postmodernism*. Bloomington: Indiana University Press, 1986.

Jameson, Fredric. 'Postmodernism, or the Cultural Logic of Late Capitalism'. *New Left Review*, 146 (1984): 53–92.

——. 'The Politics of Theory: Ideological Positions in the Postmodernism Debate'. *New German Critique*, 33 (1984): 53–66.

——. 'Postmodernism and Consumer Society'. In Hal Foster, ed. *Postmodern Culture* (London and Sydney, 1985), pp. 111–25.

——. *Postmodernism, or, The Cultural Logic of Late Capitalism*. London: Verso, 1991.

——. *The Seeds of Time*. New York: Columbia University Press, 1994.

Jordan, Glenn and Weedon, Chris. *Cultural Politics: Class, Gender, Race and the Postmodern World*. Oxford: Blackwell, 1995.

Kaplan, E. Ann, ed. *Postmodernism and Its Discontents: Theories, Practices*. London: Verso, 1988.

Kariel, Henry S. *The Desperate Politics of Postmodernism*. Amherst, Mass.: University of Massachusetts Press, 1989.

Kearney, R. 'Ethics and the Postmodern Imagination'. *Thought: A Review of Culture and Ideas*, 62: 244 (1987): 39–58.

Kellner, Douglas. *Jean Baudrillard: From Marxism to Postmodernism and Beyond*. Oxford: Polity Press, 1988.

——. *Jean Baudrillard: From Marxism to Postmodernism and Beyond*. Cambridge: Polity, 1989.

——. ed. *Postmodernism/Jameson/Critique*. Washington DC: Maisonneuve Press, 1989.

Köhler, Michael. 'Postmodernismus: Ein begriffsgeschichtlicher Überblick'. *Amerikastudien*, 22: 1 (1977): 19–46.

Kristeva, Julia. 'Postmodernism?' *Bucknell Review*, 25: 2 (1980): 136–41.

Kroker, Arthur and Kroker, Marilouise, eds. *Body Invaders: Sexuality and the Postmodern Condition*. London: Macmillan, 1988.

Kroker, Arthur. *The Possessed Individual: Technology and Postmodernity*. Basingstoke and London: Macmillan, 1992.

Laffey, J. F. 'Cacophonic Rites: Modernism and Postmodernism'. *Historical Reflections*, 14: 1 (1987): 1–32.

Lang, Berel. 'Postmodernism in Philosophy: Nostalgia for the Future, Waiting for the Past'. *New Literary History*, 18: 1 (1986): 209–23.

Lash, Scott. 'Postmodernity and Desire'. *Theory and Society*, 14: 1 (1985): 1–33.

——. *Sociology of Postmodernism*. London: Routledge, 1990.

Lawson, Hilary and Appignanesi, Lisa, eds. *Dismantling Truth: Reality in the Postmodern World*. London: Weidenfeld and Nicolson, 1989.

Lea, Kenneth. ' "In the Most Highly Developed Societies": Lyotard and Post-modernism'. *Oxford Literary Review*, 9: 1–2 (1987): 86–104.

Lemaire, Gérard-George. 'Le spectre du post-modernisme'. *Le Monde Dimanche*, 18 October 1981, xiv.

Levin, David Michael. *The Opening of Vision: Nihilism and the Postmodern Situation*. London and New York: Routledge, 1988.

Lyotard, Jean-François. *Economie Libidinale*. Paris: Minuit, 1974.

——. *The Postmodern Condition: A Report on Knowledge*. First published 1979. Trans. Geoff Bennington and Brian Massumi (Manchester: Manchester University Press, 1984).

——. *Le Postmoderne expliqué aux enfants: Corréspondance 1982–1985*. Paris: Galilée, 1986.

——. 'Notes on Legitimation', trans. Cecile Lindsay. *Oxford Literary Review*, 9: 1–2 (1987): 105–18.

——., and Thébaud, Jean-Loup. *Just Gaming*. Trans. Wlad Godzich. Manchester: Manchester University Press, 1985.

——. *The Differend: Phrases in Dispute*. Trans. Georges Van Den Abbeele. Manchester: Manchester University Press, 1988.

——. *The Lyotard Reader*. Ed. Andrew Benjamin. Oxford: Blackwell, 1989.

——. *The Inhuman: Reflections on Time*. Trans. Geoffrey Bennington and Rachel Bowlby. Cambridge: Polity Press, 1991.

——. *Toward the Postmodern*. Ed. and trans. Robert Harvey and Mark S. Roberts. Atlantic Highlands, NJ and London: Humanities Press, 1993.

——. *Political Writings*. Ed. and trans. Bill Readings and Kevin Paul Geiman. London: UCL Press, 1993.

McGowan, John P. 'Postmodern Dilemmas'. *Southwest Review*, 72: 3 (1987): 357–76.

——. *Postmodernism and Its Critics*. Ithaca and London: Cornell University Press, 1991.

Mandel, E. *Late Capitalism*. London: Verso, 1975.

Melville, Stephen. *Philosophy Beside Itself: On Deconstruction and Modernism*. Manchester: Manchester University Press, 1986.

Merquior, J. G. 'The Spider and the Bee: A Critique of Postmodern Ideology'. *Cuadernos del Norte*, 8: 42 (1987): 2–7.

Michel, Karl Markus. 'Abschied von der Moderne? Eine Komödie'. *Kursbuch*, 73 (1987): 169–96.

Milner, Andrew. 'Postmodernism'. In *Contemporary Cultural Theory: An Introduction* (London: UCL Press, 1994), pp. 135–56.

——, Thomson, Philip and Worth, Chris, eds. *Postmodern Conditions*. Oxford: Berg, 1990.

Montag, Warren. 'What Is At Stake in the Debate on Postmodernism?' In Kaplan, ed., *Postmodernism and Its Discontents*, 88–103.

Murphy, J. W. 'Cultural Manifestations of Postmodernism'. *Philosophy Today*, 30: 4 (1987): 53–8.

Murray, Robin. 'Life After (Henry) Ford'. *Marxism Today* (October 1988): 8–13.

Nichols, Bill. 'The Work of Culture in the Age of Cybernetic Systems'. *Screen*, 29: 1 (1988): 22–46.

Norris, Christopher. 'Narrative Theory or Theory-as-Narrative: The Politics of "Post-Modern" Reason'. In *The Contest of Faculties: Philosophy and Theory After Deconstruction* (London: Methuen, 1985), pp. 19–46.

——. 'Philosophy as a Kind of Narrative: Rorty on Post-Modern Liberal Culture'. In *The Contest of Faculties*, pp. 139–66.

——. 'Against Postmodernism: Derrida, Kant and Nuclear Politics'. *Paragraph*, 9 (1987): 1–30.

——. *What's Wrong With Postmodernism: Critical Theory and the Ends of Philosophy*. Hemel Hempstead: Harvester Wheatsheaf, 1989.

——. *Uncritical Theory: Postmodernism, Intellectuals and the Gulf War*. London: Lawrence and Wishart, 1992.

——. *The Truth About Postmodernism*. Oxford: Basil Blackwell, 1993.

Paden, R. 'Lyotard, Postmodernism and the Crisis in Higher Education'. *International Studies in Philosophy*, 19: 1 (1987): 53–8.

Palmer, Richard E. 'Postmodernity and Hermeneutics'. *Boundary 2*, 5–2 (1977): 363–93.

Pefanis, Julian. *Heterology and the Postmodern: Bataille, Baudrillard, and Lyotard*. Durham, NC: Duke University Press, 1991.

Peper, Jürgen. 'Postmodernismus: Unitary Sensibility?' *Amerikastudien*, 22: 1 (1977): 65–89.

Pfohl, Stephen. *Death at the Parasite Cafe: Social Science (Fictions) and the Postmodern*. Basingstoke and London: Macmillan, 1992.

Radhakrishnan, Rajagoplan. 'The Post-Modern Event and the End of Logocentrism'. *Boundary 2*, 12: 1 (1983): 33–60.

Rajchman, John. 'Postmodernism in a Nominalist Frame: The Emergence and Diffusion of a Cultural Category'. *Flash Art*, 137 (1987): 49–51.

Readings, Bill. *Introducing Lyotard: Art and Politics*. London: Routledge, 1991.

Rojek, Chris and Turner, Bryan S., eds. *Forget Baudrillard?* London: Routledge, 1993.

Rorty, Richard. 'Habermas and Lyotard on Postmodernity'. In Richard Bernstein, ed., *Habermas and Modernity*, pp. 161–76.

——. 'Le Cosmopolitisme sans émancipation: en réponse à Jean-François Lyotard'. *Critique*, 41 (1985): 570–83.

Rose, Margaret A. *The Post-modern and the Post-industrial: A Critical Analysis*. Cambridge: Cambridge University Press, 1991.

Ross, Andrew. *Universal Abandon? The Politics of Postmodernism*. Minneapolis: University of Minnesota Press, 1988.

Ryan, Michael. 'Postmodern Politics'. *Theory, Culture and Society*, 5: 2–3 (1988): 559–76.

Scherpe, K. R. 'Dramatization and Re-Dramatization of the End: The Apocalyptic Consciousness of Modernity and Post-Modernity'. *Cultural Critique*, 5 (1987): 95–129.

Schulte-Sasse, J. 'Modernity and Modernism, Postmodernity and Postmodernism: Framing the Issue'. *Cultural Critique*, 5 (1987): 5–22.

Schusterman, Richard. 'Postmodernist Aestheticism'. *Theory, Culture and Society*, 5: 2–3 (1988): 337–56.

Second of January Group. *After Truth: A Post-Modern Manifesto*. London: Inventions Press, 1986.

Seidman, Steve. *Contested Knowledge: Social Theory in the Postmodern Era*. Oxford: Blackwell, 1994.

Seidman, Steven, and Wagner, David G. *Postmodernism and Social Theory: The Debate Over General Theory*. Oxford: Blackwell, 1992.

Shapiro, Michael J. *Reading the Postmodern Polity: Political Theory as Textual Practice*. Minneapolis: University of Minnesota Press, 1992.

Shevtsova, Maria. 'Intellectuals, Commitment and Political Power: Interview With Jean Baudrillard', *Thesis Eleven*, 10–11 (1984/5), 166–75.

Sim, Stuart. *Beyond Aesthetics: Confrontations With Post-modernism and Post-structuralism*. Hemel Hempstead: Harvester Wheatsheaf, 1992.

Smart, Barry. *Modern Conditions, Postmodern Controversies*. London and New York: Routledge, 1992.

——. *Postmodernity*. London and New York: Routledge, 1993.

Sontag, Susan. 'Against Interpretation'. In Hardwick, Elizabeth, ed., *A Susan Sontag Reader* (Harmondsworth: Penguin, 1983), pp. 95–104.

Squires, Judith, ed. *Principled Positions: Postmodernism and the Rediscovery of Value*. London: Lawrence and Wishart, 1993.

Toulmin, Stephen. 'The Construal of Reality: Criticism in Modern and Postmodern Science'. In W.J.T. Mitchell, ed., *The Politics of Interpretation* (Chicago: University of Chicago Press, 1983), pp. 99–117.

Turner, Bryan S., ed. *Theories of Modernity and Postmodernity*. London: Sage, 1990.

Vattimo, Gianni. *Le avventure della differenza: Che cosa significa pensare dopo Nietzsche e Heidegger*. Milan: Garzanti, 1980.

——. *Al di là del soggetto: Nietzsche, Heidegger e l'ermeneutica*. Milan: Feltrinelli, 1981.

——. *La fine della modernità: Nichilismo ed ermeneutica nella cultura postmoderna*. Milan: Garzanti, 1985.

——. , and Rovatti, Pierre Aldo, eds. *Il pensiero debole*. Milan: Garzanti, 1983.

Wellmer, Albrecht. *The Persistence of Modernity: Essays on Aesthetics, Ethics, and Postmodernism*. Trans. David Midgley. Oxford: Polity, 1991.

White, Stephen K. *Political Theory and Postmodernism*. Cambridge: Cambridge University Press, 1991.

Wolin, Richard. 'Modernism vs. Postmodernism'. *Telos*, 62 (1984/5): 9–29.

Wood, David, ed. *Writing the Future*. London and New York: Routledge, 1990.

Zavarzadeh, Mas'ud and Morton, Donald, eds. *Theory, (Post)Modernity, Opposition*. Washington D.C.: Maisonneuve Press, 1991.

Ziolkowski, Theodore. 'Toward a Post-Modern Aesthetics?' *Mosaic*, 2: 4 (1969): 112–19.

Postmodernism and Law

Boyle, James, ed. *Critical Legal Studies*. New York: New York University Press, 1994.

Carty, Anthony, ed. *Post-Modern Law: Enlightenment, Revolution and the Death of Man*. Edinburgh: Edinburgh University Press, 1990.

Dalton, Clare. 'An Essay in the Deconstruction of Contract Doctrine', *Yale Law Review*, 94 (1985): 999–1114.

Douzinas, Costas, Warrington, Ronnie and McVeigh, Shaun. *Postmodern Jurisprudence: The Law of Text in the Text of Law*. London and New York: Routledge, 1991.

Douzinas, Costas, Goodrich, Peter, and Hachamovitch, Yifat, eds. *Politics, Postmodernity and Critical Legal Studies: The Legality of the Contingent*. London and New York: Routledge, 1994.

Fish, Stanley. *Doing What Comes Naturally: Change, Rhetoric, and the Practice of Theory in Literary and Legal Studies*. Oxford: Clarendon, 1989.

——. *There's No Such Thing as Free Speech and It's a Good Thing, Too*. New York and Oxford: Oxford University Press, 1994.

Fitzpatrick, Peter. *The Mythology of Modern Law*. London and New York: Routledge, 1992.

Frug, Mary Joe. *Postmodern Legal Feminism*. London: Routledge, 1992.

Goodrich, Peter. *Legal Discourse: Studies in Linguistics, Rhetoric and Legal Analysis*. Basingstoke and London: Macmillan, 1987.

——. *Languages of Law*. London: Weidenfeld and Nicolson, 1990.

——. *Oedipus Lex: Psychoanalysis, History, Law*. (Berkeley and London: University of California Press, 1995).

Peller, Gary. 'The Metaphysics of American Law'. In Boyle, ed., *Critical Legal Studies*, pp. 448–503.

Posner, Richard. *The Problems of Jurisprudence*. Cambridge, Mass.: Harvard University Press, 1990.

Unger, Roberto. *Knowledge and Politics*. New York: Free Press, 1975.

——. *The Critical Legal Studies Movement*. Cambridge, Mass.: Harvard University Press, 1986.

Postmodernism and Architecture

Akkerman, J. S. 'Why Classicism? (Observations on Post-Modern Architecture)'. *Harvard Architecture*, 5 (1987): 78–9.

Amery, Colin. *A Celebration of Art and Architecture: The National Gallery Sainsbury Wing*. London: National Gallery Publications, 1991.

Benevole, L. 'Piazze For Everyone'. *Casabella*, 51: 533 (1987): 29–30.

Coleman, A. 'Whither Post-Modern Housing?' *Architectural Design*, 56: 10 (1986): 70–2.

Crook, J. Mordaunt. *The Dilemma of Style: Architectural Ideas From the Picturesque to the Postmodern*. London: John Murray, 1987.

Egenter, N. 'Foundation for an Anthropological Theory of Architecture (What Has the Nestbuilding Behaviour of the Higher Apes To Do With Post-Modern Architecture?). *A and U: Architecture and Urbanism*, 197 (1987): 99–108.

Frampton, Kenneth. 'Towards a Critical Regionalism'. In Foster, Hal, ed., *Postmodern Culture* (London and Sydney: Pluto Press, 1985), pp. 16–30.

——. 'Reflections on Postmodernism and Architecture'. *Cuadernos del Norte*, 8: 42 (1987): 54–7.

Iovine, J. V. 'Die Revision der Moderne: Postmodernism on Display at Williams College'. *Architectural Review*, 175: 7 (1987): 191.

Jencks, Charles. *The Language of Post-Modern Architecture*. 6th edn. London: Academy Editions, 1991.

——. , ed. *Post-Modern Classicism, Architectural Design*, 5–6 (1980).

Jones, P. B. 'Where Do We Stand: A Lecture About Modernism, Post Modernism and the Neglected Possibility of a Responsive Architecture'. *A and U: Architecture and Urbanism*, 198 (1987): 14–30.

Kolb, David. *Postmodern Sophistications: Philosophy, Architecture, and Tradition*. Chicago: University of Chicago Press, 1990.

Portoghesi, Paolo. *After Modern Architecture*. Trans. Meg Shore. New York: Rizzoli, 1982. Revised and updated as *Postmodern: The Architecture of the Postindustrial Society*. New York: Rizzoli, 1983.

Schmerz, M. F. 'Preservation and Postmodernism: A Common Cause'. *Architectural Review*, 175: 7 (1987): 9.

Venturi, Robert. *Complexity and Contradiction in Architecture*. 2nd edn. New York: Museum of Modern Art and Graham Foundation, 1972.

Venturi, Robert, Scott Brown, Denise and Izenour, Steven. *Learning From Las Vegas*. Cambridge, Mass.: MIT Press, 1977.

Postmodernism and Art

Benjamin, Andrew. *Art, Mimesis and the Avant-Garde: Aspects of a Philosophy of Difference*. London: Routledge, 1991.

Burgin, Victor. *The End of Art Theory: Criticism and Postmodernity*. London: Macmillan, 1986.

Carrier, D. 'Michael Kassler: A Painter of Nature in the Era of Postmodernist Art', *Art Magazine*, 61: 9 (1987), 32–3.

Collins, Michael. *Towards Post-Modernism: Design Since 1851*. London: British Museum, 1987.

Crimp, Douglas. *On the Museum's Ruins*. Cambridge, Mass.: MIT Press, 1993.

Davis, Douglas. *Artculture: Essays on the Post-Modern*. New York: Harper and Row, 1977.

——. 'Late Postmodern: The End of Style?' *Art in America*, 75: 6 (1987): 15.

Dilnot, Clive. 'What is the Post-Modern?' [Review of Foster, *Postmodern Culture* and Lyotard, *Postmodern Condition*.] *Art History*, 9: 2 (1986): 245–63.

Foster, Hal. *Recodings: Art, Spectacle, Cultural Politics*. Port Townsend: Bay Press, 1985.

Gottlieb, Carla. *Beyond Modern Art*. New York: E. P. Dutton, 1976.

Greenberg, Clement. *The Notion of 'Post-Modern'*. 4th Sir William Dobell Memorial Lecture, University of Sydney, 1980. Sydney: Bloxham and Chambers, 1980.

——. 'Modern and Postmodern'. *Arts Magazine*, 54 (1980): 64–6.

Jencks, Charles, ed. *The Post-Avant-Garde: Painting in the Eighties*. London: Academy Editions, 1987.

Kramer, Hilton. 'Postmodern: Art and Culture in the 1980s'. *The New Criterion*, 1: 1 (1982): 36–42.

——. *The Revenge of the Philistines: Art and Culture, 1972–1984*. New York: Free Press, 1985.

Krauss, Rosalind. *The Originality of the Avant-Garde and Other Modernist Myths*. Cambridge, Mass.: MIT Press, 1985.

Kuspit, Donald. *Signs of Psyche in Modern and Postmodern Art*. Cambridge: Cambridge University Press, 1993.

Levin, Kim. 'Farewell to Modernism'. *Arts*, 54 (1979): 90–2.

Lovejoy, Margot. *Postmodern Currents: Art and Artists in the Age of Electronic Media*. Ann Arbor: UMI Research Press, 1989.

McEvilley, Thomas. *The Exile's Return: Towards a Redefinition of Painting for the Post-Modern Era*. Cambridge: Cambridge University Press, 1993.

Melville, Stephen, 'Notes on the Reemergence of Allegory, the Forgetting of Modernism, the Necessity of Rhetoric and the Conditions of Publicity in Art and Criticism'. *October*, 19 (1981): 55–92.

Melville, Stephen, and Readings, Bill, eds. *Vision and Textuality*. Basingstoke and London: Macmillan, 1995.

Nairne, Sandy, with Dunlop, Geoff and Wyver, John. *State of the Art: Ideas and Images in the 1980s*. London: Chatto and Windus, 1987.

Oliva, Achille Bonito. 'The International Trans-Avantgarde'. *Flash Art*, 104 (1982): 36–43.

Orton, Fred. *Figuring Jasper Johns*. London: Reaktion, 1994.

Owens, Craig. 'The Allegorical Impulse: Toward a Theory of Postmodernism', Part 1: *October*, 12 (1980): 67–86. Part 2: *October*, 13 (1980): 59–80.

Perloff, Marjorie. *The Futurist Moment: Avant-Garde, Avant-Guerre and the Language of Rupture*. Chicago and London: University of Chicago Press, 1986.

Phillipson, Michael. *Painting, Language and Modernity*. London: Routledge and Kegan Paul, 1985.

Sandler, Irving. 'Modernism, Revisionism, Pluralism, and Post-Modernism'. *Art Journal*, 40 (1980): 345–7.

Spalding, Frances. 'Simon Watney and His Friends in a Postmodernist Age'. *Burlington Magazine*, 129: 1009 (1987): 251–2.

Tagg, John. 'Postmodernism and the Born-Again Avant-Garde'. *Block* (1985/6): 3–7.

Thackara, John, ed. *Design After Modernism: Beyond the Object*. New York and London: Thames and Hudson, 1988.

Watney, Simon. 'Roger Fry and His Friends in a Postmodern Age'. *Burlington Magazine*, 129: 1009 (1987): 250–1.

Wolfe, Tom. *The Painted Word*. New York: Bantam Books, 1976.

Postmodernism and Photography

Abbas, M. A. 'Photography/Writing/Postmodernism'. *Minnesota Review*, n.s. 23 (1984): 91–111.

Andre, Linda. 'The Politics of Postmodern Photography'. *Minnesota Review*, n.s. 23 (1984): 17–35.

Burgin, Victor, ed. *Thinking Photography*. London: Macmillan, 1982.

Crimp, Douglas. 'The Photographic Activity of Postmodernism'. *October*, 15 (1980): 91–100.

Godeau, Abigail Solomon. 'Winning the Game When the Rules Have Been Changed: Art Photography and Postmodernism'. *Screen*, 25: 6 (1984): 88–102.

——. 'Living With Contradictions: Critical Practices in the Age of Supply-Side Aesthetics'. *Screen*, 28: 3 (1987): 2–22.

Squiers, Carol, ed. *The Critical Image: Essays on Contemporary Photography*. Seattle: Bay Press, 1990.

Postmodernism and Literature

Adams, Robert Martin. 'What Was Modernism?' *Hudson Review*, 31 (1978): 29–33.

Alexander, Marguerite. *Flights From Realism: Themes and Strategies in Postmodernist British and American Fiction*. London: Edward Arnold, 1990.

Allen, Donald and Butterick, George E. *The Postmoderns: The New American Poetry Revised*. New York: Grove Press, 1982.

Alpert, Barry. 'Post-Modern Oral Poetry: Buckminster Fuller, John Cage and David Antin'. *Boundary* 2, 3 (1975): 665–82.

Alter, Robert. *Partial Magic: The Novel as a Self-Conscious Genre*. Berkeley: University of California Press, 1975.

——. 'The Self-Conscious Moment: Reflections on the Aftermath of Modernism'. *TriQuarterly*, 33 (1975): 209–30.

Altieri, Charles. 'From Symbolist Thought to Immanence: The Ground of Postmodern American Poetics'. *Boundary* 2, 1 (1973): 605–41.

——. 'Postmodernism: A Question of Definition'. *Par Rapport*, 2 (1979): 87–100.

Altieri, Charles. 'The Postmodernism of David Antin's *Tuning'*. *College English*, 48:1 (1986): 9–25.

Andrews, Bruce, and Bernstein, Charles. *The L=A=N=G=U=A=G=E Book*. Carbondale and Edwardsville: Southern Illinois University Press, 1984.

Antin, David. 'Modernism and Postmodernism: Approaching the Present in American Poetry'. *Boundary* 2, 1 (1972): 98–133.

Bakhtin, Mikhail. *The Dialogic Imagination*. Ed. Michael Holquist, trans. Cary Emerson and Michael Holquist. Austin: University of Texas Press, 1981.

Barry, T. F. 'Postmodern Longings for the Static Moment: On Recent Handke Criticism'. *German Quarterly*, 60: 1 (1987): 88–98.

Barth, John. 'The Literature of Exhaustion'. Repr. in Bradbury, Malcolm, ed. *The Novel Today: Contemporary Writers on Modern Fiction*. Glasgow: Fontana Press, 1977.

——. 'The Literature of Replenishment: Postmodernist Fiction'. *Atlantic Monthly*, 245: 1 (1980): 65–71.

Beebe, Maurice. 'What Modernism Was'. *Journal of Modern Literature*, 3 (1974): 1065–84.

Benison, Jonathan. 'Science Fiction and Postmodernity'. In *Postmodernism and the Re-Reading of Modernity*, eds. Francis Barker, Peter Hulme and Margaret Iversen (Manchester: Manchester University Press, 1992), pp. 138–58.

Bertens, Hans and D'haen, Theo, eds. *Postmodern Fiction in Europe and the Americas*. ('Postmodern Studies', 1). Amsterdam and Atlanta, GA: Rodopi, 1988.

——. *History and Post-War Writing*. ('Postmodern Studies', 3). Amsterdam and Atlanta, GA: Rodopi, 1990.

——. *Postmodern Characters: A Study of Characterization in British and American Postmodern Fiction*. ('Postmodern Studies', 4). Amsterdam and Atlanta, GA: Rodopi, 1991.

——. *Neo-Realism in Contemporary American Fiction*. ('Postmodern Studies', 5). Amsterdam and Atlanta, GA: Rodopi, 1992.

——. *Postmodern Fiction in Canada*. ('Postmodern Studies', 6). Amsterdam and Atlanta, GA: Rodopi, 1992.

——. *British Postmodern Fiction*. ('Postmodern Studies', 7). Amsterdam and Atlanta, GA: Rodopi, 1993.

——. *Liminal Postmodernisms: The Postmodern, The (Post-)Colonial, and the (Post-)Feminist*. ('Postmodern Studies', 8). Amsterdam and Atlanta, GA: Rodopi, 1994.

——. *Narrative Turns and Minor Genres in Postmodernism*. ('Postmodern Studies', 11). Amsterdam and Atlanta, GA: Rodopi, 1995.

Blasing, Mutlu Konuk. *Politics and Form in Postmodern Poetry: O'Hara, Bishop, Ashbery and Merrill*. Cambridge: Cambridge University Press, 1996.

Broderick, Damien. *Reading By Starlight: Postmodern Science Fiction*. London: Routledge, 1995.

Brooker, Peter. *New York Fictions: Modernity, Postmodernism, the New Modern*. London: Longman, 1995.

Bukatman, Scott. *Terminal Identity: The Virtual Subject in Postmodern Science Fiction*. Durham, NC and London: Duke University Press, 1993.

Burke, Ruth E. *The Games of Poetics: Ludic Criticism and Postmodern Fiction*. New York: P. Lang, 1994.

Butler, Christopher. *After the Wake: An Essay on the Contemporary Avant-Garde*. Oxford: Oxford University Press, 1980.

Butterick, George. 'Editing Postmodern Texts'. *Sulfur*, 11 (1984): 113–40.

Cage, John. *Empty Words*. Middletown: Wesleyan University Press, 1981.

Calinescu, Matei and Fokkema, Douwe, eds. *Exploring Postmodernism*. Amsterdam and Philadelphia: John Benjamins, 1988.

Caramello, Charles. *Silverless Mirrors: Book, Self and Postmodern American Fiction*. Tallahassee: Florida University Press, 1983.

Clausen, Christopher. 'A Comment on the Postmodernism of David Antin'. *College English*, 48: 5 (1987): 11–27.

Connor, Steven. *Samuel Beckett: Repetition, Theory and Text*. Oxford: Basil Blackwell, 1988.

——. 'Reading: The *Contretemps*'. In *Strategies of Reading: Dickens and After*, *Yearbook of English Studies*, 26 (1996): 232–48.

Couturier, Maurice. *Representation and Performance in Postmodern Fiction*. Montpellier: Université Paul Valery, 1983.

Cornwell, Neil. *The Literary Fantastic: From Gothic to Postmodernism*. London: Harvester Wheatsheaf, 1990.

Cunningham, Valentine. *In the Reading Gaol: Postmodernity, Texts and History*. Oxford: Blackwell, 1994.

Dear, Glenn. *Postmodern Canadian Fiction and the Rhetoric of Authority*. Montreal: McGill–Queen's University Press, 1994.

Ebert, Teresa L. 'The Convergence of Postmodern Innovative Fiction and Science Fiction', *Poetics Today*, 1 (1980), 91–104.

Eco, Umberto. 'Postmodernism, Irony, and the Enjoyable'. In *Postscript to The Name of the Rose*. New York: Harcourt Brace Jovanovitch, 1984.

Elam, Diane. *Romancing the Postmodern*. London: Routledge, 1992.

Federman, Raymond, ed. *Surfiction: Fiction Now and Tomorrow*. Chicago: Swallow Press, 1975, 2nd edn, 1981.

——. 'Fiction Today or the Pursuit of Non-Knowledge'. *Humanities in Society*, 1:2 (1978): 115–31.

Ferrer, Daniel. 'ModoPost: A Postmodern Reconsideration of the *Avant-Texte*'. In *Writing the Future*, ed. David Wood (London and New York: Routledge, 1990), pp. 30–6.

Fiedler, Leslie. 'Cross That Border – Close That Gap'. First published, 1969, repr. in *The Collected Essays of Leslie Fiedler*, Vol. 2. (New York: Stein and Day, 1971), pp. 461–85.

Fokkema, Douwe, ed. *Literary History, Modernism, and Postmodernism*. Amsterdam and Philadelphia: John Benjamins, 1984.

Fokkema, Douwe and Bertens, Hans, eds. *Approaching Postmodernism*. Amsterdam and Philadelphia: John Benjamins, 1986.

Gass, William H. *Fiction and the Figures of Life*. New York: Alfred A. Knopf, 1970.

Graff, Gerald. 'The Myth of the Postmodernist Breakthrough'. *Tri-Quarterly*, 26 (1973): 383–417.

——. 'Babbit at the Abyss: The Social Context of Postmodern American Fiction'. *TriQuarterly*, 33 (1975): 305–37.

Hafrey, Leigh. 'The Gilded Cage: Postmodernism and Beyond'. *TriQuarterly*, 56 (1983): 126–36.

Hartman, Geoffrey. *Criticism in the Wilderness: The Study of Literature Today*. New Haven: Yale University Press, 1980.

——. *Saving the Text: Literature/Derrida/Philosophy*. Baltimore Md. and London: Johns Hopkins University Press, 1981.

Hassan, Ihab. *The Dismemberment of Orpheus: Toward a Postmodern Literature*. New York: Oxford University Press, 1982.

——. *Paracriticisms: Seven Speculations of the Times*. Urbana: University of Illinois Press, 1975.

Hayman, David. 'Double-distancing: An Attribute of the "Post-Modern" Avant-Garde'. *Novel*, 12 (1978): 33–47.

Hoffmann, Gerhard. 'The Fantastic in Fiction: Its "Reality" Status, Its Historical Development and Its Transformations in Postmodern Narration'. *REAL (Yearbook of Research in English and American Literature)*, 1 (1982): 267–364.

——. 'Social Criticism and the Deformation of Man: Satire, the Grotesque and Comic Nihilism in the Modern and Postmodern American Novel'. *Amerikastudien*, 28 (1983): 141–203.

Hoffman, Gerhard, Horning, Alfred and Kunow, Rüdiger. ' "Modern," "Postmodern," and "Contemporary" as Criteria for the Analysis of 20th-Century Literature'. *Amerikastudien*, 22 (1977): 19–46.

Howe, Irving. 'Mass Society and Post-Modern Fiction'. *Partisan Review*, 26 (1959): 420–36.

——. *The Decline of the New*. New York: Harcourt, Brace, and World, 1970.

Hutcheon, Linda. *Narcissistic Narrative: The Metafictional Paradox*. Waterloo, Ont.: Wilfred Laurier University Press, 1980.

——. 'Beginning to Theorize Postmodernism'. *Textual Practice*, 1: 1 (1987): 10–31.

——. 'The Politics of Postmodernism: Parody and History'. *Cultural Critique*, 5 (1987): 179–207.

——. *A Poetics of Postmodernism: History, Theory, Fiction*. (New York and London: Routledge, 1988.

——. *The Canadian Postmodern: A Study of Contemporary English–Canadian Fiction*. Toronto: Oxford University Press, 1988.

Kafalenos, Emma. 'Fragments of a Partial Discourse on Roland Barthes and the Postmodern Mind'. *Chicago Review*, 35 (1985): 72–94.

Klinkowitz, Jerome. *Literary Disruptions: The Making of a Post-Contemporary American Fiction*. Urbana: University of Illinois Press, 1975, 2nd edn, 1980.

Klinkowitz, Jerome and Knowlton, James. *Peter Handke and the Postmodern Transformation: The Goalie's Journey Home*. Columbia: University of Missouri Press, 1983.

Kutnik, Jerzy. *The Novel as Performance: The Fiction of Ronald Sukenick and Raymond Federman*. Carbondale, Ill.: Southern Illinois University Press, 1986.

LeClair, Tom and McCaffery, Larry, eds. *Anything Can Happen: Interviews With American Novelists*. Urbana: University of Illinois Press, 1983.

Lee, Alison. *Realism and Power: Postmodern British Fiction*. London: Routledge, 1990.

Lodge, David. *The Modes of Modern Writing: Metaphor, Metonymy and the Typology of Modern Literature*. London: Edward Arnold, 1977.

——. 'Modernism, Antimodernism, Postmodernism'. In *Working With Structuralism* (London: Routledge and Kegan Paul, 1981), pp. 3–16.

Lumsden, C. J. 'The Gene and the Sign: Giving Structure to Post-modernity', *Semiotica*, 62: 3–4 (1986): 191–206.

McCaffery, Larry. *The Metafictional Muse: The Works of Robert Coover, Donald Barthelme and William H. Gass*. Pittsburgh: University of Pittsburgh Press, 1982.

McConnell, Frank. 'The Corpse of the Dragon: Notes on Postromantic Fiction'. *TriQuarterly*, 33 (1975): 273–304.

McCaffery, Larry. *Storming the Reality Studio: A Casebook of Cyberpunk and Postmodern Fiction*. Durham, NC: Duke University Press, 1992.

McHale, Brian. 'Modernist Reading, Postmodernist Text: The Case of *Gravity's Rainbow*'. *Poetics Today*, 1: 1–2 (1982): 85–110.

——. 'Writing About Postmodern Writing'. *Poetics Today*, 3:3 (1982): 211–27.

——. *Postmodernist Fiction*. New York and London: Methuen, 1987.

——. *Constructing Postmodernism*. London and New York: Routledge, 1992.

Malmgren, Carl Darryl. *Fictional Space in the Modernist and Postmodernist American Novel*. Lewisburg Pa.: Bucknell University Press, 1985.

Maltby, Paul. *Dissident Postmodernists: Barthelme, Coover, Pynchon*. Philadelphia: University of Pennsylvania Press, 1991.

Marshall, Brenda K. *Teaching the Postmodern: Fiction and Theory*. New York and London: Routledge, 1992.

Mazzaro, Jerome. *Postmodern American Poetry*. Urbana: University of Illinois Press, 1980.

Morrissette, Bruce. 'Post-Modern Generative Fiction: Novel and Film'. *Critical Inquiry*, 2 (1975): 253–62.

Nägele, Rainer. 'Modernism and Postmodernism: The Margins of Articulation'. *Studies in Twentieth-Century Literature*, 5: 1 (1980): 5–25.

Newman, Charles. *The Post-Modern Aura: The Act of Fiction in an Age of Inflation.* Evanston, Ill.: Northwestern University Press, 1985.

Olsen, Lance. 'Deconstructing the Balzacian Mode: Postmodern Fantasy'. *Extrapolation*, 28: 1 (1987) 45–51.

——. *Ellipse of Uncertainty: An Introduction to Postmodern Fantasy.* London: Greenwood Press, 1987.

——. *Circus of the Mind in Motion: Postmodernism and the Comic Vision.* Detroit, Mich.: Wayne State University Press, 1990.

Olson, Charles. 'The Act of Writing in the Context of Post-Modern Man', *Olson: The Journal of the Charles Olson Archives*, 2 (1974): 28.

Pasanen, O. 'Postmodernism: An Interview With William Spanos'. *Arbeiten aus Anglistik und Amerikanistik*, 11: 2 (1986); 195–209.

Paterson, Janet M. *Moments postmodernes dans le roman québecois.* Edition augmentée. Ottowa: Presse de l'Université d'Ottowa, 1993.

Perloff, Marjorie. *The Poetics of Indeterminacy: Rimbaud to Cage.* Princeton NJ: Princeton University Press, 1981.

——. *The Dance of the Intellect: Studies in the Poetry of the Pound Tradition.* Cambridge, Cambridge University Press, 1986.

——. *Poetic License: Essays on Modernist and Postmodernist Lyric.* Evanston, Ill.: Northwestern University Press, 1990.

Pfeil, Fred. *Another Tale to Tell: Politics and Narrative in Postmodern Culture.* London: Verso, 1990.

Poirier, Richard. *The Performing Self: Compositions and Decompositions in the Languages of Contemporary Life.* New York: Oxford University Press, 1971.

Pinsker, Sanford. '*Ulysses* and the Post-Modern Temper'. *Midwest Quarterly*, 15 (1974): 406–16.

Pütz, Manfred. 'The Struggle of the Postmodern: Books on a New Concept in Criticism'. *Kritikon Litterarum*, 2 (1973): 225–37.

Pütz, Manfred and Freese, Peter, eds. *Postmodernism in American Literature: A Critical Anthology.* Darmstadt: Thesen, 1984.

Rabaté, Jean-Michel. ' "Rien N'Aura Eu Lieu Que Le Lieu": Mallarmé and Postmodernism'. In *Writing the Future*, ed. David Wood (London and New York: Routledge, 1990), pp. 37–54.

Readings, Bill and Schaber, Bennet, eds. *Postmodernism Across the Ages: Essays For A Postmodernity That Wasn't Born Yesterday.* Syracuse NY: Syracuse University Press, 1993.

Robinson, Alan. 'James Fenton's "Narratives": Some Reflections on Postmodernism'. *Critical Quarterly*, 29:1 (1987): 81–93.

Rother, James. 'Parafiction: The Adjacent Universes of Barth, Barthelme, Pynchon, and Nabokov'. *Boundary* 2, 5 (1976): 21–43.

Salami, Mahmoud. *John Fowles's Fiction and The Poetics of Postmodernism.* Rutherford: Fairleigh Dickinson University Press, 1992.

Schmitz, Neil. 'Gertrude Stein as Postmodernist: The Rhetoric of *Tender Buttons'*. *Journal of Modern Literature*, 3 (1974): 1203–18.

Scholes, Robert. *Structural Fabulation: An Essay on Fiction of the Future*. Notre Dame, Ind.: University of Notre Dame Press, 1975.

——. *Fabulation and Metafiction*. Urbana: University of Illinois Press, 1979.

Schwartz, R. A. 'Postmodernist Baseball'. *Modern Fiction Studies*, 33: 1 (1987): 35–49.

Spanos, William V. 'The Detective and the Boundary: Some Notes on the Postmodern Literary Imagination'. *Boundary* 2, 1 (1972): 147–68.

——. 'De-struction and the Question of Postmodernist Literature: Toward a Definition'. *Par Rapport*, 2 (1979): 107–22.

——, ed. *Martin Heidegger and the Question of Literature: Toward a Postmodern Literary Hermeneutics*. Bloomington: Indiana University Press, 1979.

Stark, John O. *The Literature of Exhaustion: Borges, Nabokov, and Barth*. Durham, NC: Duke University Press, 1974.

Stark, Michael. ' "The Murder of Modernism": Some Observations on Research Into Expressionism and the Post-Modernism Debate'. In Richard Sheppard, ed. *Expressionism in Focus* (Blairgowrie: Lochee Publications, 1987), pp. 27–45.

Szegedy-Maszák, Mihály. 'Postmodernism in Hungarian Literature: Péter Esterházy's "Agnes" '. *Zeitschrift für Kulturaustausch*, 34 (1984): 150–6.

Tani, Stefano. *The Doomed Detective: The Contribution of the Detective Novel to Postmodern American and Italian Fiction*. Carbondale and Edwardsville: Southern Illinois University Press, 1984.

Tarn, Nathaniel. 'Fresh Frozen Fenix: Random Notes on the Sublime, the Beautiful, and the Ugly in the Postmodern Era'. *New Literary History*, 16:2 (1985): 417–26.

Thiher, Allen. *Words in Reflection: Modern Language Theory and Postmodern Fiction*. Chicago: University of Chicago Press, 1984.

Thompson, Jon. *Fiction, Crime, and Empire: Clues to Modernity and Postmodernism*. Urbana.: University of Illinois Press, 1993.

Updike, John. 'Modernist, Postmodernist, What Will They Think of Next?' *The New Yorker*, 10 September 1984: 136–42.

Varsava, Jerry A. *Postmodern Fiction, Mimesis, and the Reader*. Tallahassee: Florida State University Press, 1990.

Vizenour, Gerald, ed. *Narrative Chance: Postmodern Discourse on Native American Indian Literatures*. Albuquerque: University of New Mexico Press, 1989.

Wasson, Richard. 'Notes on a New Sensibility'. *Partisan Review*, 36 (1969), 460–77.

——. 'From Priest to Prometheus: Culture and Criticism in the Post-Modern Period'. *Journal of Modern Literature*, 3 (1974): 1188–1202.

Waugh, Patricia. *Metafiction: The Theory and Practice of Self-Conscious Fiction*. London and New York: Methuen, 1984.

——. *Feminine Fictions: Revisiting the Postmodern*. London and New York: Routledge, 1989.

Waugh, Patricia. *Practising Postmodernism Reading Modernism*. London: Edward Arnold, 1992.

Wilde, Alan. *Horizons of Assent: Modernism, Postmodernism and the Ironic Imagination*. Baltimore and London: Johns Hopkins University Press, 1981.

——. 'Strange Displacements of the Ordinary: Apple, Elkin, Barthelme, and the Problem of the Excluded Middle'. *Boundary* 2, 10 (1982): 177–99.

Witschi, Beat. *Glasgow Urban Writing and Postmodernism: A Study of Alisdair Gray's Fiction*. Frankfurt am Main: P. Lang, 1991.

Zadworna-Fjellestad, Danuta, and Björk, Lennart, eds. *Criticism in the Twilight Zone: Postmodern Perspectives in Literature and Politics*. Stockholm: Almqvist and Wiksell, 1990.

Zurbrugg, Nicholas. *The Parameters of Postmodernism*. London: Routledge, 1993.

Postmodernism and Performance

Auslander, Philip. 'Towards a Concept of the Political in Postmodern Theatre'. *Theatre Journal*, 39: 1 (1987): 20–34.

Auslander, Philip. *Presence and Resistance: Postmodernism and Politics in Contemporary American Performance*. Ann Arbor: University of Michigan Press, 1992.

Benamou, Michel and Carmello, Charles. *Performance in Postmodern Culture*. Milwaukee: Centre for Twentieth-Century Studies, 1977.

Birrenger, Johannes. *Theatre, Theory, Postmodernism*. Bloomington: Indiana University Press, 1991.

Blau, Herbert. *Bloodied Thought: Occasions of Theatre*. New York: Performing Arts Journal Publications, 1982.

——. *Take Up the Bodies: Theater at the Vanishing Point*. Urbana: University of Illinois Press, 1982.

——. 'The Remission of Play'. In Hassan Ihab and Hassan Sally, eds. *Innovation/Renovation: New Perspectives on the Humanities* (Madison: University of Wisconsin Press, 1983), pp. 161–88.

——. 'Ideology and Performance'. *Theatre Journal*, 35: 4 (1983): 441–60.

——. *The Eye of Prey: Subversions of the Postmodern*. Bloomington: Indiana University Press, 1987.

Brater, Enoch and Cohn, Ruby, eds. *Around the Absurd: Essays on Modern and Postmodern Drama*. Ann Arbor: University of Michigan Press, 1990.

Campbell, Patrick, ed. *Analysing Performance: A Critical Reader*. Manchester: Manchester University Press, 1996.

Connor, Steven. 'The Flag on the Road: Bruce Springsteen and the Live'. *New Formations*, 3 (1987): 129–37.

——. 'Postmodern Performance'. In Campbell, ed. *Analysing Performance*, pp. 107–24.

Corrigan, Robert W. 'The Search for New Endings: The Theatre in Search of a Fix, Part III'. *Theatre Journal*, 36: 1 (1984): 153–63.

Derrida, Jacques. 'The Theater of Cruelty and the Closure of Representation'. In *Writing and Difference*, trans. Alan Bass (London: Routledge and Kegan Paul, 1978), pp. 169–95.

——. 'La Parole Soufflée'. In *Writing and Difference*, pp. 232–50.

Davy, Kate. *Richard Foreman and the Ontological-Hysteric Theater*. Ann Arbor: UMI Research Press, 1981.

Dort, Bernard. 'The Liberated Performance'. Trans. Barbara Kerslake. *Modern Drama*, 25:1 (1982): 60–8.

Durand, Régis. 'Theatre/SIGNS/Performance: On Some Transformations of the Theatrical and the Theoretical'. In Hassan Ihab and Hassan Sally, eds, *Innovation/Renovation: New Perspective on the Humanities* (Madison: University of Wisconsin Press, 1983), pp. 211–24.

Féral, Josette. 'Performance and Theatricality: The Subject Demystified'. Trans. Terese Lyons. *Modern Drama*, 25: 1 (1982): 170–81.

Forte, Jeanie. 'Women's Performance Art: Feminism and Postmodernism'. *Theatre Journal*, 40: 2 (1988): 217–35.

Fuchs, Elinor. 'The Theatre After Derrida', *Performing Arts Journal*, 26/7 (1985), 163–73.

Kaye, Nick. *Postmodernism and Performance*. Basingstoke and London: Macmillan, 1994.

Kershaw, Baz. 'The Politics of Performance in a Postmodern Age'. In Campbell, ed. *Analysing Performance*, pp. 133–52.

Leabhart, Thomas. *Modern and Post-Modern Mime*. Basingstoke and London: Macmillan, 1989.

Marranca, Bonnie, *Theatrewritings*. New York: Performing Arts Journal Publications, 1984.

Mehta, Xerxes. 'Some Versions of Performance Art'. *Theatre Journal*, 36:1 (1984): 165–98.

Pavis, Patrice. 'The Classical Heritage of Modern Drama: The Case of Postmodern Theatre'. Trans. Loren Kruger. *Modern Drama*, 29: 1 (1986): 1–22.

Pontbriand, Chantal. ' "The eye finds no fixed point on which to rest . . . " '. Trans. C. R. Parsons. *Modern Drama*, 25: 1 (1982): 154–62.

Savran, D. *The Wooster Group, 1975–1985: Breaking the Rules*. New York: Theater Communications Group, 1988.

Sayre, Henry. 'The Object of Performance: Aesthetics in the Seventies'. *Georgia Review*, 37: 1 (1983): 169–88.

Schechner, Richard. 'News, Sex, and Performance Theory'. In Hassan Ihab and Hassan Sally, eds, *Innovation/Renovation: New Perspectives on the Humanities* (Madison: University of Wisconsin Press), pp. 189–210.

——. *Performative Circumstances From the Avant-Garde to Ramlila*. Calcutta: Seagull Books, 1983.

Simard, Rodney. *Postmodern Drama: Contemporary Playwrights in America and Britain*. Lanham, Md.: University Presses of America/American Theatre Association, 1984.

Ulmer, Gregory L. *Applied Grammatology: Post(e)-Pedagogy from Jacques Derrida to Joseph Beuys*. Baltimore Md. and London: Johns Hopkins University Press, 1985.

Wright, Elizabeth. *Postmodern Brecht: A Re-Presentation*. London: Routledge, 1988.

Postmodern Dance

Banes, Sally *Terpsichore in Sneakers: Post-Modern Dance*. Boston: Houghton Mifflin, 1980.
——. *Writing Dancing in the Age of Postmodernism*. Hanover, NH: Wesleyan University Press/University Press of New England, 1994.
Briginshaw, Valerie. 'Postmodern Dance and the Politics of Resistance'. In Campbell, Patrick, ed., *Analysing Performance* (Manchester: Manchester University Press, 1996), pp. 125–32.
——. *Out of Line: The Story of New British Dance*. London: Dance Books, 1992.
Rainer, Yvonne. 'A Quasi Survey of Some "Minimalist" Tendencies in the Quantitatively Minimal Dance Activity Midst the Plethora, or an Analysis of *Trio A*'. In *Work 1961–73* (Halifax, Nova Scotia: Press of the Nova Scotia College of Art and Design; New York: New York University Press, 1974), pp. 63–9.
——. 'Some Retrospective Notes on a Dance for 10 People and 12 Mattresses Called "Parts of Some Sextets," Performed at the Wadsworth Atheneum, Hartford, Connecticut, and Judson Memorial Church, New York, in March 1965', *Tulane Drama Review*, 10 (1965): 168–78.
Thomas, H. *Dance, Gender and Culture*. Basingstoke and London: Macmillan, 1993.

Postmodernism and Music

Attali, Jacques. *Noise: The Political Economy of Music*. Trans. Brian Massumi. Manchester: Manchester University Press, 1985.
Boone, Charles. 'Has Modernist Music Lost Power?'. In Hoesterey, Ingeborg, ed. *Zeitgeist in Babel: The Postmodernist Controversy* (Bloomington: Indiana University Press, 1991), pp. 207–15.
Brett, Philip, Thomas, Gary C., and Wood, Elizabeth, eds. *Queering the Pitch: The New Gay and Lesbian Musicology*. New York and London: Routledge, 1994.
Clément, Catherine. *Opera, or the Undoing of Woman*. Trans. Betsy Wing. Minneapolis: University of Minnesota Press, 1988.
Dunn, Leslie C. and Jones, Nancy A., eds. *Embodied Voices: Representing Female Vocality in Western Culture*. Cambridge: Cambridge University Press, 1994.
Frith, Simon and Goodwin, Andrew, eds. *On Record: Rock, Pop and the Written Word*. New York: Pantheon, 1990.
Hermand Jost. 'Avant-Garde, Modern, Postmodern: The Music (Almost) Nobody Wants To Hear'. In Hoestery, Ingeborg, ed. *Zeitgeist in Babel: The Postmodernist Controversy* (Bloomington: Indiana University Press, 1991), pp. 192–206.

Kramer, Lawrence. *Classical Music and Postmodernist Knowledge*. Berkeley: University of California Press, 1995.

Lindenberger, Herbert. 'From Opera to Postmodernity: On Genre, Style, Institutions'. *Genre*, 20: 3–4 (1987): 259–84.

Lipsitz, George. *Dangerous Crossroads: Popular Music, Postmodernism, and the Poetics of Place*. London: Verso, 1994.

McClary, Susan. *Feminine Endings: Music, Gender, and Sexuality*. Minneapolis: University of Minnesota Press, 1991.

McNeilly, Kevin. 'Ugly Beauty: John Zorn and the Politics of Postmodern Music', *Postmodern Culture*, 5: 2 (1995).
http://www.village.virginia.edu/pmc/issue.195/mcneilly.195. html

Miller, Simon, ed. *The Last Post: Music After Modernism*. Manchester: Manchester University Press, 1993.

Potter, K. 'Robert Ashley and Post-Modernist Opera'. *Opera*, 38: 4 (1987): 388–94.

Postmodern TV and Film

Baudrillard, Jean. *The Evil Demon of Images*. Trans. Paul Foss and Paul Patton. Sydney: Power Institute of Fine Art, 1985.

Boyd-Bowman, Susan. 'Imaginary Cinematheques: The Postmodern Programmes of INA'. *Screen*, 28: 2 (Spring, 1987): 103–17.

Denzin, Norman. '*Blue Velvet*: Postmodern Contradictions'. *Theory, Culture and Society*, 5: 2–3 (1988): 461–73.

——. *Images of Postmodern Society: Social Theory and Contemporary Cinema*. London: Sage, 1991.

Eco, Umberto. 'A Guide to the Neo-Television of the 1980s'. *Framework*, 25 (1984): 18–25.

Friedberg, Anne. *Window Shopping: Cinema and the Postmodern*. Berkeley: University of California Press, 1993.

Frith, Simon, Goodwin, Andrew, and Grossberg, Lawrence, eds. *Sound and Vision: The Music Television Reader*. London: Unwin and Hyman, 1991.

Gitlin, Todd, ed. *Watching Television*. New York: Pantheon, 1986.

Grossberg, Lawrence. 'The In-Difference of Television'. *Screen*, 28: 2 (1987): 28–46.

Jameson, Fredric. 'On Magic Realism in film'. *Critical Inquiry*, 12 (1986): 301–25.

——. 'Reading Without Interpretation: Postmodernism and the Video-Text'. In Derek Attridge, Alan, Durant, Nigel, Fabb, and Colin McCabe, eds, *The Linguistics of Writing: Arguments Between Language and Literature* (Manchester: Manchester University Press, 1987), pp. 199–233.

Kaplan, E. Ann. *Rocking Around the Clock: Music Television, Postmodernism and Consumer Culture*. London and New York: Methuen, 1987.

———. 'Feminism(s)/postmodernism(s): MTV and Alternative Women's Videos and Performance Art'. In Campbell, Patrick, ed. *Analysing Performance: A Critical Reader* (Manchester: Manchester University Press, 1996), pp. 82–103.

Mellencamp, Patricia. 'Images of Language and Indiscreet Dialogue: "The Man Who Envied Women" '. *Screen*, 28: 2 (1987): 87–102.

Morris, Meaghan. 'Tooth and Claw: Tales of Survival and *Crocodile Dundee*'. In *The Pirate's Financée: Feminism, Reading, Postmodernism* (London: Verso, 1988), pp. 241–69.

Roberts, John. 'Postmodern Television and the Visual Arts'. *Screen*, 28: 2 (1987): 118–27.

Sharrett, C. 'Sustaining Romanticism in a Postmodernist Cinema: An Interview With Syberborg'. *Cinéaste*, 15: 3 (1987): 18–20.

Wyver, John. 'Television and Postmodernism'. In Appignanesi, Lisa, ed., *Postmodernism: ICA Docments 5* (London: ICA, 1986), pp. 52–4.

Postmodernism and Popular Culture

Certeau, Michel de. *The Practice of Everyday Life*. Trans. Stephen Rendall. Berkeley: University of California Press, 1984.

Chambers, Iain. *Urban Rhythms: Pop Music and Popular Culture*. New York: St. Martin's Press, 1985.

———. 'Maps for the Metropolis: A Possible Guide to the Present'. *Cultural Studies*, 1: 1 (1987): 1–21.

Collins, Jim. *Uncommon Cultures: Popular Culture and Post-Modernism*. New York and London: Routledge, 1989.

Docker, John. *Postmodernism and Popular Culture: A Cultural History*. Cambridge: Cambridge University Press, 1994.

Eco, Umberto. *Travels in Hyper-Reality*. Trans. William Weaver. New York: Harcourt, Brace, Jovanovitch, 1986.

Emberley, Julia. 'The Fashion Apparatus and the Deconstruction of Postmodern Subjectivity'. *Canadian Journal of Political and Social Theory*, 11: 1 (1987): 38–50.

Faurschou, Gail. 'Fashion and the Cultural Logic of Postmodernity'. *Canadian Journal of Political and Social Theory*, 11: 1 (1987): 68–84.

Gitlin, Todd. 'Postmodernism: Roots and Politics'. In Angus, Ian and Jhally, Sut, eds. *Cultural Politics in Contemporary America* (New York and London: Routledge, 1989), pp. 347–60.

Goodwin, Andrew. 'Sample and Hold: Pop Music in the Age of Digital Reproduction'. *Critical Quarterly*, 30: 3 (1988): 34–49.

Grossberg, Lawrence. ' "I'd Rather Feel Bad Than Not Feel Anything At All": Rock and Roll, Pleasure and Power'. *Enclitic*, 8 (1984): 94–110.

———. 'The Politics of Music: American Images and British Articulations'. *Canadian Journal of Political and Social Theory*, 11: 1 (1987): 144–51.

——. *We Gotta Get Out of This Place: Popular Conservatism and Postmodern Culture*. New York and London: Routledge, 1992.

Grossberg, Lawrence, Nelson, Cary and Treichler, Paula, eds. *Cultural Studies*. New York and London: Routledge, 1992.

Hebdige, Dick. *Subculture: The Meaning of Style*. London: Methuen, 1979.

——. 'Posing . . . Threats, Striking . . . Poses: Youth, Surveillance and Display'. *SubStance*, 37/38 (1983): 68–88.

——. 'A Report on the Western Front: Postmodernism and the "Politics" of Style'. *Block*, 12 (1986–7): 4–26.

——. *Cut 'N' Mix: Culture, Identity and Caribbean Music*. London: Comedia, 1987.

——. 'The Impossible Object: Towards a Sociology of the Sublime', *New Formations*, 1: 1 (1987): 47–76.

——. *Hiding in the Light: On Images and Things*. London: Comedia, 1988.

Kaite, Berkeley. ' "Obsession" and Desire: Fashion and the Postmodern Scene'. *Canadian Journal of Political and Social Theory*, 11: 1 (1987): 84–9.

Lipsitz, George, 'Cruising Around the Historical Bloc: Postmodernism and Popular Music in East Los Angeles'. *Cultural Critique*, 5 (1986–7): 157–77.

Mercer, Kobena. 'Black Hair/Style Politics'. *New Formations*, 3 (1987): 33–54.

McRobbie, Angela. 'Postmodernism and Popular Culture'. In Appignanesi, Lisa, ed., *Postmodernism: ICA Documents 5* (London: ICA, 1986), pp. 54–7.

——. *Postmodernism and Popular Culture*. London: Routledge, 1994.

Modleski, Tania, ed. *Studies in Entertainment*. Bloomington: Indiana University Press, 1987.

Schwichtenberg, Cathy, ed. *The Madonna Connection: Representational Politics, Subcultural Identities, and Cultural Theory*. Boulder: Westview, 1993.

Wilson, Elizabeth. *Adorned in Dreams: Fashion and Modernity*. London: Virago, 1985.

Wollen, Peter. 'Fashion/Orientalism/The Body'. *New Formations*, 1 (1987): 5–33.

Postmodernism and Spatial Theory

Bondi, Liz. 'Feminism, Postmodernism and Geography: Space For Women?' *Antipode*, 22 (1990): 156–67.

Bondi, Liz and Domosh, Mona. 'Other Figures in Other Places: On Feminism, Postmodernism and Geography'. *Environment and Planning D: Society and Space*, 10 (1992): 199–214.

Davis, Mike. 'Urban Renaissance and the Spirit of Postmodernism'. *New Left Review*, 151 (1985): 106–13.

——. *City of Quartz: Excavating the Future in Los Angeles*. London: Verso, 1990.

Dear, Michael. 'Postmodernism and Planning'. *Environment and Planning D: Society and Space*, 4 (1986): 367–84.

——. 'The Premature Demise of Postmodern Urbanism'. *Cultural Anthropology*, 6 (1991): 535–48.

Gregory, Derek. *Geographical Imaginations*. Oxford: Basil Blackwell, 1994.

Harvey, David. *The Condition of Postmodernity: An Enquiry Into the Origins of Social Change*. Oxford: Blackwell, 1989.

Lefebvre, Henri. *The Production of Space*. Trans. Donald Nicholason-smith Oxford: Blackwell, 1991.

Ley, David. 'Modernism, Post-modernism and the Struggle For Place'. In John Agnew, and James Duncan, eds. *The Power of Place: Bringing Together Geographical and Sociological Imaginations* (London: Unwin Hyman, 1989), pp. 44–65.

Macmillan, Bill. 'Postmodern Morality Plays'. *Antipode*, 24 (1992): 300–26.

Morris, Meaghan. 'The Man in the Mirror: David Harvey's "Condition" of Postmodernity'. *Theory, Culture and Society*, 9 (1992): 253–79.

Rose, Gillian. *Feminism and Geography: The Limits of Geographical Knowledge*. Cambridge: Polity, 1993.

Soja, Edward W. *Postmodern Geographies: The Reassertion of Space in Critical Social Theory*. London: Verso, 1989.

Stratton, Jon. *Writing Sites: A Genealogy of the Postmodern World*. London: Harvester Wheatsheaf, 1990.

Virilio, Paul. 'The Last Vehicle'. In Jean Baudrillard et al, *Looking Back On The End of the World*, ed. Dietmar Kamper and Christoph Wulf, trans. David Antal (New York: Semiotext(e), 1989), pp. 106–19.

Zukin, Sharon. 'The Postmodern Debate Over Urban Form'. *Theory, Culture and Society*, 5 (1988): 431–46.

Feminism and Postmodernism

Assiter, Alison. *Enlightened Women: Modernist Feminism in a Postmodern Age*. London: Routledge, 1995.

Benhabib, Seyla. *Situating the Self: Gender, Community, and Postmodernism in Contemporary Ethics*. Oxford: Polity, 1992.

Brodribb, Somer. *Nothing Mat(t)ers: A Feminist Critique of Postmodernism*. Melbourne: Spinifex Press, 1992.

Butler, Judith. *Gender Trouble: Feminism and the Subversion of Identity*. London and New York: Routledge, 1990.

——. *Bodies That Matter: The Discursive Limits of 'Sex'*. London: Routledge, 1993.

Cornell, Drucilla. *Philosophy of the Limit*. London and New York: Routledge, 1992.

——. *Transformations: Recollective Imagination and Sexual Difference*. London: Routledge, 1993.

Creed, Barbara. 'From Here to Modernity: Feminism and Postmodernism'. *Screen*, 28: 2 (1987): 47–68.

Doan, Laura, ed. *The Lesbian Postmodern*. New York: Columbia University Press, 1994.

Flax, Jane. 'Postmodernism and Gender Relations in Feminist Theory'. *Signs*, 12: 4 (1987): 621–43.

———. *Disputed Subjects: Essays on Psychoanalysis, Politics, and Philosophy*. New York and London: Routledge, 1993.

Fraser, Nancy and Nicholson, Linda. 'Social Criticism Without Philosophy: An Encounter Between Feminism and Postmodernism'. *Theory, Culture and Society*, 5: 2–3 (1988): 373–94.

Fraser, Nancy. *Unruly Practices: Power, Discourse and Gender in Contemporary Social Theory*. Cambridge: Polity Press, 1989.

Haraway, Donna. 'A Cyborg Manifesto: Science, Technology and Socialist-Feminism in the Late Twentieth Century'. In *Simians, Cyborgs and Women: The Reinvention of Nature* (London: Routledge, 1991), pp. 149–81.

Hekman, Susan. *Gender and Knowledge: Elements of a Postmodern Feminism*. Oxford: Polity, 1990.

Lovibond, Sabina. 'Feminism and Postmodernism', *New Left Review*, 178 (1989): 5–28.

McCormick, Richard. *Politics and the Self: Feminism and the Postmodern in West German Literature and Film*. Princeton, NJ: Princeton University Press, 1991.

Jardine, Alice. *Gynesis: Configurations of Woman and Modernity*. Ithaca and London: Cornell University Press, 1985.

Mellencamp, Patricia. 'Images of Language and Indiscreet Dialogue: "The Man Who Envied Women" '. *Screen*, 28: 2 (1987): 87–102.

Moi, Toril. 'Feminism, Postmodernism and Style: Recent Feminist Criticism in the United States'. *Cultural Critique*, 9 (1988): 3–22.

Morris, Meaghan, *The Pirate's Fiancée: Feminism, Reading, Postmodernism*. London: Verso, 1988.

Nicholson, Linda, ed. *Feminism/Postmodernism*. New York and London: Routledge, 1990.

Owens, Craig. 'Feminism and Postmodernism'. In Foster, ed., *Postmodern Culture* (London and Sydney: Pluto Press, 1985), pp. 57–82.

Probyn, Elizabeth. 'Bodies and Anti-bodies: Feminism and the Postmodern'. *Cultural Studies*, 1: 3 (1987): 349–60.

Spretnak, Charlene. *States of Grace: The Recovery of Meaning in the Postmodern Age* (San Francisco: Harper San Francisco, 1991).

Suleiman, Susan Robin. 'Feminism and Postmodernism: A Question of Politics'. In Hoesterey, Ingeborg, ed. *Zeitgeist in Babel: The Postmodernist Controversy* (Bloomington: Indiana University Press, 1991), pp. 111–31.

Wolmark, Jenny. *Aliens and Others: Science Fiction, Feminism and Postmodernism*. Hemel Hempstead: Harvester Wheatsheaf, 1993.

Postmodernism and Postcoloniality

Adams, Ian and Tiffin, Helen, eds. *Past the Last Post: Theorizing Post-Colonialism and Post-Modernism*. New York and London: Harvester Wheatsheaf, 1991.

Appiah, Kwame Anthony. 'Is the Post- in Postmodernism the Post-in Postcolonial?', *Critical Inquiry*, 17 (1991): 336–57.
During, Simon. 'Postmodernism or Post-Colonialism Today'. *Textual Practice*, I:1 (1987): 32–47.
Richard, Nelly. 'Postmodernism and Periphery'. *Third Text*, 2 (1987/8): 5–12.

Postmodern Ethnography and Anthropology

Clifford, James and Marcus, George E., eds. *Writing Culture: The Poetics and Politics of Ethnography*. Berkeley, Los Angeles and London: University of California Press, 1986.
Clifford, James. *The Predicament of Culture: Twentieth-Century Ethnography, Literature, and Art*. Cambridge, Mass.: Harvard University Press, 1988.
Geertz, Clifford. *Local Knowledge: Further Essays in Interpretive Anthropology*. New York: Basic Books, 1986.
Tyler, Stephen A. *The Unspeakable: Discourse, Dialogue, and Rhetoric in the Postmodern World*. Madison: University of Wisconin Press, 1987.
Wolf, Margery. *A Thrice-Told Tale: Feminism, Postmodernism and Ethnographic Responsibility*. Stanfordca. Stanford University Press, 1992.

Bibliography of Postmodernism

McCaffery, Larry, ed. *Postmodern Fiction: A Bio-Bibliography*. London: Greenwood Press, 1986.
Madsen D. *Postmodernism: A Bibliography, 1926–1994*. Amsterdam and Atlanta, Ga: Rodopi, 1995.

Special Issues of Journals

Amerikastudien, 22: 1 (1977). On Postmodernism.
Boundary 2, 20: 3 (1993). The Postmodernism Debate in Latin America.
Bucknell Review, 25 (1980). Romanticism, Modernism, Postmodernism.
Caliban, 12 (1975). On Postmodernism.
Chicago Review, 32: 2–3 (1983). Postmodern Literature and Criticism.
Cuadernos del Norte, 8:42 (1987). On Postmodernism.
Cultural Critique, 5 (1987). Modernity and Modernism; Postmodernity and Postmodernism.
Drama Review, 19: 1 (1975). Post-Modern Dance.
Genre, 20:3–4 (1987). Postmodern Genres.
Krisis, 2 (1984). Negative Thinking, Crisis, Postmodernism.
Krisis, 3–4 (1985). Postmodernism: Search for Criteria.

Minnesota Review, n.s. 23 (1984). The Politics of Postmodernism.
Modern Literature, 3 (1974). From Modernism to Postmodernism.
New German Critique, 22 (1981). Habermas and Postmodernism.
New German Critique, 33 (1984) On Postmodernism.
New Literary History, 3:1 (1971). Modernism and Postmodernism.
Par Rapport, 2:2 (1979). On Postmodernism.
Postmodern Culture (electronic journal) 1990– .
http://www.village.virginia.edu/pmc/contents.html
Screen, 28:2 (1987). On Postmodernism.
Salmagundi, 67 (1985). Responses to Newman's *The Post-Modern Aura*.
Theory, Culture and Society, 2:3 (1985). *The Fate of Modernity*.
Theory, Culture and Society, 5:2–3 (1988). Postmodernism.
TriQuarterly, 26 (1973). On Postmodernism.
TriQuarterly, 30 (1974). On Postmodernism.
TriQuarterly, 32 (1975). On Postmodernism.
TriQuarterly, 33 (1975). On Postmodernism.
Wallace Stevens Journal, 7 (1983). Stevens and Postmodern Criticism.

Postmodernism and Religion

Aichele, George, et. al. *The Postmodern Bible*. New Haven Conn: Yale University Press, 1995.

Allen, Diogenes, et. al. *Postmodern Theology: Christian Faith in a Pluralist World*. San Francisco: Harper and Row, 1989.

Astell, Ann W., ed. *Divine Representations: Postmodernism and Spirituality*. New York: Paulist Press, 1994.

Berry, Phillipa and Wernick, Andrew, eds. *Shadow of Spirit: Postmodernism and Religion*. London: Routledge, 1992.

Gellner, Ernest. *Postmodernism, Reason and Religion*. London and New York: Routledge, 1992.

Griffin, David Ray. *God and Religion in the Postmodern World: Essays in Postmodern Theology*. Albany, NY: State University of New York Press, 1989.

Griffin, David Ray, Beardslee, William A. and Holland, Joe. *Varieties of Postmodern Theology*. Albany, NY: State University of New York Press, 1989.

Ingraffia, Brian D. *Postmodern Theory and Biblical Theology: Vanquishing God's Shadow*. Cambridge: Cambridge University Press, 1995.

Jasper, David, ed. *Postmodernism, Literature, and the Future of Theology*. New York: St. Martin's Press, 1992.

Taylor, Mark C. *ERRING: A Postmodern A/Theology*. Chicago and London: University of Chicago Press, 1984.

——. *Disfiguring: Art, Architecture, Religion*. Chicago: University of Chicago Press, 1992.

——. *Notes*. Chicago: University of Chicago Press, 1993.

Thiselton, Anthony C. *Interpreting God and the Postmodern Self: On Meaning, Manipulation and Promise*. Edinburgh: T & T Clark, 1995.
Winquist, Charles E. *Desiring Theology*. Chicago: University of Chicago Press, 1995.

Readers and Anthologies

Brooker, Peter, ed. *Modernism/Postmodernism*. London: Longman, 1992.
Docherty, Thomas, ed. *Postmodernism: A Reader*. Hemel Hempstead: Harvester Wheatsheaf, 1993.
Hutcheon, Linda and Natoli, Joseph, eds. *A Postmodern Reader*. Albany, NY: State University of New York Press, 1993.
Jencks, Charles. *The Post-Modern Reader*. London: Academy Editions, 1992.
Waugh, Patricia, ed. *Postmodernism: A Reader*. London: Edward Arnold, 1992.

Index